"十四五"职业教育国家规划教材

"十三五"职业教育国家规划教材
高等职业教育专业英语系列教材

实用旅游英语

主　编　龚聪琮　刘　娜
副主编　邵　杰　罗海锋
参　编　王　柠　孙　川
主　审　齐智英

机械工业出版社

本书是"十四五"职业教育国家规划教材，分为三章，共 10 个单元。第一章介绍旅游准备，包括办理护照和办理签证两个单元；第二章介绍旅游种类，包括历史人文游、自然奇观游和红色旅游三个单元；第三章介绍旅游要素，包括吃——餐饮服务，住——宾馆服务，行——交通服务，游——旅游服务，购——购物服务五个单元。

每个单元又分为五个模块，即 Warm-Up, Conversations, Readings, Practical Writing 和 Typical Scenic Spot，其中在 Conversations 和 Readings 模块上加注参考译文，并在 Readings 模块的 Integrated Exercises of Skills 部分加注了习题答案。

本书适用于高等职业院校教学，也可供酒店、机场、景区景点、旅行社、外事机构、公司、教育和旅游局等部门相关人员参考使用。

为方便教学，本书配备电子课件、教案等教学资源。凡选用本书作为教材的教师均可登录机械工业出版社教育服务网 www.cmpedu.com 注册后免费下载。如有问题请致电 010-88379375 联系营销人员，服务 QQ：945379158。

图书在版编目（CIP）数据

实用旅游英语/ 龚聪琮，刘娜主编. —北京：机械工业出版社，2017.10（2025.2 重印）

高等职业教育专业英语系列教材

ISBN 978-7-111-58307-3

Ⅰ.①实… Ⅱ.①龚… ②刘… Ⅲ.①旅游-英语-高等职业教育-教材 Ⅳ.①F59

中国版本图书馆 CIP 数据核字（2017）第 264757 号

机械工业出版社（北京市百万庄大街 22 号　邮政编码 100037）
策划编辑：赵志鹏　　责任编辑：赵志鹏
责任印制：刘　媛
涿州市般润文化传播有限公司印刷
2025 年 2 月第 1 版·第 13 次印刷
184mm×260mm·20 印张·484 千字
标准书号：ISBN 978-7-111-58307-3
定价：49.50 元

电话服务	网络服务
客服电话：010-88361066	机 工 官 网：www.cmpbook.com
010-88379833	机 工 官 博：weibo.com/cmp1952
010-68326294	金 书 网：www.golden-book.com
封底无防伪标均为盗版	机工教育服务网：www.cmpedu.com

关于"十四五"职业教育
国家规划教材的出版说明

为贯彻落实《中共中央关于认真学习宣传贯彻党的二十大精神的决定》《习近平新时代中国特色社会主义思想进课程教材指南》《职业院校教材管理办法》等文件精神，机械工业出版社与教材编写团队一道，认真执行思政内容进教材、进课堂、进头脑要求，尊重教育规律，遵循学科特点，对教材内容进行了更新，着力落实以下要求：

1. 提升教材铸魂育人功能，培育、践行社会主义核心价值观，教育引导学生树立共产主义远大理想和中国特色社会主义共同理想，坚定"四个自信"，厚植爱国主义情怀，把爱国情、强国志、报国行自觉融入建设社会主义现代化强国、实现中华民族伟大复兴的奋斗之中。同时，弘扬中华优秀传统文化，深入开展宪法法治教育。

2. 注重科学思维方法训练和科学伦理教育，培养学生探索未知、追求真理、勇攀科学高峰的责任感和使命感；强化学生工程伦理教育，培养学生精益求精的大国工匠精神，激发学生科技报国的家国情怀和使命担当。加快构建中国特色哲学社会科学学科体系、学术体系、话语体系。帮助学生了解相关专业和行业领域的国家战略、法律法规和相关政策，引导学生深入社会实践、关注现实问题，培育学生经世济民、诚信服务、德法兼修的职业素养。

3. 教育引导学生深刻理解并自觉实践各行业的职业精神、职业规范，增强职业责任感，培养遵纪守法、爱岗敬业、无私奉献、诚实守信、公道办事、开拓创新的职业品格和行为习惯。

在此基础上，及时更新教材知识内容，体现产业发展的新技术、新工艺、新规范、新标准。加强教材数字化建设，丰富配套资源，形成可听、可视、可练、可互动的融媒体教材。

教材建设需要各方的共同努力，也欢迎相关教材使用院校的师生及时反馈意见和建议，我们将认真组织力量进行研究，在后续重印及再版时吸纳改进，不断推动高质量教材出版。

机械工业出版社

前 言
Preface

《实用旅游英语》是"十四五"职业教育国家规划教材,通过动态修订,贯彻落实党的二十大精神进教材、进课堂、进头脑的要求。

党的二十大报告提出,"增强中华文明传播力影响力""坚持以文塑旅、以旅彰文""全面提升国际传播效能"。随着"一带一路"倡议的推进,中国与"一带一路"沿线国家旅游合作越来越密切,因此急需高素质的旅游从业人员,尤其是既掌握较扎实的专业知识又具备较强的英语口语交际能力的旅游英语人才。

1. "职业导向"编写理念

本教材根据高等职业教育的特点,改变传统学科型的课程形式,构建以职业能力为核心的模块式教材体系,体现知识学习和技能训练兼顾的原则,加强学生专业旅游知识的同时,重视实用英语技能和职场交际能力的培养,重点打造学生的"专业知识能力+职业素养能力+英语语言能力"。

2. 增强文化自信,坚持"以文塑旅、以旅彰文"

本书通过"历史人文游""自然奇观游""红色旅游"等部分介绍了我国众多经典旅游景点,增强文化自信和民族自豪感,将红色旅游文化融入教学,突出革命传统和爱国主义等红色文化的传承与创新。"餐饮服务"单元则以美食为窗口,介绍了我国各地菜系。本书通过图文和微课视频,近观食物之美,远眺中华美食所根植的文化渊源,尽享中国饮食文化的魅力;同时教会学习者必备的英语技能,用英文讲好中国故事,为传播中华文明做出自身的贡献,落实立德树人根本任务。

3. "多元化"编写团队

团队由"教学名师+专业教师+双师型教师"构成,具备严谨的治学态度和高度的责任心,拥有丰富的旅游、酒店专业知识和多年从事高职一线英语教学的经验,因此编写的教材更加符合学生的认知结构和知识结构。

4. 内容新颖、实用

本书的主要内容以旅游过程为主线,旅游工作环节为导向,以职业技能需求细化分析为依据,以满足岗位技能要求为目标。内容涵盖旅游手续、旅游种类和旅游要素。把旅游专业知识、跨文化旅游交际能力及英语语言运用能力结合在一起,以学生为中心、以旅游活动为环境、以旅游交际为目的,由浅入深,循序渐进,培养学生在未来职业岗位中完成旅游任务、实现旅游交际活动所需要的能力,重视实用英语技能和职场交际能力的培养。

本书内容新颖、实用,不仅可以帮助学习者提高英语听说能力、阅读能力,以及英汉双语互译能力,而且可以帮助其了解旅游文化并掌握旅游行业的新理论、新术语,开阔视野。

5. 布局科学,实现混合式学习

从交际功能的角度出发,本书通过二维码融入微课视频、景点介绍、英文朗读等线上资源,将听、说、读、写紧密结合,调动学生与教师之间的双向互动、学生之间的多向互动,最大限度地激发学生的兴趣,提升学生思考、交流及协同学习的能力。本书的最大特点是集背景知识、英语词汇、常用口语、技能训练于一体,创造真实的旅游情境,使学生能在真实的视听旅游情境中学习、操练旅游英语,以及学习、掌握相关的旅游知识。

本书分为三章,共 10 个单元,每个单元围绕一个旅游环节来安排内容和设计任务。第一章介绍旅游准备,内容涉及办理护照和办理签证;第二章介绍旅游种类,内容涉及历史人文游、自然奇观游和红色旅游;第三章介绍旅游要素,内容涉及吃——餐饮服务,住——宾馆服务,行——交通服务,游——旅游服务,购——购物服务。每个单元又分为五个模块,即 Warm-Up, Conversations, Readings, Practical Writing 和 Typical Scenic Spot,计划 8~10 个学时。Conversations 和 Readings 模块配有相关词汇和短语,并加注了参考译文。在 Readings 模块的 Integrated Exercises of Skills 部分加注了习题答案。此外,每单元还提供一处中英文对照的热门旅游景点,以扩充阅读量,增加学习趣味性。

本书由具有丰富旅游、酒店专业知识和多年从事一线英语教学的专家和教师编写。全书由龚聪琮、刘娜主编并负责统稿,具体分工如下:刘娜编写第一、二单元及其课后练习、答案和译文,王柠编写第三、四单元及其课后练习、答案和译文,邵杰编写第五、六单元及其课后练习、答案和译文,龚聪琮编写第七、八单元及其课后练习、答案和译文,罗海锋编写第九、十单元及其课后练习、答案和译文,孙川负责整理编写词汇表和附录部分。河南工业职业技术学院的齐智英教授任本书主审,齐教授对本书提出了很多宝贵意见和建议;河南工业职业技术学院的外籍教师 Sean Paul Koch 也对本书给予了帮助,在此一并表示衷心感谢。

本书在编写过程中参考和借鉴了业内众多学者和同行的研究成果和文献资料,在此表示衷心感谢。

由于编者水平有限,不足之处在所难免,敬请各位专家和读者不吝赐教,批评指正,以便下次修订时完善。

编　者

二维码索引
QR Code Index

序号	名称	二维码	页码	序号	名称	图形	页码	序号	名称	图形	页码
1	Unit1-C1		2	11	Unit6-C1		104	21	微课：护照		3
2	Unit1-C2		3	12	Unit6-C2		106	22	微课：故宫		19
3	Unit2-C1		21	13	Unit7-C1		124	23	微课：古都		47
4	Unit2-C2		23	14	Unit7-C2		126	24	微课：黄山		57
5	Unit3-C1		42	15	Unit8-C1		143	25	微课：红旗渠		86
6	Unit3-C2		44	16	Unit8-C2		144	26	微课：美食		111
7	Unit4-C1		59	17	Unit9-C1		161	27	微课：酒店		129
8	Unit4-C2		61	18	Unit9-C2		162	28	微课：问路		147
9	Unit5-C1		78	19	Unit10-C1		179	29	微课：日月潭		193
10	Unit5-C2		81	20	Unit10-C2		181				

Contents

Preface

QR Code Index

Chapter One Preparation for Travelling ………………………… 1

   Unit 1 Passport Applications ………………………… 2
      Part I　Warm-Up ………………………… 2
      Part II　Conversations ………………………… 2
      Part III　Readings ………………………… 7
      Part IV　Practical Writing ………………………… 15
      Part V　Typical Scenic Spot ………………………… 19

   Unit 2 Visa Affairs ………………………… 21
      Part I　Warm-Up ………………………… 21
      Part II　Conversations ………………………… 21
      Part III　Readings ………………………… 27
      Part IV　Practical Writing ………………………… 35
      Part V　Typical Scenic Spot ………………………… 38

Chapter Two Categories of Tourism ………………………… 41

   Unit 3 Historical and Cultural Relics Tour ………………………… 42
      Part I　Warm-Up ………………………… 42
      Part II　Conversations ………………………… 42
      Part III　Readings ………………………… 47
      Part IV　Practical Writing ………………………… 54
      Part V　Typical Scenic Spot ………………………… 56

   Unit 4 Natural Wonders Tours ………………………… 59
      Part I　Warm-Up ………………………… 59
      Part II　Conversations ………………………… 59
      Part III　Readings ………………………… 64

      Part IV　Practical Writing ……………………………………… 72
      Part V　Typical Scenic Spot …………………………………… 75

Unit 5　Red Resorts Tours ……………………………………………… 78
      Part I　Warm-Up ………………………………………………… 78
      Part II　Conversations ………………………………………… 78
      Part III　Readings ……………………………………………… 86
      Part IV　Practical Writing ……………………………………… 95
      Part V　Typical Scenic Spot …………………………………… 99

Chapter Three　Elements of Tourism ……………………………… 103

Unit 6　Food ………………………………………………………………… 104
      Part I　Warm-Up ………………………………………………… 104
      Part II　Conversations ………………………………………… 104
      Part III　Readings ……………………………………………… 111
      Part IV　Practical Writing ……………………………………… 120
      Part V　Typical Scenic Spot …………………………………… 122

Unit 7　Accommodation ………………………………………………… 124
      Part I　Warm-Up ………………………………………………… 124
      Part II　Conversations ………………………………………… 124
      Part III　Readings ……………………………………………… 129
      Part IV　Practical Writing ……………………………………… 138
      Part V　Typical Scenic Spot …………………………………… 141

Unit 8　Transportation ………………………………………………… 143
      Part I　Warm-Up ………………………………………………… 143
      Part II　Conversations ………………………………………… 143
      Part III　Readings ……………………………………………… 147
      Part IV　Practical Writing ……………………………………… 156
      Part V　Typical Scenic Spot …………………………………… 158

Unit 9　Travelling ………………………………………………………… 161
      Part I　Warm-Up ………………………………………………… 161
      Part II　Conversations ………………………………………… 161
      Part III　Readings ……………………………………………… 164
      Part IV　Practical Writing ……………………………………… 173
      Part V　Typical Scenic Spot …………………………………… 176

Unit 10	**Shopping**	179
	Part I　　Warm-Up	179
	Part II　 Conversations	179
	Part III　Readings	183
	Part IV　 Practical Writing	191
	Part V　　Typical Scenic Spot	193

Appendix A	参考译文	196
Appendix B	习题答案	240
Appendix C	词汇表	272
Appendix D	世界著名景观中英文对照	294
Appendix E	中国菜名中英文对照	298
Appendix F	常用公共标识语中英文对照	305
Appendix G	酒店词汇	307
Reference		310

Chapter One
Preparation for Travelling

◈ Unit 1　Passport Applications
◈ Unit 2　Visa Affairs

Unit 1 Passport Applications

Part I Warm-Up

How to get a passport?
- Prepare your photograph for the passport.
- Take with you your ID card and residence registration booklet (*hukou*), both originals and photocopies.
- Fill in the form as required.
- Apply for your passport in person at the local Exit and Entry Administration.

Part II Conversations

Conversation 1   Apply for a Passport

A: I want to travel to America for some time.

B: You must have a passport if you want to go abroad.

A: Oh, I forgot it.

B: Then you will have to delay your travel, because the passport application usually takes 10 days.

A: Well. Can you explain to me how to get a passport?

B: OK. You should prepare your residence registration booklet and ID card well, and go to the Exit and Entry Administration Bureau to manage it.

A: I was unlucky to lose my ID card two days ago.

B: Don't worry. You can take the temporary ID card to apply for the passport.

A: Thank you.

(*10 days later*)

A: Good news! I get my passport.

B: Congratulations!

A: This is my first time to apply for a passport. Without your explanation, I could not

Chapter One Preparation for Travelling

have applied for the passport successfully.

B: It's my pleasure. By the way, what is the validity period of your passport?

A: It's a month.

 New Words

delay	[dɪˈleɪ]	v. & n. 延期；耽搁
application	[ˌæplɪˈkeɪʃ(ə)n]	n. 应用；申请
explain	[ɪkˈspleɪn; ek-]	v. 说明；解释
residence	[ˈrezɪd(ə)ns]	n. 住宅；居住
migration	[maɪˈgreɪʃ(ə)n]	n. 迁移；移民
manage	[ˈmænɪdʒ]	v. 经营；控制；设法；处理；应付过去
temporary	[ˈtemp(ə)rərɪ]	adj. 暂时的，临时的 n. 临时工
explanation	[ˌekspləˈneɪʃ(ə)n]	n. 说明，解释；辩解
validity	[vəˈlɪdɪtɪ]	n. 有效性；正确性

 Phrases and Expressions

go abroad　　　　　　　　去国外
residence registration booklet　　户口簿
ID card　　　　　　　　　身份证

Conversation 2　　Customs Inspection

A: Can I see your passport, please?

B: Is this line for non-residents?

A: Yes it is. Residents can queue up in the lines to my right.

B: OK. Here's my passport.

A: What's the expiration date on your passport?

B: I think it's soon, maybe in a few months. It was renewed in Beijing, so the new expiry date is on the last page.

A: I see. Yes, you'll need to renew your passport in a few months. Make sure you don't let it expire while you are in the UK.

B: I won't.

A: Do you have anything to declare?

B: No, I don't have anything to declare.

A: How long will you be staying in the UK?

B: I'll be here for about a year.

A: What is the purpose of your stay?

B: I'll be studying. I'm doing an MBA at Nottingham University.

A: Where will you be staying?

B: I have a housing contract with the university. I'll be in a dorm room on campus.

A: How do you plan on paying for your living costs and tuition fees while you are here?

B: My father has already paid for that in advance. Here are the receipts.

A: OK. Have a good day. Here's your passport and documents back.

B: Thank you very much.

 New Words

non-resident	[ˌnɒnˈrezɪdənt]	n. 非居民 adj. 非驻留的
expire	[ɪkˈspaɪə; ek-]	v. 期满；终止；死亡；呼出（空气）
expiry	[ɪkˈspaɪrɪ; ek-]	n. 满期，逾期；呼气；终结
expiration	[ekspɪˈreɪʃ(ə)n]	n. 呼气，终结；届期
renew	[rɪˈnjuː]	v. 使更新；续借；重申；更新；重新开始
declare	[dɪˈkleə]	v. 宣布，声明；宣称
tuition	[tjuːˈɪʃ(ə)n]	n. 学费；讲授
fee	[fiː]	n. 费用；酬金；小费 v. 付费给……
receipt	[rɪˈsiːt]	n. 收到；收据；收入 v. 收到
document	[ˈdɒkjʊm(ə)nt]	n. 文件，公文 v. 用文件证明

 Phrases and Expressions

queue up	排队等候
expiration date	有效期
housing contract	住宿合同
dorm room	学生公寓
tuition fee	学费
in advance	提前

Chapter One　Preparation for Travelling

 Practical Patterns

1. What is the validity period of my passport?
   我的护照有效期是多久?

2. Please come here to get your passport on time.
   请按时来这里领取护照。

3. You can get your passport by express delivery.
   你可以通过快递领取你的护照。

4. This is the first time for me to apply for a passport.
   这是我第一次申请护照。

5. September 28th, 2017 is the expiration date of your passport.
   你的护照到期日是 2017 年 9 月 28 日。

6. May I have a customs declaration form, please?
   请给我一份海关审报表,好吗?

7. Please give this declaration card to that officer at the exit.
   请将这张申报卡交给出口处的官员。

8. May I see your passport, your customs and health declaration forms, please?
   请您出示护照、海关申报表和体检表,好吗?

9. Please fill out this certificate of Entrustment, so that when your baggage arrives, we can go through the customs formalities for you.
   请您填写一张委托书,这样行李抵达后,我们可以代您接受海关检查。

10. You must go through customs inspection if you transfer in Los Angeles.
    如果您在洛杉矶转机,需要在那通过海关检查。

11. Our baggage has cleared customs.
    我们的行李已经通过了安全检查。

12. Where will the customs procedure take place?
    海关手续在哪儿办理?

13. You're not supposed to bring fresh fruits. We are going to confiscate them.
    不准携带新鲜水果。我们将予以没收。

14. Have you any contraband in your luggage?
    你的行李里有违禁物品吗?

Task I　Complete the following dialogues by translating the Chinese in the brackets.

(C: Customs Officer　T: Traveller)

C: Do you have anything to declare?

T: _____ (没有什么东西要申报的,我只是替孩子们带了些小礼品。)

C: What's their value?

T: Way under the duty-free allowance. _____
（我为女儿买了张唱片，为儿子买了本书，为我妻子买了条项链。）

C: May I see the necklace? There's a duty on some types of jewelry even if the total of your purchases is under the amount you are allowed.

T: _____（当然可以。给你。但我确信不用完税。）

C: You are right. There's no duty on it. Thank you for your cooperation. I'm sorry that I had to trouble you.

T: _____（没关系。检查每一件入境物品是你的工作。谢谢你对我这么客气。）

Task II   Using the given words and expressions to make a conversation with your partner according to the situation.

Situation 1: The summer vacation is coming. Liu Ming and his girl friend Wang Shanshan are going to travel to America together. Now they are talking about how to apply for a passport.

Situation 2: You are an overseas Chinese coming back to visit your relatives and bringing with you some presents for them, including some electric appliances. Now you are going through the customs formalities.

 Useful Words and Eexpressions

go for an interview 面试	fill in a form 填表
get a visa 得到签证	process an application 处理申请
hand in an application 提交申请	fill out an application 填写申请
show your identity card 出示身份证	present documents 提交文件
approve an application 同意申请	reject an application 拒绝申请

 Useful Sentences

1. It takes you quite a long time to apply for a passport.
   申请护照需要花上好长一段时间。

2. Oh, I just remembered something! I have to apply for a passport.
   哦，我刚刚想起一件事！我需要去申请一个护照。

3. You have to apply for a passport in advance.
   你必须提前申请护照。

4. In order to obtain a passport, you must first fill in the official form.

Chapter One Preparation for Travelling

要申请护照，你必须先填写正式表格。

5. Put your carry-on luggage on the belt, please.
   请把您的手提行李放在传送带上。
6. Now put everything from your pockets in this tray and come through the detector.
   现在请把口袋里的东西掏出来放在这里，从检测器走过。
7. OK. Go through the gate, please.
   好的，请通过安全门。
8. You may go now. Please take your things. I wish you a happy journey.
   您可以走了。请带好您的东西，祝您旅途愉快。
9. All the leaving passengers must go through this gate. Will you please put your suitcase and that box on the belt?
   所有旅客都必须从这个检查口通过。请把您的手提箱和那个盒子放在传送带上好吗？
10. We'll check you by hand. What do you think?
    我们用手检，您看如何？

Part III Readings

Text A

Planning Your Vacations

On your next vacation, where do you want to stay in the US? Or maybe you would like to go somewhere outside of the US but you don't want to cross any oceans. Or maybe you would prefer to see Asia, Africa or Europe. There are many destinations to choose from, both stateside and internationally.

There are many places to see in California. Maybe you would prefer to go skiing in Colorado. How about seeing the historical sites of the south or maybe the northeast? Have you considered Alaska? There are many different places that you could visit, and each one brings something different to the table. Here in America you can see many places that have affected the condition of our country.

If you go to Central or South America, then you can see thriving cultures set against what are still considered to be wild and uninhabited. You can see something fairly similar in South Africa but with a whole different culture and with an extremely different kind of wild. Perhaps the bustling cities of North Africa, sometimes called the Middle East, are more to your taste. What about the ancient cultures mixed with cutting edge technologies in parts of Asia? Then you have Europe, with some of the most travelled areas in the world.

Each area does bring in a totally different perspective so that within each general area there are more specific areas. If you are looking for something as vague as someplace with a small population and minimal inhabitation, then you can look at parts of Australia, Asia, Canada, South America, South Africa, Northern Europe and Russia.

If you want bustling cities, then you have your pick of many on every continent and just about every country. There are many places that could be recommended, such as Rome, Paris, the Amazon in Brazil, the white peaks of the Andes, London, Northern Ireland, Hong Kong, Manila, and the outback. Take your pick. It is probably safe to say that most people have an idea of where they want to go, but if you don't, take a look around. There are literally millions of places.

 New Words

stateside	[ˈsteɪtsaɪd]	*adj.* 美国本土的 *adv.* 在美国国内
historical	[hɪˈstɒrɪk(ə)l]	*adj.* 历史的；史学的
consider	[kənˈsɪdə]	*v.* 考虑；认为；细想
affect	[əˈfekt]	*v.* 影响；感染
uninhabited	[ˌʌnɪnˈhæbɪtɪd]	*adj.* 无人居住的，杳无人迹的
extremely	[ɪkˈstriːmli; ek-]	*adv.* 非常，极其
ancient	[ˈeɪnʃ(ə)nt]	*adj.* 古代的；古老的，过时的
technology	[tekˈnɒlədʒi]	*n.* 技术；工艺
perspective	[pəˈspektɪv]	*n.* 观点；远景
specific	[spəˈsɪfɪk]	*adj.* 特殊的，特定的；明确的
vague	[veɪg]	*adj.* 模糊的；不明确的
population	[ˌpɒpjʊˈleɪʃ(ə)n]	*n.* 人口
bustling	[ˈbʌslɪŋ]	*adj.* 熙熙攘攘的；忙乱的
continent	[ˈkɒntɪnənt]	*n.* 大陆，洲，陆地 *adj.* 自制的，克制的
recommend	[ˌrekəˈmend]	*v.* 推荐，介绍
literally	[ˈlɪt(ə)rəli]	*adv.* 照字面地；逐字地；不夸张地

Chapter One Preparation for Travelling

Phrases and Expressions

cross oceans   漂洋过海
prefer to   更喜欢
How about …?   ……怎么样？
cutting edge technology 尖端科技

Integrated Exercises of Skills

Task I Discuss with partners and then answer the questions according to the passage.

1. If you go to Central or South America, what can you see?
2. If you are looking for something as vague as someplace with a small population and minimal inhabitation, where would you look at?
3. Where can you feel the ancient cultures mixed with cutting edge technologies?
4. If you want to go to bustling cities, where would you like to go? Please recommend some places.
5. Please talk with your partner about the places you like best.

Task II Fill in the blanks with the suitable words given below, changing the form where necessary.

| specific | consider | uninhabited | vague | affect |
| population | recommend | extremely | historical | prefer |

1. This _____ novel illustrates the breaking up of feudal society in microcosm.
2. We all _____ what you said to be unbelievable.
3. How did that experience _____ you?
4. Which one would you _____, tea or coffee?
5. The region is _____ except for a few scattered mountain villages.
6. Although I am _____ busy and am working very hard, the pressures are not the same.
7. We should make a concrete analysis of each _____ question.
8. One must not be _____ on matters of principle.
9. The _____ gravitates towards the city.
10. Can you _____ some to me?

Task III Translate the sentences into Chinese.

1. Or maybe you would like to go somewhere outside of the US but you don't want to

cross any oceans.
_____

2. There are many destinations to choose from, both stateside and internationally.
_____

3. You can see something fairly similar in South Africa but with a whole different culture and with an extremely different kind of wild.
_____
_____

4. What about the ancient cultures mixed with cutting edge technologies in parts of Asia?
_____

5. Each area does bring in a totally different perspective so that within each general area there are more specific areas.
_____
_____

Task IV Reading comprehension.

Immigration

As the passengers leave the large aircraft, Alice Baker and Henry Fisher step forward to greet them. Ms. Baker and Mr. Fisher are passenger service agents. They represent, or act for, their country's airline. They serve, or take care of passengers.

"Welcome," says Mr. Fisher, "We're glad to have you visit our country. If you will please follow us, we'll take you to the immigration area." The deplaning passengers follow the passenger service agents into the large terminal building.

In the terminal building are the immigration, customs and baggage areas as well as ticket and reservation desks for many airlines. There are also waiting rooms, shops, restaurants and other facilities for the travellers' comfort. "Will immigration take long?" Mrs. Silver, one of the passengers, asks as they follow Ms. Baker through the long hallway in the terminal.

"I don't think so," answers Ms. Baker. "There are many immigration officials. They will take care of tourists as quickly as possible." "Good," says Mr. Silver, "We're all tired of being cooped up on the plane. We're eager to get started seeing your country." As the passengers enter the immigration area, they see people lined up in front of high counters, or desks. An immigration officer sits behind each counter. Hanging from the ceiling over one group of counters is a large sign reading: TOURISTS - VISITORS. Ms. Baker directs Mr. and Ms. Silvers to the section. "It shouldn't take

Chapter One Preparation for Travelling

very long," she tells them as they get on line. "Please be sure to have your immigration information card, your passports, visas and other documents ready. I hope you'll enjoy your stay in our country."

In the immigration area, the passenger service agents answer questions and help the people waiting in line. Some people are returning to the country from trips to other places. They are either nationals or residents of the country.

Although "immigrate" means to come into a country with the intention of settling there, all persons entering a country must go through immigration, no matter how short their stay will be. Their documents and identification must be checked by an immigration official. In this way, a country keeps track of the people entering and knows the countries from which tourists and visitors come. Tourists and other visitors must fill out the immigration information cards to explain their purpose of entering the country.

It takes longer for immigrants and returning nationals or residents to go through immigration. That is why there are usually separate lines for each group. The officials are anxious to let visitors go through immigration as quickly and easily as possible.

I. Vocabulary Review. Choose the correct word or phrase to complete each sentence.

1. _____ is an official document issued by a country to its citizens or residents that permits them to leave and re-enter the country.
   A. A passport   B. A visa
   C. A customs declaration   D. An immigration card

2. _____ is a special endorsement by a country to allow a foreigner to enter the country.
   A. A passport   B. A visa
   C. A customs declaration   D. An immigration card

3. _____ examine the travel record and identification documents of all people entering a country.
   A. Customs officials   B. First officers
   C. Passenger service agents   D. Immigration officers

4. An official who is _____ can spoil a tourist's entire vacation by creating a bad impression.
   A. polite   B. courteous   C. rude   D. friendly

II. Questions for discussion.

1. What is Ms. Baker's job?
2. How does she represent the airline?
3. What are there in the terminal building?

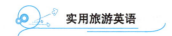

4. What does "immigrate" mean? Why must all persons entering a country go through immigration?

5. Why are there separate lines for groups of nationals, residents and tourists?

Text B

Customs Check

According to American Customs Hints for Visitors (Non-Residents)[1], foreigners coming to America can bring the following articles free of charge:

1) Personal belongings—goods used by oneself, not to be sold. This includes clothing, jewelry, electrical equipment and sports equipment.

2) Household utensils—furniture, carpets, and equipment for work. But they are supposed to be for personal use only and not to be sold.

3) Gifts—Entering the U.S., you can bring $100 worth of presents, but you have to stay in the United States for at least 72 hours. Moreover, in the past six months, you shouldn't bring any of the same gifts into the country.

4) Cigarettes and alcohol—Adults may bring 0.95L of wine, 300 cigarettes, and 1.35 kg of tobacco.

After arriving in America, your documents will be checked by the customs officer. You must fill in a customs declaration form[2] and show your inoculation certificate[3] and passport. Having received your baggage, you should hand in your customs declaration form and luggage check.

Customs inspectors examine the luggage of all travellers to the country. All articles acquired abroad must be declared—that is, they must be identified and their value must be given to an inspector. If a person fails to declare an article or understates its value, the article may be taken away and the individual may be fined. In the United States, articles totaling up to $400 are exempt (free from any duty) if they meet certain regulations. For example, the articles must be for personal use, and the person's trip must last at least 48 hours.

Having arrived at your destination, you should make your way to the city. Normally, an airport is very far from a city, so you may take a shuttle bus that runs every half an hour. The transportation is very convenient, but the shuttle bus will not send you to the exact place where you want to go.

▶ **Notes**

[1] American Customs Hints for Visitors (Non-Residents)

Chapter One Preparation for Travelling

美国游客（非居民）海关条例

[2] customs declaration form 海关申报表

无论是美国公民还是持有观光、学生等签证的非美国公民，每一位到达美国的人士都必须填写一份海关申报表；若整个家庭出行，一个家庭只需填写一份。在飞往美国的飞机上，机组工作人员会给大家发这张表，需要你填写个人及所携带物品的基本信息，入关时交给海关人员。美国关口要确保没有违禁物品随旅客入境。该表有中、英文两版，有需要的话，可直接向机组成员索要中文版申报单（填写的时候还是要用英文）。

[3] inoculation certificate 接种证书

为了维护本国的利益、有效控制疫情传播和蔓延，世界各国对于外国入境者都要求出示其由本国的卫生检疫机关或国立医院签发的健康证明书，不少国家还要检查艾滋病检验证书和预防接种证书——黄皮书，对没有相关的卫生检疫证书的外国入境者，将拒绝其入境。

New Words

charge	[tʃɑːdʒ]	n. 费用；掌管；控告 v. 使充电；指责
belonging	[bɪˈlɒŋɪŋ]	n. 所有物；行李；附属物
worth	[wɜːθ]	n. 价值
jewelry	[ˈdʒuːəlri]	n. 珠宝；珠宝类
electrical	[ɪˈlektrɪk(ə)l]	adj. 有关电的；电气科学的
equipment	[ɪˈkwɪpm(ə)nt]	n. 设备；器材
carpet	[ˈkɑːpɪt]	n. 地毯；地毯状覆盖物
cigarette	[sɪɡəˈret]	n. 香烟
adult	[ˈædʌlt; əˈdʌlt]	adj. 成年的；成熟的 n. 成年人
suppose	[səˈpəʊz]	v. 假设；认为；推想；猜想；料想
document	[ˈdɒkjʊm(ə)nt]	n. 文件，公文；证件
declaration	[dekləˈreɪʃ(ə)n]	n.（纳税品等的）申报；宣布
inspector	[ɪnˈspektə]	n. 检查员；巡视员
identify	[aɪˈdentɪfaɪ]	v. 确定；识别，辨认出；认同；一致
abroad	[əˈbrɔːd]	adv. 在国外；到海外 adj. 国外的 n. 海外；异国
destination	[ˌdestɪˈneɪʃ(ə)n]	n. 目的地，终点
inoculation	[ɪˌnɒkjʊˈleɪʃn]	n. 接种
regulation	[reɡjʊˈleɪʃ(ə)n]	n. 管理；规则

Phrases and Expressions

free of charge	免费
electrical equipment	电器设备
personal belongings	私人物品
household utensils	家庭用品
customs inspector	海关检察员
inoculation certificate	接种证书

 Integrated Exercises of Skills

Task I Work in groups and discuss the following questions.

1. What articles are free of charge when foreigners coming to America bring?
2. What will customs inspector do if a person fails to declare an article or understates its value?
3. In the United States, how much the articles totaling up to are exempt (free from any duty) if they meet certain regulations?
4. How much wine can adults bring?
5. What should you do when you've received your baggage?

Task II Complete the brackets according to the text.

　　After arriving in America, your documents will be checked (1) _____. You must fill in a (2) _____ form and show your (3) _____ and passport. Having received your (4) _____, you should hand in your (5) _____ and luggage check.

　　Customs inspectors examine the luggage of all travellers to the country. All articles acquired abroad must be (6) _____ —that is, they must be identified and their value must be given to an inspector. If a person fails to declare an article or understates its value, the article may be (7) _____ and the individual may be fined. In the United States, articles totaling up to $400 are (8) _____ (free from any duty) if they meet certain regulations. For example, the articles must be for (9) _____ use, and the person's trip must last (10) _____ 48 hours.

Task III Fill in the blanks with the suitable words given below, changing the form where necessary.

check	destination	abroad	fail
worth	identify	equipment	suppose

Chapter One Preparation for Travelling

1. They have all the _____ and advice you will need.
2. She is actively _____ with our plans.
3. You should not deprecate your own _____.
4. _____ he isn't out, how can I do then?
5. Some goods made in China cost more than they do _____.
6. Don't let down even if you're nearing the _____.
7. You'll have to stay in after school if you still _____ to pass the examination.
8. Please _____ out these names and numbers.

Task IV   Translate the sentences into Chinese.

1. Entering the U. S. , you can bring $100 worth of presents, but you have to stay in the United States for at least 72 hours.

   _____
   _____

2. After arriving in America, your documents will be checked by the customs officer.

   _____
   _____

3. Customs inspectors examine the luggage of all travellers to the country.

   _____
   _____

4. If a person fails to declare an article or understates its value, the article may be taken away and the individual may be fined.

   _____
   _____

5. For example, the articles must be for personal use, and the person's trip must last at least 48 hours.

   _____
   _____

······ Part IV   Practical Writing ······

Arrival/Departure Record 入境/离境记录

入境美国的外籍旅客需要填写两份表格，一份是美国海关申报表（Custom Declaration），一份是 I-94 出入境卡（I-94 Form）。

I-94 出入境卡对于入境美国的外籍旅客非常重要，该卡上记载该旅客可在美国停留的有效日期，通常由美国移民官订在旅客的护照上。在旅客离开美国时，该卡必须要交给航空公司，而航空公司则转交给美国移民局，以建立该旅客出入美国的记录，否则将来该旅客有可能会被美国拒绝入境。

I-94 Arrival/Departure Record Instructions
（I-94 入境/离境记录说明）

This form must be completed by all persons except U.S. citizens, returning resident, aliens with immigrant visas, and Canadian citizens, visiting or in transit.

Type or print legibly with pen in ALL CAPITAL LETTERS. Use English. Do not write on the back of this form.

This form is in two parts. Please complete both the Arrival Record (Item 1 through 13) and the Departure Record (Item 14 through 17).

Item 7—If you are entering the United States by land, enter LAND in this space. If you are entering the United States by ship, enter SEA in this space. When all items are completed, present this form to the U.S. Immigration and Naturalization Service Inspector.

除了美国公民、美国侨民、持有移民签证的外国人，访问或过境的加拿大公民外，（其他）所有人员都必须填写此表。

请用大写字母打字或用笔填写清楚。请用英文填写。不要在此表背面写任何字。

此表包括两部分，请填写入境记录（第1项至第13项）和出境记录（第14项至第17项）两部分。

第7项内容说明——如果你从陆路进入美国，请在空格内填写"LAND"。如果你是搭乘船进入美国，请在空格内填写"SEA"。填写完毕后，请将此表交给美国移民局官员。

I-94 Arrival Record
（I-94 入境记录）

1. Family Name（姓）_____
2. First (Given) Name（名）_____
3. Birth Date (Day/Mo/Yr)（生日（日/月/年））_____
4. Country of Citizenship（国籍）_____
5. Sex (Male or Female)（性别（男填 MALE 或女填 FEMALE））_____
6. Passport Number（护照号码）_____
7. Airline&Flight Number（航空公司和班机号码）_____
8. Country Where You Live（居住国）_____
9. City Where You Boarded（你在哪个城市登机）_____
10. City Where Visa Was Issued（在哪个城市取得签证）_____
11. Date Issued (Day/Mo/Yr)（取得签证日期（日/月/年））_____
12. Address While in the United State (Number and Street)（在美国的住址（门牌号及街

Chapter One Preparation for Travelling

名) _____
13. City and State（在美国的住址（市名及州名））_____

Departure Number 89073853 1 01（离境号码 89073853 1 01）

Immigration and Naturalization Service（移民局）

I-94 Departure Record

（I-94 离境记录）

14. Family Name（姓）_____
15. First（Given）Name（名）_____
16. Birth Date（Day/Mo/Yr）（生日（日/月/年））_____
17. Country of Citizenship（国籍）_____

Task Suppose you are going to spend your holiday in the U.S., please fill the Arrival/Departure Record according to your own situation.

美国海关出入境登记表（I-94 FORM）（中英文对照）	
U.S. Department of Justice OMR 1115-4077 Immigration and Naturalization Service	美国司法部 OMR 1115-407 移民局
Welcome to the United State	欢迎来到美国
Admission Number 233414639 09	登记号码（＊举例说明） 233414639 09
I-94 Arrival/Departure Record Instructions	**I-94 入境/离境记录说明**
This form must be completed by all persons except U.S. citizens, returning resident aliens with immigrant visas, and Canadian Citizens visiting or in transit.	除了美国公民、美国侨民、持有移民签证的外国人，访问或过境的加拿大公民外，（其他）所有人员都必须填写此表。
Type or print legibly with pen in ALL CAPITAL LETTERS. Use English. Do not write on the back of this form.	请用大写字母打字或用钢笔或用圆珠笔清楚填写。请用英文填写。不要在此表背面填写任何东西。
This form is in two parts. Please complete both the Arrival Record（Item 1 through 13）and the Departure Record（Item 14 through 17）.	此表包括两部分，请填写入境记录（第 1 项至第 13 项）和离境记录（第 14 项至第 17 项）两部分。
When all items are completed, present this form to the U.S. Immigration and Naturalization Service Inspector.	填写完毕后，请将此表交给美国移民局官员。
Item 7—If you are entering the United States by land, enter LAND in this space. If you are entering the United States by ship, enter SEA in this space.	第 7 项内容说明——如果你从陆地进入美国，请在空格内填写"LAND"，如果你乘船进入美国，请在空格内填写"SEA"。

（续）

Form I-94 (10-01-85) N	I-94 表 (10-01-85) N
Admission Number 233414639 09	登记号码 233414639 09
Immigration and Naturalization Service	移民局
I-94 Arrival Record	I-94 入境记录
1. Family Name _____	1. 姓
2. First (Given) Name _____	2. 名
3. Birth Date (Day/Mo/Yr) _____	3. 生日（日/月/年）
4. Country of Citizenship _____	4. 国籍
5. Sex (Male or Female) _____	5. 性别（男填 MALE 或女填 FEMALE）
6. Passport Number _____	6. 护照号码
7. Airline & Flight Number _____	7. 航空公司和航班号
8. Country Where You Live _____	8. 居住国
9. City Where You Boarded _____	9. 你在哪个城市登机
10. City Where Visa Was Issued _____	10. 在哪个城市取得签证
11. Date Issued (Day/Mo/Yr) _____	11. 取得签证日期（日/月/年）
12. Address While in the United State (Number and Street)	12. 在美国的住址（门牌号及街名）
13. City and State _____	13. 在美国的住址（市名及州名）
Departure Number 233414639 09	离境号码 233414639 09
Immigration and Naturalization Service	移民局
I-94 Departure Record	I-94 离境记录
14. Family Name _____	14. 姓
15. First (Given) Name _____	
16. Birth Date (Day/Mo/Yr) _____	15. 名
16. 生日（日/月/年）	
17. Country of Citizenship _____	17. 国籍

Chapter One　Preparation for Travelling

······ Part V　Typical Scenic Spot ······

Forbidden City

The Palace Museum, known as the Forbidden City, was the home to 24 Ming and Qing emperors, off-limits to the public for 500 years. It stands in the center of Beijing, covering 720,000 square meters, owning 800 buildings and 9,999 rooms, constituting a priceless testimony to Chinese civilization during the Ming and Qing dynasties. It is the largest and most magnificent group of palaces existing in China and a treasure house of various relics. It is also perfectly maintained.

The Forbidden City was inaccessible to the common people during the reign of the emperors. Even the highest civil and military officers could not enter it without good reason. The Forbidden City is one of the architectural wonders of the world. The construction took 14 years and was finished in 1420. The former Palace's outer court, with its halls of Supreme, Central and Preserved Harmony and side buildings, was where the emperor handled the state affairs and held grand ceremonies. The three main and six eastern and western palaces form the inner court, where the emperor dealt with daily government affairs, and where the imperial family lived. The last dynasty fell in 1911, but Emperor Puyi still lived in the inner court. In 1925, it was converted into a museum and opened to the public.

In 1987, the Palace was inscribed on the UNESCO World Cultural Heritage List.

How to Get There and Get Around

Buses No. 1, 2, 4, 10, 20 or 101 stop at Tiananmen, Front Gate of the Palace. Trolley buses No. 103 and No. 109 stop by the North Gate.

Opening Time

8:30-17:00, last admission at 16:10 in summer and 15:40 in winter.

Admission Fee

60 yuan/person.

Tips

1) Photography is strictly forbidden in the halls and palaces.

2) At Meridian Gate, you can rent a guide tape with player, in various languages to introduce you to different places in the City. The tape can be returned at North Gate as you exit.

Neighborhood

The hill in Jingshan Park opposite North Gate offers a panoramic view of the Forbidden City.

职业素养

　　文化是旅游的灵魂，旅游是文化的载体。党的二十大报告明确要求，"坚持以文塑旅、以旅彰文，推进文化和旅游深度融合发展"。所谓"以文塑旅"，就是要用文化去塑造旅游，文化是旅游的方向。所有看似旅游活动的表象，底层都是为了体验当地文化。旅游要加强对文化的弘扬和传播，文化要为旅游提供内涵和支撑。

Unit 2 Visa Affairs

······ **Part I Warm-Up** ······

Apply for a visa

1. **Qualifications**

A foreigner who is invited to China for visit, study, lecture or business tour or for scientific, technical, and culture exchanges, short-term refresher course or job-training needs applying for a visa.

2. **Formalities**

1) Handing over the originals of the valid passport for examination.

2) The original of the certificate of check-in in ××× (issued by the hotel or the police substation of the area where the lodging takes place).

3) Submitting the Foreigner Visa and Residence Permit Application From completely filled up and one recent 2-inch half-length, bareheaded and full-faced photograph.

3. **Time limit of handling**

With 5 working days, if the application documents are complete. If there is no temporary lodging proof, we need 6 working days. In special circumstances, it takes only 4 working days.

4. **Fee standard**

For details, you can see the Visa Fee Standard of Reciprocal Countries and Non-Reciprocal Countries, issued by the State Development and Planning Commission and the Ministry of Finance.

5. **Duration time:** 3months or 6 months.

6. **Numbers of Entry:** Zero, Single, Double.

······ **Part II Conversations** ······

听一听

Conversation 1   Apply for a Visa

Todd: So, Lucinda, you were saying that your boyfriend Kwame really likes New Zealand, so are you guys going to move back to New Zealand?

Lucinda: Yes. We're actually leaving at the end of this month on the 30th of November.

Todd: Oh, really. You're moving. He's moving for good?

Lucinda: Yes, yes. We're both moving there to work.

Todd: So, was it difficult for him to get a visa? Or, is it quite easy to go to New Zealand?

Lucinda: There are a lot of things they want you to have before you can apply for the visa. Such as, you need to prove that you're living together, certain things like that.

Todd: You mean as a married couple you have to show...

Lucinda: Right, right. There is because his visa is under partnership. If he was going to New Zealand for work, then he would have to show that he had worked in New Zealand. But since it's under partnership, even though it's a work visa, he doesn't need to have worked in New Zealand. And he has to prove that he's been living with me for one year, and that we have a stable relationship.

Todd: Wow. How do you prove that you've been living together? What kind of things do you do?

Lucinda: We have to show a letter from our landlord, and we also have to show photos of us together from different times. We also have to have letters from friends. I think there maybe twenty letters from friends and families from both my side and his side showing that we've been together for a certain time. And they recommend the visa, etc. Yeah, quite complicated.

Todd: What about the paperwork process? Is it pretty easy or is it difficult?

Lucinda: The paperwork's very easy. Apart from the house certificate, we have to go through as many medical examinations as you can think possible, with six vials of blood taken. Apart from that, the actual filling out of forms is very easy. There's only, I think, a number of pages to fill out, because there're no children or other people involved. It's only him and me so there are only a few pages actually to fill out on forms.

Todd: OK. And he has to have a medical examination just to make sure that he doesn't have...

Lucinda: He doesn't have any illnesses that New Zealand doesn't have or certain tests will have to be taken to see if he's healthy, I guess. I don't know why they do that, but they want to know that someone doesn't have any too serious health problems. Because once you are in New Zealand, you can enjoy quite a good health care system, so they don't want to be taking on some person that's just going to New Zealand for certain health care benefits.

Todd: Well, that's great that you guys are going together and good luck with your life in New Zealand.

Lucinda: Thank you.

Chapter One Preparation for Travelling

New Words

guy	[gaɪ]	n.	男人，家伙
prove	[pruːv]	v.	证明；显示
couple	[ˈkʌp(ə)l]	n.	对；夫妇
partnership	[ˈpɑːtnəʃɪp]	n.	合伙
certificate	[səˈtɪfɪkɪt]	n.	证书；执照，文凭
stable	[ˈsteɪb(ə)l]	adj.	稳定的；牢固的；坚定的
apartment	[əˈpɑːtm(ə)nt]	n.	公寓；房间
complicated	[ˈkɒmplɪkeɪtɪd]	adj.	难懂的，复杂的
basically	[ˈbeɪsɪk(ə)li]	adv.	主要地，基本上
process	[ˈprəʊses]	n.	过程，进行
vial	[ˈvaɪəl]	n.	小瓶；药水瓶
blood	[blʌd]	n.	血液；血统
involve	[ɪnˈvɒlv]	v.	有关；卷入
actually	[ˈæktjʊəli; -tʃʊ-]	adv.	实际上；事实上
illness	[ˈɪlnəs]	n.	病；疾病
test	[test]	n. 试验；检验 v. 试验；测试
once	[wʌns]	adv. 一次；曾经 conj. 一旦

Phrases and Expressions

for good	永久地；一劳永逸地
as long as	只要；和……一样长
apart from	除……之外；并且
fill out	填写
taking on	承担；接纳
a certain amount of	一定数量的

Conversation 2　　Conditions of Applying for a Visa

A: I have heard that you are going to Singapore for an international educational conference next month. Is it true?

B: Yes, if everything goes smoothly.

A: Wonderful. It is really a valuable chance to get to know some knowledge frontier as well as the latest teaching skills. Isn't it marvelous? Congratulations!

B: Thank you. But the procedures for going abroad are very complicated. It's a big headache. I really do not know how to make it. I have heard that the procedures to apply for a business visa are not that easy.

A: Don't worry so much. I went to attend an international meeting last year, and I know there are some requirements to be satisfied if you are applying for a business visa, but it is not that difficult as you have imagined. Firstly you need to have an invitation letter, which is a necessity, because the officer in the visa office will need this to confirm that there are really some proper business reasons for you to go to their country and without any ill intention.

B: OK. I see. That means the invitation letter is the basic document I need to have. Then I will e-mail the organizer of this conference to provide me with an invitation letter.

A: And the Immigration Bureau will ask you to be physically healthy, no criminal record, and no threat to the national security. That means you have to ask the personnel department of your school to provide a certificate to confirm that you do not have any of the problems.

B: OK. This is not difficult.

A: So, we are almost there. It is not that complicated as you imagined, huh?

B: Yes. You are right. Thank you so much. You are really helpful. I am really honored to have a friend like you.

 New Words

smoothly	[ˈsmuːðli]	adv.	平滑地；流畅地，流利地
frontier	[ˈfrʌntɪə; frʌnˈtɪə]	n.	前沿；边界；国境
marvelous	[ˈmɑːvələs]	adj.	了不起的；非凡的；不平常的
procedure	[prəˈsiːdʒə]	n.	程序，手续
headache	[ˈhedeɪk]	n.	头痛；麻烦
attend	[əˈtend]	v.	出席；照料；致力于
requirement	[rɪˈkwaɪəm(ə)nt]	n.	要求；必需品
satisfied	[ˈsætɪsfaɪd]	adj.	感到满意的
imagine	[ɪˈmædʒɪn]	v.	想象；臆断
necessity	[nɪˈsesɪti]	n.	需要；必然性；必需品
confirm	[kənˈfɜːm]	v.	确认；证实
intention	[ɪnˈtenʃ(ə)n]	n.	意图；目的
document	[ˈdɒkjʊm(ə)nt]	n.	文件，公文
provide	[prəˈvaɪd]	v.	提供；规定
criminal	[ˈkrɪmɪn(ə)l]	n.	罪犯
security	[sɪˈkjʊərəti]	n.	安全；保证

Chapter One　Preparation for Travelling

 Phrases and Expressions

go smoothly	顺利；进展顺利
as well as	也；和……一样；不但……而且
business visa	商务签证
an invitation letter	一封邀请函
Immigration Bureau	移民局

 Practical Patterns

1. Excuse me. Can you tell me how to apply for a visa to France?
   Can you tell me what I need to apply a visa to France?
   Can you tell me how you give me a visa to France?
   打扰了，请问怎样申请到法国的签证？

2. If you want to apply for a visa, you must go to consulate to find the consul.
   You need to go to consulate to find the consul to apply for a visa.
   For applying a visa, you have to go to the consulate to find the consul.
   如果你想申请签证，你必须去领事馆找领事。

3. I will have an interview with the visa official this Thursday.
   I will go for an interview for a visa this Thursday.
   I will interview with the visa official this Thursday.
   这个周四办理签证的官员要对我进行面试。

4. How did the interview go?
   What about your interview?
   How was your interview?
   面试怎么样？

5. The consular officer just asked me a few questions.
   I only had a few questions from the consular officer.
   I was asked a few questions by the consular officer.
   领事官就问了我几个问题。

6. Have you got your visa yet?
   Have you got hold of the visa?
   Did you succeed in getting the visa?
   你拿到签证了吗？

7. I was ordered to leave the country because my visa was due.
   My visa had expired and I might return to my country.
   Because of my visa is at maturity, I have to leave the country.

25

因为我的签证到期了，我被命令离开这个国家。

8. I heard most of the study visas are approved.

   Most of the study visas are said to be approved.

   If you want to study abroad, most of the visas will be approved.

   听说留学的签证大部分都会批准。

Task I   Complete the following dialogues by translating the Chinese in the brackets.

A: _____（我要去美国参加一个销售会议，所以我想申请一个商务签证。）

B: OK. Do you mind if I ask you a few questions?

A: Not at all. Go ahead.

B: OK. _____（首先，您能告诉我您的姓名和出生年月日吗?）

A: Sure. I am Helena and I was born on April, 27th, 1981.

B: So, you just said you would attend a conference there, _____（您能不能详细说一下这次会议，还有您收到邀请函了吗?）

A: Of course. That is an annual sales conference held by Leech Company of America, and we have much business with the company, _____（所以我被邀请去参加此次会议。）

B: When do you prepare to depart?

A: _____（我是打算下个月出发去美国。）

B: OK. _____（好的，我们会尽快办好您的签证。）

Task II   Using the given words and expressions to make a conversation with your partner according to the situation.

Student A

Imagine that you are going to travel abroad on holiday. Think of what you are going to do and answer Student B's questions.

Student B

You want to find out about Student A' holiday plans. Ask questions using the following prompts.

Where / spend / holiday /...?

When / leave/...?

How / apply for / a visa / ...?

Have / got / visa /...?

Chapter One Preparation for Travelling

Will / interview / for a visa /...?
How many days / stay / there /...?

······ Part III   Readings ······

Text A

Visa Application

Just getting accepted to an American college or university does not guarantee that you will get a visa. And getting a visa just lets you arrive in the United States. It does not guarantee that an immigration officer will permit you to enter the country. Travel documents come from the State Department, but immigration is the responsibility of the Department of Homeland Security.

The State Department has a website with all the rules for getting a visa. The address is unitedstatesvisas. gov. "Unitedstatesvisas" is all one word.

If you are requesting a visa for the first time, you will probably have to go to an American embassy or consulate. You will need to bring a government form sent to you by your American school that shows you have been accepted. You will also need banking and tax records that show you have enough money to pay for your education. And be prepared to provide evidence that you will return to your home country after your studies end.

All of these are very important in satisfying the requirements to apply for a visa. A consular official will also take your picture and your fingerprints.

Foreign students must contact their local embassy or consulate to request an interview and to get some information which includes directions about how and where to pay the visa application charge. The cost is two hundred dollars. You should apply for the visa as soon as you have been accepted to a school in the United States. The government needs time to perform a background investigation. You cannot receive a visa more than one hundred twenty days before the start of your program. And if you are coming as a student for the first time, you cannot enter the country more than thirty days before classes begin. Once you enter the United States, you can stay there for the entire period of your study.

 New Words

guarantee	[gær(ə)nˈtiː]	v. 保证；担保
immigration	[ˌɪmɪˈgreɪʃn]	n. 外来移民；移居
responsibility	[rɪˌspɒnsɪˈbɪlɪti]	n. 责任，职责；义务
rule	[ruːl]	n. 统治；规则
request	[rɪˈkwest]	n. & v. 请求；需要
probably	[ˈprɒbəbli]	adv. 或许；很可能
embassy	[ˈembəsi]	n. 大使馆
consulate	[ˈkɒnsjʊlət]	n. 领事馆
tax	[tæks]	v. 向……课税；使负重担 n. 税金；重负
record	[ˈrekɔːd]	v. 记录；录音 n. 记录，档案；唱片
education	[ˌedjʊˈkeɪʃ(ə)n]	n. 教育；培养
evidence	[ˈevɪd(ə)ns]	n. 证据；迹象 v. 证明
fingerprint	[ˈfɪŋgəprɪnt]	n. 指纹；手印 v. 采指纹
interview	[ˈɪntəvjuː]	n. & v. 采访；面试
government	[ˈgʌv(ə)nm(ə)nt]	n. 政府；管辖
information	[ˌɪnfəˈmeɪʃ(ə)n]	n. 信息，资料；情报
perform	[pəˈfɔːm]	v. 执行；表演
background	[ˈbækgraʊnd]	n. 背景 v. 做……的背景
investigation	[ɪnˌvestɪˈgeɪʃ(ə)n]	n. 调查；调查研究
entire	[ɪnˈtaɪə; en-]	adj. 全部的；整个的

 Phrases and Expressions

State Department	（美国）国务院
Department of Homeland Security	国土安全部
American embassy or consulate	美国大使馆或领事馆
tax records	纳税记录
background investigation	背景调查

Chapter One Preparation for Travelling

 Integrated Exercises of Skills

Task I Discuss with partners and answer the following questions according to the text.

1. Will you get a visa if you accept a college or university admission letter?
2. If you get a visa, does it guarantee that an immigration officer will permit you to enter the country?
3. If you are requesting a visa for the first time, where will you probably have to go?
4. Why should you also need banking and tax records when you are requesting a visa?
5. Where must foreign students contact to request an interview and to get some information?

Task II Fill in the blanks with the suitable words given below, changing the form where necessary.

| guarantee | request | record | fingerprint | education |
| information | rule | probably | responsibility | evidence |

1. But even that does not _____ they will be achieved.
2. I'm afraid I can't shoulder such a _____.
3. If one of us breaks a _____, we all should be punished.
4. We _____ the favor of a reply at your earliest convenience.
5. That photograph _____ won't enlarge well.
6. What he said was completely spread on the _____.
7. His rudeness rooted in his lack of _____.
8. Let me adduce more _____.
9. A _____ can identify you at birth, death and any time in between.
10. I'm giving you this _____ for the record.

Task III Translate the sentences into Chinese.

1. Travel documents come from the State Department, but immigration is the responsibility of the Department of Homeland Security.
   _____
   _____

2. You will need to bring a government form sent to you by your American school that shows you have been accepted.
   _____
   _____

3. And be prepared to provide evidence that you will return to your home country after your studies end.

4. You should apply for the visa as soon as you have been accepted to a school in the United States.

5. And if you are coming as a student for the first time, you cannot enter the country more than thirty days before classes begin.

Task IV Reading comprehension.

Baggage and the Customs Inspector

The Silvers enter the baggage area where the baggage from their flight is already being unloaded.

The personal property that passengers take with them on a trip is called "baggage", or "luggage". For people who work on airlines, there are three kinds of baggage. One is the hand or carry-on luggage that people keep with them in the passenger cabin of the aircraft. Then there is the baggage that is carried in the special baggage compartment of the passenger's plane. This is called "checked baggage".

A third kind of luggage is called "unaccompanied baggage". It does not go on the same plane with the passenger, the owner of the baggage. Sometimes a person will make a stop somewhere in the middle of a trip but will send the luggage to the final stop.

The Silvers see that the baggage from their flight is entering the baggage area on a conveyor belt, which carries the luggage from the plane outside the terminal into the baggage area where the passengers can get them.

At the far end of the room are several rows of short conveyor belts, waist high. People place their luggage on these conveyor belts, which carry the bags to a counter where they are inspected, or examined, by the customs inspectors.

Simone Clark is one of the customs inspectors behind the counter. Her job is to examine the contents of all baggage brought into the country and to watch for contraband and smugglers. However, she knows that most travellers and tourists are not smugglers. Her country does not tax the personal things visitor or tourist bring into the country. The country is anxious for tourists to enjoy its hospitality. Most tourists bring only the personal things they will need for their trip. They do not bring things for resale. Instead, they usually buy the country's products to remember the trip or to take home as gifts.

Mrs. Clark must be a diplomat in her job.

Chapter One Preparation for Travelling

Tourist or visitors often get upset when customs inspectors go through their luggage. They get angry with the inspector even when they know it is the official's job. Mrs. Clark tries not to annoy people who are coming to enjoy the hospitality of her country. She tries to be as polite as possible and not to mess or disturb their clothing and other belongings. Often she doesn't even inspect their suitcase. After many years on the job, Mrs. Clark is a good judge of people.

I. Choose the correct word or phrase to complete each sentence.

1. The baggage that is carried in a special compartment of the plane on which the passenger is flying is called _____ baggage.
   A. carry-on   B. tagged   C. checked   D. unaccompanied
2. The baggage comes into the baggage area from the aircraft on a _____.
   A. counter   B. conveyor belt
   C. claim check   D. baggage compartment
3. The job of _____ is to examine the contents of all baggage brought into the country.
   A. immigration officers   B. customs inspectors
   C. flight attendant   D. tax collectors
4. A person who brings into or sends out of a country an item illegally is a _____.
   A. passenger   B. smuggler
   C. contraband   D. customs inspector

II. Questions for discussion.

1. What are the three kinds of baggage for people who work on airlines?
2. How is luggage brought into the baggage area?
3. What are some of the things Mrs. Clark must watch for?
4. Why do people sometimes get angry with customs inspectors?
5. Why doesn't Mrs. Clark inspect most tourists' luggage?

Text B

How to Reduce Your Waiting Time

Following these tips will help you reduce your waiting time at the security checkpoint.

Before You Go to the Airport

- Do not pack or take Prohibited Items to the airport.
- Place valuables such as jewelry, cash and laptops in carry-on baggage only.
- Tape your business card to the bottom of your laptop.
- Avoid wearing clothing, jewelry and accessories that contain metal. Metal items may set off the alarm on the metal detector.
- Avoid wearing shoes that contain metal or have thick soles or high heels. Many types of footwear will require additional screening even if the metal detector is not alarmed.
- Put all undeveloped film and cameras with film in your carry-on baggage. Checked baggage screening equipment will damage undeveloped film.
- Declare firearms & ammunition to your airline and place them in your checked baggage. If you wish to lock your baggage, use a TSA[1]-recognized lock[2].
- Do not take lighters or prohibited matches to the airport. Do not pack wrapped gifts and do not take them to the checkpoint. Wrap on arrival or ship your gifts prior to your departure. TSA may have to unwrap packages for security reasons.

While at the Airport

Each adult traveller needs to keep available his/her airline boarding pass and government-issued photo ID until exiting the security checkpoint. Due to different airport configurations, at many airports you will be required to show these documents more than once.

 New Words

tip	[tɪp]	n. 小建议，小窍门
security	[sɪˈkjʊərəti]	n. 安全；保证 adj. 安全的；保密的
prohibit	[prə(ʊ)ˈhɪbɪt]	v. 阻止，禁止
valuable	[ˈvæljʊb(ə)l]	adj. 有价值的；贵重的 n. 贵重物品
laptop	[ˈlæptɒp]	n. 笔记本电脑
tape	[teɪp]	n. 胶带；磁带 v. 录音；用带子捆扎

Chapter One Preparation for Travelling

bottom	[ˈbɒtəm]	n. 底部；末端
accessory	[əkˈses(ə)ri]	n. 配件；附件；[常作复数]（妇女的）装饰品
undeveloped	[ˌʌndɪˈveləpt]	adj. 未开发的；不发达的；（胶片）未冲洗的
alarm	[əˈlɑːm]	n. 闹钟；警报
heel	[hiːl]	n. 脚后跟；踵
require	[rɪˈkwaɪə]	v. 要求；命令
film	[fɪlm]	n. 电影；胶卷
damage	[ˈdæmɪdʒ]	n. & v. 损害；损毁；赔偿金
declare	[dɪˈkleə]	v. 宣布，声明，声明
lock	[lɒk]	v. 锁上；隐藏；锁住；卡住
lighter	[ˈlaɪtə]	n. 打火机；点火者
prior	[ˈpraɪə]	adj. 优先的；在先的；adv. 在前，居先
ammunition	[ˌæmjʊˈnɪʃ(ə)n]	n. 弹药，军火
wrapped	[ræpt]	adj. 有包装的
configuration	[kənˌfɪgəˈreɪʃ(ə)n]	n. 配置，布局；外形

 Phrases and Expressions

security checkpoint　　　　安全检查处
Prohibited Items　　　　　　明令禁止的物品
carry-on baggage　　　　　　随身携带的包裹
business card　　　　　　　　名片
high heel　　　　　　　　　　高跟鞋
metal detector　　　　　　　金属检测器
wrapped gifts　　　　　　　　有包装的礼物
boarding pass　　　　　　　　登机牌

 Notes

1. TSA 是指 U.S. Transportation Security Administration 的缩写，意为"美国运输安全管理局"。
2. a TSA-recognized lock，称海关锁，亦俗称关锁，又称 TSA 认证锁。海关锁是指美国海关对转关行李货物及运输海关监管货物进行安全性检测，须保证货物在运输过程中的安全性而采用国际海关全球通用的万能 TSA 专用钥匙。

 Integrated Exercises of Skills

Task I　Discuss with partners and answer the following questions according to the text.

1. Where should you place your valuables before you go to the airport?
2. Why don't you wear clothing that contains metal?
3. If you're wearing shoes that contain metal or have thick soles or high heels, what will you probably have to face?
4. If you want to send your friend a beautiful wrapped gift box, what can you do?
5. If you have to take firearms & ammunition when you take a plane, what can you do?

Task II　Fill in the blanks with the suitable words given below, changing the form where necessary.

valuable	declare	prohibit	wrap	bottom
require	security	prior	alarm	film

1. Their talk ran upon the problems of social welfare and social _____ system.
2. We are _____ from drinking alcohol during working hours.
3. If this time is so _____—for ourselves and our companies—how do we get more of it?
4. The children carefully printed their names in capitals at the _____ of their pictures.
5. The air-raid _____ went on drilling away from the gate.
6. What clause do you _____ in the contract?
7. With this instant _____ the picture develops in only one minute.
8. You'd better _____ the camera to the official.
9. I look out at this audience filled with not only many friends and colleagues, but people who have served in _____ administrations.
10. He _____ the present in pretty paper for his girlfriend.

Task III　Translate the sentences into Chinese.

1. Place valuables such as jewelry, cash and laptops in carry-on baggage only. Tape your business card to the bottom of your laptop.

_____
_____

2. Many types of footwear will require additional screening even if the metal detector is

not alarmed.

3. Put all undeveloped film and cameras with film in your carry-on baggage. Checked baggage screening equipment will damage undeveloped film.

4. Do not pack wrapped gifts and do not take them to the checkpoint.

5. Due to different airport configurations, at many airports you will be required to show these documents more than once.

Part IV Practical Writing

VISA APPLICATION FORM OF THE PEOPLE'S REPUBLIC OF CHINA
中华人民共和国签证申请表

请用印刷体大写填写（Please write in block letters）

1. 外文姓 Surname _____ 外文名 Given name _____
2. 性别 Sex：□男/M □女/F   照片 Paste your Photo here
3. 中文姓名 Chinese name (If any)：_____
4. 曾用名 Former name (If any)：_____
5. 出生日期 Date of birth： 年   月   日
   _____ Y _____ M _____ D
6. 出生地点（省/市）Place of birth：_____ City _____ Province
7. 国籍 Nationality：_____
8. 曾有过何国籍 Former nationality (If any)：_____
9. 职业 Occupation：_____
10. 工作单位 Employer's name：_____
    电话：Tel. No. _____
11. 家庭住址 Home address：_____
    电话：Tel. No. _____

12. 护照种类 Passport type：

    □外交 Diplomatic　　　□公务（官员）Service（Official）　　　□普通 Ordinary

    □其他旅行证件 Other travel document：

    护照号码 Passport No.：_____

    有效期至 Valid until：_____

    发照机关 Issued by：_____

13. 申请赴中国事由 Purpose of journey to China：_____

14. 前往地点 Place to visit in China：_____

15. 邀请单位名称或邀请人姓名、地址、电话

    Name，address and phone of the inviting organization or person to be visited in China：

    单位名称/姓名 Name：_____

    地址 Address：_____

    电话 Tel. No.　_____

16. 拟入境日期：　　　年　　　月　　　日

    Intended date of entry：_____Y _____M _____D

17. 每次停留天数 Duration of each stay：_____天 days

18. 拟入境次数 Number of entries：

    □一次 Single　　　　　　　　　　□二次 Double

    □半年多次 Multiple for half year　　□一年多次 Multiple for one year

    □一次过境 Single transit　　　　　□二次过境 Double transit

19. 是否申请过赴华签证？Have you ever applied for a Chinese visa before?

    是 Yes□　　　否 No□

20. 是否被拒绝过来华签证？Have you ever been declined for your Chinese visa application?

    是 Yes□　　　否 No□

    被拒时间、地点 If ever declined，when and where?　_____

21. 使用同一护照的同行人 Accompanying persons included in passport：

    姓名 Full name _____

    出生日期 Date of birth _____

    与申请人的关系 Relationship to applicant _____

    　　　年　　　月　　　日

    _____Y _____M _____D

22. 我谨声明我已如实和完整地填写了上述内容，并对此负责。

    I hereby declare that the information given above is true, correct and complete. I shall bear the responsibility for the above information.

　　年　　　月　　　日　　　　　签名

_____ Y _____ M _____ D　　Signature：

请认真阅读背面的注意事项。

Please read "Notes" carefully on the back.

注意事项

一、申请人的护照有效期不能少于半年，且必须有两张空白签证页。

二、申请人需填写一张签证申请表，并提供一张二寸护照照片，以及其他与申请事项有关的材料。

三、申请人必须如实、完整地填写申请表格和签名，并对所填写的内容负责。申报情况或提供材料不实或不完整，将可能导致签证被拒绝。由此产生的一切后果由申请人自行承担。

四、持标有"X""Z""D""J－1"字签证者，必须在入境后30天内到所在地区公安机关办理居留手续。

五、申请人赴华必须带足旅费，在华期间必须遵守中国的法律法规，不得在中国境内从事与申请签证时申报事由无关的活动。

六、未经批准，不得在中国境内任职或就业。

Notes

1. Applicant's passport should be valid for at least 6 months and have 2 blank visa pages.

2. Applicant is required to submit one visa application form. One 2″ passport photo and other documents related to application.

3. Applicant is required to fill the application form faithfully，completely and shall bear the responsibility for all the filled information. The application for a visa may be declined if the applicant fails to provide true and complete information or documents. The applicant shall bear all the consequences arising therefore.

4. The person holding types of X, Z, D, or J－1 visa shall go through residential formalities in the local public security department within 30 days since the date of entry.

5. Applicants shall carry with sufficient finances to cover all expenditures in China and shall abide by Chinese law and Regulations. Without approval，applicant is not permitted to do activities irrelevant to his or her statement when he or she applies the visa.

6. Employment in the territory of China is prohibited without approval.

Task Suppose you are going to spend your holiday abroad, please fill the visa application above according to your own situation.

Part V Typical Scenic Spot

Harbin International Ice and Snow Festival and Harbin Ice and Snow World

Harbin International Ice and Snow Festival

The Harbin International Ice and Snow Festival, started in 1985, is held annually from January 5 and lasts for over one month. Harbin is the capital city of Heilongjiang Province that holds China's original and greatest ice artwork festival which attracts hundreds of thousands of local people and visitors from all over the world.

The city's location in northeast China accounts for its arctic climate which provides abundant natural ice and snow. Subsequently the "Ice City" of Harbin is recognized as the cradle of ice and snow art in China and is famous for its exquisite and artistic ice and snow sculptures. The fabulous Ice Lantern Festival was the forerunner of the current festival and is still the best beloved part of the overall event in the opinion of those who come to Harbin each year.

The first ice lanterns were a winter-time tradition in northeast China. People made ice lanterns and put them outside their houses or gave them to children to play with during some of the traditional festivals. Thus the ice lantern began its long history of development. With novel changes and immense advancement in techniques, today we can marvel at the various delicate and artistic ice lanterns on display. Nowadays, ice lantern in broad sense refers to a series of plastic arts using ice and snow as raw material combining ice artworks with colored lights and splendid music. The specific patterns of ice lantern include ice and snow sculptures, ice flowers, ice architectures and so on. Harbin Ice and Snow Festival provides the visitors each year a whole new world of ice and snow. The best collections of ice artworks are exhibited in three main places: the Sun Island Park, Harbin Ice and Snow World, and Zhaolin Park.

Today, Harbin Ice and Snow Festival is not only an exposition of ice and snow art, but also an annual cultural event for international exchange. Every year, there are many ice sculpture experts, artists and fans from America, Canada, Japan, Singapore, Russia, China, etc. gathering in Harbin to participate ice sculpting competitions and to communicate with each other in the ice and snow world. Also, Harbin ice lanterns have been exhibited in most of China's main cities as well as in many countries in Asia, Europe, North America, Africa and Oceania. For more than 40 years Harbin's natural resource of ice and snow has been fully explored to provide joy and fun for visitors to the city. Now during the festival, many sporting competitions are also popular including ice-skating, sledding and so on. Weddings, parties and other entertainments are now very much a feature of this ice world, adding their own contribution to the celebrations of this great festival of art, culture, sports and tourism.

Harbin Ice and Snow World

First set-up by the Harbin Municipal Government in 1999, Harbin Ice and Snow World is by far the largest ice and snow art exhibition in the world. It is not only has art attractions, but also has beautiful night views, recreational activities and many forms of entertainment. Furthermore, the festival is constantly evolving and each year brings with it a new theme, providing visitors with a totally unique experience from one year to the next.

The ice carvings at the Harbin Ice and Snow World are regarded as some of the world's finest examples of ice art with visitors able to admire some of the largest and most majestic ice-sculpted masterpieces. Each of these ice carvings are designed in some way related to the festival's theme, enabling travellers to sample a variety of cultural flavors. For example, in its first year the festival's layout was designed around the idea of "Prosperous China and High-Flying Longjiang", with the ice carvings depicting the rapid development of the country. In 2005, the theme was "Friendship between China and Russia", with all the sculptures fashioned in a typical Russian style. Among them were replicas of some of Russia's most famous architecture, such as the Winter Palace, and Moscow's Red Square.

One of the highlights for any visitor to the festival is to visit the site at night when multicolored lights set underground illuminate the sculptures, revealing a whole new colorful dimension to the exhibits. The contrasts of the bright and dazzling lights against the dark night sky make the works look all the more spectacular.

Harbin Ice and Snow World is also a centre for various forms of recreation and entertainment, with a variety of opportunities on offer. Visitors will be amazed by the magnificent ice buildings, including an ice maze, ice bar, and even an ice hotel. If you are a fan of snow sports, then there is also the chance to participate in activities such as ice rock-climbing, skating, skiing, sliding, snow fights, ice golf, and ice archery. In addition to all this, special performances based on the festival theme are put on throughout the event which will no doubt greatly entertain those in search of something a little less physically-demanding.

Understandably, the best time to travel to Harbin is during the winter. The Harbin International Ice and Snow Festival is held either in late December or in early January, and for those who dream of a proper winter experience, Harbin Ice and Snow World is the place to make those dreams become a reality.

职业素养

党的二十大报告提出,增强中华文明传播力影响力。坚守中华文化立场,讲好中国故事、传播好中国声音,展现可信、可爱、可敬的中国形象;全面提升国际传播效能,形成同我国综合国力和国际地位相匹配的国际话语权;深化文明交流互鉴,推动中华文化更好走向世界。在文旅融合发展的大背景下,旅游是促进各国民众相互交流和理解,实现民心相通的重要手段和渠道。近年来,微博、微信等社交媒体和各种专业旅游网站是人们获取旅游信息、选择旅游产品的主要渠道。因此,在我国文化"走出去"过程中,利用好新媒体、讲好中国故事,是旅游文化对外传播的重要任务。

Chapter Two
Categories of Tourism

◇ Unit 3　Historical and Cultural Relics Tour

◇ Unit 4　Natural Wonders Tours

◇ Unit 5　Red Resorts Tours

Unit 3 Historical and Cultural Relics Tour

•••••• Part I Warm-Up ••••••

Historical and Cultural Sight means the landscape which is formed in the history with the profound nationality as well as historical and cultural connotation and is manifested in the materialized form. Historical and Cultural Relics Tour refers to the visit and sightseeing to the cultural and historical landscape.

•••••• Part II Conversations ••••••

Conversation 1   A Visit to the Summer Palace

Jack Smith: Do you know the Summer Palace?

Wade Vinson: Yes, I do. The Summer Palace is in Beijing, and it is a beautiful place.

Jack Smith: You are right. The Summer Palace is located in Beijing's northwest suburb, and it consists, in the main, the Longevity Hill and the Kunming Lake.

Wade Vinson: Could you tell me who wrote the name of the Summer Palace?

Jack Smith: The name of the Summer Palace, Yiheyuan Park (Park of Nurtured Harmony) is inscribed in gold in this name board in the handwriting of Emperor Guangxu of the Qing dynasty.

Wade Vinson: That's great. I think that is a good name. Do you know about Emperor Qianlong?

Jack Smith: Of course, I know about him a lot. In the winter of 1749, or the 14th year of the Qianlong reign of the Qing dynasty, Emperor Qianlong gave the place a major face-lift in preparation for his mother's 60th birthday. The Kuming Lake was dredged on a large scale.

Wade Vinson: I have read a book about the history of the Qing dynasty, and I know the major remains expended a large sum of money and consumed great manpower and material resources.

Jack Smith: Yes. It also took the workers so much time. After a dozen years of spadework,

Chapter Two　Categories of Tourism

the Garden of Limpid Ripples (Qingyiyuan) appeared on the map of Beijing as an immense imperial garden famed for its picturesque landscape.

Wade Vinson: Could you tell me who changed the Garden of Limpid Ripples to the name of the Summer Palace?

Jack Smith: In 1860, the Anglo-French Allied Force burned the Garden of Limpid Ripples together with Yuanmingyuan and some other famous imperial gardens. In 1886, or the 12th year the Guangxu reign, the Empress Dowager Cixi had the burned garden rebuilt on the debris, and in 1888, Cixi named the garden "Yiheyuan" or "Summer Palace".

Wade Vinson: Oh, that's great.

Jack Smith: However, in 1900, the Summer Palace was plundered and destroyed by the Allied Forces of Britain, America, Germany, France, Russia, Japan, Italy and Austrlia. The Summer Palace was rebuilt in 1903.

Wade Vinson: The Summer Palace has a hapless fate. But now it is very nice, covering an area of 300 hectares. There are 3,000 ancient buildings with a total floor space of approximately 70,000 square meters.

Jack Smith: Well, so many corridors, bridges, pavilions, waterside kiosks, hills, and towers are laid out in the Summer Palace, outlining the contours of the terraces to form a splendid group of classical Chinese architecture.

Wade Vinson: On December 2, 1998, the Summer Palace was designated by UNESCO as world cultural heritage. Through the years the place, with its superb artistic appeal, has enchanted many visitors from all over the world, who award it as "Paradise under Heaven".

Jack Smith: Such a wonderful place, why not go now?

 New Words

suburb	[ˈsʌbɜːb]	n.	附近；边缘部分
nameboard	[ˈneɪmbɔːd]	n.	名称牌；站名牌；招牌
dredge	[dredʒ]	v.	疏浚（河道等）
spadework	[ˈspeɪdwɜːk]	n.	铲土活儿；挖槽工作
immense	[ɪˈmens]	adj.	无限的；无边无际的
picturesque	[ˌpɪktʃəˈresk]	adj.	似画的；自然美的
plunder	[ˈplʌndə]	v.	掠夺；抢劫
hapless	[ˈhæplɪs]	adj.	运气不佳的；不幸的
appproximate	[əˈprɒksɪmɪt]	adj.	位置接近的，紧靠的，紧邻的
architecture	[ˈɑːkɪtektʃə]	n.	建筑学；建筑业
designate	[ˈdezɪgneɪt]	v.	标示；标明；指出

43

Phrases and Expressions

a dozen years of spadework	十余年的土方工程
a large scale of face-lift	大规模的翻修或改建
Anglo-French Allied Force	英法联军
consume manpower and material resources	耗费人力物力
Empress Dowager Cixi	慈禧太后
Garden of Limpid Ripples（Qingyiyuan）	清漪园
Kunming Lake	昆明湖
Longevity Hill	万寿山

Conversation 2   A Visit to Badaling

Ben Huston: I would like to visit Badaling. Would you like to go with me?
Mrs. Wright: Yes. But where is Badaling?
Ben Huston: Badaling is in the north of Juyong Pass. The ancient said that the formidability of Juyong Pass lies in Badaling. If Juyong Pass is the gateway to Beijing, then Badaling is its lock and key.
Mrs. Wright: When was Badaling built?
Ben Huston: It was built in 1505. The Great Wall in this area was repaired in large scale by Qi Jiguang during the period of 1569 to 1573. The Great Wall here is of imposing manner.
Mrs. Wright: Do you know the average height and width of the Great Wall at Badaling?
Ben Huston: The Great Wall at Badaling stands at an average height of 7.8 meters, 6.5 meters wide at the base and 5.8 meters at the top. Watchtowers or battlements were built at intervals of three hundred to five hundred meters.
Mrs. Wright: As the earliest sections of the Great Wall to be opened up as a tourist attraction, Badaling has become an emblem of the Ming-dynasty Great Wall, and enjoys a reputation that is the envy of other sections on the Great Wall.
Ben Huston: You are right.
Mrs. Wright: Let's go.

New Words

gateway	[ˈgeɪtweɪ]	n. 门口；出入口；门道
lock	[lɒk]	n. 锁；闩 v. 锁上
impose	[ɪmˈpəʊz]	v. 利用；欺骗；施加影响

Chapter Two   Categories of Tourism

average	[ˈævərɪdʒ]	n. 平均；平均数
interval	[ˈɪntəvəl]	n. 间隔；间距；幕间休息
emblem	[ˈembləm]	n. 象征；徽章；符号
reputation	[repjuˈteiʃən]	n. 名誉；声望
envy	[ˈenvi]	n. 嫉妒；羡慕

 Phrases and Expressions

Juyong Pass 居庸关
the average height and width 平均高度和宽度
watchtowers or battlements 瞭望塔或城垛
Ming-dynasty Great Wall 明代长城

 Practical Patterns

1. Do you know the Summer Palace?
   你知道颐和园吗？

2. The Summer Palace is located in Beijing's northwest suburb, and it consists, in the main, the Longevity Hill and the Kunming Lake.
   颐和园位于北京西北郊区，它主要由万寿山和昆明湖组成。

3. I think that is a good name.
   我认为这是一个不错名字。

4. I know him a lot.
   我非常了解他。

5. The Kuming Lake was dredged on a large scale.
   昆明湖也是在这次大规模疏浚过程中行成的。

6. I know the major remains expended a large sum of money and consumed great manpower and material resources.
   我了解到此次工程花费了一大笔金钱，消耗了巨大的人力和物力。

7. Could you tell me who changed the Garden of Limpid Ripples to the name of the Summer Palace?
   你能告诉我是谁把清漪园的名字改成颐和园的吗？

8. The Summer Palace has a hapless fate.
   颐和园有一个多灾多难的命运。

9. There are 3,000 ancient buildings with a total floor space of approximately 70,000 square meters.
   颐和园总占地面积300公顷，有3000个古代建筑，总建筑面积约为70,000平方米。

45

10. Such a wonderful place, why not go now?
    这样一个美妙的地方，为什么不去参观一下呢？

11. Would you like to go with me?
    你愿意和我一起去吗？

12. If Juyong Pass is the gateway to Beijing, then Badaling is its lock and key.
    如果说居庸关是通往北京的北大门，那么八达岭长城就是它的锁和钥匙。

13. The Great Wall here is of imposing manner.
    八达岭长城更显气势恢弘。

14. Watchtowers or battlements were built at intervals of three hundred to five hundred meters.
    每隔300米到500米建有瞭望塔或城垛。

Task I   Complete the following dialogue by translating the Chinese in the brackets.

A: Good morning. Today we're going to climb the Great Wall. _____（长城在北京的西北部。）Are you ready?

B: Yes, I am ready. _____（你了解长城吗？）

A: _____（我读过一本关于长城历史的书籍。）The Great Wall, also known as Ten-Thousand-Li Long Wall, is considered as the No.1 defense in the world. _____（每隔300米到500米建有瞭望塔或城垛。）

B: You are right. _____（1987年，长城被联合国教科文组织列为世界遗产。）

A: I was told a Chinese saying, "You are not a true man until you get to the Great Wall."

B: _____（让我们出发吧！）

Task II   Using the given words and expressions to make a conversation with your partner according to the situation.

Your friend Jim from USA is visiting the city of Hangzhou. He wants to know some details about the West Lake. You should cater to Jim's interests and help him make sense of the narration. You should try your best to ensure that your friend obtain the maximum enjoyment and satisfaction.

Student A: You
Student B: Jim

 Suggested words and expressions

reputation   名气
beautiful scenery   美景
lingering   拖延的

Chapter Two　Categories of Tourism

survive	幸存
scenery	风景
Spring Dawn at Sudi Causeway	苏堤春晓
Melting Snow on the Broken Bridge	断桥残雪
Afternoon View of Leifeng Tower	雷峰夕照
Lotus in the Breeze Crooked Courtyard	曲院风荷
Autumn Moon on Calm Lake	平湖秋月
Listening to Orioles Singing in the Willows	柳浪闻莺
Viewing Fish at Flowers Harbor	花港观鱼
Evening Bell at Nanping Hill	南屏晚钟
Three Pools Mirroring the Moon	三潭印月
Twin Peak Piercing the Clouds	双峰插云
sightsee	观光
ultimate	极限的

 Practical Patterns

It is so wonderful.

The West Lake of Hangzhou holds high reputation for...

It is said...

To demonstrate its beauty, the lake offers 10 most famous scenes as...

Shall we tour all of them?

Do you know the beauty of the West Lake lies in...

Part III　Readings

Text A

The Ancient Capital Tour

　　There are seven ancient capitals in the history of China. Different dynasties chose Beijing, Xi'an, Nanjing, Hangzhou, Kaifeng, Luoyang, and Anyang as the capitals of the state. The seven ancient capitals left us a great number of valuable cultural and historical resources. The tourists from home and abroad come to visit the scenic spots in these capital cities.

　　For example, the Imperial Palace (also called Forbidden City), Yonghe Palace, Summer Palace, Temple of Heaven, Yuanmingyuan Garden (which is originally a large imperial garden in the Qing dynasty built from 1709 onward and burnt down by the Anglo-French aggressors in 1860), and other tourist attractions in Beijing; Wild Goose Pagoda, Museum of Terracotta Warriors and Horses, Huaqing Pool in Lishan, Silk Road, and Forest of Steles and so on in Xi'an; Heavenly Mansion, Yuhuatai, Qinhuai River and others in Nanjing; Liuhe Pagoda, West Lake and so on in Hangzhou; Qingming Shanghe Picture, Dragon Kiosk, Iron Pagoda and so on in Kaifeng; Yin Ruins (which was discovered near Xiaotun Village in 1989) in Anyang. All the scenic spots in seven capital cities have occupied high situation in the tourists' favor for years. The trip to the ancient capitals seems to let the people read the historical picture scrolls again, seems to come back to the past period of once bustling with people and activity, seems to smell the printing ink as well as the breath of rouge and power in those years. There are different characteristics in seven ancient capitals, which show the ancient records and relics of different zones in different periods.

The Imperial Palace in Beijing is a case in point:

The Imperial Palace is located in the center of Beijing, also named the Forbidden City. It is not only the palace for the Emperors in Ming and Qing Dynasties in China, but also the biggest imperial palace in the world. This palace, covering an area of 72,000 square meters, is the most telling witness of 24 emperors spanned more than 500 years. It keeps 8,700 or so palaces with the floor space of 16,000 square meters. There are about one million ancient records and relics in the Museum of Imperial Palace, including the historical and cultural relics, such as palace records and relics, technological records and relics, religious records and relics, ancient artwork like calligraphy, painting, bronze, pottery, pearl and jade, silk and so on.

 New Words

capital	[ˈkæpɪtəl]	n. 首都
dynasty	[ˈdɪnəsti]	n. 王朝
resource	[rɪˈsɔːs]	n. 资源
leave	[liːv]	v. 离开；留下
originally	[əˈrɪdʒənəli]	adv. 起初；本来
occupy	[ˈɒkjupaɪ]	v. 占据，占领
scroll	[skrəʊl]	n. 卷轴，画卷；名册
bustle	[ˈbʌsl]	v. 喧闹；忙乱；充满
rouge	[ruːʒ]	n. 胭脂；口红
relic	[ˈrelɪk]	n. 遗迹；遗骸

Chapter Two Categories of Tourism

witness	['wɪtnəs]	n. 证人；目击者
locate	[lə(ʊ)'keɪt]	v. 位于
calligraphy	[kə'lɪgrəfi]	n. 书法；笔迹
bronze	[brɒnz]	n. 青铜；古铜色；青铜制品
pottery	['pɒtəri]	n. 陶器
pearl	[pɜːl]	n. 珍珠；珍品
jade	[dʒeɪd]	n. 翡翠

 Phrases and Expressions

a great number of	多数的，许多
home and abroad	国内外，海内外
scenic spot	风景区，景点
burn down	烧毁
Imperial Palace	故宫
Yonghe Palace	雍和宫
Temple of Heaven	天坛
Anglo-French aggressors	英法联军
Wild Goose Pagoda	大雁塔
Heavenly Mansion	天王府
Liuhe Pagoda	六和塔
in point	相关的；恰当的
in the center of	在中央

Integrated Exercises of Skills

Task I Please answer these questions according to the passage.

1. Would you like to tell me what the historical and cultural relics tour refers to?
2. What are the seven ancient capitals in the history of China?
3. Would you like to give me some examples about the historical and cultural relics in these scenic ancient capitals?
4. Are you interested in the ancient architecture cultural tour? Give me some example, please.

Task II Fill in the blanks with the suitable words given below, changing the form where necessary.

| in the center of | in point | burn down | leave |
| home and abroad | occupy | locate | witness |

49

1. He _____ his whole afternoon reading documents.
2. She _____ some of the food for her husband.
3. The old building _____ as crowds watched helplessly.
4. That's one of my fundamental commitments as President, both at _____.
5. Let me walk you through a case _____, one that I've been following lately.
6. The school is _____ next to the church.
7. Her account of the incident approximates to that of the other _____.
8. Who put this stone _____ the road?

Task III Translate the sentences into Chinese.

1. The seven ancient capitals left us a great number of valuable cultural and historical resources.

   _____

   _____

2. There are different characteristics in seven ancient capitals, which show the ancient records and relics of different zones in different periods.

   _____

   _____

3. The Imperial Palace is not only the palace for the Emperors in Ming and Qing Dynasties in China, but also the biggest imperial palace in the world.

   _____

   _____

4. There are about one million ancient records and relics in the Museum of Imperial Palace, including the historical and cultural relics, such as palace records and relics, technological records and relics, religious records and relics, ancient artwork like calligraphy, painting, bronze, pottery, pearl and jade, silk and so on.

   _____

   _____

5. There are seven ancient capitals in the history of China. Different dynasties chose Beijing, Xi'an, Nanjing, Hangzhou, Kaifeng, Luoyang, and Anyang as the capitals of the state.

   _____

   _____

Task IV Choose one word for each blank from a list of choices.

Zhaozhou Bridge

Zhaozhou Bridge is also __1__ Anji Bridge, and it is situated __2__ the river in Zhao County of Hebei Province. It is the the most famous ancient stone arch bridge which still exists in China. Zhao County was __3__ Zhaozhou, hence it was named Zhaozhou

Chapter Two Categories of Tourism

Bridge, which was built by Li Chun during the period of 590—608 A. D. , which was in Sui dynasty. This bridge has a __4__ arche, with the __5__ of 50. 82 meters and the __6__ of 10 meters or so. 28 independent stone arches are built in order from the south to the north. The height of each arch roll reaches 7. 23 meters with 4 small arches on the __7__ part of the bridge. This can not only reduce the weight and save the materials, but also is convenient to drain off floodwater. It is pleasing to the eyes too. The design of Zhaozhou Bridge is the first in the bridge building history all over the world, and its span was the longest at that time. Zhaozhou Bridge is an art treasure of supernatural works.

1. A. call   B. called   C. said
2. A. across   B. cross   C. through
3. A. titled   B. naming   C. named
4. A. alone   B. lonely   C. single
5. A. lengths   B. length   C. lengthy
6. A. wide   B. width   C. widen
7. A. up   B. upward   C. upper

Text B

The Temple, Hall and Grotto Tour

Religion, especially Buddhism, once brought the profound influence to Chinese culture in the history. However, all kinds of the temples, halls and grottos and so on left behind from many dynasties, are the rare art treasure. They have become the window to making better understanding of the religious culture, and have been regarded as the teaching materials for the studies of the art and history by the experts and scholars. They have also been kept as the rare art treasure in human beings' history.

The temples, halls and grottos in China mainly include Dule Temple, Wuta Temple, Hanshan Temple, Shaolin Temple, Dazhao Temple, Zhashenlunbu Temple, Zhebang Temple, Taer Temple, Labuleng Temple, Baima Temple, Foguang Temple, Nanshan Temple, Guandi Temple in Jiezhou, Wuhou Hall, Yongle Palace, Potala Palace (Figure 3-1), Mogao Grottos in Dunhuang, Maijishan Grottos, Binlingsi Grottos, Xunmier Grottos, Kezier Thousand-Buddha Grottos, Yungang Grottos, Big-Foot Stone Inscription and so on. The exquisite and beautiful grotto statues and religious paintings and arts are invaluable and incomparable treasure. The grottos started from Wei and Jin Dynasties, and they were most popular from North Wei to Sui and Tang Dynasties with a great numbers and distributed in vast places. The bigger ones in scale are Mogao Grottos in Dunhuang, Yungang Grottos in Datong, Longmen Grottos in Luoyang City, Maijishan Grottos in Gansu Province. In fact, Longmen Grottos and Yungang Grottos are mainly famous for stone inscription, however, Mogao Grottos and Maijishan Grottos are not suitable for carving and engraving due to the loose quality of stones and rocks. Therefore, Mogao Grottos in Dunhuang are famous for the frescos, but Maijishan Grottos are famous for the clay sculpture. The following is Potala Palace as an example in point:

 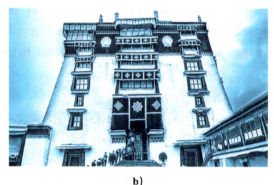

a)　　　　　　　　　　　　　　　　　　　　　b)

Figure 3-1　Potala Palace

Potala Palace is located on the Maburi Mountain in the northwest of Lasa City. It is said that Potala Palace was first constructed in the 7th century, because Songtsam Gambo (He is the founder of the Tobo Kingdom, who united many tribes inhabiting in the Tibetan Plateau in the 7th century for the first time. It was Songtsam Gambo who made Lasa the capital. Both moves helped the social progress in Tibet) wanted to entertain the bride Princess Wencheng. Potala Palace went through a great changes from the 7th century to the middle of 17th century. The existent palaces are the parts reconstructed during the year of Ming Emperor Chongzhen Regime, and the renovation of sorts for many times made Potala Palace become the scale of nowadays. Potala Palace is a project of large dimensions, and it is built near the mountain and decorated beautifully and magnificently. Potala Palace, with the real wood structure, consists of a lot of palaces, mainly including 13-storeyed and 110-meter tall red palaces and white palaces. Its imposing scale as well as unique style makes it the symbol of Tibet. Aside from that, it is also the site of an art museum and a treasure house of the cultural records and relics.

New Words

Buddhism	['bʊdɪzəm]	n. 佛教
profound	[prə'faʊnd]	adj. 深厚的,意义深远的
grotto	['grɒtəʊ]	n. 岩洞,洞穴
rare	[reə(r)]	adj. 罕见的,特殊的
include	[ɪn'kluːd]	vt. 包含,包括

Chapter Two Categories of Tourism

exquisite	[ˈekskwɪzɪt]	*adj*. 精致的；优美的
incomparable	[ɪnˈkɒmp(ə)rəb(ə)l]	*adj*. 无比的；无可匹敌的
distribute	[dɪˈstrɪbjuːt]	*v*. 分配；散布；分开
inscription	[ɪnˈskrɪpʃ(ə)n]	*n*. 题词；铭文；刻印
carve	[kɑːv]	*v*. 雕刻；开创
engrave	[ɪnˈɡreɪv]	*v*. 雕刻；铭记
clay	[kleɪ]	*n*. 黏土；泥土
dominion	[dəˈmɪnjən]	*n*. 主权，统治权
renovation	[renəˈveɪʃn]	*n*. 革新；修理
decorate	[ˈdekəreɪt]	*v*. 装饰；布置
symbol	[ˈsɪmb(ə)l]	*n*. 象征；符号

 Phrases and Expressions

be regarded as	（被）认为是
a great number	大量的
in scale	依比例
be famous for	因……而著名
due to	由于；应归于
Maburi Mountain	玛布日山
Tobo Kingdom	吐蕃王朝
go through	参加；经受
consists of	包含；由……组成
aside from that	除此之外

 Integrated Exercises of Skills

Task I Mark the following statements with "T" for true and "F" for false according to the passage.

(   ) 1. Potala Palace is located in the west of Lasa City.
(   ) 2. Mogao Grottos in Dunhuang are famous for the frescos.
(   ) 3. Maijishan Grottos are famous for the frescos, too.
(   ) 4. The grottos started from Tang Dynasties.
(   ) 5. The grottos were most popular from North Wei to Sui and Tang Dynasties with a great numbers.
(   ) 6. The Mogao Grottos and Maijishan Grottos are not suitable for carving and engraving due to the loose quality of stones and rocks.

(　) 7. Potala Palace with the real wood structure consists of a lot of palaces, mainly including 15-storeyed and 110-meter tall red palaces and white palaces.

(　) 8. Potala Palace is the official residence of the Dalai Lamas for generations of different dynasties.

Task II　Match the following temple with their regions.

1. Dule Temple　　　　　　a. the City of Beijing
2. Wuta Temple　　　　　　b. Jiangsu Province
3. Hanshan Temple　　　　　c. the City of Tianjin
4. Shaolin Temple　　　　　d. Tibet
5. Dazhao Temple　　　　　e. Henan Province

Task III　Translate the names of Temple, Hall and Grotto into Chinese.

Zhashenlunbu Temple _____

Zhebang Temple _____

Taer Temple _____

Labuleng Temple _____

Baima Temple _____

Foguang Temple _____

Nanshan Temple _____

Guandi Temple in Jiezhou _____

Wuhou Hall _____

Yongle Palace _____

Potala Palace _____

Mogao Grottos in Dunhuang _____

Maijishan Grottos _____

Binlingsi Grottos _____

Xunmier Grottos _____

Kezier Thousand-Buddha Grottos _____

Yungang Grottos _____

Big-Foot Stone Inscription _____

Part IV　Practical Writing

Welcome Speech

Making a welcome speech is the first formal communication between a tour guide

Chapter Two Categories of Tourism

and the tourists. A good tour guide should make change to their welcome speeches according to the gender, ages, and nationalities of the group. However, the following parts should be covered:

1. Ladies and gentlemen, may I have your attention, please?
2. Please take your seats. We are setting off in just a few minutes.
3. I am…, and this is our driver…
4. I would like to welcome you, our distinguished tourists, to our beautiful city.
5. Now allow me to introduce the city of… briefly to you.
6. I am very happy to be at your service.
7. Our bus number is No… Please do remember it.
8. Wish you have a pleasant and enjoyable journey.

Sample 1

(*Situation: The guide Li Hui is making a welcome speech to his tourists on the coach. He will guide his tourists to visit Suzhou City for the following days.*)

Good morning, ladies and gentlemen. On behalf of the China International Travel Service, Suzhou Branch, I would like to welcome you, our distinguished tourists, to our beautiful city. My name is Li Hui. I will be your tour guide during your stay in this city. I would like to introduce our driver to you. This is Mr. Wang; he is well-experienced, and our bus plate number is 12345. I suggest that you remember the number in order not to get on a wrong bus. I will be glad to help you at any time, so please do not hesitate to tell me if you need any help. I will do my best to make your stay an enjoyable one. Wish you have a pleasant and enjoyable journey.

Sample 2

(*Situation: In the airport lobby outside the customs, Li Chen, a guide from the China Travel Service, Beijing Branch, is meeting a tour party from the USA headed by Mr. Richard Stewart.*)

Li Chen: Excuse me, but are you Mr. Richard Stewart from the USA?
Richard Stewart: Yes. Are you our tour guide from CTS?
Li Chen: Yes. Very glad to meet you. My name is Li Chen.
Richard Stewart: Hello, Mr. Li. Thank you for coming to meet us.
Li Chen: My pleasure. How was your trip? It was quite a long flight.
Richard Stewart: Well, it was a nice flight.
Li Chen: I suppose you must be rather tired after the long flight. We have made reservation for your party at the Beijing Hotel. We shall get you to the hotel to rest as soon as possible.
Richard Stewart: Thank you. (To the group) Attention, folks. Let me introduce our

local guide Mr. Li, to you. Mr. Li from China Travel Service will act as our guide during our stay in Beijing.

Li Chen: Welcome you all to Beijing. I hope you will have a pleasant stay here. If you have any special request, please let me know. I would like to introduce our driver to you. This is Mr. Feng; he is well-experienced, and our bus plate number is 34765. I suggest that you remember the number in order not to get on a wrong bus. Shall we go to the hotel?

Richard Stewart: Fine. Let's go!

Integrated Exercises of Skills

Task I Complete the following sentences.

A: Sorry, _____, but are you Mr. Stone from Australia?

B: Oh, yes.

A: _____, Mr. Stone. I am Wang Hui from the International Hotel. And I am here to _____.

B: How do you do? Thank you very much for meeting me here.

A: You are welcome. You must _____.

B: Oh, no. It was a nice trip, so I am OK.

A: I will be your guide during your stay in China.

B: Wonderful!

A: Can I help _____? The taxi is waiting outside.

B: Thank you very much.

Task II Make a welcome speech as a guide when you are meeting Mr. Smith from British in Qingdao.

Part V Typical Scenic Spot

Chapter Two Categories of Tourism

Mount Huangshan of China

Mount Huangshan covers an area of 154 square kilometers in the southeast part of Anhui Province. Over the years visitors from home and abroad have been visiting there to marvel at its peaks, which are magnificent and elegant. Towering and extraneous-looking rocks, the green pine trees with gnarly branches and suggestive gestures, the ever-changing ocean of clouds and marvelous hot springs are the "Four Wonders".

"After visiting the five holy mountains, I decided not to see the other mountains. But after my return from Mount Huangshan, I don't even care to glance at the five holy mountains", said a Ming dynasty poet. Another saying goes, "Whoever has journeyed to the five holy mountains, he or she will never fail to feel captivated at the mere sight of the Tiandu Peak." Mount Taishan is known for its magnificence, Mount Huashan is known for its precipitousness, Mount Hengshan is known for its ethereal mass of mists and clouds, Mount Lushan is known for its flying cataracts, Mount Yandang is known for its statuesque rocks, Mount Emei is known for its soothing coolness, but Mount Huangshan is in the possession of all these salient features. The seventy-two peaks of Huangshan look as if they came into shape by cutting into the depth of the earth and elevating the land to such heights where even the clouds cease to flow. Each peak is masterpiece of the cunning labor of nature's chiseling force, but the visitor has to pluck up the courage and mount some of them to get some idea about this. The State Council designated Mount Huangshan as a key national scenic resort in 1982, and Mount Huangshan found its way into a UNESCO list of world cultural and natural heritages in 1990.

Mount Huangshan is an immense ocean of soaring peaks. For Guo Muro, a celebrated contemporary Chinese writer, the peaks were among the most spectacular of Huangshan's "Four Wonders". In 1964 he wrote a poem: "Although a popular saying has it that there are seventy-two exotic peaks of varying sized, as a matter of fact, there are seven hundred and twenty thousand ones of equal appeals. Within a circumference of eight hundred *li* the land is taken over by a sea of peaks, which are surrounded by an ocean of floating clouds. The kaleidoscopical view of this part of the world is incomparable anywhere in the world, and even if the visitor makes the attempt to make a comparison, he is simply wasting his breath. In a hundred and one ways the scenery changes in the twinkling of an eye, appearing or disappearing, thick or thin, just like in a dream-like fashion."

The entire Huangshan Mountain Range starts from Mount Jiuhua in Qingyang County, extends east to the Mount Dazhang in Jixi County, west to the Yangzhan Mountain in Yitai, and southeast to the Tianmu Mountain in Zhejiang Province. Within a circumference of several hundred kilometers the land is strewn with innumerous mountain peaks and crisscrossed by a myriad ravines and glens. Sixteen major peaks stand towering over this topographical turmoil while thirty-six smaller ones look uniquely picturesque and add a touch of grace and elegance to the landscape.

Looking northwest from the highway on the outskirts of Huicheng, the first thing that meets the eyes is the Yumen Peak, where flying birds dare not fly over and floating clouds hesitate as to where to go. But if you have mounted the Yuping Tower, nicknamed "Human World in Heaven", then you will feel the Yunmen peak is not steep at all. A look around you from the summit of the Yuping Peak shows that the mountains that meet the eyes all look so tiny. Peaks are linked with one plunging ravine after another, looking like surging waves in a choppy sea.

职业素养

党的二十大报告提到,"加大文物和文化遗产保护力度,加强城乡建设中历史文化保护传承,建好用好国家文化公园。坚持以文塑旅、以旅彰文,推进文化和旅游深度融合发展"。近年来,在文旅融合过程中,文化产业和旅游产业的边界逐步被打破,旅游成为文化产业发展的重要载体和途径,文化为旅游产业发展提供了灵魂和活力源泉。新发展阶段,文旅需求多元化、个性化特征更加突出,文创、资本、科技作为新动能,促进文旅融合业态更充分、更丰富。

Unit 4　Natural Wonders Tours

••••• **Part I　Warm-Up** •••••

There are many natural wonders in China. They includes the volcanic groups, the waterfalls, the springs, the caves, the valleys, the forests, the rivers, the mountains and so on. Natural wonders tours are very welcome because people are interested in the grotesque peaks, odd stones, strange caves, and famous rivers and so on formed by the nature. Do you remember how many natural wonders have you visited? Let me introduce some natural wonders in China.

••••• **Part II　Conversations** •••••

Conversation 1　A Visit to Three Gorges of the Yangtze River

Mary Ricardo: Do you know where the Three Gorges of the Yangtze River is?
Jimmy Smith: Yes, I do. It is in the east of Chongqing City and in the west of Hubei Province.
Mary Ricardo: The Yangtze River is the longest river in China, isn't it?
Jimmy Smith: Yes, you are right. It is also the third longest river in the world.
Mary Ricardo: Really? Where does the Yangtze River take its source?
Jimmy Smith: Exactly. The river has its source in the Geladandong Snow Mountain, the main peak of the Tanggula Range, which stands 6,621 meters above sea level on the southwestern border of Qinghai Province.
Mary Ricardo: Thank you. I know the Yangtze River flows about 6,300 kilometers in eight provinces, one autonomous region, and two municipalities.
Jimmy Smith: Well, why do the people call it "Three Gorges"?
Mary Ricardo: The Three Gorges are composed of Qutang Gorge, Wuxia Gorge, and Xiling Gorge, thus the people call the "Three Gorges".
Jimmy Smith: Oh, I see. Would you like to tell me their special characteristics?
Mary Ricardo: Yes, I'd like to. Qutang Gorge is famous for its magnificence and

59

                  precipitousness; Wuxia Gorge is known for its serenity and beauty; and Xiling Gorge has own characteristics of its swift currents and rapids.

Jimmy Smith: That is great!

Mary Ricardo: By the way, do you know which gorge is the shortest, the narrowest?

Jimmy Smith: I know that Qutang Gorge is the shortest, the narrowest, and the most magnificent of the Three Gorges.

Mary Ricardo: Furthermore, the eight-kilometer-long Qutang Gorge starts from Baidicheng in Fengjie County in the west and terminates in Daxi Town of Wushan County in the east.

Jimmy Smith: How long is Xiling Gorge?

Mary Ricardo: Xiling Gorge runs 76 kilometers between Zigui County in the west and Yichang City in the east.

Jimmy Smith: Where is the Dam of the Three Gorge Water Conservation Pivotal Project?

Mary Ricardo: The well-known Dam of the Three Gorge Water Conservation Pivotal Project is located at Sandouping in the middle of Xiling Gorge in Yichang, Hubei Province.

Jimmy Smith: How long is the Dam of the Three Gorge Water Conservation Pivotal Project?

Mary Ricardo: The Dam is 2,309 meters long and 185 meters high.

Jimmy Smith: Well, this is a great project. The Three Gorges features a unique landscape of the Yangtze River.

 New Words

gorge	[gɔːdʒ]	n. 峡谷
source	[sɔːs]	n. 来源；水源
peak	[piːk]	n. 山峰；最高点
municipality	[mjʊˈnɪsəˈpæləti]	n. 自治市或区
characteristic	[kærəktəˈrɪstɪk]	n. 特征；特性；特色
serenity	[sɪˈrenɪti]	n. 平静，宁静
magnificent	[mægˈnɪfɪs(ə)nt]	adj. 高尚的；壮丽的
furthermore	[fɜːðəˈmɔː]	adv. 此外；而且
terminate	[ˈtɜːmɪneɪt]	v. 使终止；使结束

 Phrases and Expressions

be famous for	因……而著名
in the middle of	在……中间
height above sea level	海拔高度

Chapter Two Categories of Tourism

Conversation 2   A Visit to Mount Huangshan

Alice Smith: I would like to visit Mount Huangshan. Would you like to go with me?

Christina Inglis: Yes. But where is Mount Huangshan located?

Alice Smith: Mount Huangshan is located in the southeast part of Anhui Province and covers an area of 154 square kilometers.

Christina Inglis: What is Mount Huangshan famous for?

Alice Smith: As far as I know, Mount Huangshan is famous for an ocean of soaring peaks, Huangshan pine trees, and strange shapes of Huangshan rocks and an ocean of surging clouds.

Christina Inglis: You are right, especially Huangshan pine trees. They are the representatives of the soul of Mount Huangshan. Can you name some of Huangshan pine trees?

Alice Smith: Of course, I can. The Guest-Greeting Pine has been there for the last thousand years as a symbol of Mount Huangshan and an emblem of the hospitality of the nation of China.

Christina Inglis: Do you know other pine trees?

Alice Smith: Yes, I do. The Guest-Greeting Pine is not the only tree with a personified name. There are also the Guest's Companion Pine, Seeing a-Friend-off Pine, Yearning-for-Guests Pine, Receptionist Pine, Sea-Surveying Pine, and etc. One of my friends visited Mount Huangshan last year and told me that those pine trees are very beautiful.

Christina Inglis: I can imagine that the beauty of Huangshan pine trees in spring and winter is indeed beyond description. Why not go now? I could not wait to visit Mount Huangshan.

Alice Smith: OK. I will buy two tickets at once.

 New Words

cover	['kʌvə]	v. 包括；采访
soar	[sɔː]	v. 高飞；高耸
surge	[sɜːdʒ]	v. 汹涌；蜂拥而来
representative	[reprɪ'zentətɪv]	adj. 典型的，有代表性的
emblem	['embləm]	n. 象征；徽章；符号
hospitality	[hɒspɪ'tælɪti]	n. 好客；殷勤

Phrases and Expressions

as far as I know 据我所知；就我所知
The Guest-Greeting Pine 迎客松
The Guest's Companion Pine 陪客松
The Seeing a-Friend-off Pine 送客松
The Yearning-for-Guests Pine 望客松
The Receptionist Pine 接引松
The Sea-Surveying Pine 探海松

 Practical Patterns

1. Do you know where the Three Gorges of the Yangtze River is?
   你知道长江三峡在哪里吗？

2. The Yangtze River is the longest river in China, isn't it?
   长江是中国最长的河流，是吗？

3. The river has its source in the Geladandong Snow Mountain, the main peak of the Tanggula Range, which stands 6,621 meters above sea level on the southwestern border of Qinghai Province.
   长江发源于唐古拉山脉主峰的格拉丹东雪山，它位于青海省西南部，海拔6621米。

4. I know the Yangtze River flows 6,300 kilometers in eight provinces, one autonomous region, and two municipalities.
   我知道长江全长6300千米，流经八个省、一个自治区和两个直辖市。

5. The Three Gorges are composed of Qutang Gorge, Wuxia Gorge, and Xiling Gorge, thus the people call the "Three Gorges".
   三峡是由瞿塘峡、巫峡和西陵峡组成，因此人们称为"三峡"。

6. Qutang Gorge is famous for its magnificence and precipitousness; Wuxia Gorge is known for its serenity and beauty; and Xiling Gorge has own characteristics of its swift currents and rapids.
   瞿塘峡以险峻和陡峭著称；巫峡以宁静和美丽著称；西陵峡拥有独特的激流和险滩。

7. The well-known Dam of the Three Gorge Water Conservation Pivotal Project is located at Sandouping in the middle of Xiling Gorget in Yichang, Hubei Province.
   著名的三峡大坝水利枢纽工程位于西陵峡中段的湖北省宜昌市境内的三斗坪。

8. Would you like to go with me?
   你愿意和我一起去吗？

Chapter Two　Categories of Tourism

9. As far as I know, Mount Huangshan is famous for an ocean of soaring peaks, Huangshan pine trees, and strange shapes of Huangshan rocks and an ocean of surging clouds.

   据我所知,黄山以高耸入云的山峰、千姿百态的松树、巧夺天工的奇石和如梦如幻的云海闻名于世。

10. The Guest-Greeting Pine has been there for the last thousand years as a symbol of Mount Huangshan and an emblem of the hospitality of the nation of China.

    黄山的迎客松已经存在上千年,它象征着中华民族的热情好客。

11. The Guest-Greeting is not the only tree with a personified name.

    黄山迎客松不是唯一具有人格化命名称的树。

12. I can imagine that the beauty of Huangshan pine trees in spring and winter is indeed beyond description.

    我可以想象黄山的松树在春季和冬季的美,确实难以形容。

Task I　Read the conversation again and answer the questions.

1. Where is the Three Gorges of the Yangtze River?
2. Where does the Yangtze River take its source?
3. Which river is the third longest in the world?
4. How long is The Yangtze River?
5. Where is the Dam of the Three Gorge water Conservation Pivotal Project?
6. Where is Mount Huangshan located?
7. What is Mount Huangshan famous for?
8. Can you name some of Huangshan pine trees?

Task II　Complete the following dialogue by translating the Chinese in the brackets.

A: Good morning. I would like to visit Zhangjiajie Scenic Area. _____(你愿意和我一起吗?)

B: Yes. _____(但是张家界风景区在哪啊?)

A: It is in Hunan Province of the Central China. It is very famous in China.

B: _____(有些人告诉我,我应该去游览一下张家界的黄龙洞。)

A: I would like to go, too. _____(黄龙洞总长13公里。)

B: How about the area of Huanglong Cave?

A: _____(黄龙洞占地面积12 000平方米。)

B: That is great! Let's go!

63

Task III Look at these natural wonders, discuss with your partners about their characteristics.

Diaoshuilou Waterfall	Baotu Spring	Liquid Cave	Houhua Cave
Stone Forest	Bamboo Forest	Yeliu	
Zhangjiajie Scenic Spot	Yueya Spring	Hukou Waterfall	

Part III Readings

Text A

The Natural Wonders in China

The grotesque peaks, odd stones, strange caves and famous rivers and so on are formed mostly due to the natural superlative craftsmanship and the functions of the lithology, conformation, efflorescence or weathering, erosion, aggradation, and so on. These natural masterpieces are either infinite variety of fantastic phenomena or very exotic and interesting. Some peaks towers to the sky like opening a new path, the scenery changes while you take your paces; Some peaks create lifelike images, and looks mimic perfectly; some peaks are changeable and look full of mystery; other peaks seem to be the Land of Peach Blossom-fictitious land of peace, away from the turmoil of the world and are as holy and quiet as possible. For example, the Qixingyan Cave, Ludiyan Cave, Yilingyan Cave in Guangxi Zhuang Autonomous Region, the Three Caves in Yixing City, Jiangsu Province are the fulgurite physiognomies. There are different kinds of stalactites, zigzagging underground rivers and grotesque and gaudy holes in the cave. The Bamboo Forest in the south of Sichuan Province with the bamboos everywhere and grant waterfall like the curtain, all give the tourists a great surprise. However, the Shangri-La Scenic Spot is the absolutely beautiful place and it sets off the snow peaks and valleys. All these natural wonders look like the picturesque views, which are a great attraction to the visitors who tend to linger on there or enjoy themselves so much as to forget to go home. The Wudalian Pool in Heilongjiang Province is a case in point as follows:

The Volcanic Groups in Wudalian Pool (Figure 4-1) has the good reputation as "Museum of Volcanos". It is located in Wudalianchi City in Heilongjiang Province, in a natural scenery with the volcanic geological structure. The scenic spots consist of the

Chapter Two Categories of Tourism

volcanic wimbles, volcanic bombs, karst caves and lava physiognomies with different shapes. Due to the volcanic eruption in different periods, the magmas flow into the Near River so as to separate it into several pieces and form five volcanic barrier lakes like a bunch of pearls. The Wudalian Pool consists of five lakes, fourteen mountains and calcareous or lime lava mesas, covering an area of 1,060 square kilometres, and being famous for its four characteristics, namely beautiful mountains, odd stones, deep water and splendid spring. There are a lot of ancient and neoteric volcanos, which form the thin hazes, stone forests, volcanic lavas, inverse image in the volcanic pools, ice splits in three pools, the sound of the wave striking the stones in the pond, and Hualin Spring and other scenes. In 1982, the Wudalian Pool was listed as the major state scenic spot in China.

a)

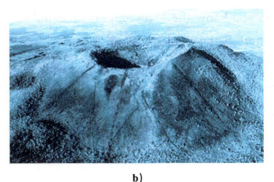
b)

Figure 4-1 Wudalian Pool

New Words

volcano	[vɒlˈkeɪnəʊ]	n.	火山
lava	[ˈlɑːvə]	n.	火山岩浆
physiognomy	[ˌfɪziˈɒnəmi]	n.	地貌;外貌
fulgurite	[ˈfʌlgjʊraɪt]	n.	闪电岩
stalactite	[ˈstæləktaɪt]	n.	钟乳石
zigzag	[ˈzɪgzæg]	v.	使成"之"字形;使曲折行进
grotesque	[grə(ʊ)ˈtesk]	n.	奇异风格;怪异的东西
gaudy	[ˈɡɔːdi]	adj.	华而不实的;俗丽的
curtain	[ˈkɜːt(ə)n]	n.	幕;窗帘
turmoil	[ˈtɜːmɔɪl]	n.	混乱,骚动
eruption	[ɪˈrʌpʃ(ə)n]	n.	爆发,喷发
separate	[ˈsep(ə)reɪt]	v.	使分离;使分开
splendid	[ˈsplendɪd]	adj.	辉煌的;灿烂的
neoteric	[niːə(ʊ)ˈterɪk]	adj.	现代的;新发明的

Phrases and Expressions

consist of	由……构成
different kinds of	各种各样
set off	出发；引起；衬托
enjoy themselves so much as to forget to go home	流连忘返
due to	由于；归于

 Integrated Exercises of Skills

Task I   Please answer these questions according to the passage.

1. Do you know the "Museum of Volcano"?
2. Where is the Wudalian Pool located?
3. How many lakes and mountains does the Wudalian Pool consist of?
4. Would you please tell me the location of the Baotu Spring?

Task II   Fill in the blanks with the suitable words given below, changing the form where necessary.

consist of	set off	different kinds of	curtain
separate	eruption	due to	splendid

1. She peered at the neighbors from behind the _____.
2. The last _____ of this volcano lasted over a year, so this cannot be ruled out.
3. Then she would go and live with her children happily, ever after thrashing rice to _____ it from the husk.
4. The peacock spreads his _____ tail.
5. They always _____ inclined regions.
6. You're muddling up _____ letters.
7. The next morning, we _____.
8. The traffic accident was allegedly _____ negligence.

Task III   Fill in the blanks with the proper forms of the words.

  The Guilin Li River is _____ (locate) in the northeast of Guangxi Zhang Autonomous Region, and it is the _____ (type) karst peak physiognomy. The hills and stones stick up, and peak clumps join together here. The Li River and its branches

Chapter Two Categories of Tourism

_____ (bypass) both the hills and stones, and it is _____ (surround) by the hills and rivers, which is _____ (comparable) elegant and beautiful. Therefore, the Li River is really _____ (worth) of the good reputation of "The Mountains and Rivers of Guilin are the _____ (fine) under Heaven".

Task IV Translate the following sentences into Chinese.

1. The Volcanic Groups in Wudalian Pool has the good reputation as "Museum of Volcanos.

   _____
   _____

2. The Shangri-La Scenic Spot is an absolutely beautiful place. Away from the turmoil of the world, it sets off the snow peaks and valleys.

   _____
   _____

3. All these natural wonders look like the picturesque views, which are a great attraction to the visitors who tend to linger on there or enjoy themselves so much as to forget to go home.

   _____
   _____

4. It is located in Wudalianchi City in Heilongjiang Province, in a natural scenery with the volcanic geological structure.

   _____
   _____

5. The Wudalian Pool consists of five lakes, fourteen mountains and calcareous or lime lava mesas, covering an area of 1,060 square kilometres, and being famous for its four characteristics, namely beautiful mountains, odd stones, deep water and splendid spring.

   _____
   _____

6. In 1982, the Wudalian Pool was listed as the major state scenic spot in China.

   _____
   _____

Text B

The End of the World

Thousands years of wandering passion, the Chinese with sentimentality strew the lovesickness into the sky, and hope to witness their love at a certain place. Those souls remaining faithful and unyielding even under severe tortures need a foothold after ten-thousand miles banishing trip. Moreover, the seek of being up to the blue sky and down the lower world after all needs a goal.

And then, we hope there is a vanishing point between heaven and earth, and yearn for a place that is the true ultima thule (the End of the World or Tianya Haijiao). Coming to Sanya City in Hainan Island, we find that the "Ultima Thule" is in fact the two simple stones (Figure 4-2).

Figure 4-2　The End of the World

After four chinesc characters— "Tianya" and "Haijiao" engraved on the two stones, the Tianya complex (or the complex of the Ultima Thule) in our heart has found its materialized carrier, thus the two stones— "Tianya" and "Haijiao" have come to be a synonym of the ultimate meaning, undertaking the rich and profound cultural connotation accumulated for hundreds and thousands of years.

In the vast south boundary of the Chinese Mainland, which is seperated from the Qiongzhou Strait, there is a solitary island. If you go straight to the south until you reach the remotest corner of the island, two stones stand upright before your eyes. Nothing is found in the south of the two stones except the vast sea and grand sky. This is called Hainan Island, "Tianya" and "Haijiao" is engraved on the two stones separately. All the Chinese probably know the stones in the south most of China. The vast sky has found the brim, and the deep blue sea has spread to the vanishing point.

The famous two stones, indicating the end of the world, are situated in the southwest seashore of Sanya City in Hainan Island, 23 kilometers away from the town, and 6 kilometers away from the Phoenix Airport. It takes more than 20 minutes by car to arrive at the gate of the Ultima Thule Scenic Spot, and there is an antithetical couplet written on both sides of the door: "A bright moon rises in Hainan, please enjoy the moment in the remotest corner of the earth", which is inspired by a poem written by Zhang Jiuling, a poet of Tang dynasty: "A bright moon rises at sea, please enjoy the moment in the remotest corner of the earth." After a second thought on the antithetical couplet, a warm sentiment rises from the bottom of the heart: "The lover still has not come back. This let the lady dreams to scatter poplar flowers, and moves around the end of the world". "The setting sun is in the west, and the heartbroken person is in the remotest corner of the earth". Maybe, the tourists from a long distance come to visit the two simple stones, and they want to recall the sentiment in their heart, and trace those unclear emotions with warmness and sorrow that they don't know about themselves.

Entering the scenic area of the Ultima Thule, you see a wide and straight bluestone road head on. The end of this road are the boundless sea. Although now it is December, trident flowers on both sides of the road are still burst vigorously under the tropical sunlight in South China, and the coconut trees still bear fruits quietly. Travelling westward along the soft beach of the sea, and passing "Haipan Nantian", "Haishi Stone" and "Nantian Pillar", there are a lot of huge stones scattered in the westmost of the scenic area. Among the stones, the one in the east looks like a huge house with perimeter of 60 meters and height of 10 meters, and on its top engraved two characters, that is, "Tianya". The side-ward inscription indicates that the words were written by Cheng Zhe, the head of Yazhou County in the 11th year of Yongzheng Regime, which was the year of 1733. We can imagine that the beach in that time might be in great desolation.

In the northwest of the stone "Tianya", a group of huge stones run out into the sea, and one of them stands upright to the sky like a huge bamboo shoot, and two characters "Haijiao" are engraved on the top. The inscription is illegible or unclear under years of erosion of the sea breeze, only Wang Yi, the name of the writer can be made out or recognized. But who is Wang Yi? This is still to be put to textual research. UP to now, most people think that Wang Yi is a local official in the Republic of China (1912–1949). Passing through the heaps of megalith or huge stones, you come to Haijiao (the end of the sea) and suddenly see the boundless sea and have no way to go underfoot. Thereupon, you suddenly realize that you have to reach the Ultima Thule, that is, the end of the world or the remotest corner of the earth.

While climbing heaps of stones and looking around, you may see a white and bright beach like jade strips spanning between the blue sky and sea. The back of the sea is surrounded by hills. The year' erosion by the ocean wave brings up these primitive stones before your eyes, and these stones stand between the vigorous sky and powerful ocean to treat sea changes into mulberry fields with distain or scorn as time flies. However, under the boundless of blue or cloudless sky, those graceful coconut trees bring forth their austral heartthrob tirelessly. All seem to look like in pictures and poems.

New Words

sentimentality	[ˌsentɪmenˈtælɪti]	n.	多愁善感
strew	[struː]	v.	散播；撒满
lovesickness	[ˈlʌvsɪknɪs]	n.	相思病
vanish	[ˈvænɪʃ]	v.	消失
ultima	[ˈʌltəmə]	adj.	最终的；最后的
Thule	[ˈθjuːliː]	n.	极北之地
engrave	[ɪnˈɡreɪv]	v.	雕刻；铭记
complex	[ˈkɒmpleks]	adj.	复杂的；合成的
undertake	[ˌʌndəˈteɪk]	v.	承担，保证
accumulate	[əˈkjuːmjʊleɪt]	v.	累积；积聚
solitary	[ˈsɒlɪt(ə)ri]	adj.	孤独的；独居的
southmost	[ˈsaʊθməʊst]	adj.	最南的
indicate	[ˈɪndɪkeɪt]	v.	表明；指出
situate	[ˈsɪtjʊeɪt]	v.	使位于；使处于
scatter	[ˈskætə]	v.	分散，散开
desolation	[ˌdesəˈleɪʃ(ə)n]	n.	荒芜；忧伤
jade	[dʒeɪd]	n.	翡翠

Phrases and Expressions

in fact	事实上，实际上
come from	来自；出生于
run out	耗尽；到期；伸向
up to now	到目前为止
faithful and unyielding	坚贞不屈
head on	迎面地

Integrated Exercises of Skills

Task I Read the passage above and decide whether the following statements are true (T) or false (F).

(　) 1. Coming to Sanya City in Hainan Island, we find that the "Ultima Thule" is in fact the two simple stones.

(　) 2. The famous two stones, indicating the end of the world, is situated in the southeast seashore of Sanya City in Hainan Island.

(　) 3. It takes more than 20 minutes by car to arrive at the gate of the Ultima Thule Scenic Spot in Haikou City.

(　) 4. A stone in the east looks like a huge house with perimeter of 60 meters and height of 10 meters.

(　) 5. In the east boundary of the Chinese Mainland, which is separated from the Qiongzhou Strait, there is a solitary island.

(　) 6. The side-ward inscription indicates that the words were written by Cheng Zhe, the head of Yazhou County in the 11th year of Yongzheng Regime, which means the year of 1733.

(　) 7. In the northwest of the stone "Tianya", a group of huge stones run out into the sea, and one of them stands upright to the sky like a huge bamboo shoot, and two characters "Haijiao" are engraved on the top.

(　) 8. Cheng Zhe is a local official in the Republic of China (1912 – 1949).

Task II　Fill in the sentences with the proper forms of the words.

1. He could not undertake to go down and pick up the litter they _____ (strew).
2. I know about the voices, the sense of _____ (vanish), the horrible envy of others.
3. That image is _____ (engrave) on my mind.
4. She discouraged me from _____ (undertake) the work.
5. None can afford to neglect the _____ (accumulate) experience of men.
6. The name of the service _____ (indicate) what it is about or what it does.
7. It is _____ (situate) in Burma as the original city of Baga.
8. The Jews are _____ (scatter) over the world.

Task III　Translate the following sentences into Chinese.

1. We hope there is a vanishing point between heaven and earth, and yearn for a place that is the true ultima thule.

_____

2. This is called Hainan Island. "Tianya" and "Haijiao" are engraved on the two stones

separately.

3. There is an antithetical couplet written on both sides of the door: "A bright moon rises in Hainan, please enjoy the moment in the remotest corner of the earth".

4. Although now it is December, trident flowers on both sides of the road are still burst vigorously under the tropical sunlight in South China, and the coconut trees still bear fruits quietly.

5. We can imagine that the beach in that time might be in great desolation.

6. In the northwest of the stone "Tianya", a group of huge stones run out into the sea, and one of them stands upright to the sky like a huge bamboo shoot, and two characters "Haijiao" are engraved on the top.

7. While climbing heaps of stones and looking around, you may see a white and bright beach like jade strips spanning between the blue sky and sea.

8. All seem to look like in pictures and poems.

Part IV Practical Writing

Registration Forms 住宿登记单

详细明了的住宿登记单,不但可以给客人留下好印象,而且可以给酒店的管理提供方便。住宿登记单分为散客和团队两种,填写方式相差较大。散客住宿登记单包括客人的姓名、性别、国籍、证件、抵离时间、房号等,团队住宿登记单包括团队名称、代码、国籍、抵离时间、联系人、房间要求、餐饮要求等。

Chapter Two Categories of Tourism

酒店前台服务人员务必认真检查客人填写的住宿登记单，这是保证每一位顾客顺利入住酒店必须完成的第一项任务。因此，熟悉该登记单的格式、内容，快速准确地完成这一套手续，对顾客和宾馆都是十分重要的。

Sample 1

Peace Hotel

Please write in block letters   REGISTRATION FORM

Surname: Levy	First Name: Logan	Sex: Male
Other Name:	Nationality: U.S.A.	Date of Birth: July 3, 1959
Certificate No.: 287129	Type of Certificate: Passport	Expiry Date: March 1, 2002
Type of Visa: F1 Port of Entry: Beijing	Valid Visa Date: March 1, 1997 Date of Entry: Oct. 2	
Arrival Date: Oct. 2 Departure Date: Oct. 10	Arrival Time: 9:00 a.m. Departure Time: 7 a.m.	
Next Destination: Tianjin	Flight No. CY3135 Departure Time: 8:15 a.m.	Company
Permanent Address: No. 206 Jackson Street, New York		
Room No.: 1208	Folio No.: 302	Booking Source: Travel Agency	Room Rate: $120/night
My account will be settled by: Cash * Credit card Voucher Company account	Please Note: I will bear all my expenses in the hotel. Safe deposit boxes are available in the guestroom. The hotel will not be liable for any items left unattended. Check out time is 12:00 noon.	
Room charge My F&B charge will be settled by Mr./Mrs. Logan Levy * All charges	Signature (guest) Receptionist Du Xiaoling	

Sample 2

A Form of Tour Group Information（旅行团信息表）

IN-HOUSE GROUP INFORMATION

Group Name: American Professor Sightseeing Group	Group Code: 0281
Arrival Date: June 11, 2001	Departure Date: June 21, 2001
ETA: 10:00 a.m. June 11 ETD: 10:25 a.m. June 21	Nationality: U.S.A.
Name of Agent: Sun Tavel Agency Tel: 32111255	Contact Person: Lu Baoguo

TYPE	No. OF RMS	ROOM NUMBER	No. OF PAS
SK	1	203	2211
ST	2	301　302	2230
DK	2	201　205	2217　2218
DT	2	207	2280　2290
JS.	3	101　102　103	2274　2275　2276
TOTAL	10		

MEAL REQUIREMENT:

DATE	TIME	BREAKFAST	LUNCH	DINNER	VENUE	REMARKS	No. OF PAS
11th	12:00		20	20	2nd Dining Room		22130
12th – 13th							

WAKE-UP CALLS:

DATE							
TIME							

RECEPTIONIST:＿＿＿＿＿＿＿＿＿＿＿＿＿＿＿＿＿＿＿
NATIONAL GUIDE:＿＿＿＿＿＿＿＿＿＿＿＿＿＿＿＿＿＿＿

White copy: Front Desk　　　Blue copy: Concierge　　　Pink copy: Operator
Yellow copy: F&B Dept　　　Green copy: Housekeeper

TOUR GROUP NAME LIST

GROUP CODE:＿＿＿＿＿＿　ARRIVAL DATE:＿＿＿＿＿＿　DEPARTURE DATE:＿＿＿＿＿＿

ROOM No.	NAME	SEX	DATE OF BIRTH	CERTIFICATE No.	VISA EXP	ADDRESS
205	Joy Kral	Male	June 11, 1965	35892457	June 11, 2001	London

REGISTERED BY: Mary Lee　　　　　　　　　　CHECK-IN BY: Mark Wu
REMARKS:＿＿＿＿＿＿＿＿＿＿＿＿＿＿＿＿＿＿＿＿＿＿

Chapter Two Categories of Tourism

 Integrated Exercises of Skills

Task I Match the following groups of words and phrases.

1. departure   a. 国籍
2. code   b. 证书
3. certificate   c. 代理人
4. visa   d. 离开
5. signature   e. 接待员
6. nationality   f. 行李
7. agent   g. 签名
8. receptionist   h. 签证
9. luggage   i. 代码

Task II Write a Registration Form according to the situation given below. Add some more information if necessary.

一个 20 人的英国商业代表团于 2015 年 12 月 8 日下午 3 点抵达上海浦东国际机场。他们将下榻于上海东方大酒店，并在上海进行为期 8 天的商务考察。他们离开上海的时间是 12 月 16 日上午 11:30。

Part V Typical Scenic Spot

Zhangjiajie Scenic of China

The City of Zhangjiajie is in the northwest part of Hunan Province, stretching over the area from between 28°52′ and 29°48′ Northern Latitude to between 109° and 111°20′ Eastern Longitude. With annual average temperature of 16℃, it has a humid subtropical climate characterized by rain-bearing monsoon wind. Covering a total area of 9,563 square kilometers, the City of Zhangjiajie governs Yongding and Wulingyuan districts as well as Cili and Sangzhi Counties.

Zhanjiajie City obtained its name from Zhangjiajie Scenic Area. Under the jurisdiction of Dayong County, the natural landscapes of Zhangjiajie were discovered in 1979 and have been exploited and opened to the public ever since. In 1985, Dayong County upgraded to city-level. Three years later, Dayong City, Cili and Sangzhi Counties merged into a single whole and rose to prefecture level for the purpose of developing tourism. Far from renowned as Zhangjiajie, Dayong assumed the name of Zhangjiajie City in 1994 with the approval of the State Council so as to promote tourism and economy.

As a tourist city being newly built, Zhangjiajie is blessed with a vast wealth of resources for tourism. Wulingyuan, which consists of Zhangjiajie National Forest Park, Suoxi Gully Natural Scenic Spot and Emperor Mountain Natural Scenic Spot, is not only one of the national major scenic areas but also put on the World Heritage List compiled by the United Nations Educational, Scientific and Cultural Organization (UNESCO). In 1982, Zhangjiajie was named as the first National Forest Park in China, followed by Tianmen Mountain. In 1986, China's first tourist drifting course was set along Maoyan River (Figure 4-3). So far, three more scenic spots of provincial level (that is, Maoyan River, Jiutian Cave and Tianmen Mountain) have been established. Scenic sites and nature preservation zones at state or provincial level cover 500 square kilometers, accounting for approximately one ninth of the total area of the city. In addition, such historical interests as Puguang Buddhist Temple and Yuhuang (Jade Emperor) Grottoes have made great cutucral attractions. Extremely appealing to the tourists at home and abroad are the customs of minorities, gripping and mysterious Kung Fu and popular martial arts.

Figure 4-3　Maoyan River

The city of Zhangjiajie is implementing the opening-up policy of basing its growth on tourism. In the wake of ten years' efforts, a new pattern of tourism has emerged, in which Zhangjiajie, Suoxi Gully and Emperor Mountain regarded are as the principal tourist attractions with Maoyan River, Jiutian Cave, Tianmen Mountain, Wulei Mountain Puguang Temple as outlying scenic areas, thus blending the mountains, rivers and caves as well as the history, culture and folklore into a whole.

The city has set up 12 excursion centers, which link 30 routes for sightseeing covering a distance of over 300 kilometers and are equipped with two cableways. Communications networks connect scenic sites. Zhangjiajie Railway Station has access to more than ten large and medium-sized cities through express trains, and the airport is open to more than 20 large and medium-sized cities. The city's telecommunications system has reached advanced level at home. The city boasts more than 400 hotels, which can accommodate for over 30,000 people. Twenty of the hotels are graded as star level. Besides, the city possesses over 40 travel agencies.

As it is becoming better known to the world and its tourist facilities improving and its ports opened, Zhangjiajie is quickening its steps to go to the world arena.

职业素养

坚持绿色发展，人与自然和谐共生。大自然是人类赖以生存发展的基本条件。尊重自然、顺应自然、保护自然，是全面建设社会主义现代化国家的内在要求。从旅游业角度来说，我们要坚持推动绿色旅游发展，改善生态环境质量，提升生态系统的质量和稳定性，树立和践行绿水青山就是金山银山的理念，站在人与自然和谐共生的高度谋划旅游业的高质量发展。

Unit 5 Red Resorts Tours

••••• Part I Warm-Up •••••

In the twenty-first century, the Red tourism is booming. Red resorts are the key to the development of effective quality of red tourism resources. Nowadays more and more people visit the Red tourist attractions.

Yan'an City becomes the vibrant center point again, which evokes the memories of the glory days of the Communist Party when its leaders entered Yan'an in 1936 following the Long March.

Fujian, the coastal province, which is opposite to Taiwan, has a significant place in China's "red history". In the late 1920s and early 1930s, Fujian was a major "red base" for the Red Army, which left behind many "red scenic spots".

Do you know other "red resorts"? Go there and enjoy your travelling.

••••• Part II Conversations •••••

Conversation 1   Trip to Xi'an City

G—guide

T1—tourist 1

T2—tourist 2

Situation: A group of tourists from Australia is visiting the ancient city Xi'an. A guide is making some explanations to them.

G: Now we are on top of the Xi'an City Wall. Here we can have a full view of the city and its ancient buildings.

T1: I can see the Dayan Pagoda we visited yesterday.

T2: I really admire the persistence and perseverance of Monk Xuan Zang for having that pagoda built.

G: Yes, he was great. If you look this way into the city, you can see the Bell Tower and the Drum Tower.

T1: I still can't figure out why they are built.

G: Well, in ancient times there were no clocks to tell the time, so people built the towers to strike bells or drums to give the time.

T1: What's the difference between striking bells and beating drums?

G: The bells were struck in the morning and the drums were beaten at dusk.

T1: So people arranged their activities by the sound of bells and drums, right?

G: That's right. This well-preserved city wall still speaks of the past glory and prosperity of ancient Xi'an. As you may know, Xi'an was the noted capital of China for 13 dynasties that lasted for more than 1100 years. It certainly abounds in historical relics. Just think of the imperial tombs around Xi'an. There are 27 tombs on the northern bank of the Wei River alone!

T2: Have they been excavated?

G: Most of them have not. But the ones that have been excavated have yielded great wonders. One of them is the Tomb of the First Emperor of the Qin Dynasty. It has yielded the terracotta troops. We shall visit it tomorrow.

T2: That's great!

G: Here we are. This is the museum of Terracotta Warriors you've been longing to visit.

T1: Oh, I've never seen such a huge museum before.

G: It's 230 meters long, 70 meters wide, and 22 meters high. You know, it's the largest one of its kind in China today. Please have a look at an ancient Chinese array of troops.

T2: It's a mighty army. Oh, that's the reviewing stand, isn't it?

G: Yes, it is. Look, all these terracotta warriors face the east, because the State of Qin in the Warring States Period was located in the west and fought eastward against the ducal states.

T1: Who are they marching in the front?

G: They are terracotta warriors, lining up in three ranks, each with 70 soldiers. They form the vanguard of the troops. Behind them are files... Look, those are infantrymen there and here are chariots. There are 38 columns, each 180 meters long. The terracotta warriors are clad in armor and the chariots are drawn by four terracotta horses. This is the main force of the army.

T1: Why are some of them standing on the northern and southern sides and some at the rear? And why are they facing outside?

G: They're flanks and rear guards. Their task was to guard against enemy attacks and outflanking.

T2: I see. This army was well organized.

G: Emperor Qin Shi Huang led his mighty army, galloped across the battlefield, defeated six ducal states and unified China. These terracotta warriors and horses reproduce the grand picture of his leading the army, fighting north and south on many fronts.

T1: It's really a mighty battlefield of the Qin Period. Were they arranged in the manner they looked when excavated?

G: Yes, they were. Let's go to the terracotta warrior vault to have a look.

T2: Oh, every soldier looks so lively, brimming with energy. They all wear helmets, armor and black boots, and each carries a spear and a dagger-axe.

G: If you have a close look you'll find that each warrior has a different facial expression and manner.

T1: These terracotta warriors are vividly moulded, true to life. It's amazing that sculpture had attained such a high artistic level at that time. I hear this is No. 1 Vault of Terracotta Warriors, and there are also No. 2 and No. 3 Vaults.

G: Yes, let's have a look.

 New Words

ancient	[ˈeɪnʃ(ə)nt]	adj. 古代的；古老的
admire	[ədˈmaɪə]	v. 钦佩；赞美 v. 钦佩；称赞
persistence	[pəˈsɪst(ə)ns]	n. 持续
perseverance	[pɜːsɪˈvɪər(ə)ns]	n. 坚持不懈
pagoda	[pəˈgəʊdə]	n. （东方寺院的）宝塔
strike	[straɪk]	v. 打，打击；敲，敲击
glory	[ˈglɔːri]	n. 光荣，荣誉；赞颂
prosperity	[prɒˈsperɪti]	n. 繁荣，成功
abound	[əˈbaʊnd]	v. 充满；富于
yield	[jiːld]	v. 生；产；结
excavate	[ˈekskəveɪt]	v. 挖掘；开凿
array	[əˈreɪ]	n. 数组，阵列；排列，列阵
vanguard	[ˈvæŋgɑːd]	n. 先锋盾；前锋
chariot	[ˈtʃærɪət]	n. 二轮战车
armor	[ˈɑːmə]	n. [军]装甲；盔甲 v. 为……装甲
gallop	[ˈgæləp]	v. 飞驰；急速进行

Chapter Two Categories of Tourism

 Phrases and Expressions

on top of	在……之上
figure out	解决；算出；想出；理解；断定
the Xi'an City Wall	西安城墙
the Dayan Pagoda	大雁塔
Monk Xuan Zang	玄奘法师
the Bell Tower	钟楼
the Drum Tower	鼓楼
Terracotta Warriors	陕西秦始皇陵兵马俑
dagger-axe	戈
the Warring States Period	战国

Conversation 2 Trip to Huangpu River

(W— Wang Ming, a guide　　T—Tourist)

W: The tour on the Huangpu River will cover a distance of 60 kilometers and take three and a half hours.

T: Does the cruiser call in anywhere?

W: No. Look. The view of the Bund.

T: There are so many buildings along the river.

W: Yes. You see, to the north of the Waibaidu Bridge is the Shanghai Mansions; the building with a green pyramidal roof is the Peace Hotel; the building of classical architectural style is the office building of the Municipal Government; and the building made of huge granite blocks is the office building of the Shanghai Customs. In this complex, there are buildings in Greek, Roman, and Spanish styles.

T: I see. They're just like an exhibition of buildings in international architectural styles. I hear, apart from buildings of the European style, there are also buildings and gardens of classical Chinese style in Shanghai.

W: That's right. Yu Garden and Guyi Garden, which we'll visit tomorrow, are examples of noted classical gardens.

T: Hey, the ships at anchor on the river are also international. This one is British; this Dutch; this Japanese; and those are Brazilian, French, Norwegian and Singaporean ships. Ah, so many ships! Ships and boats of various types have their masts towering and sirens ringing.

W: Look, there's a dock.

T: What a busy dock! Perhaps it's a containerized dock. Oh, there are also quite a number of factories.

W: Factories in Shanghai, you know, used to be concentrated on either side of the Huangpu River. Since the founding of the P. R. C, about ten industrial districts have been established in the suburbs.

T: Shanghai sure is a great city. It's both an industrial and a commercial city. It also boasts quite a number of China's first-class universities and research institutions… The river, you see, is so stretched-out here.

W: We are at Wusongkou, here.

T: So many cranes and iron towers. This must be an industrial area, right?

W: Yes. It's the construction site of the new Baoshan Iron and Steel Works. The plant is one of China's large-scale iron and steel complexes.

T: Oh, there are forts on the bank!

W: Here's the former site of the Wusong Forts.

T: They were left here after the Opium period, weren't they?

W: Right. During the Opium War, General Chen Huacheng directed his soldiers at this fort to fire at the enemy, and they destroyed several enemy gun-ships. Unfortunately, General Chen and many of his soldiers died as martyrs because they fought in isolation and used backward arms and ammunition.

T: I see. The Chinese people paid a big price for safeguarding their motherland. Look, what's that in the big waves ahead of us?

W: It's a beacon tower. It's the farthest point of our tour. The cruiser will go round the tower before it turns back.

 New Words

distance	[ˈdɪst(ə)ns]	n. 距离
mansion	[ˈmænʃ(ə)n]	n. 大厦
pyramidal	[pɪˈræmɪd(ə)l]	adj. 锥体的；金字塔形的
granite	[ˈgrænɪt]	n. 花岗岩
dock	[dɒk]	n. 码头；船坞
liberation	[lɪbəˈreɪʃ(ə)n]	n. 释放，解放
backward	[ˈbækwəd]	adj. 向后的 adv. 向后地；相反地
ammunition	[æmjʊˈnɪʃ(ə)n]	n. 弹药；军火
boast	[bəʊst]	v. 以有……而自豪

Chapter Two　Categories of Tourism

 Phrases and Expressions

the Huangpu River	黄浦江
the Bund	上海外滩
the Waibaidu Bridge	外白渡桥
the Peace Hotel	和平饭店
tell the time	报时
speak of	证明；为……提供证据
the ships at anchor	停着的船
the Opium War	鸦片战争
died as martyrs	壮烈牺牲
a beacon tower	灯塔

 Practical Patterns

1. The old tower has a long history of 2000 years.
   古塔有两千年的历史。

2. Egypt is an Arabian country with a long history.
   埃及是一个具有悠久历史的阿拉伯国家。

3. The old town dates back to the late seventeenth century.
   这座古城建于17世纪后期。

4. London dates back to 43 A. D.
   伦敦始建于公元43年。

5. This area is covered with grassland.
   这个地区为草原所覆盖。

6. Sichuan Province is made up of a basin and some mountainous areas.
   四川省是由一个盆地和山区组成的。

7. One-third of the island is covered with forest.
   这个岛的三分之一是森林。

8. Hainan Province consists of Hainan Island and neighbouring isles as well as wide sea areas.
   海南省由海南岛和附近的小岛及广阔的海域组成。

9. There are quite a lot of places of interest in Xi'an, such as the Terracotta Warriors and Horses, the old City Wall and so on.
   西安有许多名胜，如兵马俑、古城墙等。

10. Beijing has many places of interest, among which is the Forbidden City.

北京有许多名胜，其中就有故宫。

11. Hangzhou is well-known for its beautiful West Lake.
    杭州以它美丽的西湖而著名。

12. Beijing is famous as the capital of China.
    北京作为中国的首都而闻名。

13. The city lies across the river.
    这座城市位于河的两侧。

14. The new gymnasium is situated at the eastern of the city.
    这座新体育馆位于城市的东边。

15. Tibet lies at a plateau averaging over 4,000 metres above sea-level.
    西藏平均海拔 4000 米以上。

16. China lies in the east of Asia and on the western coast of the Pacific Ocean.
    中国位于亚洲东部，太平洋的西岸。

17. The beautiful town is located along the shore of the lake.
    这个美丽的公园坐落于湖的沿岸。

18. The village lies among the mountains.
    这个村子坐落在群山之中。

Task I Complete the following dialogue by translating the Chinese in the brackets.

W: Good morning, sir. What can I do for you?

G: We are going to stay for two days in Shanghai. _____?
（你能否就如何安排上海的旅游计划给我们提供一些建议？）

W: Certainly, sir. In the morning of the first day, you can visit the Shanghai Exhibition Centre. It's _____. （从我们饭店到那里步行只需 10 分钟。）The next scenic spot is the Jade Buddha Temple.

G: Is it far from there?

W: Oh, no. It is only a 5-minute ride by taxi from the temple. You can have your lunch in the temple. It serves purely vegetarian food.

G: That's wonderful. I have heard that it is a special kind of Chinese cuisine. I'd like to try such food there.

W: In the afternoon you can take a taxi to the Bund to see buildings. There are Greek, Roman and Spanish buildings built before liberation and still standing in array like an exhibition of buildings in international architectural styles. Then, you take a walk to Shanghai Museum just near the Bund. It is a national art museum with a collection of such treasures as bronzes, ceramics, paintings and calligraphy and models of

Chapter Two Categories of Tourism

different dynasties.

G: That's great. _____?（那以后你建议我去哪里?）

W: After that you can go to the Yu Garden，which is also quite near. It is a _____ _____.（典型的中国式园林）It features more than thirty halls and pavilions. You will have much to see there.

G: Is the Yu Garden in the old city town?

W: Yes，outside the Yu Garden is the "City God Temple Bazaar".（城隍庙商场）There are 130 small shops in the Bazaar dealing in various kinds of small articles of daily necessities popularly known for their being "small（小）, native（土）, special（特）and varied（多）." Another feature is its delicious snacks of different flavors. _____（你可以在那里品尝一下不同种类的点心小吃）or you can have your dinner in one of the famous restaurants such as "The Green Wave Restaurant"（碧浪餐馆）and the "Shanghai Old Restaurant".

G: I think I shall really have much to see and a lot to eat on the first day. _____?（那第二天怎样?）

W: _____.（至于第二天你可以观光一下城市的西部。）

G: Where shall we go first?

W: In the morning，you may first go to the Shanghai Zoological Garden to see the animals having their breakfast and playing tricks. Then you can go to the Longhua Temple in Longhua Area，a historic site as well as a tourist resort in Shanghai's southeast suburbs. _____.（在你们回饭店的路上，你们可以顺便去一下少年宫。）

G: I see. _____.（看来你对上海十分了解。非常感谢你告诉我的这些情况。）We always follow your suggestions.

W: Thank you. _____（希望您在上海和我们酒店过得愉快。）

Task II Make up a brief dialogue according to the situations given below（Take the text and Task I as examples）.

1. You have just met a group of tourists at the airport. You are now on the way to the hotel. The tourists are going to stay in Fujian for a day and a half. Tell them their itinerary of Red Tourism.

2. Mr. and Mrs. Brown have just checked in at your hotel. As it is their first trip to Shandong，they ask you about the "red scenic spots" in Shandong. Tell them and try to make the necessary arrangements for them.

微课：红旗渠

Part III   Readings

Text A

"Red Tourism" Can Be More Colorful

"Red tourism" is certainly a catchword in China nowadays.

By visiting "red scenic spots" historical places, sites that in one way or another have relevance to China's revolution, visitors can not only relax during a trip but also relive the People's Republic of China's resourceful "red history", a period spanning from 1921, when the Communist Party of China was born, to 1949 when new China was founded.

Although a brand new travel concept, "red tourism", is now booming in places where major revolutionary sites are located through the perfect combination of patriotic education and recreation. The National Tourism Administration even designated 2005 the "Year of Red Tourism." But "red tourism," its promoters say, "has another significance."

It is well known that most of the revolutionary sites are located in mountainous areas or remote regions which are usually economically backward. "Red tourism," therefore, seems a sensible way to help develop the local economies of such places which, in the past, sacrificed a lot to the revolutionary cause.

However, "red tourism" operators should be cautious that it does not become a fleeting fashion, but develops in a sustainable way. Simply visiting "red scenic spots" runs the risk of boring tourists. Although such places are rich in historical content, they lack variety. Making things worse is that many "red scenic spots" are scattered and isolated, which means potential visitors at times have to travel long distances to see just one or two historical sites.

The operators, therefore, must look squarely at these drawbacks and devise strategies to tackle them, if this theme of tourism is to survive and thrive. They should be aware that "red tourism" should be managed in accordance with market rules. Southeast China's Fujian Province has offered us a successful model. This coastal province, which is opposite Taiwan, has a significant place in China's "red history". In the late 1920s and early 1930s, Fujian was a major "red base" for the Red Army, which left behind many "red scenic spots". For example, the famous Gutian Meeting, a milestone in the Party's history, was held in the small town Gutian in 1929. Fujian tourism authorities, however, have not tried to develop "red tourism" by exclusively relying on exploring their abundant "red scenic spots". Instead, the province tried, rather successfully, to add "red scenic spots" to more mature travel routes, combining them with other travel resources to make them more

Chapter Two　Categories of Tourism

attractive. For example, it added the Gutian Meeting venue to an existing travel route, which includes nearby scenery that is not necessarily "red" in any way. The diversified and varied combination of "red scenic spots" and other tourism resources such as unique local culture and peculiar natural beauty, are making this kind of travel experience enlightening yet enjoyable for visitors.

　　Fujian's model, however, is just one of many possible ways to nurture "red tourism". It is hoped that other places, when developing their "red tourism", can learn from Fujian and come up with other creative ways that are suitable to their local conditions.

 New Words

catchword	[ˈkætʃwɜːd]	n. 标语，口号；流行语；口头禅
relevance	[ˈreləvəns]	n. 关联
brand	[brænd]	n. 商标，牌子；烙印
combination	[ˌkɒmbɪˈneɪʃ(ə)n]	n. 结合；组合；联合
patriotic	[ˌpeɪtrɪˈɒtɪk]	adj. 爱国的
recreation	[ˌrekrɪˈeɪʃ(ə)n]	n. 娱乐；消遣；休养
revolutionary	[revəˈluːʃ(ə)n(ə)ri]	n. 革命者　adj. 革命的
designate	[ˈdezɪgneɪt]	v. 指定；指派；把……定名为
promoter	[prəˈməʊtə]	n. 促进者；发起人
mountainous	[ˈmaʊntɪnəs]	adj. 多山的；巨大的
remote	[rɪˈməʊt]	n. 远程　adj. 遥远的；偏僻的
sensible	[ˈsensɪb(ə)l]	adj. 明智的；合理的
sacrifice	[ˈsækrɪfaɪs]	n. 牺牲　vt. 牺牲
fleeting	[ˈfliːtɪŋ]	adj. 飞逝的；转瞬间的
sustainable	[səˈsteɪnəb(ə)l]	adj. 可以忍受的；可持续的
scattered	[ˈskætəd]	adj. 分散的；散乱的
potential	[pəˈtenʃl]	adj. 潜在的；可能的 n. 潜能；可能性
squarely	[ˈskweəli]	adv. 直角地；诚实地；正好
drawback	[ˈdrɔːbæk]	n. 缺点，不利条件
devise	[dɪˈvaɪz]	n. 遗赠　v. 设计；想出；遗赠给
thrive	[θraɪv]	v. 繁荣，兴旺；茁壮成长
accordance	[əˈkɔːd(ə)ns]	n. 一致；和谐
milestone	[ˈmaɪlstəʊn]	n. 里程碑，划时代的事件

exclusively	[ɪkˈskluːsɪvli]	adv. 唯一地；专有地；排外地
abundant	[əˈbʌnd(ə)nt]	adj. 丰富的；充裕的；盛产
venue	[ˈvenjuː]	n. 发生地点；集合地点
testament	[ˈtestəm(ə)nt]	n. 确实的证明

 Phrases and Expressions

red scenic spots   红色旅游景点
the Communist Party of China   中国共产党
Gutian Meeting   古田会议
the National Tourism Administration 国家旅游局

 Integrated Exercises of Skills

Task I   Fill in the blanks with the information you learned from the reading.

1. "Red tourism" is certainly a _____ in China nowadays.
2. "Red tourism," through the perfect _____ of _____ and recreation, is now booming in places where major _____ are located.
3. The National Tourism Administration even _____ 2005 the _____.
4. However, "red tourism" operators should be _____ that it does not become a _____, but develops in a sustainable way.
5. Although such places are rich in historical content, they _____.
6. The operators, therefore, must look squarely at these _____ and devise strategies to _____ them, if this theme of tourism is to survive and thrive.
7. In the late 1920s and early 1930s, Fujian was a major _____ for the Red Army, which left behind many "red scenic spots."
8. The _____ and varied combination of "red scenic spots" and other tourism resources such as _____ local culture and peculiar natural beauty, are making this kind of travel experience _____ yet enjoyable for visitors.

Task II   Read the passage above and decide whether the following statements are true (T) or false (F).

(   ) 1. China has many "red scenic spots".
(   ) 2. Fujian has set a good example of developing "red tourism".
(   ) 3. Gutian is a small town in Hunan.
(   ) 4. 2004 is designated the "Year of Red Tourism."
(   ) 5. It is hoped that other places can learn from Fujian and come up with other

creative ways that are suitable to their local conditions.

Task III Translate the following sentences into Chinese.

1. By visiting "red scenic spots" historical places, sites that in one way or another have relevance to China's revolution, visitors can not only relax during a trip but also relive the People's Republic of China's resourceful "red history," a period spanning from 1921, when the Communist Party of China was born, to 1949 when new China was founded.

2. It is well known that most of the revolutionary sites were found in mountainous areas or remote regions which are usually economically backward.

3. The operators, therefore, must look squarely at these drawbacks and devise strategies to tackle them, if this theme of tourism is to survive and thrive. They should be aware that "red tourism" should be managed in accordance with market rules.

4. The diversified and varied combination of "red scenic spots" and other tourism resources such as unique local culture and peculiar natural beauty, are making this kind of travel experience enlightening yet enjoyable for visitors.

5. It is hoped that other places, when developing their "red tourism," can learn from Fujian and come up with other creative ways that are suitable to their local conditions.

Text B

Red Tourism

Over the nearly three decades from its establishment in 1921, the Communist Party of China (CPC) is through marched down a "red" road of revolution. It was a road of hardship, passion, romance and glory. Today, increasing numbers of Chinese with an interest in history are enthusiastically revisiting former revolutionary bases and landmark sites. This is "Red Tourism".

In December 2004, the Chinese government formulated the General Plan for the Development of Red Tourism (2004 – 2010). The plan defines the 12 major red tourist areas which best represent the progressive phases of the revolution in China. Following are some of the designated red spots.

Jinggang Mountain

Nestled in southwestern Jiangxi Province, Jinggang Mountain boasts a well-preserved ecosystem featuring precipitous cliffs and dense bamboo forests. Historically, few humans settled in the area due to limited means of access. On October 7, 1927, Mao Zedong led his troops to Maoping, Ninggang County, where he established the Red Army and the Jinggang Mountain Revolutionary Base. The conditions were rugged and the going tough. Later, during his meeting with American journalist Edgar Snow, Mao recalled the suffering time on Jinggang Mountain: "The troops had no winter uniforms, and food was extremely scarce. For months we lived practically on squash. The soldiers shouted a slogan of their own: 'Down with capitalism, and eat squash!' — for to them capitalism meant landlords and the landlords' squash."

However, attacks from Kuomintang troops were a threat fiercer than low temperatures and starvation. To shatter the seeds of communism in China, from November 1930 to September 1931, the Kuomintang government launched three "annihilation campaigns". Despite the harsh environment, Mao and his comrades soldiered on, carrying out land reforms and beating back the attacks of Kuomintang troops. In the course of its painstaking struggle, the CPC realized that peasants, making up the overwhelming majority of China's population, would play a vital role in the Chinese revolution. In his essay *A Single Spark Can Start a Prairie Fire*, Mao set forth a strategy by which the CPC would shift the focus of its effort from the cities to the countryside and establish revolutionary bases in the countryside by mobilizing and relying on peasants. In this way a long-term revolutionary war were launched with peasants as the backbone. The war would develop and expand revolutionary forces and finally capture the cities and achieve a nationwide victory.

Today Jinggang Mountain is popular with fans of red tourism. Here they can experience the hard life that Red Army soldiers endured: Wearing coarse clothes, eating brown rice and pumpkin soup, and trekking along mountainous paths while learning of their stories. Today, increasing numbers of tourists are flooding into the mountain.

Zunyi

Its prior annihilation campaigns beaten back by the Red Army, the Kuomintang

Chapter Two Categories of Tourism

troops launched an even fiercer attack on the Jinggang Mountain Revolutionary Base. In his book *The Cambridge History of China*, Professor Llord E. Eastman described: "But not until the fifth annihilation campaign of 1933 – 1934 which Chiang employed about 800,000 troops, was advised by German and Japanese advisers, and augmented his military offensive with a stringent economic blockade of the Communist areas — did he gain a nearly decisive victory over the Communists. The Communists, defeated militarily and suffering incredibly from shortages of food, summoned their last reserves of strength and courage, broke out of the Nationalist encirclement, and in October 1934 commenced what was to become the Long March."

The Long March was a milestone event in contemporary China. Professor John K. Fairbank, a leading scholar in modern and contemporary China studies, proclaimed the Long March as being almost a miracle, more documented than Moses leading his Chosen People through the Red Sea. The marchers covered 6,000 miles in a year, averaging 17 miles a day. However, this miracle was conceived under extremely harsh conditions. Southwestern China's terrain is incredibly rugged, with precipitous mountains, deep valleys and rushing rivers. There are no plains.

Thanks to Mao's military acumen, the Red Army finally routed the Kuomintang troops. From January 15 to 17, 1935, the Political Bureau of the CPC Central Committee held a conference in Zunyi, a small city in Guizhou Province. Here Mao's military strategy was acknowledged as being correct and his leadership over the Party and the Red Army was formally acknowledged.

Under Mao's leadership, in 1949 the CPC liberated the nation and founded the People's Republic of China, one of the most important chapters in the nation's history.

A gifted leader, Mao rescued the Chinese revolution from near-failure and defeated an enemy previously thought to be undefeatable. He thus became an everlasting legend in human history.

A city hidden deep in the mountains, Zunyi is a popular tourist destination. Today, at the site of the Zunyi Conference stands a memorial hall. The building remains original in appearance, and the streets and lanes in front of and behind the building are paved with stone planks. Also, in order to maintain harmony with the memorial hall, the surrounding buildings were all reconstructed into low structures with the architectural style of northern Guizhou of the early 20th Century. In addition, other memorials of the Long March, such as the Memorial Hall of Crossing the Chishui River Four Times and the Observatory in Loushan Pass Scenic Resort, have been restored and well preserved.

Yan'an

The Long March ended in northern Shaanxi Province, on the dry Loess Plateau that lacked rainfall and suffered from severe desertification. It was on this land that the Red Army created a new miracle.

American journalist Edgar Snow was one of the first Westerners to look for greater insight into the Red Army and the CPC in northern Shaanxi. Due to many years of assaults and blockades on the part of the Kuomintang government, the life the CPC and the Red Army really led remained unknown to the outside world.

Based on the trip, Snow wrote the famous book *Red Star over China*, in which he depicted the tremendous changes brought by the CPC to northern Shaanxi. Yan'an was a poor, inanimate township populated by only 10,000 residents when the Red Army arrived and made it the administrative capital of the Shaanxi-Gansu-Ningxia Border Region. The arrival of the CPC, however, injected the small town with warmth, happiness and passion, transforming it into a place admired by people around China.

From 1937 to 1947, Yan'an served as the administrative capital of the Shaanxi-Gansu-Ningxia Border Region, the seat of the CPC Central Committee, and the command center and home front of the Chinese revolution. Thus, it has long been reputed as a holy land of Chinese revolution. Here are preserved many historic sites, including Phoenix Hill, Yangjialing, Zaoyuan and Wangjiaping. The revolutionary sites — whether the Treasure Pagoda on Phoenix Hill or the cave dwellings in Yangjialing — remind visitors of the past hardship endured by the CPC.

 New Words

enthusiastically	[ɪnˌθjuːzɪˈæstɪkəli]	adv. 热心地;满腔热情地
landmark	[ˈlæn(d)mɑːk]	n. 地标;里程碑;纪念碑
define	[dɪˈfaɪn]	v. 定义;使明确;规定
progressive	[prəˈgresɪv]	n. 改革论者;进步分子
ecosystem	[ˈiːkəʊsɪstəm]	n. 生态系统
precipitous	[prɪˈsɪpɪtəs]	adj. 险峻的
dense	[dens]	adj. 稠密的;浓厚的;愚钝的
rugged	[ˈrʌgɪd]	adj. 崎岖的
suffering	[ˈsʌf(ə)rɪŋ]	n. 受难;苦楚 adj. 受苦的
scarce	[skeəs]	adj. 缺乏的,不足的
capitalism	[ˈkæpɪt(ə)lɪz(ə)m]	n. 资本主义
starvation	[stɑːˈveɪʃn]	n. 饿死;挨饿;绝食
Communism	[ˈkɒmjʊnɪz(ə)m]	n. 共产主义
annihilation	[ənaɪɪˈleɪʃ(ə)n]	n. 灭绝;消灭

Chapter Two Categories of Tourism

painstaking	[ˈpeɪnzteɪkɪŋ]	n. 辛苦；勤勉 adj. 艰苦的；勤勉的
struggle	[ˈstrʌg(ə)l]	n. 努力，奋斗；竞争 v. 奋斗，努力；挣扎
backbone	[ˈbækbəʊn]	n. 支柱；骨干
expand	[ɪkˈspænd]	v. 扩张；发展
trek	[trek]	n. & v. 艰苦跋涉
augment	[ɔːgˈment]	n. 增加；增大 v. 增加；增大
blockade	[blɒˈkeɪd]	n. 阻塞 v. 封锁
summon	[ˈsʌmən]	v. 召唤；召集；鼓起
contemporary	[kənˈtemp(ə)r(ər)i]	adj. 当代的
terrain	[təˈreɪn]	n. 地形，地势；领域
acumen	[ˈækjʊmen；əˈkjuːmen]	n. 聪明，敏锐
plateau	[ˈplætəʊ]	n. 高原

 Phrases and Expressions

soldier on	坚持着干；迎着困难干
carry out	执行，实行；贯彻
A Single Spark Can Start a Prairie Fire	星星之火，可以燎原
set forth	陈述，提出；出发；宣布
rely on	依靠，依赖
the Long March	长征

Integrated Exercises of Skills

Task I Fill in the blanks with the suitable words given below, changing the form where necessary.

feature	destination	endure	preserve
blockade	settle	rescue	miracle

1. Nestled in southwestern Jiangxi Province, Jinggang Mountain boasts a well-preserved ecosystem _____ precipitous cliffs and dense bamboo forests.
2. Historically, few humans _____ in the area due to limited means of access.
3. Here they can experience the hard life that Red Army soldiers _____: wearing coarse clothes, eating brown rice and pumpkin soup, and trekking along mountainous paths while learning of their stories.

4. A gifted leader, Mao _____ the Chinese revolution from near-failure and defeated an enemy previously thought to be undefeatable. He thus became an everlasting legend in human history.

5. A city hidden deep in the mountains, Zunyi is a popular tourist _____. Today, at the site of the Zunyi Conference stands a memorial hall.

6. In addition, other memorials of the Long March, such as the Memorial Hall of Crossing the Chishui River Four Times and the Observatory in Loushan Pass Scenic Resort, have been restored and well _____.

7. The Long March ended in northern Shaanxi Province, on a dry loess plateau that lacked rainfall and suffered from severe desertification. It was on this land that the Red Army created a new _____.

8. Due to many years of assaults and _____ on the part of the Kuomintang government, the life the CPC and the Red Army really led remained unknown to the outside world.

Task II Read the passage above and decide whether the following statements are true (T) or false (F).

(   ) 1. The Communist Party of China (CPC) marched down a "red" road of revolution from 1921 to 1949.

(   ) 2. The Long March began in 1933.

(   ) 3. The Kuomintang government launched three "annihilation campaigns" in total.

(   ) 4. Mao's military strategy was acknowledged as being correct and his leadership over the Party and the Red Army was formally acknowledged before the Long March.

(   ) 5. Yan'an served as the administrative capital of the Shaanxi-Gansu-Ningxia Border Region, the seat of the CPC Central Committee, and the command center and home front of the Chinese revolution.

Task III Translate the following sentences into Chinese.

1. Over the nearly three decades from its establishment in 1921 through the founding of the People's Republic of China in 1949, the Communist Party of China (CPC) marched down a "red" road of revolution. It was a road of hardship, passion, romance and glory.

_____

_____

Chapter Two Categories of Tourism

2. The Long March was a milestone event in contemporary China.
_____
_____

3. Here Mao's military strategy was acknowledged as being correct and his leadership over the Party and the Red Army was formally acknowledged.
_____
_____

4. Also, in order to maintain harmony with the memorial hall, the surrounding buildings were all reconstructed into low structures with the architectural style of northern Guizhou of the early 20th Century.
_____
_____

5. From 1937 to 1947, Yan'an served as the capital of the Shaanxi-Gansu-Ningxia Border Region, the seat of the CPC Central Committee, and the command center and home front of the Chinese revolution.
_____
_____

Part IV Practical Writing

Tourism Advertisement 旅游广告

旅游广告主要是指由旅游企业出资，通过各种媒介进行有关旅游产品、旅游服务和旅游信息的有偿的、有组织的、综合的、劝服性的、非人员的信息传播活动，属于狭义的广告。

在全球化背景下，中国旅游广告作为一种旅游目的地的诉求方式，更应该突出本地特色。因为人们出门旅游是为了休闲、商务或其他目的，离开他们熟悉的生活环境，追寻新奇的事物，获得各种精神上的刺激，从而更新自己对世界的观点。正是由于对未知事物的新奇感引领他们去不同的旅游目的地，因此旅游广告的定位及广告元素的选择必须以"特色为主"。这个特色至少包含以下几个方面：

1. 特色自然景观。
2. 特色人文景观。
3. 特色民族文化。
4. 特色民族习俗与人文风情。
5. 特色产品与服务。

Sample 1

5-Day Turpan & Urumqi Tour (4-Star, Private)

Museum with Accommodation Private Tour Multi-City Tour

Jan 1 – Dec 31 (Daily)

Gaochang Ruins (Figure 5-1) / Bezeklik Thousand Buddha Caves (Figure 5-2) / Jiaohe Ruins / Sugong Tower / Karez Water System / Nanshan Grassland / Xinjiang Museum / Erdaoqiao Bazaar

Accommodation: Urumqi Orient Dynasty Hotel, Turpan Sun Holiday Hotel

From CNY 2,600/ guest

Begin your 5-day tour of Xinjiang with a stop in the Uyghur oasis town of Turpan where you'll discover the fascinating karez built around 100 BC to supply water to the surrounding areas. Next stop is the underground Asanta Graves and the crumbling Gaochang Ruins. You'll also head to the Bezeklik Thousand Buddha Caves before stepping 2,000 years back in time to the ruins of the once-prosperous Silk Road city of Jiaohe. Discover the traditional Kazakh yurts of the Nanshan Grasslands before heading to Urumqi's Xinjiang Museum and the Erdaoqiao Bazaar.

Figure 5-1 Gaochang Ruins

Figure 5-2 The Bezeklik Thousand Buddha Caves

Itinerary

Day 1 Urumqi arrival

Your guide will meet you at Urumqi Airport. Look for him or her holding a Ctrip sign as you come out of your arrival gate and together you will be taken to your hotel.

Overnight at the Orient Dynasty Hotel or similar.

Day 2 Urumqi-Turpan (includes breakfast, lunch)

Turpan, the second lowest point on the earth after the Dead Sea. It's also a significant Uyghur agricultural town, thanks to the karez (well) water system, the origins of which date back to around 100 BC.

Here in Turpan you'll also visit the **Asanta Graves**, a series of underground tombs and the final resting place of the rulers of Gaochang in Tang Dynasty.

You'll then continue on to see the crumbling **Gaochang Ruins**, home to the remains of an old Buddhist monastery that dates back to the 1st century BC.

Lastly, visit the **Bezeklik Thousand Buddha Caves**. One of the largest Buddhist grotto complexes in Xinjiang, these 77 shiku (caves carved to house Buddhist images) contain

Chapter Two Categories of Tourism

frescoes and statuary ranging from the naive to the masterly.

Overnight at the Sun Holiday Hotel or similar.

Day 3 Turpan-Urumqi（includes breakfast, lunch）

Today you'll visit the **Jiaohe Ruins**, a once-prosperous, 2,000-year-old Silk Road city situated on an island in the middle of the river that flows through the Yarnaz Valley.

Afterward, head to the **Sugong Tower**, also known as "Turphan Tower" or "Emin Minaret". This is the largest Islamic minaret in China. You'll also visit the amazing ancient karez system which brought water and life to Turpan and beyond from the 1st century BC, as well as a steady stream of traders, adventurers, soldiers and merchants.

In the afternoon you'll drive to Urumqi to take in the mix of Central Asian and Chinese cultures.

Overnight at the Orient Dynasty Hotel or similar.

Day 4 Urumqi（includes breakfast, lunch）

Today you'll travel by car to the **Nanshan Pasture**; lush grasslands dotted with yurts, where Kazakhs graze their herds and enjoy the cooler temperatures. An exciting visit to a traditional Kazakh yurt will be arranged.

In the afternoon visit the **Xinjiang Museum** where you should be sure not to miss the "Loulan Beauty", the body of an Indo-European woman in her 40s with reddish-brown hair, which was remarkably well preserved by the dry desert climate for between 3,800 and 6,000 years!

You'll then head to the 130-year-old **Erdaoqiao Bazaar**, a great place to buy souvenirs and see local Uyghur and Kazakh buyers and sellers doing their trading, just like they've been doing for centuries.

Overnight at the Orient Dynasty Hotel or similar.

Day 5 Urumqi departure（includes breakfast）

After breakfast, you'll be transferred to the airport or train station where you'll depart for your next destination.

(During winter season, the grassland is covered with thick snow.)

Price Includes and Excludes

What is included?
- Experienced English-speaking tour guide;
- Admission fees, meals and transportation as listed in the itinerary;
- Accommodation as listed in the itinerary;
- Turpan-Dunhuang soft sleeper train tickets.

What is excluded?
- Tips, personal expenses or all items not included in the itinerary.

Sample 2

Su Zhou & Zhou Zhuang Water Village Day Tour

From US $ 125 per adult

Destination: Shanghai

Duration: 1 Days & 0 Nights

Tour Type: Seat-in-Coach Tours

Tour Code: SHSIC-3

Summary:

Suzhou, a cultural and historical city in east China, is celebrated around the world for its elegant gardens. Laid out within a limited area by the house, a classical garden of Suzhou is a microcosm of the world made of the basic elements of water, stones, plants and different kinds of buildings with literary allusions (Figure 5-3, Figure 5-4).

Figure 5-3　Zhou Zhuang Water Village　　Figure 5-4　Lion Grove Garden

Itinerary

- Pick up service by your tour guide and driver at 8:00 a.m.;
- Suzhou City — Driving Time (2 hours);
- Suzhou Lingering Garden — Sightseeing (1 hour 20 minutes);
- Ancient Suzhou Silk Museum — Sightseeing (40 minutes);
- Local Restaurant — Lunch (1 hour);
- Zhou Zhuang — Driving Time (2 hours);
- Zhou Zhuang Water Village — Sightseeing (1 hour 30 minutes);
- Drive back to Shanghai and drop-off service at your hotel before 6:00 p.m.

Notes

1. The approximate day tour itinerary & schedule above is for reference only, and may vary according to your travel date and group size. The itinerary & schedule is subject to change at the time when the booking order is confirmed.

2. Note: Tipping is now considered by many locals to be a part of their normal

Chapter Two　Categories of Tourism

remuneration. However, this is a matter of personal discretion.

Price Policy

Price includes:
- Pick-up and drop-off service for Shanghai downtown hotels;
- Sightseeing program for seat-in-coach tour as indicated in the itinerary;
- Meals: Lunch;
- Local English-speaking tour guide for pick-up, drop-off and sightseeing program as indicated;
- Entrance fees to scenic spots as indicated in the itinerary;
- Parking fee, toll fee wherever applicable.

Price Excludes:
- Accommodation cost;
- Flight/train ticket;
- Personal expenses such as laundry, drinks, fax, telephone call, optional activities, etc;
- Gratuities to the tour guide, driver, hotel bellboy;
- Services not mentioned in the itinerary;
- travel insurance;
- For uptown hotel, extra money will be charged.

Cancellation and Refund Policy for Tours Reservation

Cancellation in advance	Cancellation penalty
More than 30 days	No Cancellation Fee
30 – 10 days	50% of the full payment
9 – 0 days or no show	100% of the full payment

Task I Tell the differences between the two samples. Which one attracts you more?

Task II What are main features of tourism ads? Please list some points.

Task III Write a tourism advertising according to the information given below.

The Smiths from England want to have a journey to Yunnan. They only have 5 days for travelling. Try to write a perfect advertising which will attract them.

······ Part V　Typical Scenic Spot ······

Yungang Grottoes

The Yungang Grottoes are located 16km west of Datong, at the base of the low-lying sandstone Wuzhou Hills. Most were carved under the Northern Wei between 460 and 494 A. D.

The advent of the Northern Wei marked a new high point in Chinese art and culture. The Wei introduced a period of stability and, through an intelligent series of laws on marriage and land distribution, created a "melting pot" of Han and non-Han peoples. Major treatises on agriculture and river transportation were written in this period, while painting, calligraphy, and poetry all developed a new vividness and grace. But the greatest achievement of all was Buddhist grotto art.

The art of cave temples originated in (or from) India and first appeared in China at Dunhuang. However, the carvings at Dunhuang are in terracotta, whereas those at Yungang are the earliest examples of stone carvings in China. The 53 caves — including 21 major ones — contain 51,000 bas-reliefs and statues, ranging in height from just a few centimeters to 17 meters. A number of different cultural influences can be seen: India (draperies, shortened skirts, and headdresses); Persian and Byzantine (weapons, lions, and beards); and Greek (the trident and the curling acanthus leaves).

From east to west, the main caves fall naturally into three groups:

Caves 1 to 4. At the far eastern end are the first two caves, somewhat removed from the others. The square floor-plan indicates that they were built quite early. The first cave has some bas-reliefs to the life of Buddha, while the second has a delicately carved pagoda at its center. Cave 3, the largest at Yungang, contains a basic triad of a large Buddha flanked by two bodhisattvas. The elegance of their garments and the use of high relief is reminiscent of some of the carving at Longmen, indicating that the Datong figures may have been created under the Sui or early Tang dynasty.

Beyond the fourth cave are a small ravine and a monastery, consisting of several temples. The monastery dates from 1652. Historical writings suggest that there may once have been as many as 10 monasteries in these hills, but today there is no trace of them.

Caves 5 to 13. Caves 5 and 6 mark the high point of Yungang art. In the fifth cave, a colossal Buddha (16.8 meters tall) is seated in serene contemplation. Both caves, but particularly cave 6, are richly carved with episodes from religious stories and processional scenes. The interiors of these two caves have fortunately been preserved from the elements by the twin towers at their entrances. Cave 5, 6, and 7—the latter having six bodhisattvas and two lions in high relief—were restored in 1955. Cave 8 contains a number of foreign influences: the Vishunu seated on a bull, the Shiva, and a guardian bearing a trident.

Caves 7 and 8 form a pair, as do caves 9 and 10, also richly carved. Each of the latter two contains front and back chambers and fine bas-relief work at its entrance.

Chapter Two Categories of Tourism

Cave 11 was decorated in 483 A. D. , in honor of the imperial family. It contains 95 large carvings and hundreds of tiny bodhisattvas in niches around the wall. The bas-reliefs in Cave 12 provide valuable information on the architecture and musical instruments of the period. Cave 13 has another colossal Buddha, his arm supported by another figure and an enormous halo around his head.

Caves 14 to 21. The first two in this series are badly eroded, though they still contain thousands of tiny bodhisattvas in niches around the walls. The next five caves, the oldest at Yungang, were all carved in 460 A. D. during the reign of Emperor Wen Chang. Each contains a colossal Buddha whose countenance is austere and divinely remote. The early carving in these caves has a geometric, linear quality, and the decoration is not as rich or bold as it is in later caves.

After the year of 1949, the caves were declared historic monuments, and the steady erosion by wind and water was slowed down through judicious tree planning and the construction of protective barriers. Unfortunately, little could be done to restore the ravages of early 20th-century art thieves and smugglers. Hundreds of statues were beheaded and a number of bas-reliefs removed. They now reside in the art museums of Japan, Europe, and North America!

职业素养

党的二十大报告指出，"用好红色资源""传承红色基因，赓续红色血脉"。红色旅游作为一种特殊的旅游形态，在传播中华优秀传统文化、革命文化和社会主义先进文化方面发挥着重要作用。发展红色旅游要把准方向，核心是进行红色教育、传承红色基因。红色文化是红色旅游景区的灵魂，没有红色文化的滋养和熏陶，红色景区只能是徒有其表。同时，红色资源是革命老区经济发展可以利用的独有特色资源。红色旅游一方面有助于传承红色文化，以革命传统精神教育时代新人；另一方面能够帮助革命老区人民发挥当地红色文化资源优势，发展红色旅游经济，将红色文化资源转化为旅游产业优势，使红色旅游成为当地经济新的增长点。

Chapter Three
Elements of Tourism

◈ Unit 6   Food

◈ Unit 7   Accommodation

◈ Unit 8   Transportation

◈ Unit 9   Travelling

◈ Unit 10   Shopping

Unit 6 Food

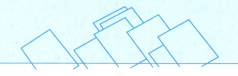

••••• Part I Warm-Up •••••

Restaurant Service Sequence

1. Greeting guests at the entrance
2. Escorting and seating guests
3. Serving beverage or water
4. Serving some snacks
5. Presenting menu and taking the order
6. Adjusting table
7. Serving the course
8. Check guest table for service needs
9. Check guests' satisfaction
10. Serving dessert
11. Preparing and presenting the bill
12. Bidding farewell to guests

••••• Part II Conversations •••••

Conversation 1   Trying Roast Duck

(W: Waiter   Mr. H: Mr. Hunt   Mrs. H: Mrs. Hunt   L: Chef Li)

W: Sit down, please. What would you like? Here's the menu.

Mr. H: Let me see... What do you prefer?

Mrs. H: It seems to me that all the dishes are so good. I really don't know where to begin?

Mr. H: I don't know either. Well, what is this restaurant famous for?

W: It is famous for its roast duck, sir.

Mr. H: Sounds wonderful. All right, let's try it. Tasting is believing.

Chapter Three　Elements of Tourism

（After a while）

W: The duck is served, sir.

Mrs. H: Excellent! Look at the appetizing brown color!

Mr. H: (to the waiter) Could you show us how this noble dish is eaten?

W: Yes, sir. First, hold a pancake in your left hand and then using some raw scallion as a brush, paint a few splashes of bean sauce on the pancake like this, and don't paint too much bean sauce on the pancake. Next, place the scallion in the middle of the pancake and add a few pieces of the roast duck with your chopsticks. Finally, roll the pancake up and enjoy!

（The waiter helps Mr. And Mrs. Hunt to use chopsticks）

Mr. H & Mrs. H: It is excellent.

Mrs. H: Could you tell us how the dish is prepared?

W: OK. A skilled chef can make more than 80 cold and hot dishes from the duck's innards, head, wings and webs to suit different tastes, and he can cut 100 to 120 slices in four or five minutes, each slice with an equal portion of skin and meat.

Mr. H: Incredible!

W: Oh, here comes Chef Li. Mr. and Mrs. Hunt, let me introduce you to a veteran chef. This is Mrs. Hunt, a friend from abroad. This is her husband Mr. Hunt. This is Chef Li.

Mr. H & Mrs. H: How do you do, Mr. Li?

Mrs. H: We're certainly enjoying your handiwork.

Mrs. H: Chef Li, would you please tell us how you roast the ducks?

L: With pleasure. The main points are the quality of the duck chosen and the type of wood burned.

Mr. H: What kind of duck do you use for roasting?

L: Plump ducks weighing 2.5 kilograms on an average.

Mrs. H: What wood is used in the roasting process?

L: Only fruit trees such as peach-trees and pear-trees are used to give the meat its unique flavor.

Mrs. H: Is there any difficulty in judging correctly the temperature and roasting time?

L: Yes. That is where the secret lies—the correct judgement. And, of course, there's the skill, too.

Mr. H & Mrs. H: Thank you very much.

L: You're welcome.

Mr. H: To tell you the truth, the smell of the duck made my mouth water.

Mrs. H: Really, I was never so hungry. Its skin is crisp and its meat so tender.

Mr. H: Truly, Chinese cooking has such a charming variety. And that makes it perfectly wonderful in color, smell and taste. I believe that only after tasting.

W: Is there anything else you would like to have?

Mr. H: No, thank you. We've had enough.

Mrs. H: We've never had anything better than this square meal.

W: It's very kind of you to say so, madam.

Mr. H: Bring me the bill, please.

W: Here it is, sir.

Mr. H: Here is one hundred yuan, please keep the change.

W: We don't accept tips. Thank you just the same.

Mrs. H: Let's go now. (Facing the waiter) Thank you for your good service.

W: Thank you. Do come again, please.

New Words

menu	[ˈmenjuː]	n. 菜单
prefer	[prɪˈfɜː]	v. 更喜欢
appetizing	[ˈæpɪtaɪzɪŋ]	adj. 开胃的；促进食欲的
pancake	[ˈpænkeɪk]	n. 薄烤饼；粉饼
scallion	[ˈskæliən]	n. 青葱
incredible	[ɪnˈkredɪb(ə)l]	adj. 难以置信的，惊人的
handiwork	[ˈhændiwɜːk]	n. 手工艺

Phrases and Expressions

be famous for　　　　　　　　因……而著名
Tasting is believing　　　　　　百闻不如一尝

Conversation 2　　Trying Seafood

(G: Guest　　W: Waiter)

G: Is this table free, waiter?

W: I'm sorry, sir, these two tables have been reserved by someone over the telephone,

Chapter Three Elements of Tourism

but that one over there is free.

G: All right.

W: It's Shanghai's crab season. Would you like to try some steamed crabs first?

G: I think I would.

   (After a while)

W: Here they are, sir.

G: Look at these monsters.

W: Monsters? You are definitely wrong. They may look ugly, but you will love them because they taste so good. Those are fresh-water crabs from a lake near Soochow.

G: Really? Could you tell me how they are prepared?

W: Well, they should be steamed. Put some water in a pot and put the tied crabs onto a meshed frame above the water. Boil the water for about twenty minutes and the crabs are ready to be served.

G: How do I eat them?

W: Break the shell with your teeth, dip the meat in a mixture of soya sauce, vinegar and sliced ginger.

G: I see... Oh, very nice. I am told crabs of Dong Ting Lake are above the rest. Is Dong Ting Lake in Hunan Province?

W: Yes. It's one of the five great lakes of China.

G: Well, are they in season now?

W: No, according to the saying "In the 9th month of the lunar calendar, eat female crabs and in the 10th month, eat male crabs." As regards the tastes, the smaller female crabs are better than the male crabs. But the claws of the bigger male crabs are much better than those of the female crabs.

G: That's right. River crabs are always preferable. Their delicious taste is a popular favorite.

W: What else will you have? Do you want to try some delicacies of autumn crab meat?

G: What do you suggest?

W: Today we have plain sauteed crab meat, sauteed shrimps and crab meat, and crab meat with beancurd.

G: That sounds good. I'd like to have them all, and a bowl of rice and a plain soup, too, please. (After a while)

W: Have you finished eating, sir?

G: Yes.

W: Is everything all right here, sir?

G: Yes, thank you. All the crab dishes were very delicious. I like them very much. Besides, your service is excellent.

W: It's very kind of you to say so. The dishes made of crab meat were prepared by the best chef in our restaurant.

G: No wonder they are so delicious! I'll come again tomorrow. How much do I owe you?

W: Sixty-five yuan in all.

G: The charges are also moderate. Here you are. Keep the change.

W: It's a pleasure to serve you, sir. But we don't take tips. Thank you all the same.

G: It's very nice of you. Good-bye.

W: Good-bye and good night.

 New Words

monster	[ˈmɒnstə]	n. 怪物
ugly	[ˈʌgli]	adj. 丑陋的
crab	[kræb]	n. 螃蟹；蟹肉
Soochow	[ˈsuːtʃaʊ]	n. 苏州
soya	[ˈsɒɪə]	n. 大豆
vinegar	[ˈvɪnɪgə]	n. 醋
plain	[pleɪn]	adj. 平的；简单的
delicious	[dɪˈlɪʃəs]	adj. 美味的；可口的
moderate	[ˈmɒd(ə)rət]	adj. 温和的；适度的

 Practical Patterns

1. It's too hot. My tongue is on fire. Can you give me some ice water?
   辣死我了！我的舌头都火辣辣的。能给我一些冰水吗？

2. How can it be so spicy? I am tearing up! The taste is too strong for me.
   怎么这么辣？都呛得我流眼泪了。这个味儿太浓了。

3. Do try some sauce. It goes perfectly with fried chicken.
   来点儿酱吧，炸鸡蘸上这种酱特别好吃。

4. That Tofu looks like it will melt in your mouth.
   豆腐看起来入口即化。

Chapter Three　Elements of Tourism

5. A visit to Beijing is not complete without a taste of Beijing roast duck.
   到了北京，怎能不尝尝北京烤鸭？

6. The plum juice was sweet and left a pleasant taste in my mouth.
   酸梅汤有点甜，让我唇齿留香。

7. I didn't expect it to taste so good.
   没想到居然这么好吃。

8. I'm sorry. The restaurant is full now. You have to wait for about half an hour. Would you care to have a drink at the lounge until a table is available?
   很抱歉，餐厅已经满座了，大约要等30分钟才会有空桌。你们介意在休息室喝点东西直至有空桌吗？

9. No, thanks. We'll come back later. May I reserve a table for two?
   不用了，谢谢。我们等一会儿再来。请替我们预订一张二人桌，可以吗？

10. By the way. Can we have a table by the window?
    顺便问一下，我们可以要一张靠近窗口的桌子吗？

11. Are you ready to order or just a minute?
    你们准备好点餐了吗？还是要再等一会儿？

12. What do you like to drink?
    你想要喝什么？

Task I Complete the following dialogues by translating the Chinese in the brackets.

1. (A: tourists; B: guide; C: waiter)

   A: Oh, I'm starving. I'd like to try some real Chinese cuisine. _____ （你给我们推荐什么），Ms. Chu？

   B: Well, it depends. You see _____ （中国有八大菜系），for instance, Sichuan cuisine and Hunan cuisine.

   A: They are both spicy hot, I've heard.

   B: That's right. If you like hot dishes, you can try some.

   A: They might be _____ （对我们来说太辣了）.

   B: Then there are Cantonese cuisine and Jiangsu cuisine. Most southerners like them.

   A: I'd like to try Cantonese food.

   B: All right. Let's go to a Hakka restaurant.

   C: Good evening. _____. （欢迎来到我们餐厅。）

B: Good evening. _____. (我们的美国客人想尝尝你们餐厅的特色菜。)

C: OK. Please be seated. Are you ready to order now?

A: What's good for today?

C: We have stuffed bean curd, sliced boiled chicken, mushroom soup etc. We also have _____ (各种各样的点心)。

A: Some chicken and vegetables, please.

C: Please wait for a moment. I'll bring them right away.

2. A: Excuse me, sir. We want to have lunch in a Chinese restaurant. _____. (我们想吃点真正的中国菜。) Can you help us?

B: Well, it depends. There are kinds of Chinese food. How about the Sichuan cuisine, and the Hunan cuisine. If you like hot dishes, you can try some.

A: They might be too hot for me. _____? (有什么特别的北京风味菜吗?)

B: There's the Beijing roast duck.

A: Oh, yes. I've heard a lot about it. I'd like very much to try it. _____? (在哪儿能吃到呢?)

B: You can find it in most restaurants, but the best place is certainly Quanjude Restaurant.

A: Is it near here?

B: _____. (不太近也不算远。) A taxi will take you there in 15 minutes, if the traffic is not too bad, I mean.

A: Well, thank you for your information. But what is the name of that restaurant again?

B: _____. (我把它写在这张纸条上。) You can show it to the taxi-driver.

A: That's very kind of you. Thanks a lot.

B: You're welcome.

Task II Using the given words and expressions to make a conversation with your partner according to the following situation.

Situation: *Mr. & Mrs. Smith go to a Sichuan food restaurant with their friend Li Xing, and a waiter is greeting them. They are ordering their dishes.*

Student A: waiter
Student B: Mr. Smith
Student C: Mrs. Smith

Chapter Three Elements of Tourism

 Suggested words and expressions

Translucent beef slices 灯影牛肉

Sliced Beef and Ox Tongue in Chili Sauce 夫妻肺片

Mapo beancurd 麻婆豆腐

Fish-Flavored Shredded Pork 鱼香肉丝

Twice-cooked pork slices 回锅肉

Kung Pao Chicken 宫保鸡丁

 Suggested sentence patterns

What is the specialty of the restaurant?

Do you have any special meals today?

What would you recommend?

What about any special Sichuan dishes?

If you like hot dishes, you can try some.

May I have a menu, please?

Can I take your order now?

Not quite. Could I have a few more minutes?

Please take my order.

Part III Readings

Text A

Chinese Food

China covers a large territory and has many nationalities, hence a variety of Chinese food with different but fantastic and mouthwatering flavor. Since China's local dishes have their own typical characteristics, generally, Chinese food can be roughly divided into eight regional cuisines, which has been widely accepted around. Certainly, there are many other local cuisines that are famous, such as Beijing cuisine and Shanghai cuisine.

Shandong Cuisine

Consisting of Jinan cuisine and Jiaodong cuisine, Shandong cuisine, clear, pure and not greasy, is characterized by its emphasis on aroma, freshness, crispness and tenderness. Shallot and garlic are usually used as seasonings so Shandong dishes tastes pungent usually. Soups are given much emphasis in Shandong dishes. Thin soup features clear and fresh while creamy soup looks thick and tastes strong. Jinan cuisine is adept at deep-frying, grilling, frying and stir-frying while Jiaodong division is famous for cooking seafood with fresh and light taste.

Shandong is the birthplace of many famous ancient scholars such as Confucious and Mencius. And much of Shandong cuisine's history is as old as Confucious himself, making it the oldest existing major cuisine in China.

Shandong is a large peninsula surrounded by the sea to the East and the Yellow River meandering through the center. As a result, seafood is a major component of Shandong cuisine. Shandong's most famous dish is the Sweat and Sour Carp. A truly authentic Sweet and Sour Carp must come from the Yellow River. But with the current amount of pollution in the Yellow River, you would be better off if the carp was from elsewhere. Shandong dishes are mainly quick-fried, roasted, stir-fried or deep-fried. The dishes are mainly clear, fresh and fatty, perfect with Shandong's own famous beer, Tsingtao Beer.

Sichuan Cuisine

Sichuan cuisine, known often in the West as Szechuan Cuisine, is one of the most famous Chinese cuisines in the world. Characterized by its spicy and pungent flavor, Sichuan cuisine, prolific of tastes, emphasizes on the use of chili. Pepper and prickly ash also never fail to accompany, producing typical exciting tastes. Besides, garlic, ginger and fermented soybean are also used in the cooking process. Wild vegetables and animals are usually chosen as ingredients, while frying, frying without oil, pickling and braising are applied as basic cooking techniques. It cannot be said that one who does not experience Sichuan food ever reaches China.

If you eat Sichuan cuisine and find it too bland, then you are probably not eating authentic Sichuan cuisine. Chili peppers and prickly ash are used in many dishes, giving it a distinctively spicy taste, called *ma* in Chinese. It often leaves a slight numb sensation in the mouth. Sichuan hotpots are perhaps the most famous hotpots in the world, most notably the *Yuan Yang* (mandarin duck) Hotpot which is half spicy and half clear.

Guangdong Cuisine

Cantonese food originates from Guangdong, the southernmost province in China. The majority of overseas Chinese people are from Guangdong (Canton), so Cantonese is perhaps the most widely available Chinese regional cuisine outside of China.

Cantonese are known to have an adventurous palate, able to eat many different kinds of meats and vegetables. In fact, people in Northern China often say that

Cantonese people will eat anything that flies except airplanes, anything that moves on the ground except trains, and anything that moves in the water except boats. Obviously, this statement is far from the truth, but Cantonese food is easily one of the most diverse and richest cuisines in China. Many vegetables originate from other parts of the world. It doesn't use much spice, bringing out the natural flavor of the vegetables and meats.

Tasting clear, light, crisp and fresh, Guangdong cuisine, familiar to Westerners, usually chooses raptors and beasts to produce originative dishes. Its basic cooking techniques include roasting, stir-frying, sauteing, deep-frying, braising, stewing and steaming. Among them steaming and stir-frying are more commonly applied to preserve the natural flavor. Guangdong chefs also pay much attention to the artistic presentation of dishes.

Fujian Cuisine

Consisting of Fuzhou Cuisine, Quanzhou Cuisine and Xiamen Cuisine, Fujian Cuisine is distinguished for its choice of seafood, beautiful color and magic taste of sweet, sour, salty and savoury. The most distinct features are their "pickled taste".

Jiangsu Cuisine

Jiangsu cuisine, also called Huaiyang Cuisine, is popular in the lower reach of the Yangtze River. Aquatics as the main ingredients, it stresses the freshness of materials. Its carving techniques are delicate, of which the melon carving technique is especially well known. Cooking techniques consist of stewing, braising, roasting, simmering, etc. The flavor of Huaiyang cuisine is light, fresh and sweet and with delicate elegance. Jiangsu cuisine is well known for its careful selection of ingredients, its meticulous preparation methodology, and its not-too-spicy, not-too-bland taste. Since the seasons vary in climate considerably in Jiangsu, the cuisine also varies throughout the year. If the flavor is strong, it isn't too heavy; if light, not too bland.

Zhejiang Cuisine

Comprising local cuisines of Hangzhou, Ningbo and Shaoxing, Zhejiang Cuisine, not greasy, Zhejiang cuisine wins its reputation for freshness, tenderness, softness, smoothness of its dishes with mellow fragrance. Hangzhou cuisine is the most famous one among the three.

Hunan cuisine

Hunan cuisine consists of local cuisines of Xiangjiang Region, Dongting Lake and Xiangxi coteau. It characterizes itself by thick and pungent flavor. Chili, pepper and shallot are usually necessaries in this division.

Anhui Cuisine

Anhui cuisine chefs focus much more attention on the temperature in cooking and are good at braising and stewing. Often hams will be added to improve taste and sugar candy added to gain the flavor.

New Words

territory	[ˈterɪt(ə)ri]	n.	领土，领域；范围
fantastic	[fænˈtæstɪk]	adj.	极好的，极出色的
mouthwatering	[ˈmaʊθˌwɔːtərɪŋ]	adj.	令人垂涎的；美味的
greasy	[ˈgriːsi]	adj.	油腻的；含脂肪多的
aroma	[əˈrəʊmə]	n.	芳香
crispness	[ˈkrɪspnɪs]	n.	易碎；清新；酥脆
tenderness	[ˈtendənəs]	n.	软；柔和；敏感
pungent	[ˈpʌn(d)ʒ(ə)nt]	adj.	辛辣的
peninsula	[pɪˈnɪnsjʊlə]	n.	半岛
prolific	[prəˈlɪfɪk]	adj.	多产的
chili	[ˈtʃɪli]	n.	红辣椒，辣椒
pepper	[ˈpepə]	n.	胡椒
prickly ash		n.	花椒
accompany	[əˈkʌmpəni]	v.	陪伴，伴随
ginger	[ˈdʒɪndʒə]	n.	姜
ferment	[fəˈment]	v.	使发酵；发酵
ingredient	[ɪnˈgriːdɪənt]	n.	原料
pickle	[ˈpɪk(ə)l]	v.	泡；腌制
braise	[breɪz]	v.	炖；蒸
distinctively	[dɪsˈtɪŋktɪvli]	adv.	特殊地；区别地
originate	[əˈrɪdʒɪneɪt]	v.	发源；发生
adventurous	[ədˈventʃ(ə)rəs]	adj.	爱冒险的；危险的
palate	[ˈpælət]	n.	味觉；上颚
saute	[ˈsəʊteɪ]	v.	炒，嫩煎
stew	[stjuː]	v.	炖，炖汤；焖
artistic	[ɑːˈtɪstɪk]	adj.	艺术的；有美感的
meticulous	[məˈtɪkjələs]	adj.	一丝不苟的
mellow	[ˈmeləʊ]	adj.	圆润的，柔和的
fragrance	[ˈfreɪgr(ə)ns]	n.	香味，芬芳

Chapter Three Elements of Tourism

Phrases and Expressions

a variety of	种种；各种各样的
be divided into	被分成……
consist of	由……组成
Confucius	孔子
Mencius	孟子

Integrated Exercises of Skills

Task I Fill in the blanks with the information you learned from the reading.

1. China's local dishes have their own _____. Generally, Chinese food can be roughly divided into _____ regional cuisines.
2. Seafood is a major component of _____ cuisine.
3. Characterized by its spicy and pungent flavor, Sichuan cuisine, prolific of tastes, emphasizes on the use of _____, _____ and _____ also never fail to accompany, producing typical exciting tastes.
4. _____ is perhaps the most widely available Chinese regional cuisine outside of China.
5. _____ is distinguished for its choice of seafood, beautiful color and magic taste of sweet, sour, salty and savory. The most distinct features are their "_____".
6. Jiangsu cuisine, also called _____, is popular in the lower reach of the Yangtze River.
7. Zhejiang cuisine wins its reputation for _____ of its dishes with mellow fragrance. _____ is the most famous one among the three.
8. Hunan cuisine characterizes itself by _____ flavor.

Task II Read the passage above and decide whether the following statements are true (T) or false (F).

(　) 1. Anhui cuisine characterizes itself by thick and pungent flavor.
(　) 2. Hunan cuisine's basic cooking techniques include roasting, stir-frying, sauteing, deep-frying, braising, stewing and steaming.
(　) 3. Zhejiang cuisine comprises local cuisines of Hangzhou, Ningbo and Shaoxing, Zhejiang cuisine.
(　) 4. Sichuan cuisine often leaves a slight numb sensation in the mouth.
(　) 5. Jiaodong cuisine is adept at deep-frying, grilling, frying and stir-frying while Jinan division is famous for cooking seafood with fresh and light taste.

Task III Translate the sentences into Chinese.

1. China covers a large territory and has many nationalities, hence a variety of Chinese food with different but fantastic and mouthwatering flavor.

2. Consisting of Jinan cuisine and Jiaodong cuisine, Shandong cuisine, clear, pure and not greasy, is characterized by its emphasis on aroma, freshness, crispness and tenderness.

3. Shandong is the birthplace of many famous ancient scholars such as Confucious and Mencius. And much of Shandong cuisine's history is as old as Confucious himself, making it the oldest existing major cuisine in China.

4. Cantonese are known to have an adventurous palate, able to eat many different kinds of meats and vegetables.

5. Sichuan hotpots are perhaps the most famous hotpots in the world, most notably the *Yuan Yang* (mandarin duck) Hotpot which is half spicy and half clear.

6. Tasting clear, light, crisp and fresh, Guangdong cuisine, familiar to Westerners, usually chooses raptors and beasts to produce originative dishes.

7. Jiangsu cuisine is well known for its careful selection of ingredients, its meticulous preparation methodology, and its not-too-spicy, not-too-bland taste.

8. Comprising local cuisines of Hangzhou, Ningbo and Shaoxing, Zhejiang cuisine, not greasy, Zhejiang cuisine wins its reputation for freshness, tenderness, softness, smoothness of its dishes with mellow fragrance.

Chapter Three Elements of Tourism

Text B

Where and How to Eat

Dining in China can prove to be a nettlesome experience, for those who are used to eating what they want. Generally speaking, most tour groups and visiting delegations will take most of their pre-paid meals at their hotels. Meals are served at designated times (usually 8 a.m., 12 noon, and 6 p.m.), at pre-assigned tables, and from a menu preselected by the hotel cooks. Unless special requests are made, breakfast will be Western-style (eggs, toast, jam, coffee, a cake or pastry); lunch and dinner are Chinese. It is usually possible to order a Chinese-style breakfast a day in advance, and if enough people to fill a table (eight or ten), a tour guide will help arrange it. It is often difficult to order individually prepared dishes (which in any case cost extra), although the large hotels will prepare special meals for visitors with special dietary requirements. In most cases, beverages, including beer, wine and sometimes alcohol, are available at an additional cost (unless covered by a pre-paid surcharge).

For the sake of convenience, the individual traveller who makes the first trip to China will usually end up taking most of their meals at their hotels. Many newer hotels now offer buffets for breakfast and lunch. Although it will entail an additional expense, eating at a local restaurant is highly recommended, both for atmosphere as well as for greater authenticity in their preparations, especially of local and regional fare, and for their wider array of offerings. You can order from the menu by looking at the prices and asking questions or by simply pointing to what looks good on other people's tables. Westerners who reside in China tend to patronize hotel restaurants or the more expensive Chinese restaurants, as the food is usually better and the premises cleaner, quieter, and less crowded.

There are a few does and don'ts in Chinese food etiquette, mostly applicable only when you dine with Chinese. Probably the most important is who pays the bill. Usually, if you are invited by Chinese, you are not expected to foot the bill. It has been customary for the host organization in China to give a welcoming dinner in honor of visiting groups or delegations. The dinner can be an elaborate banquet or a simple affair. Arriving guests are usually ushered into an anteroom and offered tea, hot towels, and about 10 to 15 minutes of light conversation with the hosts. The principal host will then signal that dinner is ready, and guests will be seated. The host will preside, sitting at a head table (Chinese tradition dictates that the seat of honor faces the door), with the highest-ranking guests (i.e., the delegation's leaders) arranged to his left and right.

A typical setting will include a small plate, a pair of chop-sticks resting on a holder (forks and knives are always available), and three glasses: for beer or soft drinks, wine, and liquor for toasts. Dishes are served according to a palate-stimulating sequence, starting with cold appetizers and continuing to 10 or more courses. A well-balanced menu will contain, at a minimum, the five basic tastes of Chinese cuisine (sour, hot, bitter, sweet and salty). Dishes alternate between crisp and tender, dry and heavily sauced. Soup is usually served after the main courses; in the south, fried rice or noodles come last. Dessert is usually fresh fruit with pastries.

Since the economic reform in the 1980s in China, great changes have taken place also in the food industry and catering services. Hotels and restaurants have been mushrooming all over the country. There are lots of eating places, and also various kinds of dishes for people to choose from. Usually, Sichuan dish and Guangdong dish can be found nearly anywhere in northern and southern China, Sichuan hotpot food has been very popular nationwide; regional and local dishes and snacks are available in localities; even foreign cuisines and fast food such as French food, Italian food, Thai food, McDonald's, Pizza Hut and Kentucky Fried Chicken are existent in major cities in the country.

 New Words

nettlesome	[ˈnetlsəm]	adj. 恼人的
pre-paid	[prɪˈpeɪd]	adj. 提前支付的
pre-assigned	[prɪˈəsaɪnd]	adj. 预定的
preselected	[prɪˈsɪlektɪd]	adj. 预选好了的
surcharge	[ˈsɜːtʃɑːdʒ]	n. 附加费
buffet	[ˈbʊfeɪ; ˈbʌfeɪ]	n. 自助餐
atmosphere	[ˈætməsfɪə]	n. 气氛
authenticity	[ɔːθenˈtɪsɪti]	n. （风味）地道
fare	[feə]	n. 伙食，车费 v. 过日子
patronize	[ˈpætrənaɪz]	v. 光顾
premises	[ˈpremɪsɪz]	n. 餐馆，房屋
etiquette	[ˈetɪket; etɪˈket]	n. 礼节
protocol	[ˈprəʊtəkɒl]	n. 礼仪
elaborate	[ɪˈlæb(ə)rət]	adj. 精心准备的
usher	[ˈʌʃə]	n. 带位员 v. 引座
anteroom	[ˈæntɪruːm]	n. 前屋
nibble	[ˈnɪb(ə)l]	v. 吃，啃

Chapter Three Elements of Tourism

setting	['setɪŋ]	n. 布置，环境
liquor	['lɪkə]	n. 白酒
prescribed	[prɪ'skraɪbd]	a. 预定了的
mushroom	['mʌʃruːm]	n. 蘑菇 v. 雨后春笋般的出现
snack	[snæk]	n. 小吃

 Phrases and Expressions

dietary requirements	进食要求
in advance	预先地
foot the bill	付账
light conversation	轻松交谈
a head table	主桌
the seat of honor	主座
seating plan	座次安排
palate-stimulating sequence	开胃程序
cold appetizers	开胃凉菜
main courses	主菜
catering services	餐饮服务

 Integrated Exercises of Skills

Task I Fill in the blanks with the information you learned.

1. Generally speaking, most tour groups and visiting _____ will take most of their pre-paid meals at their hotels.

2. Although it will _____ an additional expense, eating at a local restaurant is highly _____, both for atmosphere as well as for greater _____ in their preparations, especially of local and regional _____, and for their wider _____ of offerings.

3. Arriving guests are usually _____ into an anteroom and offered tea, hot towels, and about 10 to 15 minutes of light conversation with the hosts.

4. Westerners who reside in China tend to _____ hotel restaurants or the more expensive Chinese restaurants, as the food is usually better and the _____ cleaner, quieter, and less crowded.

5. The host will _____, sitting at a head table (Chinese tradition _____ that the seat of honor faces the door), with the _____ guests (i.e., the delegation's leaders) arranged to his left and right.

6. A _____ menu will contain, at a _____, the five basic _____ of Chinese

cuisine (sour, hot, _____, sweet and salty).

Task II   After reading the passage, try to answer the following questions.

1. Why can dining in China prove to be a nettlesome experience?
2. What should the individual travellers who make the first trip to China do for their meals?
3. What do many newer hotels now offer breakfast and lunch?
4. For what reasons is a local restaurant highly recommended?
5. What do Westerners residing in China tend to do for their meals?
6. What is the Chinese protocol in terms of seating at a dinner-table?
7. Please describe a typical setting for Chinese dining.
8. What tastes will a well-balanced menu contain?

Task III   Read the passage above and decide whether the following statements are true (T) or false (F).

(   ) 1. Most tour groups and visiting delegations will take most of their meals in their wants.
(   ) 2. Usually, if you are invited by Chinese, you are expected to foot the bill.
(   ) 3. Dishes are served according to a palate-stimulating sequence, starting with cold appetizers and continuing to 10 or more courses.
(   ) 4. Dessert is usually sent before cold dishes.
(   ) 5. It is very convenient for foreigners to eat in China. There are lots of eating places, and also various kinds of dishes.

Part IV   Practical Writing

菜单 Menu

在旅游业中,餐饮是重要的环节之一。游客中不乏美食家和烹饪高手,一份精致的菜单和诱人的菜名可令客人赏心悦目,食欲大增。菜单一般包括肉类、海鲜、蔬菜、汤、冷盘、主食、酒水等,撰写时注意分清类别,做到清晰明了。

菜名的撰写格式可以有自己的特色。从内容构成上分析,有的是把配料或修饰词前置,主料在后,如碧蓝牛排(Hunan Flower Steak)、五味茄(Aromatic Chinese Eggplant);有的则恰好相反,如干烧龙虾(Lobster with Chili Sauce);还有的由于两种材料很难区分主次,所以有平分秋色之感,如腰果虾仁(Sauteed Baby Shrimps with Cashew Nuts)。

Chapter Three Elements of Tourism

从菜单的页面设计上，有些菜单采用菜名在前，价格在后；有些餐人数和价格在前，菜名在后，等等。

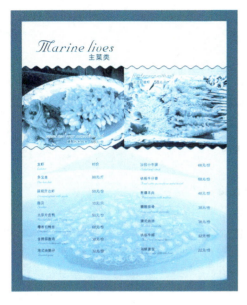

Sample 1   Sample 2

Task I Match the following groups of words and phrases.

1. broccoli beef   a. 烧烤
2. cashew   b. 冷饮
3. lobster   c. 杂烩
4. chowder   d. 龙虾
5. tuna roll   e. 甘蓝牛排
6. barbecue   f. 清炒干贝
7. lemonade   g. 腰果
8. frappe   h. 金枪鱼卷
9. Sliced Prawn with Garlic Sauce   i. 柠檬汁
10. Sauteed Scallop   j. 鱼香虾片

Task II Tell dishes following the structure and the examples.

中式菜肴的英文表达法：
a. 烹调法＋主料：
   Braised Pork 红烧猪肉
b. 烹调法＋主料＋介词（in/with）＋酱汁：
   Stir-Fried Beef in Oyster Sauce 蚝油牛肉

121

c. 主料＋介词（in/with）＋辅料：
   Chicken with Hot Pepper 辣子鸡
d. 口感＋烹调法＋主料：
   Crisp Fried Spare Ribs 香酥排骨
e. 人名/地名＋主料：
   Ma Po Bean Curd 麻婆豆腐

1. Braised Spare Ribs in Brown Sauce
2. Spared Ribs with Spiced Salt
3. Sauteed Shredded Pork in Sweet Bean Sauce
4. Mao's Family Style（Braised Pork）
5. Stewed Spare Ribs and Potatoes in Casserole
6. Boiled Beef
7. Sauteed Sliced Pork with Pepper and Chili
8. Steamed Ham in Honey Sauce
9. Sweet and Sour Spare Ribs
10. Dongpo Pig Knuckle

Task III   Write a menu according to the information given below.

一家三星级的酒店准备开业。请你给这家酒店设计一本菜谱。该菜谱须包括肉类、海鲜、蔬菜、酒水、主食。

Part V   Typical Scenic Spot

Lijiang

Lijiang is located in the Northwest of Yunnan Province. The population of Lijiang Prefecture is over 1 million involving 21 nationalities，for example，the Naxi，Yi，Lisu，Pumi，etc.

Lijiang Prefecture is the major developing tourist area of Yunnan Province. It contains beautiful natural scene，unique minority amorous feelings，age-old minority cultures，and rich tourist resources. The scenic spots are mainly scattered in Lijiang and Ninglang County. We can conclude them into "two mountains，one town，one lake，one river，one culture and one folk custom". Two mountains refer to Yulong Snow Mountains and Laojun Mountains，one town is Dayan Town，one lake refers to

Chapter Three Elements of Tourism

Lugu Lake, one river is Jinsha river, one culture is Dongba Culture and one folk custom refers to the Moso people's custom. What does that mean? I will leave it to you to discover. So you see Lijiang, with its rich resources in plants and animals, the natural beauties and the amazing minority folk customs, attracts more and more tourists from home and abroad.

Lijiang has a history of almost a thousand years. The scenes are unique and unconventional. It is one of the best-historical, cultural cities at the state level in China. It consists of three parts: Dayan, Baisha and Suhe. So why is it called Dayan? Because it is in the middle of Lijiang basin, and the Lijiang basin looks like a big inkstone, and in Chinese the pronunciation of that is "yan".

The Dayan town is famous for its old and simple architectural style and the elegant art for the lay-out of the town. In the town the Yuquan, river winds in many streams across the town and past all the houses. The roads here are parallel to the streams, and the door of each house is facing a stream. Whatever street and whatever lane you go in, there is a small stream with small bridges across it here and there. As a saying has it: A house beside a stream with a small bridge across it makes a wonderful scene which you can only find here." That's why we regard Dayan town to be the "Oriental Venice".

In the center of the ancient town, here is the Sifang Street. It is a place for country fair trades. Since ancient times, Sifang Street has been a collecting and distributing center of all kinds of products with travellers and traders coming and going everywhere. On a market day, people of different minorities in their unique costumes come here to do business and make the place crowed and noisy. If you spend a whole day here, you can experience the poetic changes here. In the morning, the street stretch its arms and woke up; in the midday, it becomes a busy man; When the night comes, the light is on, it changes into a dressed young lady; And at night it becomes quiet and fell asleep.

Why the street has a name of "Sifang"? There are two kinds of explanation: One is that the ancient leader in Lijiang named it with a meaning of "spread his power around". The other is that "Sifang" in Chinese means four directions, which implies that the street has people and goods from every area. Dayan Town is quite different from the other ancient towns in China, no town walls around it, which is mysterious.

职业素养

中国的饮食文化讲究"色、香、味、型",内容丰富且博大精深,民族特色鲜明,从古到今,历代相传又推陈出新。党的二十大报告指出,"必须坚持在发展中保障和改善民生,鼓励共同奋斗创造美好生活,不断实现人民对美好生活的向往"。这表明我国将会采取更强有力措施确保粮食安全,使国人不仅"吃饱",更要"吃好"。

Unit 7 Accommodation

••••• Part I Warm-Up •••••

Accommodation is the core of the travel business，which directly decides the visitors' satisfaction. So there are strict levels for the service. The global concept of tour guide service contains 7 meanings represented by the word **SERVICE** with 7 initial letters.

- S—smile: The tour guide is supposed to smile while rendering service to tourist.（微笑）
- E—excellent: Service should be performed in an excellent way.（出色）
- R—ready: The tour guide is constantly ready to serve tourists.（有所准备）
- V—viewing: Each tourist should be treated as a distinguished guest with his or her special needs.（看待）
- I—inviting: Tourists will want to return after he or she leaves the city or the country.（邀请）
- C—creating: The tour guide should create an amiable and harmonious environment for tourists.（创造）
- E—eye: Each tour guide pays a close attention to tourists with keen observation, anticipates their needs and provides his or her service in time which makes tourists feel that they are carefully and constantly concerned by tour guides.（眼光）

••••• Part II Conversations •••••

Conversation 1   Checking in

听一听

Situation: *Carol is talking to the Receptionist of Hilton Hotel to make a reservation for her travelling.*

Receptionist: Hello，this is Hilton Hotel. How may I help you?
Carol: Hi，I would like to make a reservation for this Friday.
Receptionist: OK. What kind of room do you want? We have single rooms，twin rooms，double rooms and suites available on Friday.
Carol: I want a single room with ocean view. Do you have one?

Chapter Three Elements of Tourism

Receptionist: Let me check. Yes.

Carol: OK. I will take it.

Receptionist: When do you check in? How long are you planning to stay? Do you have any special requirements?

Carol: I guess I am going to arrive at 9:00 in the morning and I would like to leave at 2:00 in the afternoon on Sunday. Please give me a room away from the elevator. I hate noises while I am sleeping.

Carol: Is there a pool in this hotel?

Receptionist: Yes, of course. The pool is open from 9 a.m. to 10 p.m. everyday.

Carol: Good. Then what kinds of restaurants are there in your hotel?

Receptionist: We have two Chinese restaurants and an Italian restaurant. They are all on the second floor. Also, there is a supermarket on the third floor. The Health Club is on the fourth floor.

Carol: Great! Thank you very much.

Receptionist: I'm glad to be at your service. Your room is 316. Enjoy your stay, Madam.

Carol: Thank you.

New Words

receptionist	[rɪˈsepʃ(ə)nɪst]	n.	接待员
reservation	[rezəˈveɪʃ(ə)n]	n.	预约，预订；保留
suite	[swiːt]	n.	套房
requirement	[rɪˈkwaɪəm(ə)nt]	n.	要求；必需品
elevator	[ˈelɪveɪtə]	n.	电梯；升降机
available	[əˈveɪləb(ə)l]	adj.	可获得的；有空的
view	[vjuː]	n.	风景；视野；意见
noise	[nɔɪz]	n.	噪声；杂音
pool	[puːl]	n.	水塘；泳塘
hall	[hɔːl]	n.	前厅；大厅

Phrases and Expressions

Hilton Hotel	希尔顿大酒店
single room	单人房，单人间
twin room	双人房（两个人住并配有两张单人床的房间）
double room	双人房（两个人住并配有一张双人床的房间）
check in	报到；登记
away from	远离；离开

Conversation 2 Checking out

Bell Captain: This is the Bell Captain's Desk. May I help you?
Guest: I'm going to check out soon. Could you pick up my luggage, please?
Bell Captain: Certainly, sir. May I have your room number, please?
Guest: Yes. It's 2932.
Bell Captain: Room 2932. We will send a bellman immediately. Could you wait in your room, please?
Bellman: Good morning, sir. I've come for your bags.
Guest: Thank you. Could you take these two suitcases, please? I'll bring the shoulder bag with me.
Bellman: Is there anything valuable or breakable in them?
Guest: No.
Bellman: This is your claim tag, sir. We will keep your bags at the Bell Captain's Desk. Could you pick them up there, please?
Guest: Certainly.
Bellman: Is there anything I can do for you?
Guest: No more. Thank you very much.
Bellman: I'm always at your service. Have a nice day.

 New Words

luggage	[ˈlʌɡɪdʒ]	n. 行李；皮箱
bellman	[ˈbelmən]	n. 行李员
immediately	[ɪˈmiːdɪətli]	adv. 立刻；马上
suitcase	[ˈsuːtkeɪs]	n. 手提箱；衣箱
valuable	[ˈvæljʊb(ə)l]	adj. 有价值的；贵重的
breakable	[ˈbreɪkəb(ə)l]	adj. 易碎的

 Phrases and Expressions

check out	结账；离开
Bell Captain	礼宾；侍者领班
shoulder bag	手提包
claim tag	行李标签

Chapter Three Elements of Tourism

 Practical Patterns

1. Welcome to our hotel.
   欢迎光临。

2. Can I help you?
   我能帮您什么吗?

3. What kind of room would you like, sir?
   先生,您要什么样的房间?

4. Please wait a moment. I have to check if there is a room available.
   请稍等,我查一下有没有空房。

5. Enjoy your stay with us.
   希望您在我们这里住得愉快。

6. I'm sorry, sir. Our hotel rooms are all booked at this moment. We have no vacancy.
   对不起,先生。我们已经客满,没有空房间。

7. We hope you will stay with us again.
   希望您再次光临我们酒店。

8. Would you please exchange US dollars for RMB, please?
   麻烦您替我将美元兑成人民币好吗?

9. Please, could I see your passport or other identification, madam?
   夫人,请出示您的护照或其他身份证明文件。

10. I'd like to book a double room for Tuesday next week.
    下周二我想订一间双人房。

11. I think I'll take the one with a front view then.
    我想我还是要阳面的吧。

12. How long will you be staying?
    您打算住多久?

13. I'd like to book a single room with bath from the after-noon of October 4 to the morning of October 10.
    我想订一个带洗澡间的单人房间,10月4日下午到10月10日上午用。

14. What is the rate, please?
    请问房费是多少?

15. What services come with that?
    这个价格包括哪些服务项目呢?

16. By the way, I'd like a quiet room away from the street if this is possible.
    顺便说一下,如有可能我想要一间不临街的安静房间。

Task I Complete the following dialogues by translating the Chinese in the brackets.

A: Good evening, sir. Welcome to our hotel.

B: Good evening. _____ (我们想登记入住。)

A: _____ (你有事先预订吗?)

B: Yes, I made it 5 days before. My family name is Jiang. That's spelled J-I-A-N-G.

A: OK. Let me check it. Wow, I get it. You have 19 group members totally. _____ (预订了9个单人间,5个双人间,对吗?)

B: Yes, and for three days' stay here, from today to Wednesday.

A: Right. _____ (还有其他要求吗?)

B: Yes, _____ (每个房间都要早餐,还有早晨7点的叫醒服务。)

A: No problem. I have taken them down. _____ (您还有其他需要吗?)

B: No, thanks.

A: _____ (请把护照给我,并填上这份登记卡)

Task II Using the given words and expressions to make a conversation with your partner according to the following situation.

The guest is coming to the front desk of a star hotel. He or she wants to know some details of the hotel. The receptionist introduces the hotel room and facilities carefully and helps him or her to check in.

Student A: the receptionist of Sunshine Hotel.

Student B: guests

 Suggested words and expressions

facility 设施,设备	air-condition 空调
single room 单人间	double room 双人间
suite 套房	the presidential suite 总统套房
deluxe suite 豪华套房	health club 康乐中心
aerobic gym 健身中心	sauna 蒸气浴
laundry service 洗衣服务	VISA 维萨卡(一种信用卡)
advance 预付(支)	invoice 发票
card key 电子卡钥匙	bellboy 行李员

Chapter Three　Elements of Tourism

 Suggested sentence patterns

We have single rooms, ...

The facilities of our hotel include...

How do you like...?

How many... are you going to stay here?

We need... for us to...

Are... acceptable?

Over there, ... near the left gate...

······ **Part III　Readings** ······

Text A

How to Choose a Hotel

　　Hotels in the broad sense range from bed-and-breakfast[1] family operation to megahotel of several thousands of rooms. Hotels can be classified according to the rate, location and type of guests: commercial hotel which offers drink and accommodation to business people; resort hotel may focus on attracting visitors who simply have recreational purpose, so it is often located in vacation areas; apartment hotel provides hotel rooms with fully-equipped kitchens, and it combines the luxury of a hotel and the comfort and coziness of a sweet home. There are one-bedroom and two-bedroom apartments which is an ideal choice for family with kids. Last, casino hotels are built for one purpose—to attract people who will engage in gambling.

　　Today, more and more travellers in the United States are spending nights at small houses or inns instead of hotels. They get a room for the night and the breakfast the next morning. Many of these American "bed-and-breakfast" inns are old historic buildings. Some "bed-and-breakfast" inns have only a few rooms; others are much larger. Some

129

inns do not provide telephone or television in the room, while others do. Staying at a "bed-and-breakfast" inn is much different from staying at a hotel. Usually the cost is much less. Staying at an inn is almost like visiting someone's home. The owners are glad to tell about the area and the interesting places to visit. Many travellers say they enjoy the chance to meet local families.

Sure, they all have beds and a bathroom. But when it comes to business travel, all hotels are not created equal. Check out these features that might come in handy before you book your next hotel for business travel.

1. High-Speed Internet connection in Your Room

Whether it's wireless or via an Ethernet[2] line, in-room Internet service is essential for staying on top of e-mails, working on presentations and curbing on-the-road boredom.

2. Business Centers

Need to fax or print something? Lost your computer and need to get online? Though not available in every hotel chain, a business/office center can be indispensable for on-the-road workers.

3. Room Service

Yes, it's expensive and not always good (or good for you), but when you're tired from a long day of meetings, the last thing you want to do is drive around town looking for something to eat. At the very least, you'll want the hotel to have some sort of mini-mart where you can pick up water, soda, and small bites to tide you over.

4. Workout Facilities

After too many nights of said room service meals, you may notice that your pants are a little snug. Stay healthy on the road by checking yourself into hotels that have some sort of exercise equipment.

5. Shuttle Services

Avoid having to take a cab or rent a car by booking rooms in hotels with shuttle service to/from the airport.

6. Location

Does some research before you travel, so you can find a hotel in the best location relative to your meetings or the airport, depending on your schedule.

7. Concierge Service

Available generally in major cities, concierge service can help you with everything from finding a restaurant to flagging a cab.

8. Conference Rooms

If you need to prepare for a large presentation, or just need a place for a team to work before a meeting, a conference room can be helpful. In addition, if you require significant time to set up before a meeting or have lots of samples, you might want to have clients come to your hotel for the meeting instead of schlepping large items around town.

New Words

mega	[ˈmegə]	adj. 许多；宏大的
classify	[ˈklæsɪfaɪ]	v. 分类
location	[lə(ʊ)ˈkeɪʃ(ə)n]	n. 位置；地点
commercial	[kəˈmɜːʃ(ə)l]	adj. 商业的；营利的
accommodation	[əkɒməˈdeɪʃ(ə)n]	n. 膳宿；住处
resort	[rɪˈzɔːt]	n. 度假胜地
recreational	[rekrɪˈeɪʃənl]	adj. 娱乐的；消遣的
vacation	[vəˈkeɪʃn; veɪ-]	n. 假期
combine	[kəmˈbaɪn]	v. 联合；结合
luxury	[ˈlʌkʃ(ə)ri]	n. 奢侈，奢华；奢侈品
coziness	[ˈkəʊzɪnɪs]	n. 安逸，舒适；畅快
ideal	[aɪˈdɪəl; aɪˈdiːəl]	adj. 理想的；完美的
casino	[kəˈsiːnəʊ]	n. 俱乐部，赌场
gamble	[ˈgæmb(ə)l]	n. 赌博；冒险；打赌
historic	[hɪˈstɒrɪk]	adj. 历史性的；有历史意义的
create	[kriːˈeɪt]	v. 创造；造成
essential	[ɪˈsenʃ(ə)l]	adj. 基本的；必要的
presentation	[prez(ə)nˈteɪʃ(ə)n]	n. 展示；陈述
curb	[kɜːb]	n. 抑制；控制
indispensable	[ɪndɪˈspensəb(ə)l]	n. 不可缺少的物或人
workout	[ˈwɜːkaʊt]	n. 锻炼；练习
facility	[fəˈsɪləti]	n. 设施；设备
snug	[snʌg]	adj. 紧身的
shuttle	[ˈʃʌt(ə)l]	n. 穿梭班机、公共汽车等
concierge	[ˈkɒnsɪeəʒ]	n. 门房；看门人
cab	[kæb]	n. 出租汽车
schlep	[ʃlep]	v. 拖曳；缓慢费力地行进

Phrases and Expressions

in the broad sense	广义上（而言）
range from... to...	范围从……到……

focus on	集中于
engage in	从事于（参加）
tide over	克服；度过困难时期
small bite	食品；小零食

 Notes

[1] Bed and breakfast

　　欧洲的一种简易旅馆：住宿加早餐。

[2] Ethernet 以太网

　　Ethernet 指的是由 Xerox 公司创建并由 Xerox、Intel 和 DEC 公司联合开发的基带局域网规范，是当今现有局域网采用的最通用的通信协议标准。以太网络使用 CSMA/CD（载波监听多路访问及冲突检测）技术，并以 10M/S 的速率运行在多种类型的电缆上。以太网与 IEEE802.3 系列标准相类似，包括标准的以太网（10Mbit/s）、快速以太网（100Mbit/s）和 10G 以太网（10Gbit/s）。

 Integrated Exercises of Skills

Task I According to the passage, what type of hotel would you recommend to the following persons?

A: I've been hitch-hiking（搭便车）to your city. Are there any cheap places where I could stay overnight?

B: I'm arranging the Annual Conference of company.

C: My wife and I and our two children are going by car to Beijing and would like to stop somewhere for some nights.

D: I'm a college student on summer holiday. I'm going to stay in Fenghuang Ancient City（凤凰古城）for a few days.

Task II Fill in the blanks with the suitable words given below, changing the form where necessary.

classify	accommodation	recreational	available
combine	luxury	indispensable	shuttle

1. We have a _____ bus for Expo visitors over there.
2. Good days can give your happiness while bad days can fetch you experience. Both good days and bad days are _____ in our lives.
3. Mails are _____ by men in the post office according to places.
4. Do not spend time and money on expensive shows, travel or _____ activities.

Chapter Three Elements of Tourism

5. When travelling with family or friends, make sure that the _____ you select is of high quality.
6. In this _____ resort, you can live like a king.
7. We must utilize all _____ resources.
8. Why not _____ traditions of the past with the innovations of the future.

Task III Translate the sentences into Chinese.

1. Hotels in the broad sense range from bed-and-breakfast family operation to mega-hotel of several thousands of rooms.

   _____
   _____

2. Apartment hotel combines the luxury of a hotel and the comfort and coziness of a sweet home.

   _____
   _____

3. In-room Internet service is essential for staying on top of e-mails, working on presentations and curbing on-the-road boredom.

   _____
   _____

4. At the very least, you'll want the hotel to have some sort of mini-mart where you can pick up water, soda, and small bites to tide you over.

   _____
   _____

5. In addition, if you require significant time to set up before a meeting or have lots of samples, you might want to have clients come to your hotel for the meeting instead of schlepping large items around town.

   _____
   _____

Task IV Choose one word for each blank from a list of choices.

Youth Hostel

Youth Hostel are the best places for world's young people to enjoy __1__ with less expense. The lodging can take 4 to 8 people in one room. The __2__ is between 20 to 80 per person. The guests are requested to help themselves __3__ chores such as setting and cleaning their own table, or putting sheets on their beds. But you can make friends with your roommates on the instant, and would not feel __4__.

In order to use Youth Hostel, you need to have a membership card issued by

International Youth Hostel Federation. A membership card is __5__ shortly after an application form is filled and submitted.

1. A. travel   B. to travel   C. travelling
2. A. rate   B. type   C. money
3. A. with   B. in   C. on
4. A. alone   B. lonely   C. single
5. A. issued   B. given   C. bought

Text B

Modern Hotels Today

Hotels today are quite different from those of the past. People who stay in them are generally travelling for business, touring or on vacation. So hotels are designed mainly to meet the needs of these groups.

Place to stay for a short time may be called hotels, hostels, motels or motor hotels, inns, lodges or resort.[1] Hotels, also referred to as youth hotels, are often for students walking away from home. Motels have plenty of parking space and usually near a freeway or highway. Inns are usually like Motels. Lodges and resorts, or resort hotels, are in the mountains, on the coast or near lakes.

Hotels range from the very luxurious, which charge high rates, to the small and inexpensive that fall within the affordable price range of large numbers of travellers. These hotels are rated according to established international star-rating standards.[2] Now let's see some modern hotels below.

Four Seasons Hotel, Mumbai

The Four Seasons Hotel Mumbai is perfectly placed in an area that's undergoing a process of swift gentrification and now calls itself mid-town Mumbai.

On one side, the Haji Ali Mosque landmark leads south to Colaba, and on the other the Sealink takes you north to Bandra and beyond.[3] It is, in part, because of this situational and logistical advantage that the Four Seasons has become one of the top three business hotels in Mumbai since it opened three years ago.

No other hotel offers this 360-degree view of old Bombay and new Mumbai.[4] The choice of views is comprehensive-Arabian sea view, historic mill district view, Sealink bridge (Figure 7-1) view, Mahalaxmi Temple[5] view, with a dash of construction and slums thrown in for good measure——because that is real Mumbai, not some pictures on a post-card.

Insider tip: Aer Bar (Figure 7-2),[6] the highest bar in Mumbai, takes over the entire open-air rooftop on the 34th floor of the Four Seasons. With champagne served by the glass, you can watch the sunset over the Arabian sea, spot the billion-dollar home of Mukesh Ambani[7] and get a bird's eye-view of some slums too as Mumbai's richest and poorest jostle for space.

Figure 7-1　Sealink Bridge

Figure 7-2　Aer Bar

WeChat Hotel

On the sidelines of CES in Las Vegas, Ceasars Entertainment partnered up with WeChat to give tours of new smart hotel rooms at The LINQ, a local hotel and casino. Visitors could use an App inside WeChat to control lighting, thermostats, and curtains. The connected suites will be the first of many such hotel rooms from Ceasars catering to overseas Chinese. After arriving at the room, they just need to scan a QR code to get the App. The App, which operates as a WeChat official account, was developed by Silicon Valley[8]-based Ayla Networks.

In 2013, 300,000 visitors from China travelled to Las Vegas, nearly doubling the number in the last two years. Ceasars said in a statement: "Collaborating with leading companies like Ayla and WeChat helps make our customers feel even more at home when they can interact in our resorts using technology and Apps like WeChat that they use daily."

Ceasars operates 50 casinos across the US and four other countries. The collaboration with Ceasars is one of many projects that WeChat is using to study foreign markets outside of China for new opportunities. "We aim to build up an ecosystem for merchants to leverage on WeChat O2O[9] strategies and projects. The Casears hotel project is one of many projects we are working with," Tencent spokesperson Chen said. "Other projects that connect WeChat[10] to the offline world include Easy Taxi official account implementation in Asia, Zalora project in Asia, and YOOX shopping accounts in the US, Italy, and China."

 New Words

affordable	[əˈfɔːdəbəl]	adj.	负担得起的
range	[reɪn(d)ʒ]	n.	范围；幅度
undergo	[ʌndəˈgəʊ]	vt.	经历；忍受
gentrification	[dʒentrɪfɪˈkeɪʃən]	n.	中产阶级化
mosque	[mɒsk]	n.	清真寺
logistical	[ləˈdʒɪstɪkl]	adj.	物流的；物流业的
comprehensive	[kɒmprɪˈhensɪv]	adj.	综合的；广泛的
slum	[slʌm]	n.	贫民；贫民区
spot	[spɒt]	n. 地点 v.	认出
jostle	[ˈdʒɒs(ə)l]	v.	竞争，争夺；推挤
entertainment	[entəˈteɪnm(ə)nt]	n.	娱乐；款待
casino	[kəˈsiːnəʊ]	n.	俱乐部，赌场；娱乐场
thermostat	[ˈθɜːməstæt]	n.	恒温控制器；温度调节装置
collaborate	[kəˈlæbəreɪt]	vi.	合作；勾结
ecosystem	[ˈiːkəʊsɪstəm]	n.	生态系统
leverage	[ˈlevərɪdʒ]	v.	利用；举债经营

 Phrases and Expressions

be placed	位于
a dash of	少许；一点儿
takes over	接管；接收
get a bird's eye-view of	鸟瞰
partner up with	和……进行合作

 Notes

[1] ... hotels, hostels, motels or motor hotels, inns, lodges or resort.
……旅馆、招待所、汽车旅馆或汽车酒店、客栈、旅舍或者度假村。

[2] These hotels are rated according to established international star-rating standards.
这些酒店根据制定的国际酒店星级评定标准来估价。

[3] On one side, the Haji Ali Mosque landmark leads south to Colaba, and on the other the Sealink takes you north to Bandra and beyond.
这边，地标性建筑哈吉·阿里清真寺的南面直通克拉巴区，另一边Sealink大桥带你

通往北面班德拉街区和更远的地方。

Colaba 是孟买非常有名的一个区域，也是游客集中购物地。

孟买的 Sea link 大桥是印度第一座跨海大桥，总长 5.6 公里。

[4] old Bombay and new Mumbai

孟买的名称起源于印度教女神孟巴（雪山神女化身之一，渔民的保护神），在 17 世纪大英帝国拥有该地后，地名被英语化，称为"Bombay"。1995 年，该市名称被正式改为"Mumbai"，但旧称"Bombay"仍被该市一些居民和著名机构广泛使用。

[5] Mahalaxmi Temple

马哈拉克希米寺，作为祭祀财富女神拉克希米的寺庙，这里是孟买香火最旺的宗教圣地之一，大概是因为身为"商业之都"孟买的民众，对财富有着更加执着的追求。

[6] Aer Bar

印度西海岸孟买四季酒店 34 楼的露天酒吧和休闲空间，从下午 5 点半到晚上 8 点提供"日落欢乐畅饮时光"，鸡尾酒和香槟皆为半价，音乐是爵士、疯客、House 等风格掺杂 20 世纪 80 年代和 90 年代的经典乐曲。

[7] Mukesh Ambani

穆克什·安巴尼，1957 年 4 月 19 日出生，印度商人，居住于印度孟买，毕业于斯坦福大学商学院，他是财富 500 强企业信实工业（Reliance Industries）主席，董事总经理。《福布斯》公布的 2011 年全球亿万富豪排行榜，穆克什-安巴尼位列第九。

[8] Silicon Valley

硅谷是指美国旧金山以南一片山谷，为尖端技术生产中心。

[9] O2O/Online to Offline（在线离线/线上到线下）

O2O 指将线下的商务机会与互联网结合，让互联网成为线下交易的平台，这个概念最早来源于美国。O2O 的概念非常广泛，既可涉及线上，又可涉及线下。

[10] WeChat

微信，腾讯出品的一款语音聊天应用。

Integrated Exercises of Skills

Task I Look at the list of hotel facilities.

a disco	meeting rooms
tennis courts	tour guides
a fax machine	babysitting services
a fast food snack bar	laundry service
a high-quality restaurant	car hire
a room with a view	photocopiers

Which facilities are important for

   1. a person on business?

   2. a family with small children?

   3. teenagers?

   4. a young couple on holiday?

   5. retired people?

Task II Match the following grades of hotels with their descriptions.

   1. One-Star Hotel   A. average comfort

   2. Two-Star Hotel   B. some comfort

   3. Three-Star Hotel   C. economy

   4. Four-Star Hotel   D. luxury

   5. Five-Star Hotel   E. high comfort

Task III Translate the Hotel Departments into Chinese.

Food & Beverage Department　_____

Recreation Department　_____

Rooms Division　_____

Housekeeping Department　_____

Front Office Department　_____

Accounting/Finance Department　_____

Sales & Public Relations Department　_____

Security Department　_____

Engineering Department　_____

Executive Office　_____

Human Resources Department　_____

Part IV　Practical Writing

Reply to a Letter of Complaint 投诉答复信

    投诉信是因顾客对产品、服务质量等方面不满意而向有关机构的主管或监督人员所做出的书面投诉、抱怨、质问等，其目的在于通过投诉提出的合理补偿要求，得到满意的服务。

    对投诉信的回复，必须持认真负责的态度，把投诉信看作是检验和改进工作的契机。因此，写好投诉的回复信非常重要。

Chapter Three　Elements of Tourism

投诉答复信的要点：

1) 感谢对方提出意见，对造成的损失和不便表示道歉。
2) 简单说明或解释造成错误的原因。
3) 建议解决的方法，或者已经采取的措施，防止以后发生类似情况。
4) 如果对方提出不合理的要求，语气委婉地提出你拒绝的理由。
5) 再次表示歉意，希望保持良好的关系。

回复投诉信的常用句型：

1. I feel terribly sorry to hear what you said.
2. Something must be done about it.
3. I will immediately attend to it so that I can give you a satisfactory response.
4. Please forgive what we did to you and accept our sincere apology.
5. There are three ways we can handle this situation.
6. We do wish you could be satisfied with what we have compensated for the trouble we made.
7. We have communicated with the concerned person, confirmed what you had complained, and punished him.
8. We will have him apologize to you on the day you appoint.
9. We do value your business and friendship.
10. We would have refund and hope that you could accept our sincere apology for the mess we made.

Sample 1

Dear Sir/Madam,

　　Thanks for your letter, from which we understand the situation. We are so sorry for our imperfect service and hope you could kindly forgive us. We look forward to serving you again with more satisfied service. Again please accept our sincere invitation and we will be waiting for your soon arrival.

　　With all our best regards and wishes!

　　　　　　　　　　　　　　　　　　　　　　　　　　　　　　Yours,
　　　　　　　　　　　　　　　　　　　　　　　　　　　　　　Thomas

Sample 2

Dear Mrs. Smith,

　　Thank you for your letter of 6 July.

　　I am very sorry to know that the room you stayed was not clean enough. And I learned that what you said is really the case.

　　When I received your letter, I sent one of our assistant managers to look into the matter.

He said that they had rearranged the beds in your room just a few minutes before you came in and they did not clean it thoroughly.

I am very sorry for that and I promise you that there will be no such troubles any more. Welcome you to my hotel again. I enclose a check for ＄100 as our apologies.

Sincerely yours,
Susan Keen
General Manager

Task I In which of the following places or situations have you complained? Tell your partner what you complained about and why. Then the partner tries to solve your complaint.

For instance:

A: I complained about a shirt I bought in a shop. The quality of the shirt was really poor.

B: The shopkeeper should fully refund it.

Task II Please write a reply according to this letter of complaint.

To: customerservice@hotels.com

From: John@hotmail.com

Subject: Sunshine Hotel-Shanghai

Dear Sir/Madam,

I am writing to complain about my recent stay in your hotel in Shanghai. I have stayed in your hotels many times and never had problems. However, this stay was disappointing. The room was not clean and the service was very slow. The Internet was not reliable and the hotel breakfast was poor.

Obviously, this is not satisfactory. I have stayed with your chain before, but I won't again unless something can be done about this. I look forward to receiving your response.

Kind regards,

John

Chapter Three Elements of Tourism

Task III Write a letter to answer a complaint according to the information given below.

一位客人来信抱怨说，他上个月随团旅行时，对导游的服务特别不满意，要求该导游赔礼道歉，并赔偿损失。

······ Part V Typical Scenic Spot ······

Mount WuYi

Mount Wuyi is located in Fujian Province at its boundary with Jiangxi Province running along for about 500km at an average altitude of over 1000m. The legend says that in the era of TangYao, a senior man called Peng Zu took hermitage in the mountain with his sons Wu and Yi, who first developed this area, therefore the mountain was referred to as Mt Wuyi in their honor. Yet other folks say that this was once the settlement of the ancient Minyue people governed by their King Wuyi, hence the mountain's name.

Mount Wuyi scenic area is in the southern suburb of Wuyishan City, Fujian Province, southeastern section of northern Mount Wuyi ranges, a strap about 14km long and 5km wide, covering an area of $70km^2$ about 350m above sea level in average. Geologically, the mountain is made up of low hills of red sand rocks, namely the Danxia landform. For the crustal movement of hundreds of millions of years, the topography had been changing all the time and finally created the present shooting peaks flanked by clear streams which brings to the mountain the honor of "the most miraculous and graceful in southeastern China".

Mount Wuyi is near Tropic of Cancer, seated in subtropical humid monsoon climatic zone, with an average annual temperature of about 17.90℃. The temperate and moist climate provides favorite conditions for the vegetation of Mount Wuyi, which is therefore particularly favorable for all lives all year round. As the seasons shift, the scenes offer varied interest as well. In early spring, the mountain is attractive with lively green dotted with brilliant flowers; in summer, it is the ideal resort from the seasonal heat with its cooling shade of the green trees and the bubbling brooks; in autumn, it is impressive with the azure sky, the flaming red maples, and the expanses of blooming camellia; and in winter, the evergreens brave a chilly white world that creates a special beauty. And for all seasons the sunshine, the rainfall, the mist, and the cloud all brings about unpredictable mirages of the mountain scenes.

Mount Wuyi hosts all the three dominant beliefs in China: Taoism, Buddhism, and Confucianism. Thus it is a reputed cultural mountain with a long history. The total area of this heritage is 999.75 square km, the second vast in China that have been included in *World Heritage List*. In accordance with the features of the resources, the area is subdivided into four parts: Bio-diversity quarter in the west, nine bends ecology quarter in the center, natural and cultural scenery quarter in the east, and Chengcun Village of the ancient King Minyue.

In December of 1999, UNESCO inscribed Mount Wuyi on its *World Heritage List* as a cultural and natural property of the world.

职业素养

近年来，住宿从一个旅游的基础配套项目逐渐变成了旅游的重要项目。党的二十大报告提出："发展乡村特色产业，拓宽农民增收致富渠道。""统筹乡村基础设施和公共服务布局，建设宜居宜业和美乡村。"旅游成为乡村振兴的新支点，近年来，乡村度假产品项目不断涌现，休闲度假、观光度假、体验度假、康复疗养度假和运动健身度假等各种目的和内容的度假需求也在迅速增长。住宿设施也在不断丰富，从酒店到度假村，从度假公寓到乡村民宿，从家庭客房到度假别墅等，都已成为旅游热点。国内旅游兴起和持续大幅度增长，我国人民旅游消费需求水平不断提高，成为度假区和酒店发展最强有力的支撑和最广阔的舞台。新时代人民对美好生活的需求必将推动我国旅游度假和"大住宿"产业朝向专业化、多样化、多元化、网络化、品牌化、国际化、信息化、智能化等方面更快、更好地发展。

Unit 8 Transportation

Part I Warm-Up

Is there a person who doesn't like travelling? There is hardly one. Visitors use all forms of transportation, from hiking in a wilderness to flying in a jet, to an exciting city. Transportation can include taking a chairlift up a Colorado mountainside or standing at the rail of a cruise ship looking across the blue Caribbean. Whether people travel by one of these means or by car, coach, train, taxi, motorbike, or bicycle, they are taking a trip and thus are engaging in tourism.

Then, which means of transportation would you choose if you make a plan to trip?

Part II Conversations

Conversation 1   Booking an Airline Ticket

A: Good morning. The United Airlines. What can I do for you?
B: Yes. I'd like to make a reservation to Boston next week.
A: When do you want to fly?
B: Monday, September 12.
A: We have Flight 802 on Monday. Just a moment, please. Let me check whether there're seats available. I'm sorry we are all booked up for Flight 802 on that day.
B: Then, any alternatives?
A: The next available flight leaves at 9:30 Tuesday morning September 13. Shall I book you a seat?
B: Er... it is a direct flight, isn't it?
A: Yes it is. You want to go first class or coach?
B: I prefer first class, what about the fare?
A: One way is $176.
B: OK. I will take the 9:30 flight on Tuesday.

A: A seat on Flight 807 to Boston 9:30, Tuesday morning. Is it all right, sir?

B: Right. Can you also put me on the waiting list for the 12th?

A: Certainly. May I have your name and telephone number?

B: My name is Lorus Anderson. You can reach me at 52378651.

A: I will notify you if there is a cancellation.

B: Thank you very much.

A: My pleasure.

 New Words

airline	[ˈeəlaɪn]	n. 航空公司；航线
alternative	[ɔːlˈtɜːnətɪv; ɒl-]	n. 二中择一；选择
coach	[kəutʃ]	n. 旅客车厢；经济舱
fare	[feə]	n. 票价；费用
cancellation	[ˌkænsəˈleɪʃ(ə)n]	n. 取消；删除

 Phrases and Expressions

make a reservation　　　预订；预约
book up　　　　　　　　订完；订光
direct flight　　　　　　　直达班机
first class　　　　　　　　头等舱

Conversation 2　　Renting a Car

Situation: *David wants to rent a car for the coming holiday. Now he is in the car rental agency and talking with Nick, the clerk.*

Nick: Good morning, sir. What can I do for you?

David: Good morning. I want to rent a car, please.

Nick: I think you made the right choice, coming to us. We have a wide selection of vehicles you can choose from. What kind of model do you have in mind?

David: I would like one that with a good stereo.

Nick: All our cars have stereos in them. Stereos and air conditioning are all standard with us.

David: Good. I want it for the holiday with my girlfriend. I want her to have a good time.

Nick: Oh, is that so? Well, then. Let me show you something she might like. It's on our back lot.

Chapter Three Elements of Tourism

David: This is a Porsche!

Nick: Yes. Beautiful, isn't it?

David: But I probably can't afford it. It must be really expensive.

Nick: Well, sir. You said you were looking at cars at the rental agency at the airport. Now with them you'd spend your money and get nothing for it. But you could probably rent this Porsche from us, for the same price as one of their standard cars.

David: But it doesn't get good gas mileage?

Nick: Not good as other standard cars, but it's in nice shape, isn't it?

David: Yes, it almost looks new.

Nick: Take a seat inside and see what you think. So you will take the Porsche then, sir?

David: Yes, and I want to buy the insurance too. I think it's necessary.

Nick: You're smart to buy it. How long will you need it?

David: For two weeks. Do you charge mileage?

Nick: No, it's a flat rate. Can I see your International License?

David: Sure, here it is.

Nick: Thank you, sir. You have to finish filling out the forms.

David: OK.

 New Words

selection	[sɪˈlekʃ(ə)n]	n.	选择；挑选
vehicle	[ˈviːhɪkl]	n.	车辆；交通工具
stereo	[ˈsterɪəʊ]	n.	立体声
Porsche	[ˈpɒrʃ]	n.	保时捷（德国名车品牌）
afford	[əˈfɔːd]	v.	提供；买得起
insurance	[ɪnˈʃʊər(ə)ns]	n.	保险

 Phrases and Expressions

rental agency	租赁公司
have in mind	考虑；想到
air conditioning	空调
back lot	露天区域；外景地
rental agency	租赁公司
get nothing for it	什么也得不到的
get good gas mileage	低油耗；省油
flat rate	统一费用

145

Practical Patterns

1. I want a package deal including airfare and hotel.
   我需要成套服务，包括机票和住宿。

2. I'd like to change this ticket to the first class.
   我想把这张票换成头等车。

3. I'd like to reserve a sleeper to Chicago.
   我要预订去芝加哥的卧铺。

4. I'd like two seats on today's Northwest Flight 7 to Detroit，please.
   我想订两张今天西北航空公司7班次到底特律的机票。

5. Do you have any tickets available for that date?
   你们有那天的票吗?

6. What's the fare to New York，Economy Class?
   去纽约的经济舱机票多少钱?

7. Would you please make my reservation to Chicago for tomorrow?
   请帮我预订明天去芝加哥的座位好吗?

8. What time does the plane take off? 飞机何时起飞?

9. What flights are there from Beijing to Shanghai tomorrow?
   明天从北京到上海有几趟班机?

10. If you are okay at the airport，you must be there 2 hours before the departure.
    如果保险些必须在飞机起飞前2个小时到达机场。

11. What time is the next train to Shanghai，please?
    请问下班去上海的火车几点开?

12. Do I need to change train? 我还需要转火车吗?

Task I Make up dialogues according to the following situation，and act them out in class.

Situation: You are at the Ticket Counter to buy tickets to Dubai（迪拜）. Now you are having a conversation with the Ticket Reservationist.

Task II Complete the following dialogues by translating the Chinese in the brackets.

A: Will you book a ticket to Paris for me?

B: Yes，madam. _____ .（您想什么时候离开北京?）

A: Next Monday，May 15th，2015.

B: There are several flights to Paris available on May 15th. _____.
（您想要乘坐哪一个航班?）

A: Afternoon flights preferably.

B: Yes, madam. _____.

（那天下午有两个航班：一个是下午 4 点，另一个是下午 6 点。）

A: Fine, I'd like the 4 p.m. one.

B: 4 p.m., fine. _____.

（我来准备您的机票，太太，请您稍等一下。）

A: What time do I check-in at the airport?

B: _____.

（您必须在下午点前到那里。）

A: I see. Thank you very much.

Task III Look at these modes of transportation, discuss with your partners about their functions, advantages and disadvantages.

ambulance 救护车	bike 自行车	bicycle 自行车
motorcycle 摩托车	cart 二轮马车	carriage 四轮马车
car 小汽车	jeep 吉普车	tractor 拖拉机
lorry 重型卡车	truck 卡车	coach 大客车
van 厢式货车	taxi 出租车	subway 地铁
train 火车	express 快客列车	yacht 游船
warship 军舰	aircraft 飞机	jet 喷气飞机
spaceship 宇宙飞船	helicopter 直升机	

Part III Readings

Text A

The Only Way to Travel Is on Foot

The past ages of man have all been carefully labeled by anthropologists. Descriptions like "Paleolithic Man" "Neolithic Man" etc., neatly sum up whole periods. When the time comes for anthropologists to turn their attention to the twentieth century, they will surely choose the label "Legless Man". Histories of the time will go something like this: "In the twentieth century, people forgot how to use their legs. Men and women moved about in cars, buses and trains from a very early age. There were lifts and escalators in all large building to prevent people from walking. This situation was forced upon earth dwellers of that time, because of their extraordinary way of life. In those days, people thought nothing but travelling hundreds of miles each day. But the surprising thing is that they didn't use their legs even when they went on holiday. They built cable railways, ski-lifts and roads to the top of every huge mountain. All the beauty spots on earth were marred by the presence of large car parks."

The future history books might also record that we were deprived of the use of our eyes. In a hurry to get from one place to another, we failed to see anything on the way. Air travel gives you a bird's eye view of the world or even less if the wing of the aircraft happens to get in your way. When you travel by car or train, a blurred image of the countryside constantly smears the windows. Car drivers, in particular, are forever obsessed with the urge to go on and on: they never want to stop. Is it the lure of the great motorways, or what? And as for sea travel, it hardly deserves mention. It is perfectly summed up in the words of the old song: "I joined the navy to see the world, and what did I see? I saw the sea." The typical twentieth-century traveller is the man who always says "I've been there." You mention the remotest, most evocative place names in the world like El Dorado, Kabul, Irkutsk and someone is bound to say: "I've been there." Which means: I drove through it at 100 miles an hour on the way to somewhere else.

When you travel at high speed, the present means nothing. You live mainly in the future because you spend most of your time, looking forward to arriving at some other place. But actual arrival, when it is achieved, is meaningless. You want to move on again. By travelling like this, you suspend all experience. The present ceased to be a reality: you might just as well be dead. The traveller on foot, on the other hand, lives constantly in the present. For him travelling and arriving are one and the same thing: he arrives somewhere with every step he makes. He experiences the present moment with his eyes, his ears and the whole of his body. At the end of his journey he feels a delicious physical weariness. He knows that sound and satisfying sleep will be his: the just reward of all true travellers.

 New Words

label	[ˈleɪb(ə)l]	n. 标签；商标
anthropologist	[ˌænθrəˈpɒlədʒɪst]	n. 人类学家
palaeolithic	[ˈpeɪɪəˈlɪθɪk]	adj. 旧石器时代的
neolithic	[ˈniːəˈlɪθɪk]	adj. 新石器时代的
escalator	[ˈeskəleɪtə]	n. 自动扶梯；电动扶梯
dweller	[ˈdwelə]	n. 居民，居住者
extraordinary	[ɪkˈstrɔːd(ə)n(ə)ri]	adj. 非凡的；特别的
mar	[mɑː]	v. 损伤；糟蹋
deprive	[dɪˈpraɪv]	v. 使丧失，剥夺
blur	[blɜː]	v. 使……模糊不清
constantly	[ˈkɒnst(ə)ntli]	adv. 不断地；时常地

Chapter Three Elements of Tourism

smear	[smɪə]	v. 弄脏；涂上
obsess	[əbˈses]	v. 使……着迷；使……困扰
El Dorado	[eldəˈrɑːdəʊ]	n. 埃尔多拉多
Kabul	[ˈkɑːbəl; kəˈbuːl]	n. 喀布尔（阿富汗的首都）
Irkutsk	[ɪrˈkuːtsk]	n. 伊尔库茨克（苏联东西伯利亚城市）
urge	[ˈɜːdʒ]	v. 催促；驱策
deserve	[dɪˈzɜːv]	v. 应受，应得
remote	[rɪˈməʊt]	adj. 遥远的；偏僻的
evocative	[ɪˈvɒkətɪv]	adj. 唤起的；召唤的
suspend	[səˈspend]	v. 使……延缓，推迟
weariness	[ˈwɪərɪnɪs]	n. 疲劳；厌倦
sound	[saʊnd]	adj. 酣（睡）的；健康的

 Phrases and Expressions

cable railway　　　　　　缆索铁路
ski-lift　　　　　　　　　　滑雪索道
a bird's eye view of　　　鸟瞰
even less　　　　　　　　更不用说
in particular　　　　　　　尤其，特别
obsessed with　　　　　　非常喜欢
be bound to　　　　　　　必然；一定要

 Integrated Exercises of Skills

Task I　Discuss with partners and answer the following questions according to the text.

1. How did the man go to another place in the past ages?
2. Why do anthropologists choose the label "Legless Man" for the twentieth century?
3. What are the differences for the way of life between nowadays and the ancient?
4. Do you like the way of life today? Why or why not?
5. What mode of travelling would you like to choose when you go on holiday?

Task II　Fill in the blanks with the suitable words given below, changing the form where necessary.

| deserve | urge | label | remote |
| a bird's eye view of | extraordinary | obsess with | bound |

1. If you are free, please help me _____ the products on the other side.

2. We gather some of the most beautiful and _____ scenery of France.
3. If you have a/ an _____ to smoke, please wait.
4. No matter how busy or tired you are, your family _____ this time with you.
5. If I had not been so _____ music, I might not have become a musician.
6. If we choose to _____ by the past, we will never move forward.
7. Nowadays electricity is used even in _____ mountainous regions.
8. You can have _____ of the entire area when we get to the top of the hill.

Task III Fill in the blanks with the proper forms of the words.

An airline company, esp. an international airline company, is a giant _____ (multifunction) institution, in which there are ticketing and ticket _____ (reserve) agents, airport personnel, freight transport personnel, mechanics, _____ (cater) service people, pilots and other crew members on the flight.

For more than half a century, the work of a stewardess has _____ (consider) to be both _____ (stimulate) and well-_____ (pay). Although the work is commonly regarded as women's, it is never confined to them. Men also play an important role in the work.

During flight, pilots work only in the cockpit（驾驶舱）, so passengers seldom see them in the cabin. However, the captain will greet passengers through the _____ (loudspeak). Once the plane takes off, crew members will be very busy working. Most of their work is to offer food and drinks to passengers and explain in detail points for attention. When the flights about to approach the destination, the purser will announce the landing procedures, and crew members will then make sure that all passengers and facilities in the cabin are well _____ (prepare) for the touching down of the flight. When the flight has landed, crew members will help passengers get off the plane and make farewells to the latter.

Task IV Translate the following sentences into Chinese.

1. When the time comes for anthropologists to turn their attention to the twentieth century, they will surely choose the label "Legless Man".

2. But the surprising thing is that they didn't use their legs even when they went on holiday.

3. The future history books might also record that we were deprived of the use of our eyes.

Chapter Three Elements of Tourism

4. Air travel gives you a bird's eye view of the world-or even less if the wing of the aircraft happens to get in your way.

_____

5. For him travelling and arriving are one and the same thing: he arrives somewhere with every step he makes.

_____

6. He knows that sound and satisfying sleep will be his: the just reward of all true travellers.

_____

Text B

How to Make Travel Easier

Travel is complicated, and you may face the unexpected. Frequent fliers have their favorite travel tips; some are handed down generation to generation by friends and colleagues. Any strategies to lessen the hassle become cherished keepsakes. Here are some of the most-effective techniques I use to improve the travel experience.

Get Elite Treatment

The best perks go to the top elite tiers of a frequent-flier program, generally those who fly 100,000 miles and up. But even occasional fliers can reach entry-level elite status, at 25,000 miles per year, which can help avoid missing flights when non-elite lines are long at airports.

Buy a day pass at an airline club (about $50) and get comfortable seating, TV, workspace, quiet, drinks and snacks. It's particularly worth it when things go bad: The club's experienced, unrushed airline agents can solve problems and help rebook.

Buy a seat upgrade that gets you access to priority security lines and early boarding. Also get a credit card that gives you a free checked bag and early boarding, but beware: Some cards can carry high annual fees, as much as $450 per year.

Better Ways to Pack

Customize your black rolling suitcase by tying a colorful ribbon on (but not so long that it gets caught in baggage machinery). Put a business card inside your bag. If the name tag and bag tag get eaten by airline baggage machinery, and many do, the airline will open your bag to try to identify the owner.

Beware: Never put valuables in a checked bag. The airline's liability for loss and damage is quite limited, and airlines don't offer any reimbursement for many lost items, including jewelry, electronics and valuables. If forced to check your bag at the gate because overhead bins are full, pull out valuables and electronics. Never check the suit you need for the next day, whether it is a bathing suit or a business suit. Bags may get lost and delayed.

Have a travel bag with toiletries so you're not packing that every trip. Other items to consider carrying: An umbrella, a pair of slippers if you don't want to pad around a hotel room barefoot; an empty water bottle to fill once inside security so you can avoid paying $4 a bottle at the airport store.

Zip Through Security

Airport security screening checkpoints are great places to lose important things: drivers' licenses that don't make it back to wallets, for example, or laptops that walk off with other "travellers". Here's my routine:

Cell phone, watch, keys and pens all go into my briefcase before I get in line. My ID goes back into my wallet immediately when I get it back from the agent at the TSA desk. Boarding pass goes in the same pocket every time. Liquids and laptop are carried in the same place in my bags every time so when I must be checked, I know exactly where they are. Laptop goes into one TSA plastic tub. Liquids into a second tub, along with jacket, belt and pocket change.

No jewelry that will set off the body scanner and lead to an aggressive pat-down. Wear shoes that are easy on and off.

At Home at the Hotel

Some travellers always request upper floors at hotels to lessen street noise. Others insist on lower floors so that they are within reach of fire-department ladders if there is a fire. In fact, some companies insist in contracts with hotels that their employees get rooms within four stories of the street.

Once you're checked in, spend a few minutes walking from your room to the nearest emergency stair – not the elevator. If sirens were blaring or the hallway filled with smoke, you would know which way to go.

Take your room number with you. Tear off the room number from the paper given to you at check-in and keep it in a pocket so that when you can't remember whether it is 625 or 629, you won't be lost.

 New Words

complicate	['kɒmplɪkeɪt]	v. 使复杂化
strategy	['strætɪdʒi]	n. 战略，策略
hassle	['hæs(ə)l]	n. 困难；麻烦

Chapter Three Elements of Tourism

cherish	[ˈtʃerɪʃ]	v. 珍爱
keepsake	[ˈkiːpseɪk]	n. 纪念品
perk	[pɜːk]	n. 小费；额外收入
elite	[eɪˈliːt]	n. 精英；精华
tier	[tɪə]	n. 层；等级
occasional	[əˈkeɪʒ(ə)n(ə)l]	adj. 偶然的
entry-level	[ˈentrɪ ˌlevəl]	adj. 入门的；初级的
priority	[praɪˈɒrɪti]	n. 优先；优先权
customize	[ˈkʌstəmaɪz]	v. 定做
liability	[laɪəˈbɪlɪti]	n. 倾向；可能性
reimbursement	[riːɪmˈbɜːsmənt]	n. 偿还；赔偿
toiletry	[ˈtɔɪlɪtri]	n. 化妆品；化妆用具
aggressive	[əˈgresɪv]	adj. 侵略性的；有进取心的
pat-down		搜身
emergency	[ɪˈmɜːdʒ(ə)nsi]	n. 紧急情况；突发事件
siren	[ˈsaɪərən]	n. 警笛
blare	[bleə]	v. 发嘟嘟声；发出响而刺耳的声音

 Phrases and Expressions

hand down	把……传下去
pull out	抽出；取出
set off	出发；动身
zip through	快速通过
walk off with	偷走；顺手拿走
Elite Treatment	贵宾待遇
overhead bin	舱顶行李箱
TSA (Transportation Security Administration)	美国运输安全管理局

Integrated Exercises of Skills

Task I   Work in groups and discuss the following questions.

1. Do you think travelling by air is the best mode of transportation?
2. Which technique do you think is the most important?
3. How to pack your personal staff when travelling by air?
4. Which floor is the safer one according to the author?
5. Can you list some more techniques to make the travel easier?

Task II Complete the table according to the text.

How to Make Travel Easier

Get Elite Treatment	Join a _____ program. Buy a _____ at an airline club. Buy a _____ upgrade. Get a _____.
Better Ways to Pack	Customize your black rolling suitcase by _____ _____. Put a _____ inside your bag. Never put _____ in a checked bag. Have a travel bag with _____. Other items to consider carrying: _____ _____.
Zip Through Security	Don't lose important things at airport security screening checkpoints: such as _____ and _____. No _____ that will set off the body scanner. _____ all go into my briefcase before getting in line.
At Home at the Hotel	Once you're checked in, spend a few minutes walking from _____ to _____. Take your _____ with you.

Task III Translate the following sentences into Chinese.

1. Travel is complicated, and you may face the unexpected.
   _____

2. Any strategies to lessen the hassle become cherished keepsakes.
   _____

3. The best perks go to the top elite tiers of a frequent-flier program, generally those who fly 100,000 miles and up.
   _____

4. Buy a day pass at an airline club (about $50) and get comfortable seating, TV, workspace, quiet, drinks and snacks.
   _____

5. If the name tag and bag tag get eaten by airline baggage machinery, and many do, the airline will open your bag to try to identify the owner.

Chapter Three Elements of Tourism

6. If forced to check your bag at the gate because overhead bins are full, pull out valuables and electronics.

7. Liquids and laptop are carried in the same place in my bags every time so when I must be checked, I know exactly where they are.

8. If sirens were blaring or the hallway filled with smoke, you would know which way to go.

Task IV In our daily life, we have many modes of transportation. Now talk with partners about some main modes of transportation, which one can make our travel quicker and more convenient?

Bus/Coach: A large motor vehicle, having a long body, equipped with seats or benches for passengers, usually operating as part of a scheduled service.

Subway: An underground urban railroad, usually operated by electricity (Figure 8-1).

Train (railway/railroad): Public transport provided by a line of railway cars coupled together and drawn by a locomotive (Figure 8-2).

Airplane: An aircraft that has a fixed wing and is powered by propellers or jets.

Ship: A vessel, esp. a large oceangoing one propelled by sails or engines.

Bicycle: A vehicle with two wheels in tandem, usually propelled by pedals connected to the rear wheel by a chain, and having handlebars for steering and a saddle like seat.

Magnetically Levitated Train 磁悬浮列车 (Figure 8-3)

The Shinkansen (Figure 8-4) / **bullet train (Japan)** 新干线，日本高速列车，子弹头动车

Figure 8-1 Subway

Figure 8-2 G-Series High-Speed Train

Figure 8-3　Magnetically Levitated Train

Figure 8-4　The Shinkansen

Part IV　Practical Writing

Letter of Invitation 邀请函

邀请函在形式上大体分为两种：

1. 正规的格式（formal correspondence），亦称请柬。

请柬多用第三人称，要写全名。

如果要求客人回复，请在请柬上写明"R. S. V. P"，意思是："Please reply."

2. 非正式格式（informal correspondence），即一般的邀请信。

邀请信在形式上不如请柬那样正规，但也很考究，书写时应将邀请的时间（年、月、日、时间）、地点、场合写清楚。

信函内容：

a．邀请的意图；

b．活动的时间、地点和内容；

c．表达希望对方能参加的诚意。

邀请信的回复：

a．表达感谢；

b．愉快接受，表达期待。或者谢绝邀请，并简要说明理由，表示遗憾及祝愿。

常用句型：

1) May I have the honor of your company at dinner?

2) The favor of a reply is requested.

3) It gives me the greatest pleasure to invite you to visit...

4) I do hope you can make it/ I do hope you're not too busy to come.

5) We are looking forward to meeting you at...

6) Please confirm your participation at your earliest convenience.

7) On behalf of... I am pleased to invite you to...

8) We take pleasure in inviting you to come to/visit...

9) It is very kind of you to... / Thank you so much for your invitation.

10) I am awfully/terribly sorry for not being able to... because...

11) Unfortunately, I can't come because... Thank you all the same.

Sample 1

Invitation

Mr. and Mrs. White

request the pleasure of

Mr. Frank Brow's company at dinner

on Saturday, February tenth at seven o'clock, at Hilton Hotel.

R. S. V. P

Sample 2

Dear Alice,

  Thank you very much for your invitation. It will be great pleasure for me to join you on Friday for the wonderful film. I will arrive at the cinema before eight. I look forward to meeting you on Friday.

  Thank you for invitation.

Yours,

Jane

Sample 3

July 25, 2015

Dear Louis Rogers,

  It's our great honor to invite you to visit our company, located in No. 59 Merlin Road, Futian District, Shenzhen, on August 15, 2015. This visit will provide an opportunity for you to make a better understanding of CITS, and to communicate our future tourist cooperation in detail.

  CITS Company, as one of the biggest tour agency in China, has been great progressing in tourism and service. We believe this visit will be of great benefit to our future business cooperation. Please use this invitation letter to apply for your VISA to China.

  We are all looking forward to seeing you soon, and should you have any questions, please feel free to inform me.

Yours truly,

Shawn Brown, VIP Sales

CITS Corporation

Task I Write an invitation letter according to the Chinese letter.

亲爱的帕克先生：

  我们非常高兴地邀请您出席我们定于2月10日星期六7点在希尔顿饭店举行的晚宴。我们还准备邀请一些其他的朋友，希望你们一起过得愉快。

  你真诚的，

  玛丽怀特

Task II You are going to write a reply to reject an invitation. Use the following notes.

- Greetings
- Polite rejection and reasonable explanation.
- Polite informal ending

Part V Typical Scenic Spot

Hong Kong

Situated at the southeastern tip of China, Hong Kong is ideally positioned at the centre of rapidly developing East Asia. With a total area of 1103 square kilometers, it covers Hong Kong Island, the Kowloon peninsula and the New Territories. Hong Kong, described as a "barren rock" over 150 years ago, has become a world-class financial, trading and business centre and, indeed, a great world city. Hong Kong has no natural resources, except one of the finest deep-water ports in the world. A hardworking, adaptable and well-educated workforce, coupled with entrepreneurial flair, is the bedrock of Hong Kong's productivity and creativity. Hong Kong became a Special Administrative Region (SAR) of the People's Republic of China on July 1, 1997. Under Hong Kong's constitutional document, *the Basic Law of the Hong Kong Special Administrative Region*, the existing economic, legal and social system will be maintained for 50 years. The SAR enjoys a high degree of autonomy except in defense and foreign affairs. Hong Kong is a true shopping paradise, dietary world, leisure summer resort and international cultural window.

Hong Kong Qingma Bridge

Hong Kong Qingma Bridge is the longest dual-purpose (both for driving and railroad) wire suspension type hanging bridge in the world, it is also the world's sixth longest hanging bridge of such wire suspension hanging bridge form construction. At present, Qingma Bridge has become one main-line highway to connect the Hong Kong international airport and the urban district, since its opening to traffic. Many cars, buses and trains travel across it every day. Qingma Bridge has been the Hong Kong's main construction symbol and the sightseeing scenic spot, so it attracts tourists from all over the world (Figure 8-5).

Hong Kong Disneyland

The Hong Kong Disneyland was built by the Government of Hong Kong SAR and The Walt Disney Company and officially opened on September 12, 2005. It's the world's smallest Disneyland, which consists of the Hong Kong Disneyland theme park, two hotels and retail, dining and entertainment facilities, stretching over 1.3 square kilometers on Lantau Island.

Hong Kong Disneyland is not only children's paradise bit, but also a paradise for adults returning to their childhood. Visitors who come to Hong Kong Disneyland will be temporarily away from the real world into the colorful fairy tale kingdom, enjoy mysterious fantasy travel for the future and dangerous world (Figure 8-6).

Figure 8-5   Hong Kong Qingma Bridge   **Figure 8-6   Hong Kong Disneyland**

Ocean Park Hong Kong

Ocean Park Hong Kong is world-famous marine animal museum, completed in January, 1977. Ocean Park is located at Mt. Nalang, and consists of "the Wong Chuk Hang Park" and "the Nam Long Shan Park". Both parks are connected by the sky crane, which forms a complete scenic area. By sky crane, it takes only 6 minutes for tourists to arrive at Nam Long Shan Park. It is really marvelous and exciting when you place yourself in a 6 seats birdcage shape sky cranes, roll across a whole length of 1.4 kilometers over a 200-meter altitude, and take a bird's-eye view of the whole park.

The Nam Long Shan Park has three big venues: Sea Hall, Tidal Bore Hall and Sea Theater. The Sea Hall is an ellipse building. Against a huge three-story-high glass wall, tourists may watch wonderful postures of about 400 kinds of fish and altogether 30,000 fish in water. The Tidal Bore Hall is equipped with the man-made ocean waves and the rockery. Under the electrically operated waves machine, the roaring waves might reaches as high as 1 meter. In the Sea Theater, tourists may see the marvelous shows of the well-trained dolphins and sea lions in the large tank.

There are also numerous amusement facilities in the Ocean Park, such as the crazy roller coaster, ferris wheel and so on. Tourists must have an unforgettable day in this biggest entertainment leisure center of the Southeast Asia (Figure 8-7).

Figure 8-7　Ocean Park Hong Kong

Repulse Bay

Repulse Bay is located at the south of Hong Kong Island, which is the most representative and beautiful bay in Hong Kong. The Repulse Bay is famous for its small wave, fine sand, broad beach bed, gentle slope and the warm water. The summer season is the Repulse Bay's most swinging time, the beach is thronged with visitors. After splashing in the water, people tuck in delicious grilled food as much as desired and take photos around the beach. Because of the beautiful scenery, Repulse Bay

Figure 8-8　The Repulse Bay

becomes one of the famous high-level residential districts in Hong Kong Island. These luxurious private residences have also been another unique scenic area in Hong Kong, which makes you forget to return (Figure 8-8).

职业素养

自十九大报告首次明确提出要建设"交通强国"的发展战略以来，中央到地方各级政府围绕交通强国建设进行了积极实践。党的二十大报告再次提出，"坚持把发展经济的着力点放在实体经济上，推进新型工业化，加快建设制造强国、质量强国、航天强国、交通强国、网络强国、数字中国"。目前，我国已成为世界上运输最繁忙的国家之一。根据交通强国的建设要求，到2035年，我国将基本建成"人民满意、保障有力、世界前列"的交通强国，到2050年全面建成交通强国，实现"人享其行、物优其流"。

Unit 9 Travelling

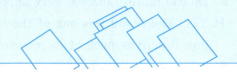

······ **Part I   Warm-Up** ······

Tourism is travel for recreational, leisure, or business purpose. There have been travelling activities long before in China and foreign countries. We can regard the migration of human beings for better life condition as the primitive "travelling". Later, travelling activities which are similar to modern tourism began with the development of productivity and flourishing of human culture. The original "travelling" are usually for some particular reasons. For example, the ancient Europeans travelled for religious reason. They would spend long time on pilgrimage to a famous church, and the ancient Chinese would make a long journey for political or educational reasons, like the kings worshiping the sacred mountains and intellectuals travelling to interpret his own thoughts.

Modern tourism began to flourish in 19th century. There came the father of modern tourism, Thomas Cook, who organized a group of people to attend Temperance Meeting. He made fairly enough profit from this activity. This incident signifies an era of modern tourism.

······ **Part II   Conversations** ······

Conversation 1   Trip to Phuket

Situation: *Bill and Jane are two overseas students in Thailand. They meet each other on the campus.*
(B: Bill   J: Jane)
B: I heard Phuket is the largest island in Thailand.
J: Yes. It's approximately the size of Singapore.
B: Where is it?

J: It is situated off the west coast of Thailand in the Andaman Sea.

B: How about its history?

J: It has a rich and colorful history. It formerly derived its wealth from tin and rubber.

B: Do you mean trade was very important to its development?

J: Yes. The island was one of the major trading routes between China and India. But now it derives much of its income from tourism.

B: Where does the name "Phuket" come from?

J: The name "Phuket" is apparently derived from the word "bukit" in Malay, which means hill. The island looks like a hill from a distance.

B: We're looking forward to seeing it.

New Words

approximately	[əˈprɒksɪmətli]	adv.	大约，近似地；近于
coast	[kəʊst]	v.	滑行；沿岸航行；沿……岸航行
		n.	海岸；滑坡
derive	[dɪˈraɪv]	v.	源于；得自；起源
rubber	[ˈrʌbə]	n.	橡胶；橡皮；合成橡胶；按摩师

Phrases and Expressions

be situated off the west coast of	位于离……西海岸不远的
derive… from	源于……
trading routes	贸易路线
look forward to	盼望

Conversation 2   Grand Canyon Tourism

A: Are there any tours for the Grand Canyon?

B: There are several tours of the Grand Canyon.

A: Have you been to our Tourist Information Center?

B: No, I haven't.

A: Would you show me where that is?

B: Sure. It's up ahead to your left.

A: I heard that some tours actually go down into the canyon. Is that true?

B: Yes. It's a great way to really see the canyon.

A: In addition, it's great exercise too, since we do a lot of hiking.

Chapter Three Elements of Tourism

B: That sounds fantastic.
A: Where do I go to sign up for that tour?
B: Go inside the Information Center. And tell them you want to go on the tour that goes down into the canyon. I will come with the next group to go down. I'll see you soon then.

 New Words

canyon	[ˈkænjən]	n. 峡谷
tourist	[ˈtʊərɪst]	n. 旅行者，观光客
hiking	[ˈhaɪkɪŋ]	n. 徒步旅行

 Phrases and Expressions

go down into	进入
do a lot of hiking	徒步旅行
sign up for	登记

 Practical Patterns

1. How about Brazil?
   去巴西怎么样？

2. We haven't been to those places yet.
   我们还没有去过那些地方呢。

3. I'd like to see the sights of Paris.
   我想领略一下巴黎的风光。

4. I can't wait to see Hong Kong.
   我迫不及待要看一看香港。

5. I'll have two days to do sightseeing in that beautiful city.
   我将在那个美丽的城市游览两天。

6. I'll spend the last two days shopping and visiting some friends in Shanghai.
   最后两天时间，我将在上海买点东西，看看朋友。

7. I've been dying to take a trip into the mountains.
   我好想到山里去旅游。

8. What places do you want to see in particular?
   有没有什么您特别想去的地方？

9. I've decided to go on a three-week tour of South-East Asia.
   我决定要参加一个为期三周的东南亚旅行团。

Task I Complete the following dialogues by translating the Chinese in the brackets.

Li: _____? （这是你在哪里照的照片？）It's so beautiful!

Chen: I took it in Hawaii. You know, I came to New York University for one year. This weekend, I travelled to Hawaii.

Li: _____? （旅行如何呢？有没有什么特别的？）

Chen: You know it was Tomb-Sweeping Day in China, so I decided to go to the cemetery there on purpose.

Li: _____? （真的？那里的人也过这个节吗？）

Chen: Not really. _____. （我只是想和家人一起过节，虽然我们身处异地。）

Li: That's very nice of you. _____? （觉得那里怎么样呢？）

Chen: _____. （和中国的墓地是很不一样的）No scare atmosphere.

Li: I see. _____. （也许是因为西方国家的人对死亡的态度吧。）

Chen: Yes. I didn't feel sorrow there. On the contrary, I began to treat death in an calm way.

Task II Make up a dialogue according to the following situation, and act them out in class.

The tourists are standing in front of the Confucius Temple. They are amazed at the good complex with a history of more than 1,000 years. Miss Chen explains the layout of the great temple before they get in.

Part III Readings

Text A

World Tourism Organization

  The United Nations World Tourism Organization (UNWTO) is the United Nations agency responsible for the promotion of responsible, sustainable and universally accessible tourism. It is the leading international organization in the field of tourism, which promotes tourism as a driver of economic growth, inclusive development and environmental sustainability and offers leadership and support to the sector in advancing knowledge and tourism policies worldwide. It encourages the implementation of the Global Code of Ethics for Tourism to maximize the contribution of tourism to socio-economic development, while minimizing its possible negative impacts, and is committed to promoting tourism as an instrument in achieving the United Nations Millennium Development Goals (MDGs) which geared towards reducing poverty and fostering sustainable development.

UNWTO's membership includes 156 countries, 6 associate members and two observers. Additionally there are some 400 affiliate members, representing the private sector, educational institutions, tourism associations and local tourism authorities, non-governmental entities with specialized interests in tourism, and commercial and non-commercial bodies and associations with activities related to the aims of UNWTO. Its headquarters are located in Madrid.

The objectives of the UNWTO are to promote and develop sustainable tourism so as to contribute to economic development, international understanding, peace, prosperity and universal respect for, and observance of, human rights and fundamental freedoms for all, without distinction as to race, sex, language or religion. In pursuing these aims, UNWTO pays particular attention to the interests of developing countries in the field of tourism.

History

The origin of UNWTO stems back to 1925 when the International Congress of Official Tourist Traffic Associations (ICOTTA) was formed at The Hague. Some articles from early volumes of the *Annals of Tourism Research* claim that the UNWTO originated from the International Union of Official Tourist Publicity Organizations (IUOTPO), although the UNWTO states that the ICOTTA became the International Union of Official Tourist Publicity Organizations first in 1934.

Following the end of the World War Ⅱ and with international travel numbers increasing, the IUOTPO restructured itself into the International Union of Official Travel Organizations (IUOTO). A technical, non-governmental organization, the IUOTO was made up of a combination of national tourist organizations, industry and consumer groups. The goals and objectives of the IUOTO were not only to promote tourism in general but also to extract the best out of tourism as an international trade component and as an economic development strategy for developing nations.

Towards the end of the 1960s, the IUOTO realized the need for further transformation to enhance its role on an international level. The 20th IUOTO general assembly in Tokyo, 1967, declared the need for the creation of an intergovernmental body with the necessary abilities to function on an international level in cooperation with other international agencies, in particular the United Nations. Throughout the period of the existence of the IUOTO, close ties had been established between the organization and the United Nations (UN), and initial suggestions were raised that the IUOTO became part of the UN.

It was by the recommendations of the UN that the new intergovernmental tourism organization was formed. In 1970, the IUOTO general assembly voted in favor of forming the World Tourism Organization (UNWTO). Based on statutes of the IUOTO and after ratifications by the prescribed 51 states, the UNWTO came into operation on November 1, 1974.

Most recently, at the fifteenth general assembly in 2003, the UNWTO general council and the UN agreed to establish the UNWTO as a specialized agency of the UN.

Structure

- General Assembly

The General Assembly is the principal gathering of the World Tourism Organization. Its members meet every two years to inspect the budget and programme of work and to discuss and debate topics of vital importance to the tourism sector. Every four years it elects a Secretary-General. The General Assembly is composed of full members and associate members. Affiliate members and representatives of other international organizations participate as observers. The World Committee on Tourism Ethics is a subsidiary organization of the General Assembly.

- Executive Council

The Executive Council is UNWTO's governing board, responsible for ensuring that the Organization carries out its work and adheres to its budget. It meets at least twice a year and is composed of 26 members elected by the General Assembly in a ratio of one for every five full members. As host country of UNWTO's headquarter, Spain has a permanent seat on the Executive Council. Representatives of the associate members and affiliate members participate in Executive Council meetings as observers.

- Regional Commissions

UNWTO has six regional commissions: Africa, the Americas, East Asia and the Pacific, Europe, the Middle East and South Asia. The commissions meet at least once a year and are composed of all the Full Members and Associate Members from that region. Affiliate Members from the region participate as observers.

- Committees

Specialized committees of UNWTO members advise on management and programme content. These include: the Programme Committee, the Budget and Finance Committee, the Statistics Steering Committee, the Environment Committee, and the Education Centers Network.

Chapter Three Elements of Tourism

- Secretariat

The Secretariat is led by Secretary-General, who supervises about 110 full-time staff at UNWTO's Madrid headquarter. These officials are responsible for implementing UNWTO's programme of work and serving the needs of members. The affiliate members are supported by a full-time Executive Director at the Madrid headquarter. The Secretariat also includes a regional support office for Asia-Pacific in Osaka, Japan, financed by the Japanese Government. The official languages of UNWTO are Arabic, English, French, Chinese, Russian and Spanish.

 New Words

sustainability	[sə'steɪnəbɪləti]	n. 持续性；永续性；能维持性
ethics	['eθɪks]	n. 伦理学；伦理观；道德标准
implementation	[ɪmplɪmen'teɪʃ(ə)n]	n. [计] 实现；履行；安装启用
millennium	[mɪ'lenɪəm]	n. 千年期，千禧年，一千年，千年纪念；黄金时代
instrument	['ɪnstrʊm(ə)nt]	n. 仪器；工具；乐器；手段；器械
foster	['fɒstə]	v. 培养；养育，抚育；抱（希望等） adj. 收养的，养育的
affiliate	[ə'fɪlɪeɪt]	n. 联号；隶属的机构等 v. 使附属；接纳，使紧密联系；参加，加入；发生联系
religion	[rɪ'lɪdʒ(ə)n]	n. 宗教；宗教信仰
extract	['ɪk'strækt]	v. 提取；取出；摘录；榨取
	['ekstrækt]	n. 汁；摘录；榨出物；选粹
ratification	[rætəfə'keɪʃən]	n. 批准；承认，认可
debate	[dɪ'beɪt]	v. 辩论，争论，讨论 n. 辩论；辩论会
executive	[ɪg'zekjʊtɪv]	adj. 行政的；经营的；执行的，经营管理的 n. 总经理；执行委员会；执行者；经理主管人员
programme	['prəʊgræm]	n. 计划，规划；节目；程序 v. 编程序；制作节目；规划；拟……计划

 Phrases and Expressions

be responsible for	为……负责
be committed to doing Sth.	致力于做某事

contribute to	有助于，对……有贡献
stem back to	起源于；上溯到
be composed of	由……组成

Task I According to the passage, give a short answer to each of the following questions.

1. What is the aim of the World Tourism Organization?
2. How many members are there in UNWTO?
3. When was the UNWTO established as a special agency of the UN?
4. What is the structure of UNWTO?
5. Where is the headquarter of the World Tourism Organization?

Task II Fill in the blanks with the suitable words given below, changing the form where necessary.

contribute	maximize	be composed of	be responsible for
participate in	commit	extract	facilitate

1. It was known that the tour group _____ many famous scientists from Asia.
2. Three club members from each organization would _____ the annual meeting.
3. You are old enough so that you should _____ your words and actions.
4. His research _____ to our understanding of this disease.
5. It is the common aim for the managers _____ the profits with the same investment.
6. However, Chinese officials have said they _____ avoiding a new round of protectionism in the global economy.
7. The communication between different peoples _____ cultural exchange.
8. Citric acid can _____ from the juice of oranges, lemons, limes or grapefruit.

Task III Translate the sentences into Chinese.

1. The United Nations World Tourism Organization (UNWTO) is the United Nations agency responsible for the promotion of sustainable and universally accessible tourism.

2. The objectives of the UNWTO are to promote and develop sustainable tourism so as to contribute to economic development, international understanding, peace, prosperity and universal respect for, and observance of, human rights and fundamental freedoms for all, without distinction as to race, sex, language or religion.

3. It was by the recommendations of the UN that the new intergovernmental tourism organization was formed.

Chapter Three Elements of Tourism

4. The Executive Council is UNWTO's governing board, responsible for ensuring that the Organization carries out its work and adheres to its budget.

5. Representatives of the associate members and affiliate members participate in Executive Council meetings as observers.

Task IV Choose one word for each blank from a list of choices.

One summer night, on my way home from work, I decided to see a movie. I knew the theatre would be air-conditioned and I couldn't face my   1   apartment.

Sitting in the theatre I had to look through the opening between the two tall heads in front of me. I had to keep changing the angle every time she leaned over to talk to him,   2   he leaned over to kiss her. Why do Americans display such   3   in a public place?

I thought the movie would be good for my English, but   4   it turned out, it was an Italian movie. After about an hour I decided to give up on the movie and   5   on my popcorn (爆玉米花). I've never understood why they give you so much popcorn! It tasted pretty good, though. After a while I heard no more of the romantic-sounding Italians. I just heard the sound of the popcorn crunching (咀嚼) between my teeth. My thought started to   6 . I remembered when I was in the Republic of Korea, I used to watch Kojak on TV frequently. He spoke perfect Korean— I was really amazed. He seemed like a good friend to me,   7   I saw him again in New York speaking   8   English instead of perfect Korean. He didn't even have a Korean accent and I felt like I had been betrayed.

When our family moved to the United States six years ago, none of us spoke any English.   9   we had begun to learn a few words, my mother suggested that we all should speak English at home. Everyone agreed, but our house became very quiet and we all seemed to avoid each other. We sat at the dinner table in silence, preferring that to   10   in a difficult language. Mother tried to say something in English but it came out all wrong and we all burst into laughter and decided to forget it! We've been speaking Korean at home ever since.

1. A. warm   B. hot   C. heated   D. cool
2. A. while   B. whenever   C. or   D. and
3. A. attraction   B. attention   C. affection   D. motion
4. A. since   B. when   C. what   D. as
5. A. concentrate   B. chew   C. fix   D. taste

6. A. wonder B. wander C. imagine D. depart
7. A. until B. because C. then D. therefore
8. A. artificial B. informal C. perfect D. practical
9. A. While B. If C. Before D. Once
10. A. telling B. uttering C. saying D. speaking

Text B

Tourism in Future

The world is at the dawn of a second Golden Age of travel— an age of voyaging on a truly global mass scale. As the twenty-first century has already arrived, people of every class and from every country will be wandering to every corner of this planet. Even one wealthy American tourist has already fulfilled his long-cherished dream to travel into space.

In the first Golden Age of travel in the nineteenth century, the steamship and the railroad fostered the first rapid expansion of travel for a new purpose: leisure curiosity. Before then, most people customarily travelled for trade, on pilgrimage, as refugees or to make war. In the era of the Industrial Revolution, newly wealthy sight-seers armed with Baedeckers began roaming afield. The literature of the nineteenth century is rich with great travel writing, including *The Innocents Abroad*[1] by American Mark Twain[2], *The Banks of the Rhine* by Frances Alexandra Dumas[3] and *Travels of Old Can*[4] by Chinese Liu E.

While the breadth and scope of the twenty-first century travel promises to be different, it will also be an echo of the past. In many ways, the near future harks back to travel's first Golden Age in the nineteenth century. Three things enhance the similarity: the sweep of technological change, the tearing down of political barriers and the rapid decline in costs that have made the impulse to see the outside world a practical urge.

Thanks to all the things mentioned above, especially the new-tech— the computer and the Internet, travellers can do more of their own planning. The electronic miracle makes it possible for people to plan and even book their trips at home from travel companies, airlines, coach buses, tour trains, hotels and so on. Through electronic gadgetry of virtual reality, many users can even partly experience a journey before they really step out of their homes.

Golden Ages are times of prosperity and achievement, but they are also eras of renewed values. The impending travel boom is liable to be the same. The entire world, with a few minor exceptions, is now open to travellers, and is likely to remain so in the foreseeable future. Smaller as the world is becoming, venturing into it will continue to provide the human with the kind of excitement and exaltation that the American writer

Henry Adams[5] experienced when he first saw the cathedral at Chartre, or that the Indian poet Rabindranath Tagore[6] had when he visited the Taj Mahal[7]. What has changed is that the cultivation and enrichment of such experiences will be more available to more people than ever before.

Like other industries, the tourism industry, undoubtedly, has created and will create a great effect either positive or negative on the human society and cultures, and on the global environment. Hence, how to keep the balance between the industry and the sustainable development of the human society is still a problem we humans have to study and tackle. The solution to the problem, to be sure, requires our long-term joint efforts.

 New Words

voyage	['vɒɪɪdʒ]	n. 航行；航程；旅行记 v. 航行；航海；飞过；渡过
steamship	['stiːmʃɪp]	n. 轮船；汽船
pilgrim	['pɪlɡrɪm]	n. 朝圣者；漫游者；（美）最初的移民 v. 去朝圣；漫游
innocent	['ɪnəs(ə)nt]	adj. 无辜的；无罪的；无知的 n. 天真的人；笨蛋
echo	['ekəʊ]	v. 反射；重复；随声附和；发出回声 n. 回音；效仿
miracle	['mɪrək(ə)l]	n. 奇迹，奇迹般的人或物；惊人的事例
gadgetry	['ɡædʒɪtrɪ]	n. 小配件；小玩意；小机件

 Phrases and Expressions

at the dawn of	在……的黎明
leisure curiosity	休闲性好奇
hark back to	回到
an echo of the past	对过去的回应
the sweep of technological change	科技变革的影响
renewed values	重新审视的价值观

 Notes

[1] *The Innocent Abroad*

《傻子出国记》是马克·吐温的旅欧报道。写的是天真无知的美国人在欧洲的旅游见闻，滑稽、诙谐，表现出美国人在欧洲封建社会及其印记面前的优越感。

[2] Mark Twain

马克·吐温，美国著名作家和演说家，一生写了大量作品，题材涉及小说、剧本、散文、诗歌等各方面，被誉为"美国文学史上的林肯"。1910年4月21日去世，享年75岁，安葬于纽约州艾玛拉。

[3] Alexandra Dumas

大仲马，法国19世纪浪漫主义作家，代表作有《亨利三世及其宫廷》（剧本）《基督山伯爵》（长篇小说）《三个火枪手》（长篇小说）等，大仲马小说大都以真实的历史作为背景，情节曲折生动，往往出人意料，有历史惊险小说之称。结构清晰明朗，语言生动有力，对话灵活机智等构成了大仲马小说的特色。大仲马也因而被后人美誉为"通俗小说之王"。

[4] *Travels of Old Can*

《老残游记》，清末中篇小说，是刘鹗（1857年10月18日—1909年8月23日）的代表作，小说以一位郎中老残的游历为主线，对社会矛盾开掘很深，尤其是他在书中敢于直斥清官（清官中的酷吏）误国，清官害民，独具慧眼地指出清官的昏庸常常比贪官更甚。同时，小说在民族传统文化精华提炼、生活哲学及艺术、女性审美、人物心理及景物描写等多方面皆达到了极其高超的境界。

[5] Henry Adams

亨利·亚当斯，美国历史学家、小说家。出生于马萨诸塞州的波士顿，1858年毕业于哈佛大学，曾任美国历史学会主席。他是亚当斯家族的成员，查尔斯·弗朗西斯·亚当斯的儿子，约翰·昆西·亚当斯的孙子。

[6] Rabindranath Tagore

拉宾德拉纳特·泰戈尔（1861—1941），印度著名诗人、文学家、社会活动家、哲学家和印度民族主义者。1913年，他以《吉檀迦利》成为第一位获得诺贝尔文学奖的亚洲人。他的诗中含有深刻的宗教和哲学的见解，泰戈尔的诗在印度享有史诗的地位，代表作《吉檀迦利》《飞鸟集》《眼中沙》《四个人》《家庭与世界》《园丁集》《新月集》《最后的诗篇》《戈拉》《文明的危机》等。

[7] Taj Mahal

泰姬陵是印度知名度最高的古迹之一，世界文化遗产，被评选为"世界新七大奇迹"。泰姬陵全称"泰姬·玛哈尔陵"，是一座白色大理石建成的巨大陵墓清真寺，是莫卧儿皇帝沙贾汗为纪念他心爱的妃子于1631年至1648年在阿格拉而建的。位于今印度距新德里200多公里外的北方邦的阿格拉（Agra）城内，亚穆纳河右侧。由殿堂、钟楼、尖塔、水池等构成，全部用纯白色大理石建筑，用玻璃、玛瑙镶嵌，具有极高的艺术价值。

Task I After reading the passage, answer the following questions.

1. Is there anyone who has been to space as a traveller?

Chapter Three Elements of Tourism

2. What is the new purpose of the first Golden Age of travel?
3. What novel did Mark Twain write related to travelling?
4. What is the influence of new-tech—the computer and the Internet?
5. What is the author's attitude towards the tourism industry?

Task II Read the passage above and decide whether the following statements are true (T) or false (F).

(   ) 1. The electronic miracle makes it impossible for people to plan and even book their trips at home from travel companies, airlines, coach buses, tour trains, hotels and so on.
(   ) 2. Before the nineteenth century, many people travelled for leisure curiosity.
(   ) 3. The first Golden Age of Travel has come into being.
(   ) 4. There are travel writings in the literature of the nineteenth century.
(   ) 5. *The Banks of the Rhine* is written by Rabindranath Tagore.

Task III According to the passage, fill in the blanks with the proper forms of the words.

In _____ of travel in the nineteenth century, the steamship and the railroad fostered the first rapid expansion of travel for a new purpose: _____. Before then, most people customarily travelled for trade, on _____, as refugees or to make war. In the era of _____, newly wealthy sight-seers armed with Baedeckers began roaming afield. The literature of the nineteenth century is rich with _____, including *The Innocents Abroad* by American Mark Twain, *The Banks of the Rhine* by Frances Alexandra Dum as and *Travels of Old Can* by Chinese Liu E.

While the breadth and scope of the twenty-first century travel promises to be different, it will also be _____. In many ways, the near future _____ travel's first Golden Age in the nineteenth century. Three things enhance the similarity: _____; the tearing down of political barriers and _____ that have made _____ to see the outside world a practical urge.

······ Part IV   Practical Writing ······

Itinerary
行程安排

Travel itineraries help keep all of your important travel arrangement information in one place for easy reference. Kept in the front of a folder full of all your brochures,

173

tickets and confirmation receipts, an itinerary gives you an easier way to find information when you are on the road than digging through all those oddly shaped papers. Whether you are writing an itinerary for yourself or for your job, the basic information you should include is the same.

Title the itinerary with the trip dates and primary destination or trip purpose. If you are preparing multiple itineraries for different people, place the name of the person for whom you are preparing the itinerary at the top of the page as well.

Detail the first flight or leg of travel with the departing location and time, arrival location and time, flight or train number and the airline or carrier. List any seat and gate information available and what time the traveller needs to be checked in by. List the reservation confirmation number and a customer service phone number in case there are any difficulties along the way.

Provide details on the second leg of travel if there is one before the first destination. If there is a connecting flight, note how much time the traveller will have to get from one flight to another so that if the first leg of travel is delayed he can make arrangements for the connection.

Include meeting and appointment information next. All meetings and travel arrangements should be listed in chronological order so the traveller can look through his itinerary and see exactly what is next based on where he has been. For meetings, list the name of the destination, the name and phone number of a contact person there, the time of the meeting and expected duration. Attach driving directions if the traveller will be driving himself to appointments.

List vehicle rental or taxicab company information at the bottom of the itinerary. If the trip will be in multiple cities or involve multiple rentals, list them at the bottom of the day they apply to. Include the name and phone number of the rental company, the type of car reserved and reservation confirmation number. Also list the pick-up day and time and the return date and time.

Detail hotel accommodations at the end of each day they apply to if there is more than one reservation or destination. Include the hotel name, address and phone number and the reservation confirmation number. Always include the check-in date and time and the check-out date and time, as well as the number of nights the reservation is for. If the traveller will be driving himself to the hotel, include driving directions from the airport or the last meeting or appointment of the day, depending on the timing.

Provide return flight or rail information last in the chronological list but before any car rental or hotel information if it is not listed chronologically. Provide all of the same information for return travel as you did for the departing flights.

Chapter Three　Elements of Tourism

Sample Ⅰ

Trip Itinerary

Day	Date	City	Touring Spots	Accommodation	Transportation
1	2015/06/15 (Mon)	London	Tower Bridge, House of Parliament and Big Ben, Buckingham Palace	PubLove @ The Crown, Battersea	Flight BA038 Beijing—London 11:15—15:10
2	2015/06/16 (Tue)	London	Hyde Park, Regent's Park, British Museum, Bond Street, The Ritz London	PubLove @ The Crown, Battersea	
3	2015/06/17 (Wed)	London	Pulteney Bridge & Pulteney Weir, Bath Abbey, Roman Baths, Sally Lunn's, Jane Austen Centre, Royal Crescent	PubLove @ The Crown, Battersea	
4	2015/06/18 (Thu)	London	Hertford Bridge, Bodleian Library, Trinity College, University of Oxford	PubLove @ The Crown, Battersea	Train London—Bath 08:30—09:59 Train Bath—London 20:13—22:08
5	2015/06/19 (Fri)		King's College, Trinity College, St John's College & Bridge of Sighs, River Granta, Corpus Clock, Mathematical Bridge	PubLove @ The Crown, Battersea	Train GW082900 London—Oxford 10:28—12:23 Train GW147200 Oxford—London 16:05—17:55
6	2015/06/20 (Sat)	Beijing			Flight BA039 London—Beijing 16:30—09:30

Sample Ⅱ

A 3-Day Tour Program in Kunming for CWNU

Day 1　Kunming (1894 meters) Arrival

Fri　　Arrival in Kunming (your own ticket). Meet your guide at airport and transfer to hotel

         The capital of Yunnan Province, Kunming is...
         Rest of the day at leisure
         Lunch and dinner at leisure
         Overnight at four star hotel
Day 2   Kunming
Sat   Buffet breakfast at hotel
         Drive along the new express way to the Stone Forest. The Stone Forest is 7 kilometers from KM and is accessible by a bus ride of 70 mins. The Stone Forest belongs to the typical karst geomorphology, it consists of...
         Visit the Flower and Bird Market...
         Lunch at local restaurant, dinner at leisure
         Overnight at four star hotel
Day 3   Kunming Departure
Sun   Buffet breakfast at hotel
         Transfer to airport for morning departure flight
         The end of the tour

Task   Write a trip itinerary for 6-day Beijing package tour.

Part V   Typical Scenic Spot

Macau

Macau is located on the southeastern coast of China, to which approximately 60 kilometers northeast is Hong Kong, an important centre for financial and trade. The city of Macau includes peninsula, Taipa island and Coloane. The territory has a total area of 32.8 square kilometers. China resumed sovereignty over Macau on December 20, 1999 and the territory has become a Special Administrative Region.

Climate

The climate is moderate to hot, with an average annual temperature of just over 20°C (68°F) and a yearly mean variation between 16°C (50°F) and 25°C (77°F). The humidity is high, which means the rainfall is abundant, with the yearly total about 1,778 millimeters. The best travelling season is autumn (October—December) when days are sunny and warm and the humidity is low. The winter (January—March) is cold but sunny. In April, the temperature starts to build up and from May to September the climate is hot and humid with rain and occasional tropical storms (typhoons).

Chapter Three Elements of Tourism

Population

The total population is estimated at approximately 455,000 with about 95% of Chinese and 5% Portuguese, Europeans and those from other regions.

Language

Chinese and Potuguese are the two official languages, with Cantonese the most widely spoken. English is Macau's third language and is generally used in trade, tourism and commerce.

Religion

There is complete freedom of worship in Macau. The main religions are Buddhism, Catholicism and Protestantism. The majorities are Buddhists while 7% are Catholics.

History

The Portuguese settled in Macau between 1554 and 1557 during the great era of Portuguese exploration initiated by Prince Henry the Navigator. Vasco da Gama made his historic voyage to India at the end of the 15th century, and in the early 16th century the Portuguese explorers moved further east and then turned north.

Jorge Alvares became the first Portuguese to set foot in Southern China in 1513 and this visit was followed by the establishment of a number of Portuguese trading centers in the area. These were eventually consolidated at Macau which boomed with a virtual monopoly on trade between China and Japan and between the two nations and Europe.

Macau also served as a vital base for the introduction of Christianity to China and Japan, an activity which provided the city with some of the most glorious, and tempestuous, moments in its history. Because of the prosperity it was enjoying and its privileged location, other European nations began casting covetous looks at Macau and plotted to seize it from Portugal. The Dutch actually tried to invade the city in 1622 but were repulsed. As time passed and other trading nations from the west sent missions to China, Macau became the summer residence for the taipans (great traders) who retreated from their "factories" in Guangzhou (better known perhaps as Canton) to await the opening of the trading season.

Hong Kong's deep-water attracted ships and trade. The economic importance of Macau declined as Hong Kong developed into one of the world's major commercial centres. Nevertheless, Macau is still regarded as an important distribution outlet for rice, fish, piece goods and other Chinese products and enjoys an active manufacturing and exporting business, mainly of textiles and garments, toys, electronics and footwear.

The Name of Macau

Macau was previously known to the Chinese as a small fishing village. The name is derived from the name of a Chinese goddess, popular with seafarers and fishermen, known as A-Ma or Ling Ma.

According to legend, a junk sailing across the South China Sea one clear day found itself in a sudden storm. Everybody on board was about to give up all hope of surviving this natural calamity, when an attractive young woman, who had boarded the ship at the very last minute, stood up and ordered the elements to calm down. Miraculously, the gale winds stopped blowing and the sea became calm. Without further incident, the junk arrived safely at the port of Hoi Keang. The young woman stepped ashore and walked to the crest of the nearby Barra Hill where, in a glowing halo of light and perfume, she ascended into heaven. On the particular spot where she set foot on land, a temple was built in homage to her. Centuries later, when Portuguese sailors landed and asked the name of the place, the natives thought they were asking for the name of temple, so replied "Ma-Gao". And so the Portuguese renamed it "Macau" according to its Chinese pronunciation.

职业素养

加大文物和文化遗产保护力度，加强历史文化保护传承；深挖民族、历史、红色、康养文化内涵，实施保护利用、研究发掘、价值提升；坚持以文塑旅，以旅彰文，推动文化和旅游深度融合发展；推动跨境旅游，推动文明传播与交流，促进各国人民相知相亲，尊重世界文明的多样性，建立一个开放包容的世界。

Unit 10 Shopping

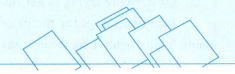

••••• Part I Warm-Up •••••

Shopping is an important part of tourist activities. Everyone loves a trip that includes a visit to a one-of-a-kind store or a unique boutique. Tourists may go shopping, especially when the tour is drawing to a close. Why not build your next vacation around the best part of the trip, and consider shopping travel as the best way to combine the fun of a vacation with the thrill of finding the perfect item to bring back home? We've already scouted out the best shopping locations for you, so take a look through our shopping destinations, and start putting your wish list together!

••••• Part II Conversations •••••

Conversation 1   The Flea Market

听一听

Todd: Hey, Melissa, we're talking about big events this week and what are some big events that you really enjoy?

Melissa: I like doing community events. I'm trying to get more involved in community events. There's a flea market this weekend.

Todd: A flea market?

Melissa: Yes.

Todd: Oh, yeah.

Melissa: At the beach side. And there's going to be lots of different eco-friendly stuff going on there, so it's kind of a mix of a reuse, resell your old stuff. Get new stuff for cheap.

Todd: OK. So for people who might not be familiar with the term flea market, can you explain?

Melissa: A flea market is basically a place where people can take old clothes, old utensils, forks, spoons, knives, things like that from the kitchen, and other house wares either sell them or give them away at a cheap price. And it's fun because the customers ... a lot of them like to come and look at all the different stuff and even maybe haggle some prices, so try to get you to give a lower price. Or if you're trying to get rid of a lot of stuff you might try to get the customer to take two things for the price of one. Things like that.

Todd: Yeah, right. Like when I was a kid I used to go to flea marts, or flea markets with my grandparents, and what I thought was great is that you can haggle.

Melissa: Yeah.

Todd: Right? Because in the U.S., you can't haggle at a store.

Melissa: Yeah, exactly. And I like haggling when I'm travelling. I try to get a good deal, so it's fun to do it at a flea market when you're selling your own stuff.

Todd: So, this weekend, are you selling or buying?

Melissa: Well, I actually don't have that much stuff to sell because I've recently moved so I've gotten rid of a lot of stuff I don't need. But I do plan bring some old pieces of clothing and things like that I want to get rid of. And yeah, I'm really into flea markets and old thrift stores and stuff like that, so I just like to see what people have. If there's something cool, I might buy it.

New Words

community	[kəˈmjuːnɪtɪ]	n. 社区；[生态] 群落；共同体；团体
flea	[fliː]	n. 跳蚤；低廉的旅馆；生蚤的动物
stuff	[stʌf]	n. 东西；材料；填充物；素材资料
		v. 塞满；填塞；让吃饱；吃得过多
utensil	[juːˈtens(ə)l]	n. 用具，器皿
haggle	[ˈhæg(ə)l]	n. 讨价还价；争论 v. 乱劈；乱砍；争论
thrift	[θrɪft]	n. 节俭；节约；[植] 海石竹

Phrases and Expressions

get involved in	卷入；参与；与……有密切关联；
be familiar with	熟悉；熟知
get rid of	扔掉；丢弃
used to do sth.	过去常常/过去曾做某事
be into sth.	对某事很感兴趣；极喜欢某事

Conversation 2   Shopping in New York

Mike: Hey, Mari, so you said New York was very diverse. What parts or neighborhoods

Chapter Three Elements of Tourism

do you like?

Mari: I really like Soho because there's lots of great shopping to do. There are really small shops and really cute restaurants and cafes, and if I'm lucky sometimes when I'm walking around or eating I see my favourite movie stars. Recently before I moved back to Japan, I was shopping on Broadway and I saw Claire Danes with her boyfriend. It was pretty cool.

Mike: So, I always hear about Central Park. Can you tell me more about Central Park?

Mari: Yeah. Central Park is obviously in the middle of Manhattan. It's really big and people go and play sports or they just hang out and walk around. If you go there on the weekends, you see a lot of joggers because the roads are closed off, so there's no car. Cars are not allowed, and in the summer time you see a lot of roller-bladers and bikers.

Mike: How big is the park?

Mari: It's really big. It goes from, I think, 56th Street to 110th, so it's pretty large.

Mike: So, what other parts?

Mari: I went to grad school at Colombia so I lived right near Harlem and I actually really like Harlem because you get a very neighborhood feeling. You hear... You see people walking on the street talking to each other. You walk by the barbershop and you know that everyone knows each other. Everyone is interested in the other. They're gossiping about people in their neighborhood.

Mike: Is there any area you don't really like?

Mari: Because I am from New York City, I really don't like going to Times Square. I feel like it's very commercial and touristy, so I really don't like Times Square, but I guess for tourists it's very exciting. It's probably very exciting, the side street vendors, the musicians and all these things. It would be exciting for tourists, but I try to avoid it.

 New Words

neighborhood	[ˈneɪbə‚hʊd]	n. 附近；街坊；接近
jogger	[ˈdʒɒgə]	n. 慢跑者；[印刷] 撞纸机
barbershop	[ˈbɑːbəʃɒp]	n. 理发店 adj. 有男声合唱之和声的
gossip	[ˈgɒsɪp]	n. 小道传闻；随笔；爱说长道短的人
		v. 闲聊；传播流言蜚语

 Phrases and Expressions

in the middle of	中部；中央；中间
hang out	闲逛，逗留

close off	隔绝；封锁
each other	彼此；互相
be interested in	感兴趣的；有兴趣的；关心的

 Practical Patterns

1. I am sorry you are on the Cash Only Lane.
   我很抱歉你现在是在只收现金的结账道上。
2. We have a clearance sale today.
   我们今天清仓大拍卖。
3. Can you give me the invoice?
   能不能给我一张发票？
4. Where are your fitting rooms?
   试衣间在哪里？
5. Does this come in other colors?
   这有其他颜色吗？
6. Do you have this in other sizes?
   有其他型号吗？
7. Can I put this on hold?
   能否为我保留几天？
8. Charge or debit? /Credit or debit?
   使用信用卡或是电子钱包？
9. Cash back?
   是否要找回现金？
10. How are you going to pay?
    你要怎么付款？

Task I Complete the following dialogues by translating the Chinese in the brackets.

A: Hi, Mark! _____ （好久不见！）
B: Hi, Alex!
A: Where have you been?
B: _____. （我刚刚从伦敦回来。）
A: _____? （你的旅途如何？）
B: It was okay. There was a lot of turbulence, though.
A: That's too bad. How long was the flight?
B: It was 10 hours.
A: _____? （中途有停留吗？）

Chapter Three　Elements of Tourism

B: Yes, in Paris, France.
A: _____ ? (你在免税商店买东西了吗?)
B: Yes. I bought two boxes of chocolate — one for me and one for you!
A: Oh, you didn't have to...
B: It was nothing.

Task II　Make up a dialogue according to the following situation, and act them out in class.

Ann wants to buy some gifts for his friends when travelling, and Kate gives him some advice.

Part III　Readings

Text A

A Shopping Paradise—Hong Kong

Famed as a shopping paradise, Hong Kong is famous for its great variety of fashion accessories, local arts and crafts, tea, jade, and jewelry. Shopping in Hong Kong has many advantages such as low price, a seemingly endless variety, and high quality. Because most products in Hong Kong don't have a tariff, the prices are usually lower than products in other places. There are also fantastic seasonal promotions when the seasons change. Hong Kong has famous name brand boutiques, as well as wonderful things that cannot be found anywhere else in the world. For those on a more limited budget, there are plenty of wonderful shopping areas that are fun to wander around and pick up less expensive, but equally fabulous items. Hong Kong has many wonderful shopping districts that offer something for everyone. Shop till you drop in your Hong Kong tours!

Tsim Sha Tsui

One of the most famous shopping areas in Hong Kong, Tsim Sha Tsui (Figure 10-1) is often known as Ladies' Street. Originally selling items strictly for women, the street has evolved and now has something for everybody. It is a great place to get souvenirs. The street sells clothing and accessories, toys, paper cuts, and artwork. At the end of the street is the Harbor Mall (Figure 10-2) which deals in high end name brand items. The mall contains the shopping areas of three different hotels.

The Causeway Bay

A typical shopping mall, the Causeway Bay (Figure 10-3) in Hong Kong is filled with all kinds of luxurious shopping malls, such as SOGO, Seibu, Mitsukoshi, Sincere, and so on. Times Square is another shopping highlight. It is also full of famous name brand products.

Stanley Market near the Sea

During the Qing Dynasty, Stanley was only a small fishing harbor, but now it is filled with European flavor. It is an outdoor market which feels like an American or European flea market. Compared with the large-scale shopping mall, shopping in Stanley Market is much cozier. The sunset is the moment when this area really shows off its uniqueness. Visitors sitting in the restaurants and bars that face the sea can enjoy the beautiful sunsets over a glass of wine.

Hong Kong is filled with smaller specialized shopping streets. The Wanchai Taiyuan Street is a street that sells toys. Antique toys, toy collections, and the newest toys can all be found here. The Sai Yeung Choi Street (Figure 10-4) sells cameras and other electrical appliance. The Fa Yuen Street is a street that sells only sporting goods. The Seafood Street is where the freshest seafood can be found. Lascar Row is where antiques, both new and old can be purchased.

Hong Kong is truly a shopper's heaven. Very few visitors can make it out of the exciting city without picking up something to take home. Since Eastern and Western cultures are both an important parts of Hong Kong, its shopping areas offer a mix of unique items. There literally is something for everyone in Hong Kong.

Figure 10-1　Tsim Sha Tsui

Figure 10-2　The Habor Mall

Figure 10-3　Causeway Bay

Figure 10-4　Sai Yeung Choi

Chapter Three Elements of Tourism

 **New Words**

paradise	[ˈpærədaɪs]	n. 天堂，至福境地
accessory	[əkˈses(ə)ri]	n. 配件；附件；[法] 从犯 adj. 副的；同谋的；附属的
advantage	[ədˈvɑːntɪdʒ]	n. 优势；利益；有利条件 v. 有利于；使处于优势；获利
fabulous	[ˈfæbjʊləs]	adj. 难以置信的；寓言中的；极好的
evolve	[ɪˈvɒlv]	v. 发展，进展；进化；逐步形成
souvenir	[suːvəˈnɪə]	n. 纪念品；礼物 v. 把……留作纪念
dynasty	[ˈdɪnəsti]	n. 王朝，朝代

Phrases and Expressions

be famous for	因为……而出名
wander around	漫游，闲逛
be filled with	充满了
feel like doing sth.	想做（喜欢）做某事
flea market	跳蚤市场，专门卖旧货的市场

Task I According to the passage, give a short answer to each of the following questions.

1. Why are the prices of most products in Hong Kong cheaper?
2. Where can we get souvenirs in Hong Kong?
3. Which market is an outdoor market, Tsim Sha Tsui, the Causeway Bay or Stanley Market?
4. Where can we get cameras in Hong Kong?
5. How do you like Hong Kong shopping?

Task II Fill in the blanks with the suitable words given below, changing the form where necessary.

| paradise | tariff | be famous for | wander around |
| evolve | purchase | be filled with | feel like |

1. The famous writer Ba Jin wrote the prose *Birds'* _____.
2. We had to _____ the truth from a mass of confused evidence.
3. America wants to eliminate _____ on items such as electronics.
4. She really _____ having a talk with him about his study at school.

185

5. The coming year _____ hardships and challenges.
6. When the children left home, she used to _____ the house as if she'd lost something.
7. He _____ this stamp at an auction.
8. Later he _____ his anti-war activities.

Task III   Translate the sentences into Chinese.

1. Famed as a shopping paradise, Hong Kong is famous for its great variety of fashion accessories, local arts and crafts, tea, jade, and jewelry.
2. For those on a more limited budget, there are plenty of wonderful shopping areas that are fun to wander around and pick up less expensive, but equally fabulous items.
3. During the Qing Dynasty, Stanley was only a small fishing harbor, but now it is filled with European flavor.
4. The sunset is the moment when this area really shows off its uniqueness.
5. Visitors sitting in the restaurants and bars that face the sea can enjoy the beautiful sunset over a glass of wine.

Task IV   Choose one word for each blank from a list of choices.

   Wise buying is a positive way in which you can make your money go further. The __1__ you go about purchasing an article or a service can actually __2__ you money or can add to the cost.

   Take the __3__ example of a hairdryer. If you are buying a hairdryer, you might think that you are making the __4__ buy if you choose one __5__ look you like and which is also the cheapest. But when you get it home you may find that it __6__ twice as long as a more expensive model to dry your hair. The cost of the electricity plus the cost of your time could well __7__ your hairdryer the most expensive one of all.

   So what principles should you __8__ when you go out shopping?

   If you keep your home, your car or any valuable possession in excellent condition, you'll be saving money in the long run.

   Before you buy a new __9__, talk to someone who owns one. If you can, use it or borrow it to check if it suits your particular purpose.

   Before you buy an expensive item, or a service, do check the price and __10__ is on offer. If possible, choose from three items or three estimates.

1. A. form   B. fashion   C. way   D. method
2. A. save   B. preserve   C. raise   D. retain
3. A. easy   B. single   C. simple   D. similar

4. A. proper B. best C. reasonable D. most
5. A. its B. which C. whose D. what
6. A. spends B. takes C. lasts D. consumes
7. A. cause B. make C. leave D. prove
8. A. adopt B. lay C. stick D. adapt
9. A. appliance B. equipment C. utility D. facility
10. A. what B. which C. that D. this

Text B

Shopping in Shanghai

Shanghai is hailed as the "Shopping Paradise" and "Oriental Paris". So if you come to the city, shopping should not be missed any more than its other charming attractions. Providing the very best of shopping has become an indispensable part of the city's tourism industry.

To welcome more visitors, Shanghai has adopted tax refund policy since July 1st, 2015 for overseas tourists. At present, there are 27 tax free stores in the city, mainly situated at Nanjing Road (Figure 10-5) and around Yuyuan Garden (Figure 10-6).

Figure 10-5   Nanjing Road   Figure 10-6   Yuyuan

Shopping areas in the city are clearly divided into "Four Streets and Four Cities". Nanjing Road (including East Nanjing Road and West Nanjing Road), one of the four streets, enjoys the reputation of No. 1 Commercial Street in China. Developed from the beginning of the 20th century, Nanjing Road has clusters of a wide variety of shops, from those that are century's old, to special ones and modern malls. In these modern times, Nanjing Road is not out done by its numerous competitors but becomes more and more prosperous. Huaihai Road, no less famous than Nanjing Road, is celebrated for its elegance. It features top-end designer brands from all over the world. North Sichuan Road offers good inexpensive merchandise and is always the first choice of ordinary people. Food and tourism are well provided on Middle Tibet Road, one of the Four Streets.

Yuyuan Tourist Mart, Xujiahui Shopping City, New Shanghai Shopping City, and Jiali Sleepless City are the bustling "Four Cities". Yuyuan Tourist Mart is the venue for specialist Chinese goods ranging from small articles, local crafts and the like to antiques, jade wares and gold and silver jewelry. The newly-established shopping and entertainment plaza, Xujiahui consists of large stores where you can obtain both costly and middle-range priced goods in abundance. New Shanghai Shopping City is on the grand scale and offers the best facilities and amenities. Located in the middle of Pudong Lujiazui Finance and Trade Zone, it is surrounded by a variety of retail outlets. Like a bright pearl on the landscape, Jiali Sleepless City facing Shanghai Railway Station, and on the Subway line 1, is a bustling commercial area.

Besides the famous "Four Streets and Four Cities", some other streets and roads are worthy of a visit.

If you just intend to buy small articles and inexpensive clothes, Hong Kong Famous Shops Street and Dimei Shopping Center beneath People's Square and Xiangyang Road will whet your appetite. In Dimei Shopping Center, clothes are competitively priced and fashionable, but you will seldom find the top brands here. With the alternation of four seasons, the small shops here sell clothes in vogue which cater for the needs of young people. You can bargain at ease.

The distinguishing feature in North Shanxi Road is its shoes. Not only abundant varieties and original styles, the prices are reasonable and moderate. If you admire Chinese-style clothes, some shops selling them on Maoming Road, Changle Road will meet your requirements. Generally clothes will be tailored to ensure a good fit.

More and more people realize the joy of having clothes tailor-made. To find the fabric, there is fabric market and tailor shops recommended here. Nan Wai Tan (South Bund) Fabric Market in Lujiabang Road is perhaps the largest fabric market you can find in the city. Take subway to Nanpu Bridge Station and walk along Lujiabang Road for a short while, you can see the market. To have anything tailor-made, get to the shop nearly one month in advance. Several fittings will undergo for it may not fit you very well at the first time. Near the fabric market, there are many tailor shops in Duojia Road. You can find various fabric materials to make curtains as well. Maoming Road and Changle Road also have some feature tailor shops.

Fuzhou Road earned its fame as "Culture Street" a century ago. The outlets here deal mainly cultural items, ranging from books, music and art… It is now the fashion for local people to wander along Fuzhou Road after work to browse through all sorts of books and magazines in the stores along the road.

Chapter Three Elements of Tourism

Dongtai Road Antique Market is a market mainly dealing with the porcelains, jade wares, bronze wares, wooden wares, calligraphy and paintings and embroidery utensils. Lots of visitors from home and aboard come to this famous market.

Of course, local food specialties should be taken into account. Houyin Fish (Noodle Fish), originated in Qingpu and Chongming counties, is scrumptious and delicious. Canned Anchovy, one of the specialties of Shanghai, is fried and exported overseas and is highly praised. Other local specialties like Pudong Chicken, Juicy Peach, Juicy Pear and so on will make your mouth water.

Local products, like Gu Embroidery (Figure 10-7), also called Luxiang Yuan Embroidery, from the Ming Dynasty (1368—1644), is now used in producing clothes, ornaments and bedding. Tapestry is divided into two types, for appreciation and daily use. It is popular among visitors because of various colors, vivid figures and visual design. A scroll of tapestry depicting the Great Wall of China is exhibited in the United Nations building. Jade sculpture, wood sculpture, and stone sculpture feature Shanghai's tourism industry with its exquisite and delicate carvings. The city was one of the original producers and exporters of Chinese silk, and silk produced here remains unique owing to its age old traditions as well as new means of production and design.

For everyday requirements, supermarkets offer a wide range of goods. You will find Carrefour, Metro, RT Mart, Hypermarkets & Shopping malls, Lotus and Hualian, etc. Most of them are located near the transportation hubs and residential areas. Furthermore, up to 100 supermarket chains and 24-hour-open Lawson Convenience Store are established for your convenience.

Figure 10-7
Gu Embroidery

New Words

indispensable	[ɪndɪˈspensəb(ə)l]	adj. 不可缺少的；绝对必要的；责无旁贷的 n. 不可缺少之物；必不可少的人
refund	[rɪˈfʌnd]	v. 退还；偿还，归还 n. 退款；偿还，偿还额
reputation	[repjʊˈteɪʃ(ə)n]	n. 名声，名誉；声望
elegance	[ˈelɪɡ(ə)ns]	n. 典雅；高雅
merchandise	[ˈmɜːtʃ(ə)ndaɪs; -z]	n. 商品；货物 v. 买卖；推销；经商
bustling	[ˈbʌslɪŋ]	adj. 熙熙攘攘的；忙乱的

plaza	[ˈplɑːzə]		n. 广场；市场，购物中心
whet	[wet]		vt. 刺激；磨快；促进
			n. 磨；开胃物；刺激物
appetite	[ˈæpɪtaɪt]		n. 食欲；嗜好
vogue	[vəʊg]		n. 时尚；流行，时髦 adj. 时髦的，流行的
fabric	[ˈfæbrɪk]		n. 织物；布；组织；构造；建筑物
undergo	[ˌʌndəˈgəʊ]		v. 经历，经受；忍受
outlet	[ˈaʊtˌlet]		n. 出路；销售点；排水口；批发商点
anchovy	[ˈæntʃəvɪ; ænˈtʃəʊvɪ]		n. 凤尾鱼；鳀鱼
embroidery	[ɪmˈbrɔɪd(ə)rɪ; em-]		n. 刺绣；刺绣品；粉饰
tapestry	[ˈtæpɪstrɪ]		n. 织锦；挂毯；绣帷 vt. 用挂毯装饰
sculpture	[ˈskʌlptʃə]		n. & v. 雕塑；雕刻；刻蚀

Phrases and Expressions

be divided into 把……分成
at present 当时，目前
in abundance 大量的，丰富充足的
on the grand scale 大规模
as well as 也

Task I After reading the passage, answer the following questions.

1. Which street is the most prosperous commercial street in China?
2. Can we buy traditional Chinese goods in New Shanghai shopping city?
3. Should we take the Subway Line 1 in order to get Jiali Sleepless City?
4. How can we get Dongtai Road antique Market?
5. Which local product can be dated back to the Ming Dynasty?

Task II Read the passage above and decide whether the following statements are true (T) or false (F).

(   ) 1. This passage mainly talks about shopping paradise in Hong kong.
(   ) 2. Shanghai has adopted tax policy since July 1st, 2015.
(   ) 3. Yang Yang is good at making Chinese traditional clothes.
(   ) 4. The distinguishing feature in North Shanxi Road is its shoes.
(   ) 5. The outlets in Fuzhou Road deal mainly cultural items.

Chapter Three Elements of Tourism

Task III   According to the passage, fill in the blanks with the proper forms of the words.

To welcome more visitors, Shanghai has adopted _____ since July 1st, 2015 among tourists from foreign countries, Hong Kong, Macau, and Taiwan. At present, there are 27 tax free stores in the city, mainly _____ at Nanjing Road and around Yuyuan Garden.

_____ in the city are clearly divided into "Four Streets and Four Cities". Nanjing Road (including East Nanjing Road and West Nanjing Road), one of the four streets, enjoys the reputation of _____ in China. Developed from the beginning of the 20th century, Nanjing Road has clusters of _____ shops, from those that are centuries old, to special ones and modern malls. In these modern times, Nanjing Road is not out done by its _____ but becomes more and more _____. Huaihai Road, no less famous than Nanjing Road, is _____ its elegance. It features top-end designer brands from all over the world. North Sichuan Road offers good _____ and is always the first choice of ordinary people. Food and tourism are well provided for on _____, one of the Four Streets.

Part IV   Practical Writing

Farewell Speech 告别辞

Tips for a Farewell Speech:

1. Show reluctance to say goodbye.
2. Look back at the sightseeing activities, extend your thanks to their understanding.
3. Ask for advice and suggestions on your service so as to improve your future work.
4. Treasure the cordial friendship with them and hope to meet them again in the future.
5. Wish tourists a pleasant journey back home or a good trip to the next stop they are to visit.

Sample

A Farewell Speech by the Local Guide

Respected Dr. Mills, leader of People-to-People Forensic Science delegation and Mrs. Mills.

Respected Mr. Lucas, leader of the delegation and Mrs. Lucas.

Ladies and gentlemen,

Time goes so quickly and your trip to China is drawing to a close. Tomorrow morning our friends will be leaving Guangzhou for Hong Kong by train. Before we part,

I would like to say a few words. Entrusted by the Ministry of Public Security, Miss Chao and I took on the responsibility of doing logistics on behalf of the China Civil International Tourist Corporation during your stay in China. Your duration of stay in this country was only two and half weeks. You visited Beijing, which is the capital of the People's Republic of China. Then the delegation was divided into two teams. Dr. Mill's team went to Shenyang and Guilin and Mr. Lucas' team toured Shanghai and Hangzhou. Shanghai and Shenyang are industrious cities, while Guilin and Hangzhou are scenic spots. In China people usually say: up above there is paradise, down below there are Suzhou and Hangzhou. Guilin claims to be second to none in scenery. (Guilin scenes are the finest under heaven.) In 1985, English newspaper *China Tourism news* sponsored a poll for the Chinese people to select the ten most popular scenic spots in China. The West Lake of Hangzhou, and mountains and waters of Guilin were on the top of the ten. Finally, the two teams came to Guangzhou by air in different directions. While the delegation members were in China, they exchanged the technical information with the Chinese professional counterparts about forensic sciences, visited several criminal science and technology research institutes, the China Criminal Police College, a jail and hospital.

The accompanying persons toured some unique place. Examples of these were a township, an arts and crafts factory, a kindergarten, jade factory, and carpet factory. The whole delegation also toured the grounds of some famous historical spots in China. They had several banquets and tasted the different varieties of Chinese food in different places. It is our belief that everything was covered, and your trip to this country was worth "all the tea in China." You were in good hands and good company. During your stay in China, the delegation members have been very co-operative, friendly, and understanding. We appreciated that very much. This is because that friendship does not go one way, it goes both ways. Friendship always benefits.

When you lead a delegation of 65 people with the assistance of our American and Canadian friends, it is easy. As the Chinese saying goes, "Nothing is more delightful than to meet friend from far away." A visit by friends from afar brings special joy. We tend to do well those things we do often.

Once your former President Abraham Lincoln said, "You can please some of the people all of the time, some of the other people some of the time, but you cannot please all of the people all of the time."

However, this is the beginning of our friendship. We believe that this friendship will continue to grow in the future.

Parting is such sweet sorrow. Happy to meet, sorry to depart and happy to meet again.

Upon your getting back to the US and Canada, would you please send our best regards to your family members, your relative, your friends, and your colleagues.

Make new friend,

But keep the old;

One is silver,

And the other is gold.

Now I propose a toast:

To the friendship among the peoples of China, the US and Canada,

To the successful visit of the delegation to China,

To your excellent co-operation and assistance during your stay in China,

To the health of Dr. Mills, leader of the delegation and Mrs. Mills,

To the health of Mr. Lucas, leader of the delegation and Mrs. Lucas,

To the health of all the delegation members, cheers!

Task I   Discuss the meanings of the following sentences with partners, which is widely used in a farewell speech.

1. Time goes so quickly and your trip to China is drawing to a close.
2. Up above there is paradise, down below there are Suzhou and Hangzhou.
3. Guilin scenes are the finest under heaven.
4. Nothing is more delightful than to meet friend from far away.
5. You can please some of the people all of the time, some of the other people some of the time, but you cannot please all of the people all of the time."

Task II   Make a farewell speech to the tourists on behalf of China International Travel Service. Remember the tips when you make a farewell speech.

Part V   Typical Scenic Spot

Sun Moon Lake

Sun Moon Lake (Figure 10-8) is the largest body of water in Taiwan China as well as a tourist attraction. Located in Yuchi Township, Nantou County, the area around the Sun Moon Lake is home to the Shao tribe. Sun Moon Lake surrounds a tiny island called Lalu. The east side of the lake resembles a sun while the west side resembles a moon, hence the name.

Sun Moon Lake is 748 meters above sea level. It is 27 meters deep and has a surface area of approximately 7.93 square kilometers. The area surrounding the lake has many trails for hiking.

While swimming in Sun Moon Lake is usually not permitted, there is an annual 3km race called the Swimming Carnival of Sun Moon Lake held around the Mid-Autumn Festival each year. In recent years the participants have numbered in the tens of thousands. Other festivities held at the same time include fireworks, laser shows, and concerts.

In the middle of the lake (between the "sun" and the "moon") is an island which has long been a sacred place for the Shao people. This island (Lalu) (Figure 10-9) is off-limits to visitors. Only the Shao people can go there to worship their ancestors. But the beauty of Sun Moon Lake is not Lalu. The beauty of Sun Moon Lake is found in the surrounding mountains. The lake and its surrounding countryside have been designated one of thirteen scenic areas in Taiwan. Wen Wu Temple (Figure 10-10) was built after the water level rose because of the building of a dam, which forced several smaller temples to be removed. Ci En Pagoda (Figure 10-11) was built by Chiang Kai-shek in 1971 in memory of his mother. Other temples of note include Jianjing Temple, Xuanzang Temple (Figure 10-12) and Xuanguang Temple.

The lake has not always looked the way it does now. At one time, Lalu (Zhuyu) was a much larger island, a pearl separating the "Sun Lake" from the "Moon Lake". But in the construction of a hydroelectric power plant, the Japanese in 1934 deepened the lake by directing water from the adjacent lakes at Puli and Yuchih. The depth changed from 6 meters to 27 meters. The surface area of the lake changed from 4.55 square kilometers to 7.73 square kilometers. The Shao people were moved from their beloved Lalu to the upper Sun Moon Village.

In older English literature, the lake was commonly referred to as Lake Candidius after the 17th century Dutch missionary Georgius Candidius. In legend, Shao hunters discovered Sun Moon Lake while chasing a white deer through the surrounding mountains. The deer eventually led them to the lake, which they found to be not only beautiful, but abundant with fish. Today, the white deer of legends is immortalized as a marble statue on Lalu Island.

After Chiang Kai-shek's Nationalist Government moved to Taiwan, the island was renamed Kuang Hua ("Glorious China") and in 1978 the local government built a pavilion where annual weddings took place. In 1999, the 9·21 earthquake destroyed the pavilion and sunk most of the island. As a result, after the 9·21 earthquake, the island was renamed in the Shao language as "Lalu".

Chapter Three   Elements of Tourism

Figure 10-8   Sun Moon Lake

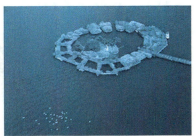

Figure 10-9   Lalu

Figure 10-10   Wen Wu Temple

Figure 10-11   Ci En Pagoda

Figure 10-12   Xuanzang Temple

职业素养

党的二十大报告明确提出,"两岸同胞血脉相连,是血浓于水的一家人"。两岸同胞应携手合作,推动两岸共同弘扬中华文化,推动中华文化走向世界,不断提高文化自信和民族自信。同时我们继续致力于促进两岸经济文化交流合作,深化两岸各领域融合发展,热忱欢迎台湾同胞来大陆旅游观光,游览大好河山,看看各地发展新貌,鼓励两岸人民互动交流,促进两岸同胞的心灵契合,实现祖国完全统一。

Appendix A

参考译文

第一章　旅游准备

第一单元　办理护照

 Part II　对话

 对话 1　申请护照

A：我想到美国旅游一段时间。
B：如果你想去国外，必须要有护照。
A：哦，我忘了这点了。
B：那你必须要推迟旅游了，因为申请护照一般需要 10 天的时间。
A：好吧。你能为我解释一下怎样拿到护照吗？
B：好的。你应该准备好户口簿和身份证，然后到出入境管理局办理。
A：很倒霉，我两天前把身份证给弄丢了。
B：不用担心，你可以携带临时身份证去申请护照。
A：谢谢。

（10 天后）

A：好消息！我拿到护照了。
B：祝贺你！
A：这是我第一次申请护照。没有你的帮忙，我恐怕不会申请成功。
B：我很乐意这么做。顺便问一下，你的护照有效期是多久啊？
A：一个月。

 对话 2　海关检查

A：请给我看看您的护照可以吗？
B：这是非居民通道吧？
A：是的，本国居民通道在我右侧。
B：好的，这是我的护照。

A：您护照的有效期是到什么时候？
B：我想好像快到了，可能还有几个月。我在北京续签过，所以最新的有效期在最后一页上。
A：我知道了。没错，您需要在最近几个月内申请办理护照延期。保证您在英国期间护照不会过期。
B：我不会让它过期的。
A：您有什么东西需要向海关申报吗？
B：没有，我没有什么要申报。
A：您打算在英国停留多久？
B：大概一年。
A：请问您来英国的目的是什么？
B：我是来上学的，我在诺丁汉大学读MBA。
A：您会住在什么地方？
B：我已经和学校签了住宿合同，就住在学校的学生公寓里。
A：请问您在读期间的住宿费和学费靠什么支付？
B：我父亲已经提前付过了，这里有缴费收据。
A：好的，祝您过得愉快。还给您护照和其他证件。
B：非常感谢！

PART III 阅读

 Text A

计划出行

你的下一个假期打算在美国哪里度过呢？或许你并不想留在美国度假了，但也不想漂洋过海。或者你想去亚洲、非洲或者欧洲，不管是国内还是国外，可选择的目的地有很多。

加利福尼亚州有很多值得一去的地方。或许你喜欢去科罗拉多州滑雪。去南部或者东北部看看历史遗迹怎么样？你是否考虑过去阿拉斯加？你可以参观很多不同的景点，每个景点都会给你带来不同的感受。在美国，你会看到很多影响了整个国家的景点。

如果你去美国中部或者南部，那么你就可以看到你可能还觉得荒芜的地方已经充满了生机勃勃的文化氛围。你可以看到一些与南非极其相似的东西，但是却有着完全不同的文化和荒芜。或者北非的喧嚣城市，有时也叫作中东，会更对你的胃口。在亚洲的某些地区有古老文化和尖端科技的完美融合，你是不是喜欢呢？当然你还可以选择欧洲，那里有世界上最受欢迎的景区。

每个地区都会给你带来不同的视角，同一地区又会有细微的不同。如果你仅仅是要寻找一个人口密度小、居民少的地方，你可以选择澳大利亚、亚洲、加拿大、南美、南非、北欧和俄罗斯的某些地方。

如果你想选择闹市，那么你在任何地方都有很多选择。值得推荐的地方也很多：罗马、巴黎、巴西亚马逊、安第斯的雪峰、伦敦、北爱尔兰、香港、马尼拉、澳大利亚内陆地区，你可以自由选择。可以说，大多数人都已经对自己的目的地有了主意，但是如果你还没有想好，仔细看看身边的各种资料，有成千上万的好去处供你选择。

Text B

海关检查

根据美国游客（非居民）海关条例，来美国的外国人可以免费携带以下物品：

1）私人物品——个人使用的物品，非卖品。包括服装、首饰、电器和体育用品。

2）家庭用品——家具、地毯和工作设备。但是这些物品仅限于个人使用，禁止买卖。

3）礼物——进入美国，你可以携带价值100美元的礼物，但是你必须在美国境内至少停留72小时。另外，在过去的6个月内你没有带相同的礼物入境。

4）烟酒——成年人可以携带0.95公升酒水，300支烟和1.35千克的烟草。

到达美国之后，海关官员会检查你的相关证件。你必须填写海关申报表，并出示你的接收证明和护照。拿到行李之后，你需要提交海关申报表和行李检查单。

海关检查员会检查每个人境者的行李。所有从境外带入的物品都必须经过申报——也就是说，它们必须经过批准才能入境，物品的价值必须上报给检查官。如果有人没有申报物品或者低报了该物品的价值，海关会没收物品并对个人进行相应的罚款。在美国，价值400美金以内的物品是免税的，但是这些物品必须符合一定的要求。例如：物品必须是供个人使用的，而且所有者必须在美国境内至少停留48小时。

到达目的地之后，你要想办法进入市区。通常情况下，机场距离市中心很远，所以你可以选择乘坐每隔半个小时发一次的机场大巴。从机场乘坐大巴非常便利，但是大巴并不能将你直接送到你的目的地。

PART V 典型景点

故宫

故宫也称紫禁城，位于北京市中心，500年中曾居住过24个皇帝，是明清两代的皇宫。故宫占地面积72万平方米，共有800多座建筑，9999间房屋，是明清时代无与伦比的杰作，是中华民族文明的结晶。它是中国最大、最完整的宫殿群，是中国文化遗产宝库。

过去的紫禁城，普通百姓是不能进入的，即使是朝中高官也不得无故入内。故宫是世界建筑史上的奇迹之一。它于1420年完工，耗时14年。故宫的前半部分叫外廷，包括太和殿、中和殿、保和殿三大殿及其两边的建筑。外廷是皇帝处理国家事务及举行重大庆典活动的地方。内廷由三个主要宫殿和东六宫、西六宫组成，内廷是皇帝处理日常事务及皇室家族居住的地方。最后一个王朝于1911年灭亡，但末代皇帝溥仪仍住在宫内。1925年，故宫改为博物馆，向公众开放。

1987年，故宫被联合国教科文组织列为世界文化遗产。

参观乘车路线

1路、2路、4路、10路、20路和101路公共汽车都经停天安门，103路和109路电车经停北门。

开放时间

8:30—17:00

（夏季停止入馆时间至16:10，冬季至15:40）

门票价格

每人60元

提示

1）故宫的宫殿、大厅等禁止拍摄。

2）午门有各种语言的导游录音带及单放机出租，离开时可在北门归还。

附近景点

在景山公园的景山上可看到故宫全景。

第二单元　办理签证

PART II　对话

对话1　申请签证

托　德：露辛达，你说过你男朋友夸梅非常喜欢新西兰，那你们是打算搬去新西兰生活吗？

露辛达：是的，实际上我们这个月底就要走了，11月30日。

托　德：哦，真的吗？你们要离开了？他是打算彻底搬走吗？

露辛达：对，没错，我们都是为了工作搬去新西兰的。

托　德：那他拿到去新西兰的签证会很难吗？还是非常简单？

露辛达：申请新西兰签证需要准备很多，比如他们会让你证明你们两个人生活在一起之类的事情。

托　德：你是说要证明你们两个是夫妻……

露辛达：对，没错，因为他申请的是配偶工作签证。如果他申请工作签证，那他就必须证明他在新西兰有工作，不过要是配偶签证，虽然也是工作签证，就不需要证明在新西兰有工作了，而是要证明他和我生活在一起超过一年的时间，且我们的关系稳定等。

托德：哇，那你们要怎么证明你们生活在一起呢？要怎么做？

露辛达：我们要出示我们居住的公寓所有人提供的证明信，还要出示我们在不同时间拍的合照。还有我们的朋友提供的证明信。我想我们大概从朋友、双方家人那里拿到了20封证明信，说明我们已经在一起一段时间了，而且他们还要提供申请签证的介绍信，等等。非常复杂。

托德：那文件手续呢？是很容易还是有难度？

露辛达：文件手续非常容易。我们除了要提供房产证明，还有6个装有血样的小瓶，还要进行尽可能多的体检项目。除此之外，填写表格非常简单。我想只有几页需要填写的内容，因为我们没有孩子，也不涉及其他人，只有他和我，所以要填的表格只有几页。

托德：他要进行体检以确定他没有……

露辛达：确定他未患有新西兰不存在的疾病，否则，还要做一些特定检查以确认他是否健康。我不知道他们为什么要这么做，不过要确定人们没有严重的健康问题，因为新西兰拥有非常良好的卫生保障体系，他们不希望接收一些只是为了追求特定的医疗福利而前往新西兰的人。

托德：嗯，你们一起搬去新西兰真是太好了，祝你们在新西兰生活顺利。

露辛达：谢谢你。

对话2　申请签证的条件

A：我听说你下个月要去新加坡参加一个国际教育会议，真是真的吗？

B：是的，假如一切都很顺利的话。

A：那真是太好了。这绝对是一次了解学术前沿知识和最先进的教学方法的大好机会。真是太棒了。祝贺你啊！

B：谢谢你。但是出国的手续很复杂啊，这是目前我最头疼的一件事了。我都不知道该怎么办。听说商务签证的程序还不简单呢。

A：你不用太过担心这个问题。我去年参加过一个国际会议，我知道要申请商务签证的话是有一些要求应该满足，但并不是像你想象的那么复杂。首先，你需要一封邀请函，这是必需的东西，因为签证官要通过你的邀请函来确认你确实有真实的商务原因要入境该国而没有其他不良意图。

B：我明白了，也就是说我首先需要的最基本的文件就是一封邀请函。那么我会给这次会议的主办方发一封电子邮件，要求他们给我发一封邀请函。

A：并且移民局会要求商务考察者身体健康，无刑事犯罪记录，对某国的国家安全不会构成威胁。所以你要到你们学校的人事部门让他们给你出具一份证明来证实你没有以上问题。

B：好的，这个并不难。

A：基本上就是这些了。没有你想象的那么复杂，是不是？

B：是啊，你说得对。真是非常感谢你。你对我帮助很大，我很荣幸能有你这样的朋友。

PART III 阅读

Text A

申请签证

仅仅拿到一所美国的学院或者大学的录取通知书并不能保证你可以拿到签证。拿到签证仅仅保证你可以到达美国，但并不保证移民局的官员会允许你进入这个国家。到美国旅行的证件由（美国）国务院签发，但移民则由国土安全局负责。

（美国）国务院的网站上列出了拿到签证的所有要求，其网址为：Unitedstatesvisas.gov。Unitedstatesvisas 是一个单词。

如果你是第一次申请签证，你可能需要去美国大使馆或领事馆。你需要带一张美国学校发给你的可以证明你已经被录取了的官方表格。同样，你需要出示银行记录和纳税记录来证明你有足够的资金来支付自己的学费。另外，准备好你求学完成后要回到自己祖国的证明。

所有这些都是你申请签证所要满足的要求，非常重要。还会有领事馆官员给你照相，并给你录指纹。

外国学生必须联系当地的大使馆或者领事馆要求进行面试，获得相关信息，包括怎样以及在哪儿支付签证费用的问题。费用为 200 美元。在被美国大学录取后你应该尽快申请签证。政府需要时间进行背景调查。你只能在开课前 120 天之内拿到签证。如果是作为学生第一次申请，那么你只能在开课前 30 天去美国。一旦去了美国，你可以在那儿停留到你学习结束。

Text B

减少等待时间

以下这些小窍门会帮助你减少在安全检查处等待的时间。

在去机场之前

- 不要携带机场明令禁止的物品。
- 珠宝首饰、现金和笔记本电脑一类的贵重物品只放在随身携带的包裹里。
- 把你的名片粘在笔记本电脑底下。
- 不要穿带有金属的衣物、首饰和装饰品。金属物会引起金属检测器报警。
- 不要穿带有金属的鞋，或者厚底的鞋，或者高跟鞋。即使金属检测警报没有响，很多种鞋子也需要进行附加的扫描。
- 把没有冲洗的胶卷和装有胶卷的相机放在随身携带的包裹里。行李扫描设备会在检查行李时损坏尚未冲洗的胶卷。

201

• 向航空公司申请携带武器和弹药，把它们放在检查的包裹中。如果你希望将自己的行李锁上，请使用 TSA 识别锁。

• 不要携带打火机或者机场明令禁止的火柴到机场。不要携带有包装的礼物，也不要将它们带到检查点。到达后再包装或者在起飞前提前将它们寄出去。TSA 需要打开包装对产品进行安全检查。

在机场时

在离开安全检查处之前，每位成年旅客都要保管好自己的登机牌和政府发放的照片 ID。出于不同的机场布局，在很多机场这些证件可能被要求出示不止一次。

PART V 典型景点

哈尔滨国际冰雪节和哈尔滨冰雪大世界

哈尔滨国际冰雪节

哈尔滨国际冰雪节创建于 1985 年，每年 1 月 5 日开幕，持续约一个多月。哈尔滨是黑龙江省省会城市，也是中国最早和最大的冰雪艺术节所在地，每年吸引了成千上万的当地和世界各国的游客。

哈尔滨位于中国东北部，北极气候为该地提供了丰富的自然冰雪，因此，"冰城"哈尔滨被认为是中国冰雪艺术的摇篮，因其精湛的冰雪雕塑艺术而闻名中外。传统的冰灯节是现行冰雪节的前身，对于每年来到哈尔滨的游人而言，冰灯节依然是整个冰雪节中他们最喜欢的部分。

第一个冰灯节源自中国东北的一个传统。人们制作各式各样的花灯挂在自家房门外或供孩子在一些传统佳节玩耍，因此冰灯就开始了其悠久的发展史。如今，在技术上有了新的变化和进步，人们可以制作和展出各种造型精美并且极具艺术性的冰灯。今天，广义上的冰灯指的是一系列造型艺术，这种艺术使用冰雪作为原料并结合了冰雕艺术的色与光和精彩音乐。冰灯的具体样式包括冰雕、冰花、冰建筑等。哈尔滨国际冰雪节每年都会给游客提供一个全新的冰雪世界。冰雕艺术的最佳收藏品主要在三个地方陈列：太阳岛公园、哈尔滨冰雪大世界和兆麟公园。

今天的哈尔滨国际冰雪节不仅是一个冰雪艺术的博览会，而且是一年一度的国际文化交流活动。每年都会有许多来自美国、加拿大、日本、新加坡、俄罗斯和中国的冰雕专家、艺术家和冰雕爱好者齐聚哈尔滨参加冰雕大赛，他们在银装素裹的世界里互相交流。此外，哈尔滨的冰灯还会在中国的一些大城市和亚洲、欧洲、北美洲、非洲和大洋洲等一些国家展出。40 多年来，哈尔滨的自然冰雪资源已被充分开发，给来访的游客提供了无尽的喜悦和乐趣。现在，在节日期间，一些体育比赛项目如滑冰、滑雪等也很受欢迎。婚礼、宴会和其他的娱乐活动如今也成了这个冰雪世界的一大亮点，这些活动为这个盛大的集艺术、文化、体育和旅游为一体的节日盛典做出了自己的贡献。

哈尔滨冰雪大世界

1999 年，哈尔滨冰雪大世界由哈尔滨市政府首次举办，是迄今为止世界上最大的

Appendix A 参考译文

冰雪艺术展览。它不仅极具艺术吸引力，而且夜景很美、活动悠闲且娱乐形式多样。此外，冰雪节每年都会推出一个新的主题，让游客有一个全新的感受。

哈尔滨冰雪大世界的冰雕被认为是世界上最美丽的冰雕艺术品，游客可以欣赏到最大最庄严的冰雕作品。每一件冰雕作品在一定程度上都是和节日的主题相关的。游客可以品味到各种各样的变化。例如，第一届冰雕节的主题就是围绕"繁荣的中国和腾飞的黑龙江"展开的，其冰雕作品反映了国家的快速发展。2005 年主题为"中俄友谊"，所有作品都是俄罗斯风格。其中包括俄罗斯一些著名建筑的复制品，如冬宫、莫斯科红场。

对于到访的游客而言，夜晚浏览会格外精彩，因为当五颜六色的地下灯光映衬着冰雕作品时，会呈现出多姿多彩的多维场景。明亮炫目的光线映衬着黑暗的天空，使每件作品看起来都更加壮观。

哈尔滨冰雪大世界也是各种休闲娱乐活动的中心，活动多种多样。游客会为壮观的如冰迷宫、冰吧甚至是冰旅馆等冰雪建筑而惊叹。如果你是滑雪运动的热爱者，那么你就会有机会参加如冰岩攀登、滑冰、滑雪、打雪仗、冰高尔夫和冰射箭等活动。除此之外，在整个节日中上演的基于冰雪节题材的一些特殊演出，无疑也会给那些平日里生活平泛的游客带来娱乐兴趣。

毫无疑问，去哈尔滨旅游的最佳时间是冬季。哈尔滨国际冰雪节在每年的 12 月底或 1 月初举办，对于那些梦想过一个特有意义的冬季的人来说，哈尔滨冰雪大世界无疑会让这些人梦想成真。

第二章　旅游种类

第三单元　历史人文游

 PART II　对话

 对话 1　参观颐和园

杰克·史密斯：你知道颐和园吗？

韦德·文森：是的，我知道。颐和园在北京，它是一个美丽的地方。

杰克·史密斯：你说的很对。颐和园位于北京西北郊区，它主要由万寿山和昆明湖组成。

韦德·文森：你能告诉我牌匾上"颐和园"这三个字是谁写的吗？

杰克·史密斯：颐和园金色牌匾上的"颐和园"（颐养和谐的公园）三个字是清朝光绪皇帝的手书。

韦德·文森：太好了。我认为这是一个不错的名字。你知道乾隆皇帝吗？

杰克·史密斯：当然，我非常了解他。清乾隆十四年（公元 1749 年），乾隆皇帝为了给他母亲庆祝 60 岁生日，而专门翻新重修了颐和园。昆明湖也是在这次大规

203

模疏浚过程中行成的。

韦德·文森：我读过一本关于清朝历史的书籍，了解到此次工程花费了一大笔金钱，消耗了巨大的人力和物力。

杰克·史密斯：是的。在耗费这么多人工的情况下，经过十几年的辛苦劳作，拥有清澈涟漪的花园（清漪园）作为一个规模宏大、风景如画的皇家园林出现在北京的地图上。

韦德·文森：你能告诉我是谁把清漪园的名字改成颐和园的吗？

杰克·史密斯：1860 年，英法联军烧毁了包括清漪园和圆明园在内的许多著名皇家园林。清光绪十二年（公元 1886 年），慈禧太后在废墟上面开始重建。1888 年，慈禧太后把它命名为"颐和园"。

韦德·文森：你的回答太详细了。

杰克·史密斯：然而，颐和园在 1900 年被八国联军再次劫掠，于 1903 年再次重建。

韦德·文森：颐和园有一个多灾多难的命运。但目前它保存还算完好，总占地面积 300 公顷（1 公顷 = 1 0000 平方米）。有 3000 个古代建筑，总建筑面积约为 70 000 平方米。

杰克·史密斯：颐和园里如此众多的走廊、桥梁、楼阁、水榭、小山、矮塔错落有致，交相辉映，形成一组灿烂的中国古典建筑群。

韦德·文森：1998 年 12 月 2 日，颐和园被联合国教科文组织列入《世界文化遗产》名录。多年来，颐和园以其精湛的艺术魅力，迷人的景色让来自世界各地的游客流连忘返。颐和园也获得了"人间天堂"的美誉。

杰克·史密斯：这样一个美妙的地方，为什么不去参观一下呢？

对话 2　游览八达岭长城

本·休斯顿：我想参观一下八达岭长城。你愿意和我一起去吗？

怀特太太：好啊。但是八达岭长城在哪儿？

本·休斯顿：八达岭长城在居庸关的北面。古代人说居庸关之所以险要就是因为坐落于八达岭长城上。如果说居庸关是通往北京的北大门，那么八达岭长城就是它的锁和钥匙。

怀特太太：八达岭长城是什么时候修建的？

本·休斯顿：它修建于 1505 年。戚继光于 1569 年到 1573 年间对此段长城进行了更大规模地加固和修复，使八达岭长城更显气势恢宏。

怀特太太：你知道八达岭长城的平均高度和宽度吗？

本·休斯顿：八达岭长城平均高 7.8 米，底部宽 6.5 米，上部宽 5.8 米，每隔 300 米到 500 米建有瞭望塔或城垛。

怀特太太：作为最早开放的旅游景点，八达岭长城已经成为明代长城的象征，它所享有盛誉远在其他段长城之上。

本·休斯顿：你说得很对。

怀特太太：咱们出发吧！

PART III 阅读

Text A

古都游

中国历史上有七大古都，历朝各代选址北京、西安、南京、杭州、开封、洛阳、安阳定都安邦，为今天留下了宝贵且丰富的历史人文资源，中外游客纷沓而至。

如北京的故宫（又名紫禁城）、雍和宫、颐和园、天坛、圆明园遗址等；西安的大雁塔、兵马俑博物馆、骊山华清池、丝绸之路、西安碑林等；南京的天王府、雨花台、秦淮河等；杭州的六和塔、西湖等；开封的清明上河园、龙亭、铁塔等；安阳的殷墟等受到游客的青睐。古都之游，人们仿佛在重翻历史的画卷，仿佛回到了那曾经繁华一时的岁月，仿佛又闻到了当年的油墨和脂粉的气息。七大古都，风格各异，展现了不同历史时期、不同地域的文物古迹。

下面以北京的故宫为例：

故宫位于北京市中心，又名紫禁城，是中国明、清两朝皇帝的宫殿，又是世界上最大的皇宫，历经 24 代帝王，已有 500 多年历史，占地 72 万平方米，现存宫殿 8700 多间，建筑面积达 16 万平方米。故宫博物院所藏文物约 100 万件，包括历史文物方面的宫廷文物、科技文物、宗教文物，古代艺术品方面的书法、绘画、青铜、陶瓷、宝玉石、丝织品等。

Text B

寺庙寺窟游

宗教，特别是佛教，在历史上曾对中国的文化产生深刻影响。然而，历代留下来的各类宗教寺庙、祠堂、石窟等，都是罕见的艺术珍品，并成为人们了解宗教文化的窗口，成为专家学者研究艺术历史的教材，更成为人类历史上不可多得的艺术宝库。

中国的寺庙、祠堂、石窟主要有独乐寺、五塔寺、寒山寺、少林寺、大昭寺、扎什伦布寺、哲蚌寺、塔尔寺、拉卜楞寺、白马寺、佛光寺、南山寺、解州关帝庙、武侯祠、永乐宫、布达拉宫、敦煌莫高窟、麦积山石窟、炳灵寺石窟、须弥山石窟、克孜尔千佛洞、云冈石窟、大足石刻等。精美绝伦的石窟造像和宗教绘画艺术，也都是无价的瑰宝。中国的石窟开凿始于魏晋，以北魏至隋唐为最盛，数量众多，分布广泛，其中规模较大的是敦煌莫高窟、大同云冈石窟、洛阳龙门石窟、甘肃麦积山石窟，其中龙门石窟和云冈石窟以石刻造像为主，而莫高窟和麦积山石窟由于石质疏松不宜雕凿，敦煌莫高窟以壁画见长，而麦积山石窟则以泥塑闻名。下面以布达拉宫为例：

布达拉宫位于拉萨市西北玛布日山上。相传为公元 7 世纪时松赞干布为迎娶文成公主而建，后经 7 世纪到 17 世纪中叶，布达拉宫几经沧桑。现存为明崇祯年间重修而成，后屡经增修，才有今日这般规模。布达拉宫规模宏大，依山垒砌，极尽富丽豪华，由无数宫殿组成，包括红宫和白宫两大部分，共13层，高达110米，全部是实木结构。建筑气势宏伟，风格奇特，成为西藏的象征。布达拉宫所藏文物众多，堪称一座艺术博物馆和文化宝库。

PART V　典型景点

中国黄山

黄山，位于安徽省东南部，面积154平方公里。黄山以其独特的雄伟、秀丽吸引着古今中外的游客；以其巍峨奇特的怪石、苍劲多姿的奇松、变幻莫测的云海和奇异的温泉，形成黄山的"四绝"。

明代就有"五岳归来不看山，黄山归来不看岳"，"任他五岳归来客，一见天都也叫奇"的盛赞。泰岳之雄伟，华山之峻峭，衡山之烟云，庐山之飞瀑，雁荡之巧石，峨眉之清凉，黄山莫不兼而有之。黄山大小七十二峰，劈地摩天、云凝霄汉。峰峰石骨无肤，登临始信方有鬼斧神工之奇。因此，1982年国务院将黄山审定为国家重点风景名胜区，1990年被联合国教科文组织作为文化和自然遗产，列入《世界遗产名录》。

黄山是一个气势磅礴的峰之海。中国现代著名文学家郭沫若先生在1961年为黄山"四绝"叫奇时，首推峰之海。他满怀激情地写道："奇峰虽云大小七十二，实则七十二万尚有奇。八百里内形成一片峰之海，更有石海缭绕之。森罗万象难比拟，纵有比拟徒费辞。瞬息万变万万变，忽隐忽显，或浓或淡，胜似梦境之迷离。"

整个黄山山脉，北起青阳的九华山，东连绩溪的大嶂山，西接黟太的羊栈岑，东南延伸至浙江的天目山；在绵亘数百里范围内，千峰叠峙，万壑纵横。在这万峰之中，三十六大峰，威武雄壮，冠盖群仑；三十六小峰，秀气横溢，多彩多姿。

在徽城郊外的公路上，向西北眺望，首先映入眼帘的是"飞鸟不敢渡，浮云往还中"的云门峰。但是，当你抵达被称为"天上人间"的玉屏楼时，顿觉云门峰一点也不奇险了。登上玉屏峰，一览众山小，那一座接一座的山峰，一条连一条的世壑，像洪峰一样汹涌，像巨浪一样排空。

第四单元　自然奇观游

PART II　对话

对话1　游览长江三峡

玛丽·里卡多： 你知道长江三峡在哪里吗？
吉米·史密斯： 当然知道。长江三峡在重庆市的东部，在湖北省的西部。

Appendix A 参考译文

玛丽·里卡多：长江是中国最长的河流，是吗？
吉米·史密斯：是的，它也是世界上第三长河流。
玛丽·里卡多：真的吗？长江的源头在哪里？
吉米·史密斯：真的。长江发源于唐古拉山脉主峰的格拉丹东雪山，它位于青海省西南部，海拔 6621 米。
玛丽·里卡多：谢谢你！我知道长江全长约 6300 公里，流经八个省、一个自治区和两个直辖市。
吉米·史密斯：那么，为什么人们称呼为"长江三峡"？
玛丽·里卡多：三峡是由瞿塘峡、巫峡和西陵峡组成，因此人们称为"三峡"。
吉米·史密斯：哦，我明白了。你能告诉我它们的特点吗？
玛丽·里卡多：当然可以。瞿塘峡以险峻和陡峭著称，巫峡以宁静和美丽著称，西陵峡拥有独特的激流和险滩。
吉米·史密斯：真是太棒了！
玛丽·里卡多：顺便问一下，你知道哪个峡谷是最短、最窄的吗？
吉米·史密斯：据我所知瞿塘峡是最短、最窄、最雄伟的峡谷。
玛丽·里卡多：此外，瞿塘峡西起奉节县西的白帝城，东至巫山县东的大溪镇，全长 8 公里。吉米·史密斯：西陵峡有多长？
玛丽·里卡多：西陵峡西起秭归县东至宜昌市，全长 76 公里。
吉米·史密斯：长江三峡大坝水利枢纽工程在哪里？
玛丽·里卡多：著名的三峡大坝水利枢纽工程位于西陵峡中段的湖北省宜昌市境内的三斗坪。
吉米·史密斯：三峡大坝有多长？
玛丽·里卡多：三峡大坝长 2309 米、高 185 米。
吉米·史密斯：嗯，这是一个伟大的工程。三峡代表长江独特的景观特点。

对话 2　游览黄山

爱丽丝·史密斯：我想去游览一下黄山。你愿意和我一起去吗？
克里斯蒂娜·英格利斯：当然可以。但是，黄山坐落在哪里？
爱丽丝·史密斯：黄山位于安徽省东南部，占地面积 154 平方公里。
克里斯蒂娜·英格利斯：黄山以什么闻名？
爱丽丝·史密斯：据我所知，黄山以高耸入云的山峰、千姿百态的松树、巧夺天工的奇石和如梦如幻的云海闻名于世。
克里斯蒂娜·英格利斯：你说得很对，尤其是黄山的松树最出名。它们代表黄山的灵魂。你能说出一些黄山有名的松树吗？
爱丽丝·史密斯：当然可以。黄山的迎客松已经存在上千年，它象征着中华民族的热情好客。

207

克里斯蒂娜·英格利斯：你知道其他的松树吗？

爱丽丝·史密斯：当然知道。以人格化命名的黄山迎客松，还有陪客松、送客松、望客松、接引松、探海松等。我的一个朋友去年去过黄山，他告诉我那些松树非常漂亮。

克里斯蒂娜·英格利斯：我可以想象黄山的松树在春季和冬季的美，确实难以形容。为什么不去呢？我都有点迫不及待了。

爱丽丝·史密斯：好的，我马上就买两张票。

PART III 阅读

Text A

中国的自然风光

自然界的奇峰、怪石、异洞、名川等，其形成多出自大自然的鬼斧神工，与岩性、构造、风化、溶蚀、沉积等作用有关。这些大自然的作品或千奇百怪，或娇趣横生。有的劈地摩天，步移景换；有的形象逼真，惟妙惟肖；有的变幻多端，神秘莫测；有的如世外桃源，纯洁静谧。例如：广西的七星岩、芦笛岩、伊岭岩，江苏的宜兴三洞，都是著名的岩溶地貌，其间有形态各异的钟乳石，有迂回流转的地下河，还有光怪陆离的洞中洞；位于四川境内的蜀南竹海，楠竹遍地，飞瀑如帘，令人称奇；而位于云南境内的香格里拉，则是一处绝美的世外桃源，映衬着雪峰与峡谷。这些自然奇观，风景如画，令游人流连忘返。下面以黑龙江省的五大连池为例：

五大连池火山群素有"火山博物馆"之誉，景观由火山喷发形成的火山锥、火山弹、溶洞及形态各异的熔岩地貌组成。它位于黑龙江省五大连池市，为火山地质自然风景。由于不同时期的火山喷发，岩浆流淌，把流经此地的纳尔河支流阻截成段，形成五个串珠般的火山堰塞湖。五大连池由五湖十四山和石灰熔岩台地构成，方圆1060平方公里，以山秀、石怪、水幽、泉奇四大特色而闻名。附近还有许多古代和近代的火山，与山色共同构成温泊云雾、石海、火山熔岩、石塘火山倒影、三池冰裂、石浪闻声、桦林温泉等景观。1982年被列为国家重点风景名胜区。

Text B

天涯海角

几千年流浪情怀，多愁善感的中国人将相思撒满天空，希望能有一处见证；数万里流放旅程，那些坚贞不屈的心灵历尽困顿颠簸，最终会有一个落脚点；此外，还有上穷碧落下黄泉的寻觅总得有个圆满的终点。

于是，我们期待天地会有尽头，渴望有那么一个地方真的就是天涯海角。来到海南岛三亚市，我们发现"天涯海角"其实就是两块简单的石头。

两块石头在刻上"天涯""海角"四个字之后，我们心中的天涯情结找到了物化的载体，成为一种终极意义上的代名词，承载着千百年积淀下来的丰富深刻的文化内涵。

在中国广袤疆域的南方，隔着白浪滔滔的琼州海峡，还有一座孤悬海外的岛屿，顺着这座海岛一直向南走去，直到海天的尽头，矗立着两块巨石，巨石之南，除了泱泱大海便是浩浩长空。这座岛屿就是海南岛，那两块巨石上，分别刻着"天涯"和"海角"。所有中国人，大概都会知道这两块矗立在天尽头的石头。昊天在此找到了边缘，沧海在此流到了尽头。

这两块标志着天地尽头的著名石头，位于海南岛三亚市西南海滨，距离市区23公里，离凤凰机场6公里。从三亚市驱车20多分钟，就可以来到天涯海角风景区的大门口，门两边有一副对联："海南生明月，天涯共此时"，改自唐朝诗人张九龄的诗句："海上生明月，天涯共此时"。细品诗联，一种温暖的感伤便缓缓从心底升起："玉郎还是不还家，教人魂梦逐杨花，绕天涯""夕阳西下，断肠人在天涯"。也许，游人不远千里万里，前来观看这两块简单的石头，就是想要追怀心中那些莫名的感伤，追怀那些带着温暖或伤痛或自己也不甚明了的情绪。

进入景区，迎面一条宽阔笔直的青石大道，路尽头是茫茫大海。即使是在12月，在南中国热带阳光的直射下，路两边艳红的三角梅仍在勃然怒放，椰树依然在静静地挂果。沿着海边细软的沙滩一路前行，经过"海判南天"，经过"海誓石"，经过"南天一柱"，在风景区的最西端，有一堆突兀峭拔的巨石，其中，东端最大的一块状如巨屋的石头，周长60米，高约10米，其顶部刻有两个大字"天涯"，旁边的题款表明，题字的是"雍正十一年"崖州知府程哲。雍正十一年，即公元1733年，料想当时的海滩该是一片荒凉。

在"天涯"石的西北，一组巨石延绵伸向大海，其中一块形似巨笋峭然向天，笋尖上刻有"海角"二字。在海风的磨蚀下，题款已经变得模糊不清，只能依稀辨认出书者的名字：王毅。但王毅是谁，仍待考证，目前多认为是民国时期的地方要员。穿行于垒石巨石之间，来到海角，忽见眼前只剩下茫茫海面，脚下再无道路可走。于是，猛然明白，自己已确实走到天涯海角，走到天地的尽头了。

爬上那些巨石，举目四望，只见一条洁白亮丽的海滩如玉带般横亘于蓝天碧海之间，海的背面是青山围绕。海浪经年累月的冲刷造就了眼前这古朴的石头，它们以屹立于海天之间的雄浑傲视沧海桑田的变迁，而艳丽晴空之下，那些婀娜的椰子树又以不倦的绿意展示着南国的柔情。一切如画、如诗。

PART V　典型景点

中国张家界景区

张家界市位于中国湖南省的西北部，地处东经109°至111°20′，北纬28°52′至29°48′之间，属中亚热带山原型季风湿润气候，年平均气温16℃。城市总面积9563平方公里，辖永定、武陵源两区和慈利、桑植两县。

张家界市因张家界风景区而得名。1979年，原大庸县辖区内张家界举世罕有的自然风光被发现并得以开发利用。1985年，大庸县撤县建市。1988年，大庸市因旅游事业发展的需要，与拥有索溪峪风景区的慈利县和拥有天子山风景区的桑植县合并升级，定为省辖地级市。1994年，为便于树立张家界的整体形象，开拓其旅游市场，促进当地经济的发展，国务院批准大庸市更名为张家界市。

张家界市是一个正在开发建设的新兴旅游城市，旅游资源极为丰富。由张家界国家森林公园、索溪峪自然风景区、天子山自然风景区三大景区构成的武陵源风景名胜区，不但是全国重点风景名胜之一，而且还被联合国教科文组织列入了《世界自然遗产名录》。1982年，张家界被命名为中国第一个国家森林公园。之后，该市境内的天门山又被命名为国家森林公园。1986年，中国第一条漂流旅游线在该市境内的茅岩河开发推出。至今，全市又新增省级风景名胜区三个（茅岩河、九天洞、天门山）。全市被列为省级、国家级风景名胜区和自然保护区的面积多达500平方公里，约占全市总面积的九分之一。此外，普光禅寺、玉皇洞石窟等若干名胜古迹成为颇具吸引力的人文旅游资源；还有当地古朴的少数民族风情和那惊心动魄、神秘莫测的民间武术硬气功，更是令中外旅游者津津乐道。

张家界市，本着以发展旅游业为立市之本的改革开放方针，经过10多年的努力，一个以张家界、索溪峪、天子山三大景区为核心景区，以茅岩河、九天洞、天门山、五雷山、普光神寺等为周边卫星景区，融山、水、洞和历史文化、民俗风情为一体的对外开放的旅游业新格局已基本形成。

全市已开发旅游参观游览区（点）12个，建成游览线30多条，建成景区游道300多公里和景区登山索道两条。景区与市区、景区与景区之间已形成公路连通网络。张家界火车站已与国内10多个大、小城市开通了旅客列车。张家界机场与国内20多个大、中城市开通了航班。张家界的邮电通信已达到国内先进水平。全市现有饭店400多家，床位总数已达3万多张，其中一星级以上饭店20家。全市现有为旅游者服务的旅行社40多家。

张家界，随着知名度的不断提高，随着旅游设施的日趋完善，随着一类口岸的建成开放，正快步走向世界。

第五单元　红色旅游

PART II　对话

对话1　游西安

（一群来自澳大利亚的游客前往古城西安。导游正在为他们做讲解。）

G：现在我们站在西安城的城墙之上。在这里，我们可以看到这个城市和它的古建筑的全景。

T1：我可以看到我们昨日去过的大雁塔。

Appendix A 参考译文

T2：我真的很佩服高僧玄奘建造佛塔的恒心和毅力。

G：是的，他很伟大。如果你从这里看向城里，就可以看到钟楼和鼓楼。

T1：我还是不明白为什么要建造它们。

G：嗯，古时候没有钟表报时，所以人们建造塔楼来敲钟或击鼓给人们报时。

T1：敲钟和击鼓之间有什么区别？

G：上午敲钟，黄昏击鼓。

T1：所以人们用钟鼓声安排活动，对不对？

G：是的。这个保存完好的城墙还告诉人们古代西安城过去的辉煌和繁荣。就像你可能知道的，西安是中国13个朝代的都城，持续了长达1100余年，当然盛产历史文物。试想西安周边的皇陵，单单渭河北岸就有27座墓葬！

T2：它们有没有被挖掘出来呢？

G：它们中的大多数都没有被挖掘。但是，已挖掘的那些就已经创造了很大的奇迹。其中之一就是秦朝始皇墓，挖掘出了兵马俑军队。我们一会儿会去游览那里。

T2：那太棒了！

G：我们到了。这就是你们一直渴望参观的兵马俑博物馆。

T1：噢，我以前从来没见过这么大的博物馆。

G：它长230米，宽70米，高22米。你知道，它是目前中国此类博物馆中最大的。请看古代中国军阵。

T2：是势力很强的军队。哦，那是看台，不是吗？

G：是的，它是。看，所有的陶俑面朝东，因为战国时期秦国的国都在西方，和东方的诸侯国打仗。

T1：走在队伍前列的是谁？

G：他们是兵马俑（武士俑），分为三列横队，每列70名士兵。他们是部队的先锋。他们后面是纵队……看，那些是步兵，这边是战车。有38列，每列180米长。兵马俑披甲穿袍，战车由四匹俑马拉车。这是主力部队。

T1：为什么有些站在南北两边，有些站在后面？他们都面朝外。

G：他们是护翼和后卫，他们的任务是保卫，防止敌人攻击和翼侧包围。

T2：我明白了。这支军队组织得很好。

G：秦始皇率领他的强大军队，驰骋沙场，打败六个诸侯国，统一了中国。这些兵马俑和马再现了他率领军队在前线南征北战的壮丽图景。

T1：它确实是秦朝大战场。刚出土的时候是这样排列的吗？

G：是的。我们去兵马俑坑看看。

T2：噢，每个士兵看起来都活灵活现，充满活力。他们都戴着头盔，身穿铠甲，脚蹬黑靴，每个士兵都手拿长矛和剑斧。

G：如果你走近看就会发现每个士兵面部表情和姿势都不一样。

T1：这些兵马俑造型生动，形象逼真。令人惊异的是那时候雕刻技术已经达到了这么高的水平。我听说这是1号坑，还有2号和3号坑。

G：是的，我们去看看吧。

对话2　游黄浦江

W：黄浦江游览有60公里长的路程，需要3个半小时。

T：游船会在什么地方（中途）靠岸吗？

W：不靠。看，外滩景观。

T：江边有很多建筑物。

W：是的。你看，外白渡桥北边是上海大厦，绿色尖顶的建筑是和平饭店，那座古典建筑风格的是市政大楼，那座巨大花岗岩建筑是上海海关大楼。在这个建筑区域，有希腊风格的，有罗马风格的和西班牙风格的建筑。

T：我明白了。它们就像世界建筑博览会。我听说，除了欧式建筑，上海还有中国古典风格的建筑和园林。

W：对极了。明天我们要参观的豫园和古猗园是著名的古典园林的代表。

T：嗨，正在江里抛锚的船也是来自各个国家的。这艘是英国的，这艘是荷兰的，这艘是日本的，那些是巴西的、法国的、挪威的和新加坡的。啊，这么多的船啊！各种不同型号的船桅杆高耸，汽笛长鸣。

W：看，有一个码头。

T：多么繁忙的码头啊！也许是集装箱码头。哦，也有很多工厂。

W：你知道，上海的工厂过去集中在黄浦江两岸。新中国成立后，在郊区建了大约10个工业园区。

T：上海的确是一个大城市。它既是工业城市，又是商业城市。同时它还拥有很多中国一流的大学和研究机构……你看，江在这里伸出一块。

W：我们这儿就是吴淞口。

T：这么多的起重机和铁塔。这里一定是一个工业园区，对吗？

W：是的。这是建设中的新宝钢厂址。你知道，这个工厂是中国大型钢铁综合企业之一。

T：啊，岸上有炮台！

W：这是吴淞炮台旧址。

T：它们是鸦片战争后留下的吗？

W：是的。在鸦片战争中，陈化成将军在这里指挥他的士兵对敌人开火，他们击毁了好几艘敌人的炮舰。由于他们孤军奋战，使用的是落后的武器和弹药，陈化成将军和许多士兵壮烈牺牲了。

T：我知道了。中国人民为保卫祖国付出了很大的代价。看到我们前面大浪中的是什么了吗？

W：是灯塔。那是我们游览的最远点。我们的船在返回前会绕灯塔一周。

PART III 阅读

"红色旅游"可以更加丰富多彩

"红色旅游"无疑是中国时下最流行的一句话。

参观"红色旅游景区"那些与中国革命有着或多或少联系的历史古迹、遗址,游客们不仅可以在旅途中放松一下心情,而且还重温了中华人民共和国足智多谋的"红色历史",这段时间从1921年中国共产党的诞生起一直跨越到1949年新中国成立。

所以,尽管"红色旅游"是一个全新的旅游概念,但是通过爱国主义教育和娱乐休闲的完美结合,目前已在那些主要革命遗址区域蓬勃发展起来。国家旅游局甚至指定2005年为"红色旅游年"。但是,红色旅游的发起人说:"红色旅游还有另外的意义"。

众所周知,大多数革命遗址建立在一般经济比较落后的山区或偏远地区。因此,"红色旅游"似乎是帮助发展这些地方经济的明智之举,毕竟过去这些地方为革命牺牲很多。

然而,"红色旅游"的经营者应该谨慎地对待此事。使它不仅仅成为一个稍纵即逝的时尚,而是要以可持续的方式发展。只是简单地游览"红色旅游景区"会存在让游客厌烦的风险。虽然这些地方都有丰富的历史内涵,但是它们缺少变化的项目种类。更糟的是,许多"红色旅游景区"是分散的、孤立的,这就意味着有时潜在的游客不得不长途跋涉,可看到的也只是一两个历史遗迹。

因此,如果这个主题旅游想要继续生存和发展,运营者就必须正视这些缺点,并且制定战略来解决这些问题。他们应该知道,"红色旅游"应按照市场规律进行管理。中国东南部的福建省已为我们提供了一个成功的典范。这个沿海省份,与台湾对面而立,是中国的一个拥有"红色历史"的显著之地。在20世纪20年代末和30年代初,福建是红军的一个非常重要的"红色基地",它留下了许多"红色旅游景区"。例如,著名的古田会议,是党的历史上的一个里程碑,就是1929年在福建古田这个小镇上举行的。但是,福建旅游局并没有试图依靠这个"红色景点"来发展丰富自己的"红色旅游"项目。相反,政府成功地尝试将"红色旅游景区"添加到比较成熟的旅游线路,让它们与其他旅游资源相结合,使其更具吸引力。比如,把古田会议场地补充到现有的旅游路线中,其中包括邻近风景区,这些不一定都是"红色遗址"。"红色旅游景区"的旅游资源和那些独特的地域文化及奇特的自然风光的多元多样化组合增强了游客的体验,也增添了游客旅途的愉快感。

然而,福建的模式可能只是许多可以用来培育"红色旅游"的可行性方法之一。希望其他地方开发他们的"红色旅游"的时候,可以从福建学习,想出其他适合当地条件的创造性的方法。

红色旅游

从1921年成立到中华人民共和国1949年成立的近30年间,中国共产党走过了一条

213

"红色"革命之路。这是困难、激情、浪漫与荣耀之路。今天,对这段历史有兴趣的中国人越来越多,他们充满热情地重新游览这些革命根据地和具有里程碑意义的地点。这就是"红色旅游"。

2004年12月,中国政府为红色旅游的制定了发展总体规划(2004—2010年)。该计划定义了最能代表中国的革命阶段12个主要红色旅游区。以下就是最重要的几个红色旅游景点。

井冈山

坐落在中国江西省的井冈山拥有保存完好的生态链,以陡峭的悬崖和茂密的竹林闻名。从历史上看,由于区域限制很少有人类在该地区定居。1927年10月7日,毛泽东率部来到宁冈县茅坪,在那里建立了红军和井冈山革命根据地。那里的条件艰苦、生活艰难。后来,在毛泽东与美国记者埃德加·斯诺会谈期间,他回顾了井冈山的艰苦时期:"部队没有冬天的衣物,食物极其匮乏。几个月来,我们几乎都是以南瓜为食。士兵们自己喊出的口号都是:'打倒资本主义!吃南瓜!'——对他们来说资本主义意味着地主和地主的南瓜。"

然而,国民党军队的袭击威胁比寒冷和饥饿更加严酷。为了粉碎共产主义在中国的种子,从1930年11月至1931年9月,国民党政府进行了三次"围剿"。尽管是在恶劣的环境下,毛泽东和他的战友们还是始终坚持开展土地改革,击退国民党军队的袭击。在艰苦斗争的过程中,中国共产党认识到,占人口绝大多数的中国农民,将在中国革命中发挥至关重要的作用。在他的文章《星星之火,可以燎原》中,毛泽东提出中共的战略重点从城市转向农村,并发动和依靠农民建立农村革命根据地。在长期的革命斗争中,这种方式下农民将会成为骨干,从而发展、壮大革命力量,最后夺取城市,实现在全国范围内的胜利。

今天,井冈山遍布红色旅游爱好者。在这里,他们可以体验到红军战士忍受的生活艰辛:穿粗布衣服,吃糙米和南瓜汤,沿山区徒步跋涉,同时学习他们的故事。如今,游客越来越多涌进山中。

遵义

国民党先前的围剿行动被红军打退,然而他们发动了更激烈的攻击来围剿井冈山革命根据地。在伊斯门教授的《剑桥中国史》一书中,教授是这样描述的:"在德国和日本顾问的建议下,1933年至1934年间,蒋介石雇佣了80万军队,增强自己的军事攻势,发动了第五次围剿行动,并对共产党地区实行严格的经济封锁,他才获得对共产党人几乎决定性的胜利。军事上的失败和食物短缺的痛苦,让共产党人集聚最后的力量和勇气打出了国民党的包围圈,于1934年10月开始了长征。"

长征是当代中国的一个里程碑事件。现当代中国研究的杰出学者费正清教授,宣告长征几乎是一个奇迹,比摩西过红海更有文献意义。长征者在一年中穿越了6000英里(1英里≈1609.34米),平均每天17英里。然而,这个奇迹是在极其恶劣的条件下发生的——中国西南地区地势崎岖、高山险峻、峡谷深邃、河流湍急、没有平原。

由于毛泽东的军事智慧,红军终于击溃了国民党军队。从1935年1月15日至17日,中共中央政治局在贵州省的一个小城市遵义市召开会议。在这里,毛泽东的军事战略被公认是正确的,正式确立了他在党和红军中的领导地位。

在毛泽东的领导下，1949年中国共产党解放了全国，成立了中华人民共和国，成为中国历史上重要的一章。

作为一个天才的领袖，毛泽东从近乎衰竭的境地挽救了中国革命，击败以前被认为是不可战胜的敌人。他也因此成为人类历史上一个永恒的传奇。

遵义是藏在深山中的城市，是著名的旅游胜地。今天，在遵义会议遗址上矗立着一座纪念馆。该建筑保留原有外观，并且周围的大街小巷都用石板铺路。此外，为了保持与纪念馆和谐，周围建筑都被改造成20世纪早期黔北的低结构建筑风格。此外，长征的其他纪念地，如四渡赤水河、娄山关风景名胜区天文台纪念馆都已恢复，且保存完好。

延安

长征在陕北结束，那里是缺少降雨和严重荒漠化的黄土高原。正是在这片土地上，红军创造了新的奇迹。

美国记者埃德加·斯诺是第一批寻求更深入地了解在陕北的中国红军和中共中央的西方人之一。由于多年来被国民党政府攻击和封锁，中国共产党和红军的生活几乎不被外面的世界所知。

根据自己的行程，斯诺写了著名的《红星照耀中国》一书，他描绘中国共产党给陕北带来的巨大变化。在红军到达时，延安是个只有10 000名居民居住的贫穷乡镇，后来它一度成为陕甘宁边区的行政首都。中国共产党的到来给这个小镇注入了温暖、快乐和激情，把它变成由中国各地万人景仰的地方。

从1937年到1947年，延安成为陕甘宁边区的首府，中共中央的所在地，中国革命的指挥中心和大后方。因此，延安长期以来一直被誉为中国革命的圣地。这里有许多保存完好的历史遗迹，包括凤凰山、杨家岭、枣园和王家坪。这些革命遗址——无论是在宝塔山上还是凤凰山上或杨家岭的窑洞——提醒着游客中国共产党过去经历的艰难岁月。

PART V 典型景点

云冈石窟

云冈石窟位于大同西16公里，在低矮的砂岩武周山脚，大多开凿于公元460—494年的北魏。

北魏的出现标志着中国艺术与文化一个新的高点。魏国的建立带来了一段时期的稳定，通过一系列有关婚姻和土地分配的法律创造了汉与非汉民族之间的"融合"。主要的有关农业和河道运输的论文都是在这个时期写出来的。而绘画、书法和诗词也变得更加活泼和雅致。但是最大的成就还是佛教石窟艺术。

石窟寺艺术源于印度，在中国首先出现在敦煌。然而，敦煌的雕刻是在赤土上，而云冈的雕刻才是中国石雕的最早例子。53个洞——包括21个主洞——有51 000个浅浮雕和雕像，高从几厘米到17米。能看到受许多不同风格影响：印度（衣饰、短裙和头饰）；波斯和拜占庭（武器、狮子和胡子）；和希腊（三叉戟、卷曲的爵床叶）。

从东到西，主窟自然分成三组：

1至4号窟。在最东端是头两个窟，有些远离其他窟。正方形的地面设计表明它们建得非常早。第一个洞有一些佛生活的浅浮雕，而第二个窟的中心有一座雕刻优美的宝塔。3号窟是云冈最大的，基本上是三个一组由一尊大佛两尊菩萨组成。优雅的衣饰和高浮雕的运用使人想起了龙门石窟，这也标志着大同的佛像在隋朝或者初唐可能就有了。

远离4号窟是一条小峡谷和一座僧院，由几个寺庙组成。这个僧院建于1652年。历史记载，在这些山里曾经可能有10座僧院，但如今已无踪迹。

5~13号窟。5号窟和6号窟标志着云冈艺术的最高点。在5号窟，一尊大佛（16.8米）静坐凝思。两个窟，特别是6号窟，都丰富地装饰着从宗教故事到宗教游行场景的事件。两个窟的内部，被两座孪生塔挡在洞口，它们被很幸运地保存好。5号、6号和7号窟——后一个有6尊菩萨和两个狮子，都是高浮雕——于1955年被修复。8号窟有许多外国人物：坐在一头公牛上的护持神，司破坏神，持三叉戟的守护神。

7号窟和8号窟形成一对，9号和10号也是，都雕刻丰富。每一组后两个都有前后间，在其入口有精美的浅浮雕作品。11号窟装饰于公元483年，是表示对皇家的敬意。它包括在洞壁神龛上95个大的雕刻和数百尊小的菩萨雕刻。12号窟的浅浮雕提供了那个时期建筑和音乐器具的有价值信息。13号窟有另外一尊大佛，他的胳膊由另一尊佛像支撑，头上笼罩巨大佛光。

14~21号窟。尽管在窟壁神龛中还保留数以千计的小菩萨，这个系列的头两个窟被严重腐蚀。另外五个是在云冈最老的，雕刻于文昌帝统治时期的公元460年。每个窟都有一尊大佛，面容严肃、庄严神圣。在这些窟中的早期雕刻具有几何、线性特质，装饰也不如后面的洞丰富和大胆。

1949年后，这些窟被宣布为历史古迹，通过明智的植树计划和防护屏障建设，风蚀和水蚀的速度慢了下来。遗憾的是，对于20世纪艺术品盗窃和走私所造成的破坏却很少有办法恢复。数以百计的雕像被砍头，大批的浅浮雕被运走。它们现在为日本、欧洲和北美的艺术博物馆所有！

第三章 旅游要素

第六单元 吃——餐饮服务

PART II 对话

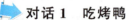
对话1　吃烤鸭

（W：服务员　Mr. H：亨特先生　Mrs. H：亨特夫人　L：李大厨）

W：请坐下。你想要什么？这是菜单。

Mr. H：让我看一下……你喜欢什么？

Mrs. H：我看似乎所有的菜都很好。我真的不知道从哪儿开始？
Mr. H：我也不知道。嗯，这家餐馆什么（菜）出名？
W：烤鸭出名，先生。
Mr. H：听起来很棒。好吧。让我们尝一尝。"百闻不如一尝"。
（过了一会儿）
W：烤鸭来了，先生。
Mrs. H：太好了！看这诱人食欲的棕褐色！
Mr. H：（对服务员）你能给我们演示一下这道高档菜怎么吃吗？
W：好的，先生。首先，左手拿一块薄煎饼，用一些生葱当刷子，在薄煎饼上涂上一层豆酱泥……像这样，不要涂太多豆酱泥在薄煎饼上……接着，把大葱放在薄煎饼中间，用你的筷子夹几片烤鸭……最后，把煎饼卷上就可以享受了！
（服务员帮助亨特夫人用筷子）
Mr. H & Mrs. H：太好吃了。
Mrs. H：你能告诉我这道菜是怎么做的吗？
W：好的。一位熟练的厨师能用鸭子的内脏、头、翅和蹼做出80多道冷热菜来以迎合不同的口味，他能在四五分钟内片出100～120片，每片的皮肉相等。
Mr. H：难以置信！
W：哦，李大厨来了。亨特先生和夫人，让我把你们介绍给经验丰富的李大厨。这是亨特夫人，国外来的朋友，这是她丈夫亨特先生，这是李大厨。
Mr. H & Mrs. H：您好，李先生。
Mrs. H：我们非常享受您的手艺。
Mrs. H：李大厨，您能告诉我这鸭子是怎么烤的吗？
L：非常荣幸。要点就是所选鸭子的质量和炉内所烧木柴的类型。
Mr. H：您用什么鸭子来烤？
L：肥嫩的鸭子平均重2.5千克。
Mrs. H：在烤的过程中用什么木头？
L：只用果木，如桃木和梨木，使鸭肉具有独特的香味。
Mrs. H：在判断正确的温度和烤制时间方面有什么难度吗？
L：有的，那是秘诀所在——正确的判断。并且，当然，也有技巧。
Mr. H & Mrs. H：非常感谢您。
L：不用客气。
Mr. H：跟你说实话，鸭子的香味使我垂涎三尺。
Mrs. H：真的，我从来没有这样饿。它的皮很脆，肉很嫩。
Mr. H：真的。中国烹饪如此丰富多彩。色、香、味都非常好。只有尝了以后我才相信。
W：您还想要别的吗？
Mr. H：不用了，谢谢你。我们都吃饱了。

Mrs. H：我们从来没有比这一顿吃的更饱了。

　　W：这样说过奖了，夫人。

Mr. H：请把账单拿过来。

　　W：给你，先生。

Mr. H：这是100元，零钱不用找了。

　　W：我们不收小费。还是要谢谢您。

Mrs. H：现在我们走吧。（面对服务员）感谢你的优质服务。

　　W：谢谢您，夫人。欢迎再来。

 对话2　吃海鲜

（G：客人　W：服务员）

G：这张桌子是空的吗，服务员？

W：抱歉，先生，这两张桌子已经被人电话预订了，但是那边那张是空的。

G：好吧。

W：（现在是）上海螃蟹上市季节。您想先来点蒸螃蟹吗？

G：我想来点吧。

（过了一会儿）

W：来了，先生。

G：看这些怪物。

W：怪物？您肯定弄错了。它们看上去有点丑，但您会喜欢它们的，因为它们尝起来味道很好。这些是靠近苏州的湖里的淡水蟹。

G：真的吗？你能告诉我它们是怎么做的吗？

W：哦，它们是蒸的。放一些水在锅里，然后把绑好的螃蟹放在蒸架上，水开约20分钟，螃蟹就可以吃了。

G：我怎么吃呢？

W：用牙剥壳，将蟹肉取出，蘸酱油、醋和姜茸吃。

G：我明白了……啊，很好。我听说洞庭湖的螃蟹是最好的。洞庭湖在湖南省吗？

W：是的，是中国的五大湖之一。

G：噢，它们现在都在时令吗？

W：不，根据谚语，"农历九月吃雌蟹，十月吃雄蟹。"至于口味，小雌蟹比雄蟹好。但大雄蟹的爪比雌蟹爪好得多。

G：那就对了。河蟹总是首选。它们鲜美的味道是最受欢迎的。

W：您还要别的什么？您想尝尝用蟹肉制作的秋季特色佳肴吗？

G：您有什么可推荐的？

W：今天我们有清炒蟹粉、炒虾蟹和蟹粉豆腐。

Appendix A 参考译文

G：听起来不错。我想都要，请再给我来碗米饭和一份素汤。

（过了一会儿）

W：吃完了吗，先生？

G：是的。

W：一切都好了吗，先生？

G：是的，谢谢你。所有蟹菜都非常美味。我非常喜欢它们。

W：您这样说真是太好了。蟹肉佳肴是由我们餐馆里最好的厨师做的。

G：难怪它们这么美味！我明天还来。我该付多少钱？

W：总共 65 元。

G：价钱也很公道。给你。零头不用找了。

W：很高兴为您服务，先生。但是我们不收小费。谢谢您。

G：你太好了！再见。

W：再见，晚安。

 PART III 阅读

Text A

中国菜

中国地域辽阔，民族众多，因此各种中国饮食口味不同，却都味美，令人垂涎。因为中国地方菜肴各具特色，总体来讲，中国饮食可以大致分为八大地方菜系，这种分类已被广为接受。当然，还有其他很多著名的地方菜系，如北京菜和上海菜。

山东菜系

山东菜系，由济南菜系和胶东菜系组成，清淡，不油腻，以其香、鲜、酥、软而闻名。因为使用青葱和大蒜作为调料，山东菜系通常很辣。山东菜系注重汤品。清汤清澈新鲜，而油汤外观厚重，味道浓重。济南菜系擅长炸、烤、煎、炒，而胶东菜系则以其烹饪海鲜的鲜淡而闻名。

山东是许多著名学者的故乡，如孔子和孟子。许多山东菜的历史和孔子一样悠久，使得山东菜系成为中国现存的最古老的主要菜系之一。

山东是个巨大的被东面的大海环绕的半岛，黄河曲折流经其中部。因此海鲜是山东菜系的主要构成。山东最著名的菜肴是糖醋鲤鱼。正宗的糖醋鲤鱼必须打捞自黄河。但是因为现在黄河的众多污染，其他地方的鲤鱼更好一些。山东菜主要是速炸、烧烤、炒或深炸。菜肴清新肥美，搭配山东本地的著名啤酒——青岛啤酒就完美了。

四川菜系

四川菜系，是世界上最著名的中国菜系之一。四川菜系以其香辣而闻名，味道多变，

219

着重使用红辣椒，搭配使用青椒和花椒，产生出经典的刺激的味道。此外，大蒜、姜和豆豉也被用于烹饪过程中。野菜和野禽常被选为原料，油炸、无油炸、腌制和文火炖煮是基本的烹饪技术。没有品尝过四川菜的人不算来过中国。

如果你吃四川菜，发现它过于"柔和"，那么你可能吃的不是正宗的四川菜。红绿辣椒被用在许多菜肴中，带来特别的辣味，在中文中称为麻，通常会在口中留下麻木的感觉。四川火锅也许是世界上最出名的火锅，尤其是半辣半清的鸳鸯火锅。

广东菜系

广东菜源自中国最南部的省份广东省。大多数华侨来自广东，因此广东菜也许是国外最广泛的中国地方菜系。

广东人热衷于尝试用各种不同的肉类和蔬菜。事实上，中国北方人常说，广东人吃天上飞的，除了飞机；地上爬的，除了火车；水里游的，除了轮船。很显然，这一陈述很不属实，但是广东菜确是种类丰富的中国菜系之一。使用很多来自世界其他地方的蔬菜，不大使用辣椒，而是注重蔬菜和肉类自身的风味。

广东菜系，味道清、淡、脆、鲜，为西方人所熟知，常用猛禽走兽来烹饪出有创意的菜肴。它的基础烹饪方法包括烤、炒、煸、炸、炖和蒸。其中蒸和炒最常用于保存天然风味。广东厨师也注重菜肴的艺术感。

福建菜系

福建菜系由福州菜、泉州菜、厦门菜组成，以其精选的海鲜，漂亮的色泽，甜、酸、咸和香的味道而出名。最特别的是它的"卤味"。

江苏菜系

江苏菜，又叫淮扬菜，流行于长江下游。以水产作为主要原料，注重原料的鲜味。其雕刻技术十分珍贵，其中瓜雕尤其著名。烹饪技术包括炖、烤、焙、煨等。淮扬菜的特色是淡、鲜、甜、雅。江苏菜系以其精选的原料，精细的准备，不辣不温的口感而出名。因为江苏气候变化很大，江苏菜系在一年之中也有变化。味道强而不重，淡而不温。

浙江菜系

浙江菜系由杭州菜、宁波菜和绍兴菜组成，不油腻，以其菜肴的鲜、柔、滑、香而闻名。杭州菜是这三者中最出名的一个。

湖南菜系

湖南菜系由湘江地区、洞庭湖和湘西的地方菜肴组成。它以其极辣的味道为特色。红辣椒、青辣椒和青葱是这一菜系中的必备品。

安徽菜系

安徽厨师注重于烹饪的温度，擅长煨炖。通常会加入火腿和方糖来改善菜肴的味道。

 Text B

进餐的场所与方式

对于那些习惯了想吃什么就吃什么的人来说，在中国吃饭是一件棘手的事。一般来说，大多数旅游团和参观团会将他们大部分预付费餐点定在下榻的酒店。餐点会在指定时间送到预定的餐桌（通常是上午8时，中午12点和下午6点），菜品由酒店厨师预选。除非特别提出请求，早餐将是西式的（鸡蛋、烤面包、果酱、咖啡、蛋糕或糕点）；午餐和晚餐都是中式的。通常可以提前一天订中式早餐，如果足够多的人能坐一桌（八个人或十个人），导游将会帮忙安排。人们往往很难单独点菜（若单独点菜，费用另计）。虽然大宾馆也会为特殊饮食要求的游客准备特别的饭菜，但在大多数情况下，饮料，包括啤酒、葡萄酒和白酒，都要支付额外的费用（除非预付费已经包含）。

为方便起见，第一次来中国的个人游客通常最终是在下榻的酒店进餐。许多较新的酒店目前提供自助早餐和午餐。尽管需要额外的费用，还是强烈建议在当地餐厅吃饭，无论是氛围，还是食材准备，都更地道，尤其是那些当地美食，还有就是更多的菜品可供选择。您可以通过价格和提问来点餐，或简单地指着别人桌上看起来好吃的点。住在中国的西方人往往光顾酒店的餐厅或更昂贵的中国餐馆，因为这些地方食物通常更好，处所也更清洁、更安静、少拥挤。

有几个能做和不该做的中国用餐礼仪，当你与中国人用餐时大多适用。也许最重要的是谁买单。在通常情况下，如果你被中国人邀请，估计你不会买单。惯例是中国的主办方会为来访的团体或代表团举办欢迎晚宴。晚餐可以是一个精心制作的宴会或者是一个简单的聚会。抵达的客人通常会被领进一个大厅，提供茶水、热毛巾，与招待方进行约10~15分钟的轻松谈话。然后主要招待人会发出信号，晚餐准备好了，嘉宾可以就座了。招待方的领导将主持，坐在主桌（中国传统决定了主座面对着门），坐在他左右的是级别最高的代表团的领导人。

主要餐具摆放包括一个小盘，一双筷子放在托架上（刀叉也可以使用的托架），还有三个杯子：啤酒或饮料杯，葡萄酒杯和用来祝酒的白酒杯。菜肴按照规定的味觉刺激顺序开始上菜，从冷盘到10个或更多的菜品。一个好的菜单将会最低限度包含中国菜的五种基本味道（酸、辣、苦、甜、咸）。菜品口味在酥嫩、干脆、重香麻辣之间交替。汤通常是主菜后送达的；在南方，炒饭或面条放在最后。甜点一般是新鲜水果与糕点。

自从中国20世纪80年代的经济改革，食品工业和餐饮服务也发生了巨大的变化。旅馆和餐馆已经如雨后春笋般出现在全国各地。有很多吃的地方，也有各种美食供人选择。通常情况下，川菜、广东菜在中国北部和南部的几乎任何地方都可以发现，地方菜和小吃也是遍地可见，甚至是外国美食和快餐，如法国美食、意大利菜、泰国菜、麦当劳、必胜客和肯德基全国各大城市都有。近年来，四川火锅已经在全国各地普及。

PART V 典型景点

丽江

丽江位于云南省西北部。丽江地区的人口超过100万，有21个民族，包括纳西族、彝族、傈僳族、普米族等。

丽江地区是云南省发展最快的旅游区。它有美丽的自然环境，独特的民族风情，古老的少数民族文化，旅游资源非常丰富。该景区主要分布在丽江市和宁蒗县。丽江被称为"两山，一镇，一湖，一河，一种文化和一种风俗"。两山是指玉龙雪山和老君山，一镇是指大研镇，一湖是指泸沽湖，一河是指金沙河，一种文化是指东巴文化，一种民俗指的是摩梭人的习俗。丽江的植物和动物资源非常丰富，自然美景和迷人的少数民族民俗风情，吸引了来自海内外越来越多的游客。

丽江古城有近千年的历史。丽江风景独特，风情独具。它是国家级历史文化名城。包括三个部分：大研、白沙和束河。那么，为什么它叫作大研？因为它位于丽江盆地的中部，看起来像一个大砚台，中文读音是"Yan"。

大研镇最著名的是其古老和简单的建筑风格和高雅艺术的布局。城内，玉泉河蜿蜒而过，穿梭在古老的民居间，河边的小路也是顺着玉泉河，古老的房屋都是面朝玉泉河的。无论你走在哪条小道或马路上，都有蜿蜒而过的小河，河上大多有桥。古语云：有河有桥的房子，是再好不过的住处了。这就是我们称大研镇为"东方威尼斯"的原因。

古镇的中心是四方街，一个热闹的集市。自古以来，四方街一直是游客、商人集散的重地。集市上每天有穿着独特服饰的少数民族人民来这里做生意，让这里成为一个无比热闹的地方。如果你花一整天在这里，你可以在这里体验诗意的变化。早上，街道伸伸懒腰苏醒了，在中午，就成了大忙人，当夜晚来临，它又变成为一个盛装的少女，深夜来临，它又静悄悄地入睡了。

为什么街名为"四方"？有两种解释：一种解释是，丽江古城的首领把它作为"扩大势力"的根据地；另一种解释是，"四方"是指四个方向，因为这里有来自各个地方的人民。大研镇完全不同于中国其他古老城镇，周围没有城墙。这是它的神奇之处！

第七单元　住——宾馆服务

 PART II　对话

对话 1　登记入住

前台：您好，这里是希尔顿酒店，请问有什么可以帮您的吗？
卡萝尔：您好，我想订一间周五的房。
前台：好的。请问您需要什么样子的房间？周五有单人间、双人双床间、双人间和套间。
卡萝尔：我想订一间带海景的单人间，可以吗？
前台：我看一下。可以。
卡萝尔：好的，那我订这间了。
前台：请问您什么时候入住？打算住几天呢？有什么特殊要求吗？

Appendix A 参考译文

卡萝尔：我想我应该周五早上 9 点入住，周日下午 2 点退房。请帮我订一间远离电梯的房间，我睡觉怕吵。

前　台：好的。没问题。

卡萝尔：饭店有游泳池吗？

前　台：有的。游泳池开放时间为每天早上 9 点到晚上 10 点。

卡萝尔：那太好了。你们酒店有什么餐厅呢？

前　台：我们有 3 个中餐厅，一个意大利餐厅，都在二楼。三楼还有一个超市，健身中心在四楼。

卡萝尔：太棒了！非常感谢。

前　台：很高兴为您服务。房间是 316。祝您愉快，女士！

卡萝尔：谢谢！

对话 2　办理离店手续

礼　宾：这里是礼宾台，有什么可以帮到您的吗？

客　人：我要退房了，你能上来帮我拿一下行李吗？

礼　宾：当然可以，先生。能告诉我您的房间号码吗？

客　人：好的，2932 房。

礼　宾：好的，2932 房。我们会马上派一名行李员上去，您在房间里等，行吗？

客　人：好的。

行李员：早上好，先生，我是来帮您拿行李的。

客　人：谢谢，你帮我拿这两个行李箱好吗，我拿背包。

行李员：里面是否有贵重物品或者易碎物品呢？

客　人：没有。

行李员：这是您的行李标签，我们会将行李放在行李台上。您到那儿取行李好吗？

客　人：好的。

行李员：您还有其他需要吗？

客　人：没有了，多谢。

行李员：很乐意为您效劳。祝您愉快！

PART III　阅读

 Text A

如何选择商务旅游酒店

从广义上来说，酒店范围从"住宿加早餐"的家庭式经营到拥有几千个房间的大型酒店不等。按照价格、位置和顾客类型，酒店可以分为：商务酒店，提供酒水、食宿给商业人士；度假酒店，主要吸引前来娱乐的游客，所以经常会设在度假胜地；公寓式酒店，提供带

223

有全套厨房设备的酒店房间,集酒店奢华与家庭的舒适安逸于一体。提供一居室和两居室,是带孩子家庭的理想选择;最后,赌场酒店,只有一个目的——吸引那些博彩、赌博的人们。

当今,越来越多的美国旅客选择入住小型旅馆或客栈,而不是酒店。他们会选择提供次日早餐的房间。在美国,很多提供住宿和早餐的快捷旅馆都是老式的历史建筑。有些这样的旅馆只有几个房间而已,而有些规模大一些。有些旅馆的房间不提供电话和电视,有些提供这些设施。住在提供住宿和早餐的快捷旅馆和住在大酒店的感觉完全不一样,通常费用要少很多。待在这样的旅馆就像拜访别人的家,店主会很乐意告诉你应该去游玩的地方和景点,很多游客表示他们很享受这种可以和当地家庭见面的机会。

当然了,每个酒店都有床和浴室(我们是这样希望的),但是商务酒店并不都是一样的。在你下次定商务酒店的时候,这些技巧可能会派上用场。

1. 房间内有高速的网络

在房间里有网络服务,不管是无线网络还是以太网,对发邮件,准备演讲和打发路上的无聊时间都是很重要的。

2. 商务中心

要打印、传真文件吗?丢了电脑,想要上网怎么办?即使不是每个连锁酒店都提供网络服务,商务中心对每个出差的职场人士来说也是必不可少的。

3. 客房服务

是的,客房服务很贵,并且不一定总是好的,但是在你开了一天冗长的会议后疲惫不堪时,你最不愿做的事情就是开着车到镇上去找吃饭的地方。至少,你会希望酒店有小型超市,让你可以买一些水、饮料、食品来填饱肚子。

4. 锻炼设施

在享受了几个晚上的客房套餐后,你会发现自己的裤子有点紧了。在你出差途中,可以在酒店的锻炼设施上做运动来保持健康。

5. 往返服务

为了避免打车或租车,订那种提供包接送到机场服务的酒店。

6. 选址

在出差前做一些调查,这样你才能根据行程,订到离会场或飞机场最近的酒店。

7. 门房服务

一般在大城市都有提供,门房服务可以帮你处理从找旅馆到打出租车的一切事情。

8. 会议室

如果你要做一场大型演讲的话,或者需要在开会前找个地方开展团队工作,这时会议室就很有作用了。另外,如果你在开会前需要大量的准备时间,或者你有很多样品要演示,你可能会让客户到你的酒店,而不是带着那么多的大样品满城转。

 Text B

当今摩登酒店

当今酒店和过去大不相同,通常人们住酒店是为出差、旅游或者度假。因此酒店的设计主要是满足这些人群的需要。

短暂停留的酒店被称为旅馆，招待所，汽车旅馆或汽车酒店，客栈，旅舍或者度假村。旅馆也指青年旅社，经常是为学生徒步旅行准备的。汽车旅馆有很多停车位，经常会在高速公路或者公路附近。客栈类似于招待所。旅舍、度假村或者度假酒店会建在山上、海边或者河边。

从超奢侈、高费用的大酒店，到小而不贵、大多数旅客都可以支付得起的小旅馆，这些酒店根据制定的国际酒店星级评定标准来估价。现在，我们看看下面的几个摩登酒店。

四季酒店，孟买

孟买四季酒店位于经历着迅速的中产阶级化的地区，现在本地人称之为孟买中城。

克拉巴区位于地标性建筑哈吉·阿里清真寺的南面，另一边 Sealink 大桥带你通往北面班德拉街区和更远的地方。因为它的环境及物流上的优势，四季酒店自从三年前开业后，一直成为孟买最佳三间商务酒店之一。

没有其他酒店能看到新旧孟买 360 度的景观。观景的选择十分全面：阿拉伯海景、历史上有名的纺织厂区景、Sealink 大桥景、马哈拉克希米寺，另外还能看到少量的工程建筑及贫民区——毕竟那里是真正的孟买，而不是一些明信片上的照片。

内幕消息：位于四季酒店的 34 楼露天楼顶，Aer Bar 是孟买最高的酒吧。一边享受香槟，一边看阿拉伯海的日落，也可看到穆克什·安巴尼价值亿万的豪宅，还可鸟瞰一些贫民区，最富有和最贫穷的人们都在争夺那些空间。

用微信控制的酒店

在拉斯维加斯举行的 CES 消费电子展上，凯撒娱乐公司与中国腾讯公司通过合作，在当地的赌场酒店 The LINQ 打造了多间全智能客房。顾客可以使用微信来控制房间的灯光、恒温器和窗帘等。智能客房是凯撒娱乐集团为了迎合中国游客做出的举动之一。到店之后，顾客只需扫描酒店的二维码便可添加凯撒娱乐集团的公众号，从而进行各项操作。这个公众号由硅谷的 Ayla 网络公司开发。

2013 年，有超过 30 万名来自中国的游客前去拉斯维加斯旅行，这一数据在过去的两年里翻了一番。凯撒娱乐集团在一份声明中表示：“通过与业界顶级公司如 Ayla 和微信合作，可以让我们的客户通过他们每天使用的微信更好地与酒店互动，从而获得宾至如归的感受。”

凯撒集团在美国和另外四个国家运营着 50 家赌场。与凯撒集团合作是微信开发海外市场的众多项目之一。腾讯发言人陈先生表示：“我们将打造一个生态系统，让商家提高微信在 O2O 战略中的地位。其他项目还包括在亚洲与 Easy Taxi 打车服务以及 Zalora 网购服务合作，以及在美国、意大利和中国与 YOOX 购物账号合作等。”

PART V 典型景点

武夷山

武夷山位于福建省与江西省的交界处，全长约 500 公里，平均海拔 1000 米以上。相传唐尧时代的长寿老翁彭祖携二子隐于此山。其长子曰"武",次子曰"夷",二人开山挖河,后人为纪念他们,就把此山称为"武夷山"。另一种说法是,此地原居住有古代闽越族人,首领名武夷君,故而得名。

武夷山风景区在福建武夷山市南郊、武夷山脉北段东南麓,呈长条形,东西宽约5公里,南北长约14公里,面积70平方公里,平均海拔350米,武夷山是由红色砂砾岩组成的低山丘陵,属丹霞地貌。几亿年以来,因地壳运动,地貌不断发生变化,构成了山峰挺拔、碧水萦回的"碧水丹山"美景,享有"奇秀甲东南"之美称。

武夷山邻近北回归线,属于亚热带湿润季风气候区,年平均气温为17.9摄氏度。夏无酷暑,冬无严寒。温暖湿润的气候为武夷山植物生长提供了优越的自然条件。因此,武夷山中竹树茂密,花草繁盛,鸟语花香,四季如春。随着时序的流转,山光水色会给人以不同的情趣:早春,山青水绿,野花红艳,明媚动人;入夏,林木交荫,处处流水潺潺,凉风习习,堪称避暑胜地;秋来,天高气爽,满山丹枫如染,茶花盛开,令人心旷神怡;冬至,寒山映日,松翠不凋,又是一种风情。至于阴晴朝暮,风烟雨雪,山川景色更是变幻莫测。

武夷山集道、佛、儒教于一身,是一座历史悠久的文化名山。总面积999.75平方公里,是迄今为止我国已申报的世界遗产中面积第二大的景点。根据区内资源的不同特征,全区划分为西部生物多样性、中部九曲溪生态、东部自然与文化景观以及城村闽越王遗址四个保护区。

1999年12月,联合国教科文组织将武夷山作为文化和自然双重遗产列入《世界遗产名录》。

第八单元　行——交通服务

 PART II　对话

 对话1　预订机票

A:早上好。美国联合航空公司。我能为您做些什么吗?

B:是的,我想订一张下周飞往波士顿的机票。

A:您想何时去?

B:周一,9月12日。

A:我们周一有802次航班。请稍等,让我查一下那天是否有座。非常抱歉802次航班的机票已订完。

B:那还有别的吗?

A:下一趟航班在9月13日周二上午9:30起飞。我要为您订个座位吗?

B:哦……是直航,对吗?

Appendix A 参考译文

A：是的。您愿意订头等舱还是经济舱的机票？
B：我想订头等舱的机票。多少钱？
A：单程是 176 美元。
B：好的，我要订周二 9:30 的机票。
A：一张 807 次航班周二早晨 9:30 飞往波士顿的机票，对吗，先生？
B：对。你能把我放到 12 号等候名单中吗？
A：当然可以。请您告诉我您的名字和联系方式。
B：我叫洛鲁斯·安德森。我的电话是 52378651，您可以和我取得联系。
A：若是取消我会通知您的。
B：非常感谢。
A：不客气。

 对话 2　租车

尼克：早上好，先生，我可以为您做些什么吗？
大卫：早上好，我想租一辆车。
尼克：你来这里真是找对人了。我们这里有很多车供你选择，你想租哪种类型呢？
大卫：我想要租一辆音响好的车子。
尼克：我们所有的车子都有音响。音响、空调都是标准配备。
大卫：那很好。我想和女朋友度假时用，我想让她玩得开心。
尼克：是这样啊？那么我让你看些她可能会喜欢的，在后面的空地。
大卫：这是保时捷。
尼克：是的，很漂亮吧！
大卫：但是我可能负担不起，一定很贵吧！
尼克：你说你在机场的租车代理商那儿看过车子。在那里你可能花了钱，还得不到东西。但是在我们这里，你可以用租他们一般车子的价格租到这辆保时捷。
大卫：但是它不省油吧。
尼克：没有普通汽车那么省油，但是它外观很漂亮啊，对吧？
大卫：没错，看起来几乎像新的一样。
尼克：坐进去看看感觉如何。那么你要租这辆保时捷了？
大卫：是的，并且我要买保险，我想它是必需的。
尼克：买保险是很明智的选择，你要租多久？
大卫：两周。你们是按公里收费吗？
尼克：不是，统一费用。我能看一下你的国际驾照吗？
大卫：当然，给你！
尼克：谢谢，先生，你需要填一下这个表格。
大卫：好的。

227

PART III 阅读

Text A

旅行的唯一方式是步行

人类学家小心翼翼地将人类以往的每一个时代都贴上标签。例如，"旧石器时代人""新石器时代人"等说法就简洁地概括了一个个完整的时代。当人类学家把他们的目光投向20世纪的时候，他们肯定会选择"无腿人"这个标签。这段时期的历史大致会这样记载："在20世纪，人类忘记了如何使用他们的腿。男子和女子从很小的时候起就坐在小汽车、公共汽车和火车里来来去去。所有的高层建筑里都装有电梯和自动扶梯，以避免人们步行。这种状况强加在这个时期地球居民的身上，是由于他们非同寻常的生活方式。那时，人们只想着每天旅行几百英里这类事情。但是，令人惊奇的是，他们即使去度假也不用他们的腿。他们建造缆索铁路、滑雪索道和道路，通向每座大山的顶峰。地球上所有的风景区都被大型停车场糟蹋了。"

未来的历史书还会说，我们的眼睛也弃置不用了。在急急忙忙从一个地方赶往另一个地方的路上，我们什么都没看到。航空旅行可以使你鸟瞰世界——要是机翼恰好挡住了你的视线，你就看得更少了。当你乘汽车或火车旅行的时候，模糊不清的乡村景象不停地映在车窗玻璃上。尤其是汽车司机，他们的头脑永远都被"向前，向前"的冲动占据着：他们从来都不停下来。到底是由于漂亮车道的诱惑，还是别的什么？至于海上旅行，简直不值一提。有一首老歌的歌词对海上旅行进行了完美的概括："哦，加入海军去看世界，我看到了什么？我看见了大海。"最典型的20世纪旅行者总是说："我已经去过那儿了"。你提到世界上最遥远、最引人遐思的地名，比如埃尔多拉多、喀布尔、伊尔库茨克，准有人说："我去过那儿。"意思是："我在去另外一个地方的路上，以100英里的时速路过那儿。"

当你以很高的速度旅行时，"现在"就毫无意义。你主要生活在未来，因为你多半时间在盼望赶到别的一个地方去。但是当你真的到达了目的地，你的到达也没有什么意义。你还要继续前行。像这样子旅行，你什么也没有经历。你的现在并不是现实，跟死亡没有什么两样。另一方面，徒步旅行者却总是生活在现在。对他来说，旅行和到达是同一件事情；他是一步一步走着来到某地的。他在用自己的眼睛、耳朵和整个身体体验现在。在他旅途的终点，他感到一种愉悦的生理疲惫。他知道他会享受深沉而甜蜜的睡眠：这是对一切真正旅行者的酬报。

Text B

如何让旅行变得轻松易行

旅行是复杂的，你可能会遇到意料之外的事情。常飞旅客有他们爱用的旅行窍门，有些人会将这些窍门通过朋友和同事代代相传。任何减少旅途麻烦的策略都能成为珍藏宝典。以下是我让旅途变轻松的一些最有效的方法。

Appendix A 参考译文

获得贵宾待遇

能获得最优待遇的是常飞旅客项目中的顶级贵宾,他们通常是飞行里程超过 100,000 英里(1 英里 = 1609.344 米)的旅客。但即使是偶尔搭飞机的旅客也有可能成为入门级贵宾,标准为每年 25,000 英里。当机场的非贵宾队伍排起长龙时,这能帮你避免错过航班。

在某家航空公司俱乐部买一张日卡(约 50 美元),就能获得舒适的座位、电视、工作空间、安静的环境、饮料和零食。出问题时,这尤其物有所值:俱乐部中经验丰富、老成稳重的航空公司服务人员能帮你解决问题并改签机票。

购买升舱座位能让你在安检时优先排队并提早登机。有些信用卡也可以让你免费托运一件行李并提早登机。但是注意:某些信用卡可能收取高额年费,最高可达每年 450 美元。

更好的打包方法

在你的黑色行李箱上绑一条彩色丝带,让行李箱变得个性化(但不要太长,以防在行李机中缠住)。在你的包里放一张名片。如果姓名牌或行李牌被航空公司的行李机吞掉(这种情况很多),航空公司会尝试开包确认行李的主人。

注意:永远不要在托运行李中放贵重物品。航空公司对行李丢失和损坏所负的责任很有限,而且航空公司对许多丢失物品,包括珠宝、电器和贵重物品,都不提供补偿。如果由于舱顶行李架已满而被迫在舱门口托运行李,那么请拿出贵重物品和电器。永远不要托运第二天你需要穿的衣服,不管是泳衣还是西装。行李可能会丢失或延迟。

准备一个洗漱用品旅行包,这样你就不用每趟旅行都打包洗漱用品。可以考虑携带的其他物品:一把雨伞、一双拖鞋(如果你不想在酒店房间里光脚走来走去的话)、一个空水瓶——这样一旦进入安检区后,你就可以用它装水,而不用花四美元在机场商店里买水喝了。

快速通过安检

机场安检扫描点是很容易丢失重要物品的地方:例如,没有装回钱包的驾照或被其他"旅客"拿走的笔记本电脑。以下是我的常规做法:

我在排队之前就将手机、手表、钥匙和笔都放进公文包里。安检工作台的人员把身份证件还给我之后,我会马上把证件放回钱包中。每次我都将登机牌放在同一个口袋中。我每次都把液体和笔记本电脑放在我包里的同一个位置,这样当我必须被检查时,就能知道它们的确切位置。我会把笔记本电脑放在一个安检塑料箱里。液体放在另一个塑料箱里,与外套、皮带和兜里的零钱放在一起。

注意不要佩戴会触发人体扫描仪并导致强制搜身的珠宝首饰,穿容易穿脱的鞋。

舒适住店

有些旅客总是要求住酒店高层房间,以减轻街面噪声。也有些人坚持要住低层房间,这样万一着火,能够得着消防梯。实际上,有些公司在与酒店签订的合同中坚持要求为员工预订距街面四层楼以内的房间。

你入住后,请花几分钟时间从你的房间走到最近的应急楼梯,而不是电梯。这样,如果警报响起，或者走廊充满烟雾，你就能知道走哪条路。

随身携带房间号码。从办理入住手续时拿到的纸上撕下房间号码，放在兜里。这样当你记不住房间号码是 625 还是 629 时，你不会迷路。

PART V 典型景点

香港

香港位于中国东南端，是发展日渐迅速的东亚地区的枢纽，地理条件优越。香港总面积达 1104 平方千米，由香港岛、九龙半岛和新界组成。早在 150 多年前，香港被形容为"荒芜之地"。时至今日，香港已发展成为一个国际金融商贸中心，跻身世界大都会之列。香港除了拥有世界上最优良的深水港外，可以说是没有其他天然资源。香港能成为一个生产力强、创意无尽的城市，在于拥有勤奋不懈、适应力强、教育程度高且富于创业精神的工作人口。香港于 1997 年 7 月 1 日回归祖国，成为中华人民共和国的特别行政区。根据《中华人民共和国香港特别行政区基本法》的规定，香港保留现有的经济、法律和社会制度，50 年不变。除防务和外交事务归中央人民政府管理外，香港特别行政区享有高度自治。香港是一个真正的购物天堂、美食世界、休闲夏日旅游胜地和世界文化窗口。

香港青马大桥

香港青马大桥是全球最长的行车铁路双用悬索式吊桥，也是全球第六长以悬索吊桥形式建造的吊桥。目前，青马大桥自开放通车以来，已成为本港一条主要连接香港国际机场及市区的干线公路。每天有很多汽车、公交车和火车穿梭于大桥之上。青马大桥已成为香港主要的建筑标志和旅游观光景点，吸引了世界各地的游客前来参观。

香港迪士尼乐园

香港迪士尼乐园是由香港政府和迪士尼公司兴建的，于 2005 年 9 月 12 日正式开园。它是世界上最小的迪士尼乐园，包含了香港迪士尼乐园主题公园、两家酒店、零售、餐饮和娱乐设施，在大屿山占地大约 1.3 平方千米。

香港迪士尼乐园不仅是孩子们的天堂，也是成年人重返童年的天堂。来到香港迪士尼乐园的游客将会暂时离开现实世界，进入五彩缤纷的童话王国，享受来自未来和危险世界的神秘幻想之旅。

香港海洋公园

香港海洋公园是世界著名的海洋动物博物馆，建成于 1977 年元月。公园位于南朗山上，由"黄竹坑公园"和"南朗山公园"组成。两者以空中吊车连接，形成一个完整的公园景区。游客乘上空中吊车，只需 6 分钟，就到了南朗山公园。置身于 6 人座的鸟笼状空中吊车中，从 200 米高空驶过 1.4 千米的全程，俯瞰整个公园的景色，真是奇妙又刺激。

南朗山公园拥有三大场馆：海洋馆、海涛馆和海洋剧场。海洋馆是一座椭圆形的建筑物，隔着高达三层的巨大玻璃壁，游客可以观看大约 400 种鱼类，共 3 万条鱼在水中的美妙姿态。海涛馆内设有人造海浪和假山,在电动浪涛机的操纵下,海水波涛起伏高达1米。在海洋剧场中,游客可以看到训练有素的海豚、海狮于巨型水池中的精彩表演。

香港海洋公园内还有疯狂过山车、摩天轮等众多游乐设施。游客在这东南亚规模最大的娱乐休闲中心里,定会度过难忘的一天。

浅水湾

浅水湾位于港岛南部,是香港最具代表性的美丽海湾。浅水湾浪平沙细,滩床宽阔,坡度平缓,海水温暖。夏令时节是浅水湾最热闹的时候,大批游客蜂拥而至。在搏浪戏水后,游客可以尽情地品尝烧烤的美味,在海边拍照留念。浅水湾的秀丽景色,使它成为港岛著名的高级住宅区之一。这些豪华私宅成为浅水湾另一独特的景区,令人流连忘返。

第九单元　游——旅游服务

对话1　普吉岛之旅

比尔和简是两名在泰国的海外留学生,他们在校园里相遇了。

比尔:我听说普吉岛是泰国最大的岛屿了。
　简:是的,他大概与新加坡的面积差不多大。
比尔:它的位置在哪儿?
　简:它位于安达曼海海域泰国的西海岸。
比尔:它的历史悠久吗?
　简:历史悠久并且绚丽多彩,主要出产锡和宝石。
比尔:你的意思是说贸易对其发展很重要了?
　简:是的,这个岛屿是中国和印度的主要贸易路线,但是现在它的收入主要依靠旅游。
比尔:为什么叫"普吉"呢?
　简:"普吉"这个名字来源于马来语"bukit",意思是"山",这座岛屿从远处看就像一座山。
比尔:我十分期待去那儿看看。

对话2　峡谷行

A:有到大峡谷的旅游团了吗?
B:有几个团去大峡谷。
A:你去过我们的旅客服务中心吗?
B:不,没去过。
A:你可以告诉我怎么走吗?
B:好的。往前走,在你的左边。
A:我听说有的旅游团真正下到峡谷里去了。是真的吗?

B：真的。那是真正参观峡谷的好方式。
A：还有，那也是个好的运动，因为我们要长距离徒步旅行。
B：听起来好极了。
A：我到哪里去报名参加呢？
B：到服务中心去。跟他们说你要参加到峡谷里去的旅游团。你在那儿付钱。我带的下一个团就是要下去的。回见！

 Text A

世界旅游组织

世界旅游组织（UNWTO）是联合国下辖的专门机构，推动了旅游业健康发展、可持续发展以及大众化发展。作为旅游领域的主要国际机构，UNWTO促使旅游业成为经济增长、包容性发展以及环境可持续发展的推动力，领导与支持旅游领域先进知识的传播及世界范围内旅游政策的制定。UNWTO倡导全球旅游业遵守行业道德，使旅游对社会经济贡献最大化，同时将其可能的负面影响降到最低。它还致力于实现联合国千年发展目标（MDGs），努力消除贫困现象和促进可持续发展。

世界旅游组织的成员包括156个国家，6个联系成员和两个观察员国。除此之外还有400多个附属会员，代表私营部门、教育机构、旅游协会、当地旅游部门、对旅游业有特殊兴趣的非政府组织以及与从事UNWTO目标有关的贸易和非贸易团体和机构。其总部位于西班牙首都马德里。

其宗旨是促进和发展旅游事业，使之有利于经济发展，国家间相互了解，和平与繁荣，为尊重人权和人类的基本自由（不分种族、性别、语言和宗教信仰）做出贡献。在实现这些目标的过程中，UNWTO特别关注发展中国家在旅游领域的利益。

历史

世界旅游组织的产生，始于1925年5月4日至9日在荷兰海牙召开的国际官方旅游者运输协会代表大会（International Congress of Official Tourist Traffic Associations，ICOTTA）。尽管世界旅游组织宣称国际官方旅游者运输协会代表大会在1934年演变为国际官方旅游宣传组织联盟，但是《旅游研究纪事》早期的一些文章却认为世界旅游组织起源于国际官方旅游宣传组织联盟（International Union of Official Tourist Publicity Organizations，IUOTPO）。

第二次世界大战使该联盟停止了活动，随着二战的结束和国际旅游人数的增加，又决定成立专门委员会研究重新恢复国际旅游宣传组织联盟的工作，将"国际官方旅游宣传组织联盟"更名为"国际官方旅行组织联盟"（International Union of Official Travel Organizations，IUOTO），作为一个技术的和非政府间的组织，国际官方旅游组织联盟主要由国家旅游机构、行业群体和消费者群体混合而成。其宗旨不仅在于促进旅游业的整体发展，还在于吸取旅游业的精华作为国际贸易的组成部分并为发展中国家的经济发展提供策略。

20世纪60年代末，IUOTO意识到需要进一步转型以提高其在国际事务中的作用。

Appendix A 参考译文

1967年第20届国际官方旅行组织联盟在东京召开，大会宣布有必要建立一个政府间的组织机构以在国际事务中与其他国际机构（尤其是联合国）进行合作，由此国际旅行组织联盟与和联合国建立了紧密的联系，最初的建议也使该组织成为联合国的一部分。

正是以联合国的建议为基础，成立了新的政府间的旅游组织。1970年，IUOTO大会投票同意成立世界旅游组织，在IUOTO和51个成员国正式批准的基础上，世界旅游组织于1974年11月1日开始运行。

最近，2003年在联合国的第15次代表大会上，世界旅游组织执行机构和联合国一致同意把世界旅游组织作为联合国的一个专门机构。

组织机构

- 全体大会

全体大会是世界旅游组织的最高权力机构。全体大会每两年召开一次，主要是审批预算报告和工作计划、审议旅游业方面的重大问题。每四年选举一次秘书长。全体大会由有投票权的代表所组成，他们代表着正式成员和行业理事成员国家和地区。联系成员和其他国际组织的代表以观察员身份参加全体大会会议。

- 执行委员会

执行委员会是世界旅游组织的行政机构，负责确保整个组织正常运转和预算控制。该委员会每年开两次会，由全体大会选举的26位委员组成（每5个正式会员产生一位委员）。作为世界旅游组织总部的主办国，西班牙在执行委员会拥有一个永久席位。行业理事成员和联系成员以观察员的身份参加执行委员会会议。

- 地区委员会

UNWTO有6个地区委员会：非洲委员、美洲委员会、东亚及太平洋委员会、欧洲委员会、中东委员会和南亚委员会。委员会由全体正式成员和所在地区的行业理事成员组成，每年至少开一次会。所在地区的联系成员以观察员的身份参加地区委员会会议。

- 专门委员会

UNWTO专门委员会的职能是就管理和项目问题提出建议。它包括：项目委员会、财经预算委员会、统计指导委员会、环境委员会和教育网络中心。

- 秘书处

秘书处由秘书长领导，他管理着马德里总部约110个专职人员，这些人员负责实施UNWTO的工作计划和服务广大成员。UNWTO的联系成员由马德里总部的一位专职行政秘书负责。秘书处还包括设在日本大阪的UNWTO亚太地区办事处，此办事处由日本政府资助。世界旅游组织的官方语言是阿拉伯语、英语、法语、中文、俄罗斯语和西班牙语。

 Text B

未来的旅游业

目前，世界正处于旅游业的第二个黄金时代的开端——一个真正意义的大众化旅游时代的开端。随着21世纪的到来，全世界的人都将周游世界。甚至一个有钱的美国人已经实现了梦寐以求的理想——太空旅游。

233

19世纪，旅游业正处于第一个黄金时代，轮船和铁路促使旅游业有了第一次飞速发展，同时旅游业首次有了一个新目标：休闲猎奇。在此之前，大多数人习惯性地进行贸易之旅，朝圣之旅，甚至是难民之旅和战争之旅。在工业革命时代，新兴的富裕阶层的观光者们身带《贝德克尔旅游指南》离家远游。19世纪的文学方面也涌现出了许多伟大的旅游作品，如马克·吐温的《傻子出国记》，大仲马的《莱茵河两岸》和刘鹗的《老残游记》。

尽管21世纪旅游业的宽度和广度与以往不同，但它仍将是对过去的回应。很多方面，未来的旅游业将重新回到19世纪旅游业的第一个黄金时代。技术变革的影响，政治壁垒的坍塌和费用的急剧下降都将使人们涌起出去看外面世界的冲动。

多亏上面提到的物品，尤其是新技术（计算机和互联网）的应用，旅游者们可以更好地计划他们的旅游。电子奇迹使人们不用出门就可以计划他们的旅途，就可以通过旅游公司预订他们的旅途、航线、巴士、观光火车以及旅馆等。随着逼真现实的电子装置的使用，很多使用者甚至在他们出门之前就可以部分地体验旅途。

黄金时代是充满财富和成就的时代，也是重塑价值观的时代，接踵而来的旅游业繁荣也是如此。毫无例外，全世界正在向游客张开了怀抱，在未来可能仍是如此。尽管世界变得越来越小，探险仍使人类产生兴奋欣喜之情，就像亨利·亚当斯第一次看到大教堂一样，又像印度诗人泰戈尔访问泰姬陵一样。与以往相比有所变化的是，更多的人会有机会有此经历。

与其他行业一样，旅游业毫无疑问已经对社会文化和全球环境产生巨大的积极影响和消极影响，未来仍将如此。因此，如何在旅游业和人类社会的可持续发展之间保持平衡仍然是我们人类必须研究和解决的一个问题。可以肯定的是，这个问题的解决需要我们长期不懈的努力。

Part V 典型景点

澳门简介

澳门位于中国东南沿海的珠江三角洲，东北约60公里便是重要的经济贸易中心香港。澳门地区由澳门半岛、氹仔和路环两个离岛组成，总面积共21.09平方公里。中华人民共和国1999年12月20日对澳门恢复行使主权，设立澳门特别行政区。

气候

澳门全年气候温和，平均气温约20℃（68°F），全年温差变化16℃（50°F）～25℃（77°F）；湿度较高，约75%～90%；全年降雨量约1,778毫米。10～12月为澳门的秋季，是旅游的理想季节，天气晴朗，气候温和，湿度低。冬季（1～3月）虽较寒冷，但阳光普照；踏入4月，温度逐渐上升；5～9月，天气炎热，气候潮湿有雨，有时有台风。

人口

总人口大约45.5万，大约95%的是中国人，5%的是葡萄牙人、欧洲人和来自其他地区的人。

语言

中文和葡萄牙语是现行官方语言。居民日常沟通普遍使用广东话。英语在澳门也很通行，在商业、旅游和贸易中使用。

Appendix A 参考译文

宗教

澳门崇尚宗教信仰自由。主要的宗教有天主教、佛教以及新教。大部分人信奉佛教,而7%的人是天主教徒。

历史

在葡萄牙王子亨利发起的葡萄牙航海大时代中,葡萄牙人在1554到1557年间开始在澳门定居,瓦斯科·达·伽马在15世纪末期到达印度,16世纪早期葡萄牙航海者进一步向东,然后向北。

1513年欧维士成为首位到达中国南部的葡萄牙人,随后在此地建立了许多葡萄牙的贸易中心,这些贸易中心最终在澳门落脚发展,当时的澳门处于中日贸易之间和中欧贸易之间的事实上的垄断地位。

澳门还是把基督教引入中国和日本的重要基地,这为澳门提供了历史上最光辉灿烂的时刻。由于其繁荣和独一无二的位置,其他欧洲国家开始用贪婪的目光注视着澳门并密谋从葡萄牙手中夺取它。1622年荷兰人试图入侵澳门但被击退。随着时间的推移和西方其他贸易国家来到中国,澳门成为富商们从广州工厂撤退后居住的夏季行宫,他们在此静待贸易季的开幕。

香港的深水吸引了商船和贸易。随着香港成为世界主要的贸易中心,澳门的经济地位逐步下降。然而,澳门仍然是大米、鱼、货物和其他中国商品的一个重要集散地,经营制造和出口业务,主要经营纺织品、服装、玩具、电子和鞋类商品。

名字由来

澳门以前是个小渔村。澳门的名字源于渔民非常敬仰的中国女神天后,又名妈祖。

根据传说,一艘渔船在一个天气晴朗、风平浪静的日子里航行,突然刮起狂风雷暴,渔民们处于危急关头。这时,一位少女站了起来,下令风暴停止。风竟然停止了,大海也恢复了平静,渔船平安地到达了海镜港。上岸后,少女朝妈阁山走去,忽然一轮光环照耀,少女化作一缕青烟。后来,人们在她登岸的地方,建了一座庙宇供奉这位娘妈。16世纪中叶,第一批葡萄牙人抵达澳门时,询问居民当地的名称,居民误以为指庙宇,答称"妈阁"。葡萄牙人以其音而译成"MACAU"。

第十单元 购——购物服务

 对话1 跳蚤市场

托德:嗨,梅丽莎,我们这周要谈论的话题是大型活动,你喜欢哪种大型活动?
梅丽莎:我喜欢社区活动。我在努力地参与社区活动。这周末有跳蚤市场。
托德:跳蚤市场?
梅丽莎:对。
托德:好。
梅丽莎:在海边举行,到时会有很多环保物品,在那里可以对旧物品进行再利用和转卖。

235

还可以以便宜的价格买到全新的物品。

托德：好，可能有些人不太了解跳蚤市场，你能解释一下吗？

梅丽莎：人们可以在跳蚤市场低价出售旧衣服、旧用具还有叉子、勺、刀等旧的厨房用具，那里很有意思，有很多人喜欢去跳蚤市场，寻找他们需要的东西，还可以讨价还价，尽量用更低的价格买到需要的东西，如果卖家要出售的旧物品比较多，那你可以用一件东西的价格买到两样物品。大概就是这样。

托德：对，没错。我小时候经常和我祖父母一起去跳蚤市场，因为可以砍价，所以我觉得很不错。

梅丽莎：对。

托德：对吧？因为美国的商店不能讨价还价。

梅丽莎：对，没错。我在旅行的时候一般都会砍价。因为要尽量买到便宜货，在跳蚤市场转卖自己的旧东西很好玩。

托德：这周末你是准备卖东西还是买东西？

梅丽莎：我没有太多的旧物品要转卖，因为我刚搬家不久，搬家时扔了很多不需要的东西，不过我打算拿几件不需要的旧衣服去跳蚤市场上卖，我真的很喜欢跳蚤市场和旧货店这样的地方，因为我对其他人的东西感兴趣。如果我看到不错的东西，那我可能会买下来。

对话 2 纽约购物

迈克：嗨，马里，你说过纽约是个多样化的城市。你最喜欢纽约的哪个地区？

马里：我非常喜欢苏豪区，因为那里是个非常棒的购物去处。苏豪区有很多小店、不错的餐厅和咖啡厅，如果幸运的话，在苏豪区漫步或是吃饭还会看见电影明星，我回日本之前在百老汇大道购物时看到了克莱尔·丹尼斯和她男友。那真是太酷了。

迈克：我经常听人提到纽约中央公园。你能说下中央公园的情况吗？

马里：好，很显然，纽约中央公园位于曼哈顿中心。中央公园非常大，人们会去那里进行体育活动，或是只是去那里散步。如果周末去中央公园，你会看到很多人在那里慢跑，因为中央公园里面的路是隔离的，所以没有汽车。汽车不能进入中央公园，夏天有很多人在中央公园滑旱冰和骑自行车。

迈克：中央公园有多大？

马里：非常大。我想面积大概有从纽约第 56 大街到第 110 大街那么大，非常大。

迈克：那其他地方呢？

马里：我在哥伦比亚大学念的研究生，当时我住在哈莱姆区附近，我非常喜欢哈莱姆区，因为那里让人有亲切感。那里的人们在路上遇到都会互相聊天。去理发店的话会发现人们之间互相都认识。所有人都对其他人的事情感兴趣。他们会闲谈社区里发生的事。

迈克：有没有你不喜欢的地区？

马里：我来自纽约市，所以我不喜欢时代广场。我认为时代广场太商业化了，而且旅游味道太浓，我非常不喜欢时代广场，不过游客很喜欢那里。我认为，时代广场的灯光、街边的商贩还有音乐人都会让游客感觉兴奋。时代广场对游客来说可能是个令人兴奋的地方，但是我会尽量不去那里。

Part III 阅读

Text A

购物天堂——香港

作为著名的购物天堂，香港以其时尚饰品、工艺品、手工艺品、茶、翡翠、珠宝等种类繁多而闻名，香港购物物美价廉，商品琳琅满目。由于香港大多数产品没有关税，其价格通常低于其他地方。当然随着季节变化，也有一些精彩的季节促销。香港有著名的名牌精品店以及在世界其他地方找不到的好东西。对于那些预算有限的人来说，这里有许多绝佳的商业街可以徜徉其中，挑选一些物美价廉的商品。同样，香港也有许多繁华的购物区可以给每个人提供想要的东西。可以一直买到香港之旅结束！

尖沙咀

尖沙咀是香港最著名的商业街之一，通常被称为女士一条街。起初销售商品仅限于女性物品，现在这条街已经发展成可以为任何人提供商品，是一个买纪念品的好地方。这条街出售服装、服饰、玩具、剪纸和艺术品。街尾是海港商城，主要经营高端品牌，其购物中心包含三个不同酒店的购物区域。

铜锣湾

铜锣湾是一个典型的购物中心，里面充满了各种各样的高档豪华购物商店，如崇光、西武、三越、真诚等。时代广场是另外一个购物的亮点，里面全是名牌产品。

斯坦利市场附近的海

在清代，斯坦利只是一个小渔港，但现在它是充满欧洲风情。这是一个露天市场，就像美国或欧洲的跳蚤市场。与大型购物中心相比，在斯坦利市场购物更温馨。当日落时，这个地区真正显示了它的独特性。游客坐在面朝大海的餐厅和酒吧，可以边喝酒边欣赏到美丽的日落。

香港有很多小型特色购物街。湾仔太原街从前是卖玩具的，古董玩具、收藏玩具和最新的玩具都可以在这里找到。西洋菜街卖相机等电器。花园街是一条只卖体育用品的街。在海鲜街可以找到最新鲜的海鲜。摩罗街是新旧古董交易的地方。

香港确实是购物者的天堂。很少有游客能做到没有买东西就离开这座令人兴奋的城市。由于中西文化都是香港的重要组成部分，其购物区提供一些中西合璧的独特项目。香港简直为每一个人都准备了礼品。

Text B

"购"在上海

上海被誉为"购物天堂"和"东方巴黎"。如果你来到这座城市，与其他迷人的景点相比购物更不应该错过。提供最好的购物已成为上海旅游业中不可缺少的一部分。

为了迎接更多的游客，2015年7月1日上海在海外游客以及中国香港、澳门和台湾游客中实施了退税政策。目前，全市有27个免税店，主要位于南京路和豫园周边。

上海的购物区可以明确地划分为"四街四城"。南京路（包括南京东路和南京西路）是四街之一，享有中国第一商业街的声誉。从20世纪早期开始发展，南京路有各种各样的百年老店和现代的购物中心。在现代，南京路并没有由于其众多竞争对手而衰败，而是变得越来越繁荣。淮海路没有南京路那么有名，但也以其高雅品位而出名，因为它的特色就是来自世界各地的高端品牌设计师。四川北路提供物美价廉的商品，通常是普通人的首选。人们也可以在西藏中路（四街之一）就餐和旅游。

豫园商城、徐家汇商城、新上海商业城、嘉里不夜城是繁华的"四城"。豫园商城专门提供有中国特色的商品，其商品包括一些小物件，当地的工艺品、古玩、玉器、金银首饰等。新成立的购物娱乐广场——徐家汇商城，主要由大型商店组成，在此可以买到大量高档价位和中档价位的商品。新上海商业城规模宏大，能够提供最好的设备和设施。位于浦东中部的陆家嘴金融贸易区，其四周是各种零售店。嘉里不夜城就像一颗璀璨的明珠，在上海火车站对面，临近地铁1号线，是一个繁华的商业区。

除了著名的"四街四市"之外，其他的一些街道和道路都值得一游。

如果你只打算买小商品和廉价衣服，人民广场下面的香港名店街和迪美购物中心以及襄阳路都能激起你的欲望。在迪美购物中心，衣服相对便宜时尚，但是在这里你很少会发现顶级品牌。随着四季的交替，可以在此买到能满足年轻人需求的时尚服装。你可以放心自由地进行交易。

陕西北路的特色是鞋，不仅种类繁多、款式新颖，而且价格合理。如果你喜欢中国风格的衣服，茂名路的一些商店有售。长乐路也会满足你的要求。一般的衣服会量身定制，确保符合你的身材。

越来越多的人意识到定制服装的乐趣。如果想要购买布料，强烈推荐这里的布料市场和裁缝店。陆家浜路的南外滩面料市场也许是这座城市里最大的面料市场。坐地铁到南浦桥站，沿着陆家浜路走一会儿，就到达市场了。想做什么衣服，需要提前一个月到店预定。一些配件还需要加工因为开始它可能并不很适合你。面料市场附近的多稼路有许多裁缝店。你可以找到做窗帘的各种布料。茂名路和长乐路也有一些特色的裁缝店。

福州路一个世纪前就是文化街。这里的店铺主要经营文化商品，包括书籍、音乐和艺术品等，对当地人来说，工作之余漫步福州路，翻阅各种书籍和杂志就是一种时尚。

东台路古玩市场主要经营瓷器、玉器、青铜器、木器、书画以及刺绣用具。来自海内外的很多游客都会来到这个著名的市场。

当然，特产食品应该考虑在内。银鱼（面条鱼）源于青浦和崇明，美味可口。罐装油炸鱼凤尾鱼是上海的特产，远销海外，受到高度赞扬。其他特产如浦东鸡、水蜜桃、多汁梨等都会让你流口水。

顾绣，又称泸元刺绣，源于明朝（1368—1644），现在用于生产服装、饰品、床上用品。织锦分为两种类型——供欣赏的和日常使用的。它深受游客喜爱，因为其色彩多样、人物生动、设计逼真。一幅描绘中国长城的织锦正在联合国大楼展出。玉雕、木雕和石雕以其精美细腻的雕工构成了上海旅游业的特色。上海是中国丝绸的原产地之一，也是中国丝绸的出口商。由于其悠久的传统和新颖的生产及设计工艺，此地出产的丝绸仍然拥有独一无二的地位。

超市提供各种各样的产品以满足日常需求。你会发现家乐福、麦德龙、大润发购物中心，莲花和华联等大超市大多临近交通枢纽和住宅区。此外，又建立了100家连锁超市和24小时开业的开劳森便利店以方便你的日常生活。

Part V 典型景点

日月潭

日月潭是台湾最大的淡水湖，同时也是旅游景点，位于南投县鱼池乡。日月潭周边地区是邵族的家乡。日月潭环绕一座小岛，名为拉鲁岛，潭的东面像一轮太阳，而西面像一轮弯月，因此得名日月潭。

日月潭海拔748米，27米深，湖面达7.93平方公里，湖周围地区有很多徒步旅行轨道。

通常不允许在日月潭游泳，但每年中秋节前后都会举办3千米长的"日月潭游泳嘉年华"，近年来都有数以万计的参与者参加，同时还举办烟火表演、激光展出和音乐会。

潭的中间即日潭和月潭的中间有一座小岛，它是邵族的圣地，这座小岛（拉鲁岛）平时不允许游客访问，只有邵族人可以去那儿祭祀祖先。但是日月潭的美景并不在拉鲁岛，而在环绕四周的大山。日月潭和四周的乡村一直是台湾13个风景区之一。文武庙建于一些小庙搬走之后（由于建坝水位升高）。慈恩塔是蒋介石为了纪念他的母亲于1971年修建的。值得一提的其他寺庙还有鉴经寺、玄奘寺和玄光寺。

过去的日月潭与现在不同，在过去拉鲁岛（珠屿岛）是个更大的岛屿，像一颗珍珠把日潭和月潭分割开来。但是由于水力发电厂的修建，日本人在1934年引入临近湖泊的湖水使湖水的深度从6米增加到27米，湖面从原来的4.55平方公里扩大到7.73平方公里。邵族人被迫从他们深爱的拉鲁岛搬入海拔更高的日月谷。

在早期的英语文学中，日月潭通常被称为干治士湖，它是以17世纪后的荷兰传教士干治士命名的。传说邵族猎人们穿过山林尾随追踪白鹿时发现了日月潭。这只白鹿最终把他们带到日月潭，他们发现这里不仅风景秀丽，还盛产鱼类。在拉鲁岛上，白鹿的传说就永生为一个大理石雕像。

蒋介石政府迁入台湾后，该岛屿被命名为光华岛。1978年当地政府修建了月下老人亭，以供每年举行集体婚礼。1999年，9·21大地震毁坏了月下老人亭，岛屿大部分下沉。9·21大地震之后，该岛屿又被重新以邵族语命名为拉鲁岛。

Appendix B

习题答案

Unit 1 Passport Applications

PART II Conversations

Task I Complete the following dialogues by translating the Chinese in the brackets.

C: Do you have anything to declare?

T: No, nothing. I've only got some presents for my children.

C: What's their value?

T: Way under the duty-free allowance. I've bought a disc for my daughter, a book for my son, and a necklace for my wife.

C: May I see the necklace? There's a duty on some types of jewelry even if the total of your purchases is under the amount you are allowed.

T: Certainly. Here you are. But I'm sure there is no duty on it.

C: You are right. There's no duty on it. Thank you for your cooperation. I'm sorry that I had to trouble you.

T: Never mind. Checking every imported article is your duty. Thank you for your kindness.

Task II Using the given words and expressions to make a conversation with your partner according to the situation.

(Z: Zencius, an Overseas Chinese   C: Customs Officer)

Z: Is the Customs examination here?

C: That's right. Your passport, please.

Z: Here it is.

C: Is all your luggage here?

Z: Yes, this is all mine.

C: May I have your luggage declaration, please?

Z: Certainly. Here you are.

C: Have you anything to declare?

Z: No, nothing. I've nothing in these suitcases but personal effects, some underwear and clothing.

C: Would you mind opening this one, please?

Z: Not at all.

（*The Customs Officer looks inside the suitcases*）

C: What's inside this package?

Z: Presents for some of my relatives. They're glass vases and so on.

C: Got any tobacco? Spirits?

Z: I've got 200 cigarettes, but no spirits.

C: Well, you've got two electric shavers here. We can pass only one shaver for each passenger, free. The other one will only be allowed as imported shaver on payment of duty.

Z: How much will the duty amount to?

PART III Readings

Text A

Task I Discuss with partners and then answer the questions according to the passage.

1. I can see thriving cultures set against what are still considered to be wild and uninhabited.
2. I can look at parts of Australia, Asia, Canada, South America, South Africa, Northern Europe and Russia.
3. In parts of Asia.
4. Such as Rome, Paris, the Amazon in Brazil, the white peaks of the Andes, London, Northern Ireland, Hong Kong, Manila, and the Outback.
5. 答案略。

Task II Fill in the blanks with the suitable words given below, changing the form where necessary.

1. historical   2. consider   3. affect   4. prefer   5. uninhabited
6. extremely   7. specific   8. vague   9. population   10. recommend

Task III Translate the sentences into Chinese.

1. 或许你并不想留在美国度假了，但也不想漂洋过海。
2. 不管是国内还是国外，可选择的目的地都有很多。
3. 你可以看到一些与南非极其相似的东西，但是却有着完全不同的文化和荒芜。
4. 在亚洲的某些地区有古老文化和尖端科技的完美融合，你是不是喜欢呢？
5. 每个地区都会给你带来不同的视角，同一地区又会有细微的不同。

Task IV Reading comprehension.

I. 1. A   2. B   3. D   4. C

II. 1. She is a passenger service agent. She represents, or acts for, her country's airline. She serves, or takes care of passengers.

2. She greets the deplaning passengers, leads them to the immigration area, and answers their questions.

3. In the terminal building are the immigration, customs, and baggage areas, as well as ticket and reservation desks for many airlines.

4. It means to come into a country with the intention of settling there.
This is because their documents and identification must be checked by an immigration official. In this way, a country keeps track of the people entering and knows the countries from which tourists and visitors come.

5. It takes longer for returning nationals or residents to go through immigration.

 Text B

Task I Work in groups and discuss the following questions.

1. Personal belongings, household utensils, gifts, cigarettes and alcohol.
2. The article may be taken away and the individual may be fined.
3. $400.
4. 0.95L.
5. I should hand in my customs declaration form and luggage check.

Task II Complete the brackets according to the text.

1. by the customs officer   2. customs declaration   3. inoculation certificate
4. baggage   5. customs declaration form   6. declared
7. taken away   8. exempt   9. personal   10. at least

Task III Fill in the blanks with the suitable words given below, changing the form where necessary.

1. equipment   2. identified   3. worth   4. Supposing
5. abroad   6. destination   7. fail   8. check

Task IV Translate the sentences into Chinese.

1. 进入美国，你可以携带价值100美元的礼物，但是你必须在美国境内至少停留72小时。
2. 到达美国之后，海关官员会检查你的相关证件。
3. 海关检察员会检查每个入境者的行李。

4. 如果有人没有申报物品或者低报了该物品的价值，海关会没收物品并对个人进行相应的罚款。

5. 例如：物品必须是供个人使用的，而且所有者必须在美国境内至少停留48小时。

PART IV Practical Writing

答案略。

Unit 2 Visa Affairs

PART II Conversations

Task I Complete the following dialogues by translating the Chinese in the brackets.

A: <u>I am going to America to attend a sales conference, so I'd like to apply for a visitor visa.</u>

B: OK. Do you mind if I ask you a few questions?

A: Not at all, go ahead.

B: OK. First, <u>may I have your name and birth date, please?</u>

A: Sure, I am Helena and I was born on April 27th, 1981.

B: So, you just said you would attend a conference there, <u>could you please tell me in detail what this conference is about and do you have the invitation?</u>

A: Of course. That is an annual sales conference held by Leech company of America, and we have much business with the company, <u>so I was invited to the conference.</u>

B: When do you prepare to depart?

A: <u>I was planning to leave for America next month.</u>

B: OK. <u>We will make your visa ready as soon as possible.</u>

Task II 答案略。

 Text A

Task I Discuss with partners and answer the following questions according to the text.

1. No, I won't.

2. No, getting a visa just lets me arrive in the United States.

3. I will probably have gone to an American embassy or consulate.

4. Because I need to prove that I have enough money to pay for my education.

5. Their local embassy or consulate.

Task II Fill in the blanks with the suitable words given below, changing the form where necessary.

1. guarantee   2. responsibility   3. rule   4. request   5. probably
6. record   7. education   8. evidence   9. fingerprint 10. information

Task III Translate the sentences into Chinese.

1. 旅游证件由（美国）国务院签发。但移民则由国土安全部负责。
2. 你需要带一张美国学校发给你的可以证明你已经被录取了的官方表格。
3. 另外，准备好你求学完成后要回到自己祖国的证明。
4. 在被美国大学录取后，你应该尽快申请签证。
5. 如果是作为学生第一次申请，那么你只能在开课前30天去美国。

Task IV Reading comprehension.

I. 1. C   2. B   3. B   4. B

II. 1. The hand or carry-on luggage, checked baggage, and unaccompanied baggage.
   2. The baggage from their flight is entering the baggage area on a conveyor belt, which carries the luggage from the plane outside the terminal into the baggage area where the passengers can get them.
   3. She must watch for contraband and smugglers.
   4. Because customs inspectors go through their luggage, mess or disturb their clothing and other belongings.
   5. Because they are tourists coming to enjoy the hospitality of her country.

 Text B

Task I Discuss with partners and answer the following questions according to the text.

1. Place valuables such as jewelry, cash and laptops in carry-on baggage only.
2. Because metal items may set off the alarm on the metal detector.
3. The metal detector may set off the alarm. Many types of footwear will require additional screening even if the metal detector is not alarmed.
4. Wrap the box on arrival, or ship your gifts prior to your departure.
5. Declare firearms & ammunition to your airline and place them in your checked baggage.

Task II Fill in the blanks with the suitable words given below, changing the form where necessary.

1. security   2. prohibited   3. valuable   4. bottom   5. alarm
6. require   7. film   8. declare   9. prior   10. wrapped

Task III Translate the sentences into Chinese.

1. 珠宝首饰、现金和笔记本电脑一类的贵重物品只放在随身携带的包裹里。把你的名片粘在笔记本电脑底下。
2. 即使金属检测警报没有响，很多种鞋子也需要进行附加的扫描。
3. 把没有冲洗的胶卷和装有胶卷的相机放在随身携带的包裹里。行李扫描设备会在检查行李时损坏尚未冲洗的胶卷。
4. 不要携带有包装的礼物．也不要将它们带到检查点。
5. 出于不同的机场布局，在很多机场这些证件可能被要求出示不止一次。

PART IV Practical Writing

答案略。

Unit 3 Historical and Cultural Relics Tour

PART II Conversations

Task I Complete the following dialogue by translating the Chinese in the brackets.

A: Good morning. Today we're going to climb the Great Wall. <u>The Great Wall is in the northwest of Beijing</u>. Are you ready?

B: Yes, I am ready. <u>Do you know the Great Wall?</u>

A: <u>I have read a book about the history of the Great Wall</u>. The Great Wall, also known as Ten-Thousand-Li Long Wall, is considered the No. 1 defense in the world. Watchtowers or battlements were built at intervals of three hundred to five hundred meters.

B: You are right. <u>The Great Wall was designated by UNESCO as world cultural heritage in 1987.</u>

A: I was told a Chinese saying, "You are not a true man until you get to the Great Wall."

B: Let's go.

Task II Using the given words and expressions to make a conversation with your partner according to the situation.

A: Jim, here is the West Lake.
B: Wow, it is so wonderful!

A: The West Lake of Hangzhou holds high reputation for its beautiful scenery.

B: Look, it is raining. It would be nicer if it didn't rain.

A: Do you know the beauty of the West Lake lies in a lingering charm that survives the change of hours in a day, and of different weather, of seasons in a year?

B: Great. It is said there are ten famous sceneries, but I know only one of them, Spring Dawn at Sudi Causeway.

A: To demonstrate its beauty, the lake offers 10 most famous scenes as Spring Dawn at Sudi Causeway, Melting Snow on the Broken Bridge, Afternoon View of Leifeng Tower, Lotus in the Breeze Crooked Courtyard, Autumn Moon on Calm Lake, Listening to Orioles Singing in the Willows, Viewing Fish at Flowers Harbor, Evening Bell at Nanping Hill, Three Pools Mirroring the Moon, Twin Peak Piercing the Clouds.

B: Shall we tour all of them?

A: Yes. We will sightsee not only all of the ten wonderful sceneries but also Hangzhou's silk products, which is very popular to the world. We will enjoy the elegantly fragrant, high quality Longjing tea, the ultimate product of all kinds of tea.

PART III Readings

Text A Integrated Exercises of Skills

Task I Please answer these questions according to the passage.

1. The historical and cultural relics tour refers to the visit and sightseeing to the cultural and historical landscape.

2. The seven ancient capitals in the history of China are Beijing, Xi'an, Nanjing, Hangzhou, Kaifeng, Luoyang, and Anyang. The seven ancient capitals left us a great number of the valuable and rich cultural and historical resources. The tourists from home and abroad come to visit the scenic spots in these capital cities.

3. I'd like to. For example, the Imperial Palace (also called Forbidden City), Yonghe Palace, Summer Palace, Temple of Heaven, Yuanmingyuan Garden (which is originally a large imperial garden in the Qing dynasty built from 1709 onward and burnt down by the Anglo-French aggressors in 1860) and other tourist attractions in Beijing; Wild Goose Pagoda, Museum of Terracotta Warriors and Horses, Huaqing Pool in Lishan, Silk Road, and Forest of Steles in Xi'an and so on; Heavenly Mansion, Yuhuatai, Qinhuai River and others in Nanjing; Liuhe Pagoda, West Lake and so on in Hangzhou; Qingming Shanghe Picture, Dragon Kiosk, Iron Pagoda and so on in Kaifeng; Yin Ruins (which was discovered near Xiaotun Village in 1989) in Anyang.

4. There are a lot of enduring or monumental ancient architectural engineering in several

thousand-year civilization history of Chinese nation, and up to now they are still glittering bright brilliance. For example, the grand ten-thousand-li Great Wall, Imperial Palace, Temple of Heaven, Wild Goose Pagoda and so on.

Task II Fill in the blanks with the suitable words given below, changing the form where necessary.

1. occupied   2. left   3. burned down   4. home and abroad
5. in point   6. located   7. witness   8. in the center of

Task III Translate the sentences into Chinese.

1. 七大古都为今天留下了宝贵且丰富的历史人文资源。
2. 七大古都，风格各异，展现了不同历史时期、不同地域的文物古迹。
3. 故宫既是中国明、清两朝皇帝的宫殿，又是世界上最大的皇宫。
4. 故宫博物院所藏文物约100万件，包括历史文物方面的宫廷文物、科技文物、宗教义物、古代艺术品方面的书法、绘画、青铜、陶瓷、宝玉石、丝织品等。
5. 中国历史上有七大古都，历朝各代选址北京、西安、南京、杭州、开封、洛阳、安阳定都安邦。

Task IV Choose one word for each blank from a list of choices.

1. B 2. A 3. C 4. C 5. B 6. B 7. C

 Text B   Integrated Exercises of Skills

Task I Read the passage above and decide whether the following statements are true (T) or false (F).

1. F 2. T 3. F 4. F 5. T 6. T 7. F 8. T

Task II Match the following temple with their regions.

1-c 2-a 3-b 4-e 5-d

Task III Translate the names of Temple, Hall and Grotto into Chinese.

Zhashenlunbu Temple   扎什伦布寺
Zhebang Temple   哲蚌寺
Taer Temple   塔尔寺
Labuleng Temple   拉卜楞寺
Baima Temple   白马寺
Foguang Temple   佛光寺
Nanshan Temple   南山寺

Guandi Temple in Jiezhou　解州关帝庙
Wuhou Hall　武侯祠
Yongle Palace　永乐宫
Potala Palace　布达拉宫
Mogao Grottos in Dunhuang　敦煌莫高窟
Maijishan Grottos　麦积山石窟
Binlingsi Grottos　炳灵寺石窟
Xunmier Grottos　须弥山石窟
Kezier Thousand-Buddha Grottos　克孜尔千佛洞
Yungang Grottos　云冈石窟
Big-Foot Stone Inscription　大足石刻

PART IV　Practical Writing—Welcome Speech

Task I　Complete the following sentences.

A: Sorry, <u>excuse me</u>, but are you Mr. Stone from Australia?

B: Oh, yes.

A: <u>Welcome to China</u>, Mr. Stone. I am Wang Hui from the International Hotel, and I am here to <u>wait for you</u>.

B: How do you do? Thank you very much for meeting me here.

A: You are welcome. You must <u>be very tired</u>.

B: Oh, no. It was a nice trip, so I am OK.

A: I will be your guide during your stay in China.

B: Wonderful!

A: Can I help <u>you with your luggage</u>? The taxi is waiting outside.

B: Thank you very much.

Task II　Make a welcome speech as a guide when you are meeting Mr. Smith from British in Qingdao.

A: Excuse me, but are you Mr. Smith from the Britain?

B: Yes. Are you our tour guide from CTS?

A: Yes. Very glad to meet you. My name is Wang Chen.

B: Hello, Mr. Wang. Thank you for coming to meet me.

A: My pleasure. How was your trip? It was quite a long flight.

B: Well, it was a nice flight.

A: I suppose you must be rather tired after the long flight. I have made reservation for you at the Qingdao Hotel. We shall get you to the hotel to rest as soon as possible.

B: Thank you.

A: I hope you will have a pleasant stay here. If you have any special request, please let me know. I would like to introduce our driver to you. This is Mr. Feng. He is well-experienced, and our bus plate number is 34765. I suggest that you remember the number in order not to get on a wrong bus. Shall we go to the hotel?

B: Fine. Let's go!

Unit 4   Natural Wonders Tours

PART II   Conversations

Task I   Read the conversation again and answer the questions.

1. It is in the east of Chongqing City and in the west of Hubei Province.
2. The Yangtze River has its source in the Geladandong Snow Mountain, the main peak of the Tanggula Range.
3. The Yangtze River.
4. The Yangtze River flows 6,300 kilometers in eight provinces, one autonomous region, and two municipalities.
5. It is located at Sandouping in the middle of Xiling Gorget in Yichang, Hubei Province.
6. Mount Huangshan is located in the southeast part of Anhui Province and covers an area of 154 square kilometers.
7. As far as I know, Mount Huangshan is famous for an ocean of soaring peaks, Huangshan pine trees, and strange shapes of Huangshan stones and ocean of surging clouds.
8. Of course, I can. The Guest-Greeting Pine has been there for the last thousand years as a symbol of Mount Huangshan and an emblem of the hospitality of the nation of China.

Task II   Complete the following dialogue by translating the Chinese in the brackets.

A: Good morning. I would like to visit Zhangjiajie Scenic Area. Would you like to come with me?

B: Yes. But where is Zhangjiajie Scenic Area?

A: It is in Hunan Province of the Central China. It is very famous in China.

B: Somebody tells me that I should go to see Huanglong Cave in Zhangjiajie.

A: I think so, too. The total length of Huanglong Cave is 13 kilometers.

B: How about the area of Huanglong Cave?

A: It occupies an area of 12,000 square meters.

B: That is great! Let's go!

Task III 答案略。

PART III　Readings

Text A　Integrated Exercises of Skills

Task I　Please answer these questions according to the passage.

1. I know that the Volcanic Groups in Wudalian Pool in Heilongjiang Province has the good reputation as "Museum of Volcano".
2. The Volcanic Groups in Wudalian Pool is located in Heilongjiang Province, in a natural scenery with the volcanic structure.
3. Due to the volcanic eruption in different periods, the magmas flow into the Near River so as to separate it into several pieces and form five volcanic barrier lakes like a bunch of pearls. The Wudalian Pool consists of five lakes, fourteen mountains and calcareous or lime lava mesas, covering an area of 1,060 square meter.
4. Yes, I'd like to. The Baotu Spring is located in Jinan City, the capital city of Shangdong Province.

Task II　Fill in the blanks with the suitable words given below, changing the form where necessary.

1. curtain　　2. eruption　　3. separate　　4. splendid
5. consist of　6. different kinds of　7. set off　　8. due to

Task III　Fill in the blanks with the proper forms of the words.

　　The Guilin Li River, is <u>located</u> in the northeast of Guangxi Zhang Autonomous Region, and it is the <u>typical</u> karst peak physiognomy. The hills and stones stick up, and peak clumps join together here. The Li River and its branches <u>bypass</u> both the hills and stones, and it is <u>surrounded</u> by the hills and rivers, which is <u>incomparable</u> elegant and beautiful. Therefore, the Li River is really <u>worthy</u> of the good reputation of "The Mountains and Rivers of Guilin are the <u>finest</u> under Heaven".

Task IV　Translate the following sentences into Chinese.

1. 黑龙江省的五大连池火山群，素有"火山博物馆"之誉。
2. 云南境内的香格里拉，则是一处绝美的世外桃源，映衬着雪峰与峡谷。
3. 这些自然奇观，风景如画，令游人流连忘返。
4. 五大连池位于黑龙江省五大连池市，为火山地质自然风景。
5. 五大连池由五湖十四山和石灰熔岩台地构成，方圆1060平方千米，以山秀、石怪、水幽、泉奇四大特色而闻名。
6. 1982年五大连池被列为国家重点风景名胜区。

Text B　Integrated Exercises of Skills

Task I　Read the passage above and decide whether the following statements are true (T) or false (F).

1. T　2. F　3. F　4. T　5. F　6. T　7. T　8. F

Task II　Fill in the sentences with the proper forms of the words.

1. strewed　2. vanishing　3. engraved　4. undertaking
5. accumulated　6. indicating　7. situated　8. scattered

Task III　Translate the following sentences into Chinese.

1. 我们期待天地会有尽头，渴望有那么一个地方真的就是天涯海角。
2. 这座岛屿就是海南岛，那两块巨石上，分别刻写着"天涯"和"海角"。
3. 门两边有一副对联："海南生明月，天涯共此时"。
4. 即使是在12月，在南中国热带阳光的直射下，路两边艳红的三角梅仍在勃然怒放，椰树依然在静静地挂果。
5. 料想当时的海滩该是一片荒凉。
6. 在"天涯"石的西北，一组巨石延绵伸向大海，其中一块形似巨笋峭然向天，笋尖上刻有"海角"二字。
7. 爬上那些巨石，举目四望，只见一条洁白亮丽的海滩如玉带般横亘于蓝天碧海之间，海的背面是青山围绕。
8. 一切如画、如诗。

PART IV　Practical Writing

Task I　Match the following groups of words and phrases.

1-d　2-i　3-b　4-h　5-g　6-a　7-c　8-e　9-f

Task II　答案略。

Unit 5　Red Resorts Tours

PART II　Conversations

Task I　Complete the following dialogue by translating the Chinese in the brackets.

W: Good morning, sir. What can I do for you?

G: We are going to stay for two days in Shanghai. Could you give us some suggestions about how to arrange the itinerary in Shanghai?

W: Certainly, sir. In the morning of the first day, you can visit the Shanghai Exhibition Centre. It's only a 10-minute walk from our hotel to the place. The next scenic spot is the Jade Buddha Temple.

G: Is it far from there?

W: Oh, no. It is only a 5-minute ride by taxi from there. You can have your lunch in the temple. It serves purely vegetarian food.

G: That's wonderful. I have heard that it is a special kind of Chinese cuisine. I'd like to try such food there.

W: In the afternoon, you can take a taxi to the Bund to see buildings, Greek, Roman and Spanish built before liberation and still standing in array like an exhibition of buildings in international architectural styles. Then, you take a walk to Shanghai Museum just near the Bund. It is a national art museum with a collection of such treasures as bronzes, ceramics, paintings and calligraphy and models of different dynasties.

G: That's great. Then where would you suggest me to go after that?

W: After that, you go to the Yu Garden, which is also quite near. It is a typical Chinese garden. It features more than thirty halls and pavilions. You will have much to see there.

G: Is the Yu Garden in the old city town?

W: Yes, outside the Yu Garden is the "City God Temple Bazaar". （城隍庙商场）There are 130 small shops in the Bazaar dealing in various kinds of small articles of daily necessities popularly known for their being "small（小）, native（土）, special（特） and varied（多）." Another feature is its delicious snacks of different flavors. You can taste different kinds of refreshments or you can have your dinner in one of the famous restaurants such as "The Green Wave Restaurant"（碧浪餐馆）and the "Shanghai Old Restaurant".

G: I think I shall really have much to see and a lot to eat on the first day. How about the second day, then?

W: As to the second day, you can visit the western part of the city.

G: Where shall we go first?

W: In the morning, you may first go to the Shanghai Zoological Garden to see the animals having their breakfast and playing tricks. Then you can go to the Longhua Temple in Longhua Area, a historic site as well as a tourist resort in Shanghai's southeast suburbs. You can make a detour to the Children's Palace on your way back to the hotel.

G: I see. It seems that you know Shanghai very well. Thank you very much for telling me this information. We always follow your suggestions.

W: Thank you. Hope you enjoy your stay in Shanghai and at our hotel.

Task II 答案略。

PART III Readings

 Text A Integrated Exercises of Skills

Task I Fill in the blanks with the information you learned from the reading.

1. catchword
2. combination; patriotic education; revolutionary sites
3. designated; "Year of Red Tourism"
4. cautious; fleeting fashion
5. lack variety
6. drawbacks; tackle them
7. "red base"
8. diversified; unique; enlightening

Task II Read the passage above and decide whether the following statements are true (T) or false (F).

  1. T 2. T 3. F 4. F 5. T

Task III Translate the following sentences into Chinese.

1. 参观"红色旅游景区"那些与中国革命有着或多或少联系的历史古迹、遗址，游客们不仅可以在旅途中放松一下心情，而且还重温了中华人民共和国内容丰富的"红色历史"，这段时间从1921年中国共产党的诞生起一直跨越到1949年新中国成立。
2. 众所周知，大多数革命遗址建立在山区或偏远地区一般经济比较落后的地方。
3. 因此，如果这个主题旅游想要继续生存和发展，运营者就必须正视这些缺点，并且制定战略来解决这些问题。他们应该知道，"红色旅游"应按照市场规律进行管理。
4. "红色旅游景区"的旅游资源和那些独特的地域文化及奇特的自然风光的多元多样化组合增强了游客的体验，也是增添了游客旅途的愉快感。
5. 希望其他地方开发他们的"红色旅游"的时候，可以从福建学习，想出其他适合当地条件的创造性的方法。

 Text B Integrated Exercises of Skills

Task I Fill in the blanks with the suitable words given below, changing the form where necessary.

1. featuring 2. settled 3. endured 4. rescued

5. destination 6. preserved 7. miracle 8. blockades

Task II Read the passage above and decide whether the following statements are true (T) or false (F).

  1. T 2. F 3. F 4. F 5. T

Task III Translate the following sentences into Chinese.

1. 从1921年成立到中华人民共和国1949年成立的近30年间，中国共产党走过了一条"红色"革命之路。这是困难、激情、浪漫与荣耀之路。
2. 长征是当代中国的一个里程碑事件。
3. 在这里，毛泽东的军事战略被公认是正确的，正式确立了他在党和红军中的领导地位。
4. 此外，为了保持与纪念馆和谐，周围的建筑都被改造成20世纪早期黔北的低结构建筑风格。
5. 从1937年到1947年，延安成为陕甘宁边区的首府，中共中央的所在地，中国革命的指挥中心和大后方。

PART IV Practical Writing

Task I 答案略。

Task II What are main features of tourism ads? Please list some points.

  It should conclude some pictures to attract people；

  It should have a schedule；

  It should have the price；

  It should contain the introductions of the places you will go.

Task III 答案略。

Unit 6 Food

PART II Conversations

Task I Complete the following dialogues by translating the Chinese in the brackets.

1. (A: tourists；B: guide；C: waiter)

  A: Oh, I'm starving. I'd like to try some real Chinese cuisine. <u>What would you recommend</u>, Ms. Chu?

  B: Well, it depends. You see, <u>there are eight famous Chinese cuisines</u>, for instance,

Sichuan cuisine and Hunan cuisine.

A: They are both spicy hot, I've heard.

B: That's right. If you like hot dishes, you can try some.

A: They might be <u>too hot for me.</u>

B: Then there are Cantonese cuisine and Jiangsu cuisine. Most southerners like them.

A: I'd like to try Cantonese food.

B: All right. Let's go to a Hakka restaurant.

C: Good evening. <u>Welcome to our restaurant!</u> .

B: Good evening. <u>Our American guests would like to try your specialty of the restaurant.</u>

C: OK. Please be seated. Are you ready to order now?

A: What's good for today?

C: We have stuffed bean curd, sliced boiled chicken, mushroom soup etc. We also have <u>all kinds of snacks.</u>

A: Some chicken and vegetables, please.

C: Please wait for a moment. I'll bring them right away.

2. A: Excuse me, sir. We want to have lunch in a Chinese restaurant. <u>We'd like to try some real Chinese cuisine.</u> Can you help us?

B: Well, it depends. There are kinds of Chinese food. How about the Sichuan cuisine, and the Hunan cuisine. If you like hot dishes, you can try some.

A: They might be too hot for me. <u>What about any special Beijing dishes?</u>

B: There's the Beijing roast duck.

A: Oh, yes. I've heard a lot about it. I'd like very much to try it. <u>Where can I find it?</u>

B: You can find it in most restaurants, but the best place is certainly Quanjude Restaurant.

A: Is it near here?

B: <u>Not too near but not too far either.</u> A taxi will take you there in 15 minutes, if the traffic is not too bad, I mean.

A: Well, thank you for your information. But what is the name of that restaurant again?

B: <u>Let me write it down on this slip of paper for you.</u> You can show it to the taxi-driver.

A: That's very kind of you. Thanks a lot.

B: You're welcome.

Task II 答案略。

PART III Readings

 Text A Integrated Exercises of Skills

Task I Fill in the blanks with the information you learned from the reading.

1. typical characteristics; eight
2. Shandong
3. chili; Pepper; prickly ash
4. Cantonese
5. Fujian cuisine; pickled taste
6. Huaiyang cuisine
7. freshness, tenderness, softness, smoothness; Hangzhou cuisine
8. thick and pungent

Task II Read the passage above and decide whether the following statements are true (T) or false (F).

  1. F 2. F 3. T 4. T 5. F

Task III Translate the sentences into Chinese.

1. 中国地域辽阔，民族众多，因此各种中国饮食口味不同，却都味美，令人垂涎。
2. 山东菜系，由济南菜系和胶东菜系组成，清淡，不油腻，以其香、鲜、酥、软而闻名。
3. 山东是许多著名学者的故乡，如孔子和孟子。许多山东菜的历史和孔子一样悠久，使得山东菜系成为中国现存的最古老的主要菜系之一。
4. 广东人热衷于尝试用各种不同的肉类和蔬菜。
5. 四川火锅也许是世界上最出名的火锅，尤其是半辣半清的鸳鸯火锅。
6. 广东菜系，味道清、淡、脆、鲜，为西方人所熟知，常用猛禽走兽来烹饪出有创意的菜肴。
7. 江苏菜系以其精选的原料，精细的准备，不辣不温的口感而出名。
8. 浙江菜系由杭州菜、宁波菜和绍兴菜组成，不油腻，以其菜肴的鲜、柔、滑、香而闻名。

 Text B Integrated Exercises of Skills

Task I Fill in each of the blanks in the following sentences the missing letters, words or phrases.

1. delegations; pre-paid
2. entail; recommended; authenticity; fare; array
3. ushered
4. patronize; premises

5. preside; dictates; highest-ranking

6. well-balanced；minimum；tastes；bitter

Task II　答案略。

Task III　Read the passage above and decide whether the following statements are true (T) or false (F).

  1. F　2. F　3. T　4. F　5. T

PART IV　Practical Writing

Task I　Match the following groups of words and phrases.

1. e　2. g　3. d　4. c　5. h　6. a　7. i　8. b　9. j　10. f

Task II　Tell dishes following the structure and the examples.

1. 酱烧排骨　2. 椒盐肉排　3. 京酱肉丝　4. 毛家红烧肉
5. 砂锅土豆排骨　6. 白灼牛肉　7. 回锅肉片　8. 蜜汁火方
9. 糖醋排骨　10. 东坡肘子

Task III　答案略。

Unit 7　Accommodation

PART II　Conversations

Task I　Complete the following dialogues by translating the Chinese in the brackets.

A：Good evening，sir. Welcome to our hotel.

B：Good evening. <u>We would like to check in.</u>

A：Do you have a reservation?

B：Yes，I made it 5 days before. My family name is Jiang. That's spelled J - I - A - N - G.

A：OK. Let me check it. Wow，I get it. <u>You have 19 group members totally. You have reserved nine single rooms and five double rooms，haven't you?</u>

B：Yes，and for three days' stay here，from today to Wednesday.

A：Right. <u>Do you have any other requirements?</u>

B：Yes，<u>breakfast for each room and morning calls at 7 o'clock.</u>

A：No problem. I have taken them down. <u>Is there anything I can do for you?</u>

B: No, thanks.

A: Your passports, please. And please fill in this registration form.

Task II Using the given words and expressions to make a conversation with your partner according to the situation.

A: Good evening. Can I help you?

B: Good evening. Could you kindly introduce the hotel rooms and facilities for me?

A: My pleasure. Here is our price list for all sorts of guest rooms. We have single rooms, double rooms, suites, deluxe suites and a presidential suite.

B: How about the room facilities?

A: All the rooms and suites are well-furnished and air-conditioned.

B: How about the restaurant?

A: There are two Chinese restaurants and one Western restaurant on the first floor, the second floor and the third floor respectively. On the top floor and in the lobby are a disco bar and a coffee bar.

B: That's great!

A: Besides, our hotel has outstanding recreational facilities: a bowling center, an outdoor swimming pool, two tennis courts, a health club, an aerobics gym, sauna, a hair and beauty salon and laundry service.

B: I see. (To the receptionist) Okay, I'll take it.

A: What kind of room do you prefer? And how many nights are you going to stay here?

B: A double room with a bath for three nights.

A: OK. Please give me your passports.

B: Need two?

A: Sure. We need the form to be filled out.

B: OK. Here you are.

A: (After finishing the forms) Here are your passports. A double room for three nights amounts to a total of US $ 270. But you are supposed to pay an advance of $ 470. When you check out, we'll return the rest to you.

B: I see. Are credit cards acceptable?

A: Yes. Major cards like VISA are acceptable.

B: Here you are.

A: Thank you. Here is your VISA card, your invoice and the card key to Room 405 on the fourth floor. The elevators are on your right side, just opposite the coffee bar. Our bellboy will help you with your baggage and guide you to your room. Please remember our check-out time is 12:30 at noon.

B: Thanks so much. See you!

A: It's so nice of you. Have a wonderful stay here!

PART III Readings

Text A Integrated Exercises of Skills

Task I According to the passage, what type of hotel would you recommend to the following persons?

 A. "Bed-and-Breakfast" Inns or Expressed Hotel
 B. Commercial Hotel
 C. Apartment Hotel
 D. Resort Hotel

Task II Fill in the blanks with the suitable words given below, changing the form where necessary.

1. shuttle   2. indispensable   3. classified   4. recreational
5. accommodation   6. luxury   7. available   8. combine

Task III Translate the sentences into Chinese.

1. 从广义上来说，酒店的范围从"住宿加早餐"的家庭式经营到拥有几千个房间的大型酒店。
2. 公寓式酒店集酒店奢华与家庭的舒适安逸于一体。
3. 在房间里有网络服务，对发邮件，准备演讲和打发路上的无聊时间都是很重要的。
4. 至少，你会希望酒店有小型超市让你可以买一些水、饮料、食品来填饱肚子。
5. 另外，如果你在开会前需要大量的准备时间，或者你有很多样品要演示，你可能会让客户到你的酒店，而不是带着那么多的大样品满城转。

Task IV Choose one word for each blank from a list of choices.

 1. C   2. A   3. A   4. B   5. A

Text B Integrated Exercises of Skills

Task I 答案略。

Task II Match the following grades of hotels with their descriptions.

 1 – C 2 – B 3 – A 4 – E 5 – D

Task III Translate the Hotel Departments into Chinese.

  Hotel Departments   酒店部门名称
  Food & Beverage Department 餐饮部

Recreation Department	康乐部
Rooms Division	房务部
Housekeeping Department	客房部
Front Office Department	前厅部
Accounting/Finance Department	财务部
Sales & Public Relations Department	营销公关部
Security Department	安全部
Engineering Department	工程部
Executive Office	行政办公室
Human Resources Department	人力资源部

PART IV Practical Writing

Task I 答案略。

Task II Please write a reply according to this letter of complaint.

To: John@hotmail.com
From: customerservice@hotels.com
Subject: RE: Sunshine Hotel-Shanghai
Dear John,
Please accept our apologies for the service you received in our hotel. Our customers are usually satisfied with our service, but unfortunately, we were not up to our usual standard. I attach a voucher（代金券）that gives you 50% discount on your next stay.
Once again I apologize for the poor service.
Kind regards,
Susan

Task III Write a letter to answer a complaint according to the information given.

Dear Sir,
　　We fully understand the situation, and we researched the issue as soon as we heard from you. It's our mistake, please accept our sincere apology to you. The tour guide has been dismissed and we will give you a special 15% discount next time. If you disagree, please do let us know and we will do our best to find the best solution for you.
　　We thank you for your kind concern and letter with which we can promote ourselves, with which we can approach to the perfect.

Yours Sincerely,
Lisa Green
Assistant Manager

Unit 8 Transportation

PART II Conversations

Task I Make up dialogues according to the following situation, and act them out in class.

A: I would like to know if it is a direct flight to Dubai?

B: Sorry, No. You need to transfer to a connect flight midway.

A: Too bad. I hate transferring during a flight. It is too complicated.

B: You have to do it. But it takes only about 30 minutes.

A: Really? It used to cost a few hours.

B: It has become more time saving.

A: OK. Good. I want two side-by-side tickets in the Economy cabinet. Thank you.

B: All right.

Task II Complete the following dialogues by translating the Chinese in the brackets.

A: Will you book a ticket to Paris for me?

B: Yes, madam. <u>When do you intend to leave Beijing?</u>

A: Next Monday, May 15th, 2015.

B: There are several flights to Paris available on May 15th. <u>Which fight do you prefer?</u>

A: Afternoon flights preferably.

B: Yes, madam. <u>There are two flights available that day: one at 4p.m., the other one at 6p.m.</u>

A: Fine, I'd like the 4p.m. one.

B: 4pm, fine. <u>I'll fix your ticket, madam. Please wait a little moment.</u>

A: What time do I check-in at the airport?

B: <u>You must be there by 3p.m.</u>

A: I see. Thank you very much.

Task III 答案略。

PART III Readings

▶ **Text A** Integrated Exercises of Skills

Task I 答案略。

Task II Fill in the blanks with the suitable words given below, changing the form where necessary.

1. label 2. extraordinary 3. urge 4. deserve
5. obsessed with 6. be bound 7. remote 8. a bird's eye view of

Task III Fill in the blanks with the proper forms of the words.

An airline company, esp. an international airline company, is a giant <u>multifunctional</u> institution, in which there are ticketing and ticket <u>reservation</u> agents, airport personnel, freight transport personnel, mechanics, <u>catering</u> service people, pilots and other crew members on the flight .

For more than half a century, the work of a stewardess has <u>been considered</u> to be both <u>stimulating</u> and well-<u>paid</u>. Although the work is commonly regarded as women's, it is never confined to them. Men also play an important role in the work.

During flight, pilots work only in the cockpit, so passengers seldom see the m in the cabin. However, the captain will greet passengers through the <u>loudspeaker</u>. Once the plane takes off, crew members will be very busy working. Most of their work is to offer food and drinks to passengers and explain in detail points for attention. When the flights about to approach the destination, the purser will announce the landing procedures, and crew members will then make sure that all passengers and facilities in the cabin are well <u>prepared</u> for the touching down of the flight. When the flight has landed, crew members will help passengers get off the plane and make farewells to the latter.

航空公司，特别是国际航空公司，是一个具有许多复杂功能的巨大机构。它有售票和订票代理商、机场服务人员、运货服务人员、机修工、饮食服务人员、飞行员以及飞机上的其他工作人员等。

半个多世纪以来，空中小姐的工作一直被认为是一份刺激而又报酬很高的职业。虽然这份职业通常被认为是女人的工作，但这绝不限于女人，男人也在这个领域起着重要的作用。

在飞行时，飞行员只在飞机的驾驶舱里工作，所以乘客很少见到他们，但机长会通过扬声器向乘客问好。飞机一起飞，舱内服务人员就变得特别忙。她们的工作大部分是给乘客供应饭食和饮料，还要详细解说需要注意的事项。当飞机快到目的地时，飞机事务长就会通知有关着陆程序，机内服务人员检查乘客和机舱是否已备着陆。着陆后，她们帮助乘客下机并道别。

Task IV Translate the following sentences into Chinese.

1. 当人类学家把他们的目光投向20世纪的时候，他们肯定会选择"无腿人"这个标签。
2. 但是，令人惊奇的是，他们即使去度假也不用他们的腿。
3. 未来的历史书还会说，我们的眼睛也弃置不用了。
4. 航空旅行可以使你鸟瞰世界——要是机翼恰好挡住了你的视线，你就看得更少了。
5. 对他来说，旅行和到达是同一件事情；他是一步一步走着来到某地的。
6. 他知道他会享受深沉而甜蜜的睡眠；这是对一切真正旅行者的酬报。

Text B　Integrated Exercises of Skills

Task I　答案略。

Task II　Complete the table according to the text.

How to Make Travel Easier

Get Elite Treatment	Join a <u>frequent-flier</u> program. Buy a <u>day pass</u> at an airline club. Buy a <u>seat</u> upgrade. Get a <u>credit card</u>.
Better Ways to Pack	Customize your black rolling suitcase by <u>tying a colorful ribbon</u>. Put a <u>business card</u> inside your bag. Never put <u>valuables</u> in a checked bag. Have a travel bag with <u>toiletries</u>. Other items to consider carrying: <u>An umbrella, a pair of slippers, an empty water bottle</u>.
Zip Through Security	Don't lose important things at airport security screening checkpoints: such as <u>drivers' licenses</u> and <u>laptops</u>. No <u>jewelry</u> that will set off the body scanner. <u>Cell phone, watch, keys and pens</u> all go into my briefcase before getting in line.
At Home at the Hotel	Once you're checked in, spend a few minutes walking from <u>your room</u> to <u>the nearest emergency stair</u>. Take your <u>room number</u> with you.

Task III　Translate the following sentences into Chinese.

1. 旅行是复杂的，你可能会遇到意料之外的事情。
2. 任何减少旅途麻烦的策略都能成为珍藏宝典。
3. 能获得最优待遇的是常飞旅客项目中的顶级贵宾，他们通常是飞行里程超过 100,000 英里的旅客。
4. 在某家航空公司俱乐部买一张日卡（约 50 美元），就能获得舒适的座位、电视、工作空间、安静的环境、饮料和零食。
5. 如果姓名牌或行李牌被航空公司的行李机吞掉（这种情况很多），航空公司会尝试开包确认行李的主人。
6. 如果由于舱顶行李架已满而被迫在舱门口托运行李，那么请拿出贵重物品和电器。
7. 我每次都把液体和笔记本电脑放在我包里的同一个位置，这样当我必须被检查时，就能知道它们的确切位置。
8. 这样，如果警报响起，或者走廊充满烟雾，你就能知道走哪条路。

Task IV 答案略。

• • • • • PART IV Practical Writing • • • • •

Task I Write an invitation letter according to the Chinese letter.

Feb. 2, 2014
Dear Mr. Parker,
We should be so happy to have you come to dinner with us on Saturday, February 10th at 7: 00, at Hilton Hotel. We are inviting some other friends and hope you will enjoy each other's company.
Sincerely yours,
Mary White

Task II You are going to write a reply to reject an invitation. Use the following notes.

Hi Luke,

　　Thanks for inviting me to your birthday party. I'd like to but we're away at a wedding on that day, so it's a pity.

　　Happy birthday and hope you have a good day.

Cheers,
Mogan

Unit 9　Travelling

• • • • • Part II • • • • •

Task I Complete the following dialogues by translating the Chinese in the brackets.

Li: <u>Where did you take the picture?</u> It's so beautiful!

Chen: I took it in Hawaii. You know, I came to New York University for one year, this weekend, I travel to Hawaii.

Li: <u>So how did your travel? Anything special</u> ?

Chen: You know it was Tomb-Sweeping Day in China, so I decided to go to the cemetery there on purpose.

Li:　Really? Did people there spend the Day?

Chen: Not really. <u>I just want to spend the Day with my family though we are not in the same place.</u>

Li: That's very nice of you. <u>And how did you like there?</u>

Chen: It has great differences here in China. No scare atmosphere.

Li: I see. That's maybe because of people's attitude towards deaths in western countries.

Chen: Yes. I didn't feel sorrow there. On the contrary. I began to treat death in an calm way.

Task II Make up a dialogue according to the following situation, and act them out in class.

(A= Miss Chen Xiaoping; B= Mr. Brown)

A: Well, the temple in front of us is the Confucius Temple. It is a memorial temple for people to offer sacrifices to Confucius.

B: Wow, what a grand temple it is! It looks like the Imperial Palace in Beijing.

A: I agree. In fact, it was built according to the layout of an imperial palace. From what ever angle you look at the Confucius Temple, it is all the same: magnificent and resplendent.

B: How many buildings are there in the temple?

A: The Temple is quite big. The whole building complex includes three halls: one pavilion, and three ancestral temples. It is divided into nine courtyards. Altogether, there are 466 rooms and 54 gateways.

B: I couldn't expect that there are so many buildings in the temple. No wonder it looks like a royal palace. I'm afraid we'll get lost.

A: Well, I'd like to tell you the layout of the temple. The main buildings lies along a north to south axis, and the attached buildings stand symmetrically on both sides. We'll visit the main buildings you won't lose your way.

B: That's good ideas.

(*In front of the Gateway*)

A: This is the first gateway of the gateway of the Confucius Temple. It is called the Golden Sound and Jade Vibration Gateway.

B: I'd be interested in knowing why the gateway is connected with gold and jade.

A: In Chinese tradition, what the saint said is considered very valuable like gold and jade. Mencius believed the voice of such a great thinker like Confucius is golden and can make jade vibrate.

B: I see.

A: Now, we come to the special stone which you may not have seen before. It is the Steles of Dismounting. On the steles writes "officials should dismount here".

B: They look strange. Could you explain why officials dismount here?

A: In ancient times, officials must dismount horses or sedan chairs and walk on foot to show their respect for Confucius when they passed by the temple.

B: That's good. I know many people respect Confucius in the world. Confucius Temples were established in other countries such as Korea and Japan.

A: Right. When you are in China, do as the Chinese do. So we have to park our coach outside the gateway.

Part III

Text A

Task I According to the passage, give a short answer to each of the following questions.

1. The objectives of the UNWTO are to promote and develop sustainable tourism so as to contribute to economic development, international understanding, peace, prosperity and universal respect for, and observance of, human rights and fundamental freedoms for all, without distinction as to race, sex, language or religion.
2. UNWTO's membership includes 156 countries, 6 associate members and 2 observers. Additionally there are some 400 affiliate members.
3. In 2003.
4. It includes General Assembly, Executive Council, Regional Commissions, Committees, Secretariat.
5. In Madrid.

Task II Fill in the blanks with the suitable words given below, changing the form where necessary.

1. are composed of   2. participate in   3. be responsible for   4. contributed
5. to maximize   6. are committed to   7. facilitates   8. be extracted

Task III Translate the sentences into Chinese.

1. 世界旅游组织（UNWTO）是联合国下辖的专门机构，推动了旅游业健康发展、可持续发展以及大众化发展。
2. 其宗旨是促进和发展旅游事业，使之有利于经济发展、国家间相互了解、和平与繁荣，为尊重人权和人类的基本自由（不分种族、性别、语言和宗教信仰）做出贡献。
3. 正是以联合国的建议为基础，成立了新的政府间的旅游组织。
4. 执行委员会是世界旅游组织的行政机构，负责确保整个组织正常运转和预算控制。
5. 行业理事成员和联系成员以观察员的身份参加执行委员会会议。

Task IV Choose one word for each blank from a list of choices.

1-5 BCCDB   6-10 BABDD

Text B

Task I After reading the passage, answer the following questions.

1. Yes, one wealthy American tourist has already fulfilled his long-cherished dream to travel into space.
2. Leisure curiosity.
3. *The Innocent Abroad*.
4. Travellers can do more of their own planning. The electronic miracle makes it possible for people to plan and even book their trips at home from travel companies, airlines, coach buses, tour trains, hotels and so on.
5. The author thinks that the tourism industry, undoubtedly, has created and will create a great effect either positive or negative on the human society and cultures, and on the global environment.

Task II Read the passage above and decide whether the following statements are true (T) or false (F).

1. F 2. F 3. T 4. T 5. F

Task III According to the passage, fill in the blanks with the proper forms of the words.

In <u>the first Golden Age</u> of travel in the nineteenth century, the steamship and the railroad fostered the first rapid expansion of travel for a new purpose: <u>leisure curiosity</u>. Before then, most people customarily travelled for trade, on <u>pilgrim age</u>, as refugees or to make war. In the era of <u>the Industrial Revolution</u>, newly wealthy sight-seer armed with baedekers began roaming afield. The literature of the nineteenth century is rich with <u>great travel writing</u>, including *The Innocents Abroad* by American Mark Twain, *The Banks of the Rhine* by Frances Alexandra Dumas and *Travels of Old Can* by Chinese Liu E.

While the breadth and scope of the twenty-first century travel promises to be different, it will also be <u>an echo of the past</u>. In many ways, the near future <u>harks back to</u> travel's first Golden Age in the nineteenth century. Three things enhance the similarity: <u>the sweep of technological change</u>; the tearing down of political barriers and <u>the rapid decline in costs</u> that have made the impulse to see the outside world a practical urge.

Part IV Practical Writing

A Trip Itinerary for 6-day Beijing Package Tour

Day 1 Arrive in Beijing

Arrive in Beijing, the capital of the People's Republic of China. Meet the guide on arrival and get to the hotel.

Day 2 Beijing

Begin the day with a visit to Tiananmen Square, then, move on to the Forbidden City. After lunch, visit the Temple of Heaven. A Peking Duck Dinner concludes the first full day activities in China.

Day 3 Beijing

Visit the Summer Palace. In the afternoon, visit the Yonghe Lama Temple.

Day 4 Beijing

Today's highlight is the visit to the Great Wall. A short drive away is the stature-lined Shen-lu (Spirit Road) leading to the Ming Tombs. Tere are some marvelous stone sculptures. The Ming Tombs are the graveyard for deceased emperors the Ming Dynasty. Rest of the day is free.

Day 5 Beijing

Visit the Fragrance Hill in the morning. After lunch, take a walk through some old "Hutongs", and enjoy a characteristic dumpling dinner at a local restaurant.

Day 6 Return Home

Get to the airport and board homebound flight.

Unit 10　Shopping

Task I　Complete the following dialogues by translating the Chinese in the brackets.

A: Hi, mark! <u>Long time no see!</u>

B: Hi, Alex!

A: Where have you been?

B: <u>I just got back from London.</u>

A: <u>How was your flight?</u>

B: It was okay. There was a lot of turbulence, though.

A: That's too bad. How long was the flight?

B: It was 10 hours.

A: <u>Did you have a layover?</u>

B: Yes, in Paris, France.

A: <u>Did you buy anything in the duty-free stores?</u>

B: Yes, I bought two boxes of chocolate – one for me and one for you!

A: Oh, you didn't have to …

B: It was nothing.

Task II Make up a dialogue according to the following situation, and act them out in class.

Ann: I'd like to buy some gifts for some friends. Would you give me some advice?
Kate: Sure. I think you'd better buy something typically Chinese.
Ann: That's a good idea. Where can I buy some typical Chinese products?
Kate: You may/can go to the Arts and Crafts Store on the 5th floor.
Ann: Is it far from here?
Kate: No. It's only a five-minute walk here.
Ann: Oh, great. How are the prices there?
Kate: The prices at the Arts and Crafts Store are quite reasonable. If you'd like to go there, I'll come with you.
Ann: Oh, that's very kind of you. Thank you.
Kate: You're welcome. /My pleasure.

Part III Readings

Text A

Task I According to the passage, give a short answer to each of the following questions.

1. Because most products in Hong Kong don't have a tariff.
2. Tsim Sha Tsui.
3. Stanley Market
4. The Sai Yeung Choi Street.
5. Hong Kong is truly a shopper's heaven. Very few visitors can make it out of the exciting city without picking up something to take home.

Task II Fill in the blanks with the suitable words given below, changing the form where necessary.

1. paradise   2. evolve   3. tariffs   4. feels like
5. will be filled with   6. wander around   7. purchased   8. be famous for

Task III Translate the sentences into Chinese.

1. 作为著名的购物天堂，香港以其时尚饰品、工艺品、手工艺品、茶、翡翠、珠宝等种类繁多而闻名。
2. 对于那些预算有限的人来说，这里有许多有美妙的商业街可以徜徉其中，挑选一些物美价廉的商品。
3. 在清代，斯坦利只是一个小渔港，但现在它充满欧洲风情。
4. 当日落时，这个地区真正显示了它的独特性。
5. 游客坐在面朝大海的餐厅和酒吧，可以边喝酒边欣赏到美丽的日落。

Task IV Choose one word for each blank from a list of choices.

1—5 C A C B C   6—10 B B A A A

 Text B

Task I After reading the passage, answer the following questions.

1. Nanjing Road
2. No, we can buy them in Yuyuan Tourist Mart.
3. Yes, Jiali Sleepless City is on the subway way Line 1.
4. Take Public Bus No. 17, 18, 23, 864.
5. Gu Embroidery.

Task II Read the passage above and decide whether the following statements are true (T) or false (F).

1. F 2. F 3. T 4. T 5. T

Task III According to the passage, fill in the blanks with the proper forms of the words.

To welcome more visitors, Shanghai has adopted <u>tax refund policy</u> since July 1st, 2015 for tourists from outside mainland China. At present, there are 27 tax-free stores in the city, mainly <u>situated</u> at Nanjing Road and around Yuyuan Garden.

<u>Shopping areas</u> in the city are clearly divided into "Four Streets and Four Cities". Nanjing Road (including East Nanjing Road and West Nanjing Road), one of the four streets, enjoys the reputation of <u>No. 1 Commercial Street</u> in China. Developed from the beginning of the 20th century, Nanjing Road has clusters of <u>a wide variety of</u> shops from those that are centuries old, to special ones and modern malls. In these modern times, Nanjing Road is not out done by its <u>numerous competitors</u> but becomes more and more <u>prosperous</u>. Huaihai Road, no less famous than Nanjing Road, is <u>celebrated for</u> its elegance. It features top-end designer brands from all over the world. North Sichuan Road offers good <u>inexpensive merchandise</u> and is always the first choice of ordinary people. Food and tourism are well provided on <u>Middle Tibet Road</u>, one of the Four Streets.

Part IV Practical Writing

Task I Translate the following sentences into Chinese.

1. 光阴似箭,你到中国的旅途马上就结束了。
2. 上有天堂,下有苏杭。

3. 桂林山水甲天下。
4. 有朋自远方来不亦乐乎？
5. 你可能会让一些人一直高兴，也可能会让一部分人高兴一段时间，但你不可能让所有人一直高兴。

Task II Make a farewell speech to the tourists on behalf of China International Travel Service. Remember the tips when you make a farewell speech.

My distinguished guests,

　　How time flies! After over ten days, your trip to China is drawing to an ending. You will leave Guangzhou for Hong Kong tomorrow morning. At this moment, I would like to say some words on behalf of our China International Travel Service.

　　First of all, we thank you for coming. Though ten days is not long enough for you to see in China, it is long enough for us to build up our friendship. You have witnessed the changes that have occurred in China since 1978 while you have communicated with some ordinary Chinese people in the streets, on the campuses and in factories. You have visited some big cities, Beijing as the capital city, Shanghai as the engine of China's economy, Xi'an as the home of Chinese culture and Guilin as the symbol of charming landscape, etc. You have visited the beautiful countryside to witness farm life, as well, and to smell flower fragrance in the mountains, breathe fresh air by the seashore, appreciate a fantastic cave and swim in a clean river. You have tasted mysterious but charming Chinese culture, such as Chinese handicrafts, Peking Opera, ancient mausoleums of emperors and minority culture from mountain areas. And I believe that the speed of modernization is also impressive to you. All this will certainly promote your understanding of the economic and social development of China, and strengthen further business and cultural cooperation between our two countries.

　　Next, we would thank you again for your great patience, cooperation and understanding, which have made our job easier. The tour couldn't have been that successful without your support.

　　Lastly, we do hope that this goodbye is just the beginning of our friendship. Confucius, the greatest teacher in Chinese history, said that, "there is nothing more delightful than to meet friends afar." I believe that our friendship will grow fast and I would like to welcome you back, sometime in the future. Upon your return to Great Britain, please bring my friendship home, and my best wishes to your families, your relatives, your friends and your colleagues.

　　Now I propose a toast:

　　To the friendship between the people in our two countries!

　　To your successful visit to China!

　　Cheers!

Appendix C

词 汇 表

Unit 1

New Words

delay	[dɪˈleɪ]	v. & n. 延期；耽搁
application	[ˌæplɪˈkeɪʃ(ə)n]	n. 应用；申请
explain	[ɪkˈspleɪn; ek-]	v. 说明；解释
residence	[ˈrezɪd(ə)ns]	n. 住宅；居住
migration	[maɪˈgreɪʃ(ə)n]	n. 迁移；移民
manage	[ˈmænɪdʒ]	v. 经营；控制；设法；处理；应付过去
temporary	[ˈtemp(ə)rəri]	adj. 暂时的，临时的　n. 临时工
explanation	[ˌekspləˈneɪʃ(ə)n]	n. 说明，解释；辩解
validity	[vəˈlɪdɪti]	n. 有效性；正确性
non-resident	[ˌnɒnˈrezɪdənt]	n. 非居民　adj. 非驻留的
expire	[ɪkˈspaɪə; ek-]	v. 期满；终止；死亡；呼出（空气）
expiry	[ɪkˈspaɪrɪ; ek-]	n. 满期；逾期；呼气；终结
expiration	[ˌekspɪˈreɪʃ(ə)n]	n. 呼气；终结；届期
renew	[rɪˈnjuː]	v. 使更新；续借；重申；更新；重新开始
declare	[dɪˈkleə]	v. 宣布，声明；宣称
tuition	[tjuːˈɪʃ(ə)n]	n. 学费；讲授
fee	[fiː]	n. 费用；酬金；小费　v. 付费给……
receipt	[rɪˈsiːt]	n. 收到；收据；收入　v. 收到
document	[ˈdɒkjʊm(ə)nt]	n. 文件，公文　v. 用文件证明
stateside	[ˈsteɪtsaɪd]	adj. 美国本土的　adv. 在美国国内
historical	[hɪˈstɒrɪk(ə)l]	adj. 历史的；史学的
consider	[kənˈsɪdə]	v. 考虑；认为；细想

Appendix C 词汇表

单词	音标	释义
affect	[əˈfekt]	v. 影响；感染
uninhabited	[ˌʌnɪnˈhæbɪtɪd]	adj. 无人居住的，杳无人迹的
extremely	[ɪkˈstriːmli; ek-]	adv. 非常，极其
ancient	[ˈeɪnʃ(ə)nt]	adj. 古代的；古老的，过时的
technology	[tekˈnɒlədʒi]	n. 技术；工艺
perspective	[pəˈspektɪv]	n. 观点；远景
specific	[spəˈsɪfɪk]	adj. 特殊的，特定的；明确的
vague	[veɪɡ]	adj. 模糊的；不明确的
population	[ˌpɒpjʊˈleɪʃ(ə)n]	n. 人口
bustling	[ˈbʌslɪŋ]	adj. 熙熙攘攘的；忙乱的
continent	[ˈkɒntɪnənt]	n. 大陆，洲，陆地 adj. 自制的，克制的
recommend	[ˌrekəˈmend]	v. 推荐，介绍
literally	[ˈlɪt(ə)rəli]	adv. 照字面地；逐字地；不夸张地
charge	[tʃɑːdʒ]	n. 费用；掌管；控告；v. 使充电；指责
belonging	[bɪˈlɒŋɪŋ]	n. 所有物；行李；附属物
worth	[wɜːθ]	n. 价值
jewelry	[ˈdʒuːəlri]	n. 珠宝；珠宝类
electrical	[ɪˈlektrɪk(ə)l]	adj. 有关电的；电气科学的
equipment	[ɪˈkwɪpm(ə)nt]	n. 设备；器材
carpet	[ˈkɑːpɪt]	n. 地毯；地毯状覆盖物
cigarette	[ˌsɪɡəˈret]	n. 香烟
adult	[ˈædʌlt; əˈdʌlt]	adj. 成年的；成熟的 n. 成年人
suppose	[səˈpəʊz]	v. 假设；认为；推想；猜想；料想
document	[ˈdɒkjʊm(ə)nt]	n. 文件，公文；证件
declaration	[ˌdekləˈreɪʃ(ə)n]	n. (纳税品等的) 申报；宣布
inspector	[ɪnˈspektə]	n. 检查员；巡视员
identify	[aɪˈdentɪfaɪ]	v. 确定；识别，辨认出；确定；认同；一致
abroad	[əˈbrɔːd]	adv. 在国外；到海外 adj. 国外的 n. 海外；异国
destination	[ˌdestɪˈneɪʃ(ə)n]	n. 目的地，终点
inoculation	[ɪˌnɒkjʊˈleɪʃn]	n. 接种
regulation	[ˌreɡjʊˈleɪʃ(ə)n]	n. 管理；规则

273

Phrases and Expressions

- go abroad 去国外
- residence registration booklet 户口簿
- ID card 身份证
- migration office 出入境管理处
- queue up 排队等候
- expiration date 有效期
- housing contract 住宿合同
- dorm room 学生公寓
- tuition fee 学费
- in advance 提前
- cross oceans 漂洋过海
- prefer to 更喜欢
- How about...? ……怎么样?
- historical 历史遗迹
- cutting edge technology 尖端科技
- free of charge 免费
- electrical equipment 电器设备
- personal belongings 私人物品
- household utensils 家庭用品
- customs inspector 海关检察员

Unit 2

New Words

guy	[gaɪ]	n. 男人,家伙
prove	[pruːv]	v. 证明;显示
couple	[ˈkʌp(ə)l]	n. 对;夫妇
partnership	[ˈpɑːtnəʃɪp]	n. 合伙
certificate	[səˈtɪfɪkɪt]	n. 证书;执照,文凭
stable	[ˈsteɪb(ə)l]	adj. 稳定的;牢固的;坚定的
apartment	[əˈpɑːtm(ə)nt]	n. 公寓;房间
complicated	[ˈkɒmplɪkeɪtɪd]	adj. 难懂的,复杂的
basically	[ˈbeɪsɪk(ə)li]	adv. 主要地,基本上
process	[ˈprəʊses]	n. 过程,进行;
vial	[ˈvaɪəl]	n. 小瓶;药水瓶
blood	[blʌd]	n. 血液;血统
involve	[ɪnˈvɒlv]	adj. 有关的;卷入的;复杂的
actually	[ˈæktjʊəli; -tʃʊ-]	adv. 实际上;事实上
illness	[ˈɪlnəs]	n. 病;疾病
test	[test]	n. 试验;检验 v. 试验;测试
once	[wʌns]	adv. 一次;曾经 conj. 一旦
smoothly	[ˈsmuːðli]	adv. 平滑地;流畅地,流利地
frontier	[ˈfrʌntɪə; frʌnˈtɪə]	n. 前沿;边界;国境
marvelous	[ˈmɑːvələs]	adj. 了不起的;非凡的;不平常的

Appendix C 词汇表

单词	音标	释义
procedure	[prə'siːdʒə]	n. 程序，手续
headache	['hedeɪk]	n. 头痛；麻烦
attend	[ə'tend]	v. 出席；照料；致力于
requirement	[rɪ'kwaɪəm(ə)nt]	n. 要求；必需品
satisfied	['sætɪsfaɪd]	adj. 感到满意的 v. 使满意（satisfy 的过去式）
imagine	[ɪ'mædʒɪn]	v. 想象；臆断
necessity	[nɪ'sesɪti]	n. 需要；必然性；必需品
confirm	[kən'fɜːm]	v. 确认；证实
intention	[ɪn'tenʃ(ə)n]	n. 意图；目的
document	['dɒkjʊm(ə)nt]	n. 文件，公文
provide	[prə'vaɪd]	v. 提供；规定
criminal	['krɪmɪn(ə)l]	n. 罪犯
security	[sɪ'kjʊərəti]	n. 安全；保证
guarantee	[gær(ə)n'tiː]	v. 保证；担保
immigration	[ɪmɪ'greɪʃn]	n. 外来移民；移居
responsibility	[rɪˌspɒnsɪ'bɪlɪti]	n. 责任，职责；义务
rule	[ruːl]	n. 统治；规则
request	[rɪ'kwest]	n. & v. 请求；需要
probably	['prɒbəbli]	adv. 或许；很可能
embassy	['embəsi]	n. 大使馆
consulate	['kɒnsjʊlət]	n. 领事馆
tax	[tæks]	v. 向……课税；使负重担 n. 税金；重负
record	['rekɔːd]	v. 记录；录音 n. 记录，档案；唱片
education	[edjʊ'keɪʃ(ə)n]	n. 教育；培养
evidence	['evɪd(ə)ns]	n. 证据；迹象 v. 证明
fingerprint	['fɪŋgəprɪnt]	n. 指纹；手印 v. 采指纹
interview	['ɪntəvjuː]	n. & v. 采访；面试
government	['gʌv(ə)nm(ə)nt]	n. 政府；管辖
information	[ɪnfə'meɪʃ(ə)n]	n. 信息，资料；情报
perform	[pə'fɔːm]	v. 执行；表演
background	['bækgraʊnd]	n. 背景 v. 做……的背景
investigation	[ɪnˌvestɪ'geɪʃ(ə)n]	n. 调查；调查研究
entire	[ɪn'taɪə; en-]	adj. 全部的；整个的
tip	[tɪp]	n. 小建议，小窍门

security	[sɪˈkjʊərəti]	n. 安全；保证 adj. 安全的；保密的
prohibit	[prə(ʊ)ˈhɪbɪt]	v. 阻止，禁止
valuable	[ˈvæljʊb(ə)l]	adj. 有价值的；贵重的 n. 贵重物品
laptop	[ˈlæptɒp]	n. 笔记本电脑
tape	[teɪp]	n. 胶带；磁带 v. 录音；用带子捆扎
bottom	[ˈbɒtəm]	n. 底部；末端
accessory	[əkˈses(ə)ri]	n. 配件；附件；[常作复数]（妇女的）装饰品
undeveloped	[ˌʌndɪˈveləpt]	adj. 未开发的；不发达的
alarm	[əˈlɑːm]	n. 闹钟；警报
heel	[hiːl]	n. 脚后跟；踵
require	[rɪˈkwaɪə]	v. 要求；命令
film	[fɪlm]	n. 电影；胶卷
damage	[ˈdæmɪdʒ]	n. &v. 损害；损毁；赔偿金
declare	[dɪˈkleə]	v. 宣布，声明；声明
lock	[lɒk]	v. 锁上；隐藏；锁住；卡住 n. 锁；水闸
lighter	[ˈlaɪtə]	n. 打火机；点火者
prior	[ˈpraɪə]	adj. 优先的；在先的 adv. 在前，居先
ammunition	[ˌæmjʊˈnɪʃ(ə)n]	n. 弹药；军火
wrapped	[ræpt]	adj. 有包装的
configuration	[kənˌfɪɡəˈreɪʃ(ə)n]	n. 配置，布局；外形

 Phrases and Expressions

- for good 永久地；一劳永逸地
- as long as 只要；和……一样长
- apart from 除……之外；并且
- fill out 填写
- taking on 承担；接纳
- a certain amount of 一定数量的
- go smoothly 顺利；进展顺利
- as well as 也；和……一样；不但……而且
- business visa 商务签证
- an invitation letter 一封邀请函
- immigration Bureau 移民局
- State Department 美国国务院
- Department of Homeland Security 美国国土安全部
- American embassy or consulate 美国大使馆或领事馆
- tax records 纳税记录
- background investigation 背景调查
- security checkpoint 安全检查处
- Prohibited Items 明令禁止的物品
- carry-on baggage 随身携带的包裹
- business card 名片
- high heel 高跟鞋

Appendix C 词汇表

- metal detector 金属检测器
- wrapped gifts 有包装的礼物
- boarding pass 登机牌

Unit 3

 New Words

suburb	[ˈsʌbɜːb]	n. 附近；边缘部分
nameboard	[ˈneɪmbɔːd]	n. 名称牌；站名牌；招牌
dredge	[dredʒ]	v. 疏浚（河道等）
spadework	[ˈspeɪdwɜːk]	n. 铲土活儿；挖槽工作
immense	[ɪˈmens]	adj. 无限的；无边无际的
picturesque	[ˌpɪktʃəˈresk]	adj. 似画的；自然美的
plunder	[ˈplʌndə]	v. 掠夺；抢劫
hapless	[ˈhæplɪs]	adj. 运气不佳的；不幸的
approximate	[əˈprɒksɪmɪt]	adj. 位置接近的，紧靠的，紧邻的
architecture	[ˈɑːkɪtektʃə]	n. 建筑学；建筑业
designate	[ˈdezɪgneɪt]	v. 标示；标明；指出
gateway	[ˈgeɪtweɪ]	n. 门口；出入口；门道
lock	[lɒk]	n. 锁；闩 v. 锁上
impose	[ɪmˈpəʊz]	v. 利用；欺骗；施加影响
average	[ˈævərɪdʒ]	n. 平均；平均数
interval	[ˈɪntəvəl]	n. 间隔；间距；幕间休息
emblem	[ˈembləm]	n. 象征；徽章；符号
reputation	[ˌrepjuˈteɪʃən]	n. 名誉；声望
envy	[ˈenvi]	n. 嫉妒；羡慕
capital	[ˈkæpɪtəl]	n. 首都
dynasty	[ˈdɪnəstɪ]	n. 王朝
resource	[rɪˈsɔːs]	n. 资源
leave	[liːv]	vt. 离开；留下
originally	[əˈrɪdʒənəli]	adv. 起初；本来
occupy	[ˈɒkjʊpaɪ]	v. 占据，占领
scroll	[skrəʊl]	n. 卷轴，画卷；名册
bustle	[ˈbʌsl]	v. 喧闹；忙乱；充满
rouge	[ruːʒ]	n. 胭脂；口红
relic	[ˈrelɪk]	n. 遗迹；遗骸

277

witness	['wɪtnəs]	n.	证人；目击者
locate	[lə(ʊ)'keɪt]	v.	位于
calligraphy	[kə'lɪgrəfi]	n.	书法；笔迹
bronze	[brɒnz]	n.	青铜；古铜色；青铜制品
pottery	['pɒtəri]	n.	陶器
pearl	[pɜːl]	n.	珍珠；珍品
jade	[dʒeɪd]	n.	翡翠
Buddhism	['bʊdɪzəm]	n.	佛教
profound	[prə'faʊnd]	adj.	深厚的，意义深远的
grotto	['grɒtəʊ]	n.	岩洞，洞穴
rare	[reə(r)]	adj.	罕见的，特殊的
include	[ɪn'kluːd]	v.	包含，包括
exquisite	['ekskwɪzɪt]	adj.	精致的；优美的
incomparable	[ɪn'kɒmp(ə)rəb(ə)l]	adj.	无比的；无可匹敌的
distribute	[dɪ'strɪbjuːt]	v.	分配；散布；分开
inscription	[ɪn'skrɪpʃ(ə)n]	n.	题词，铭文；刻印
carve	[kaːv]	v.	雕刻；开创
engrave	[ɪn'greɪv]	v.	雕刻；铭记
clay	[kleɪ]	n.	粘土；泥土
dominion	[də'mɪnjən]	n.	主权，统治权
renovation	[ˌrenə'veɪʃn]	n.	革新；修理
decorate	['dekəreɪt]	v.	装饰；布置
symbol	['sɪmb(ə)l]	n.	象征；符号

Phrases and Expressions

- a dozen years of spadework 十余年的土方工程
- a large scale of face-lift 大规模的翻修或改建
- Anglo-French Allied Force 英法联军
- consume manpower and material resources 耗费人力物力
- Empress Dowager Cixi 慈禧太后
- Garden of Limpid Ripples（Qingyiyuan）清漪园

- Kunming Lake 昆明湖
- Longevity Hill 万寿山
- Juyong Pass 居庸关
- the average height and width 平均宽度和高度
- watchtowers or battlements 瞭望塔或城垛
- Ming-dynasty Great Wall 明长城
- a great number of 多数的，许多
- home and abroad 国内外，海内外

Appendix C 词汇表

- scenic spot 风景区，景点
- burn down 烧毁
- Imperial Palace 故宫
- Yonghe Palace 雍和宫
- Temple of Heaven 天坛
- Anglo-French aggressors 英法联军
- Wild Goose Pagoda 大雁塔
- Heavenly Mansion 天王府
- Liuhe Pagoda 六和塔
- in point 相关的；恰当的
- in the center of 在中央
- be regarded as （被）认为是
- a great number 大量的
- in scale 依比例
- be famous for 因……而著名
- due to 由于；应归于
- Maburi Mountain 玛布日山
- Tobo Kingdom 吐蕃王朝
- go through 参加；经受
- consists of 包含；由……组成
- aside from that 除此之外

Unit 4

 New Words

gorge	[gɔːdʒ]	n. 峡谷
source	[sɔːs]	n. 来源；水源
peak	[piːk]	n. 山峰；最高点
municipality	[mjʊˈnɪsəˈpæləti]	n. 自治市或区
characteristic	[kærəktəˈrɪstɪk]	n. 特征；特性；特色
serenity	[sɪˈrenɪtɪ]	n. 平静，宁静
magnificent	[mægˈnɪfɪs(ə)nt]	adj. 高尚的；壮丽的
furthermore	[fɜːðəˈmɔː]	adv. 此外；而且
terminate	[ˈtɜːmɪneɪt]	v. 使终止；使结束
cover	[ˈkʌvə]	v. 包括；采访
soar	[sɔː]	v. 高飞；高耸
surge	[sɜːdʒ]	v. 汹涌，蜂拥而来
representative	[reprɪˈzentətɪv]	adj. 典型的，有代表性的
emblem	[ˈembləm]	n. 象征；徽章；符号
hospitality	[hɒspɪˈtælɪti]	n. 好客；殷勤
volcano	[vɒlˈkeɪnəʊ]	n. 火山
lava	[ˈlaːvə]	n. 火山岩浆
physiognomy	[ˌfɪzɪˈɒnəmi]	n. 地貌；外貌
fulgurite	[ˈfʌlgjʊraɪt]	n. 闪电岩
stalactite	[ˈstæləktaɪt]	n. 钟乳石
zigzag	[ˈzɪgzæg]	v. 使成"之"字形；使曲折行进

grotesque	[grə(ʊ)ˈtesk]	n.	奇异风格；怪异的东西
gaudy	[ˈgɔːdi]	adj.	华而不实的；俗丽的
curtain	[ˈkɜːt(ə)n]	n.	幕；窗帘
turmoil	[ˈtɜːmɔɪl]	n.	混乱，骚动
eruption	[ɪˈrʌpʃ(ə)n]	n.	爆发，喷发
separate	[ˈsep(ə)reɪt]	v.	使分离；使分开
splendid	[ˈsplendɪd]	adj.	辉煌的；灿烂的
neoteric	[ˌniːə(ʊ)ˈterɪk]	adj.	现代的；新发明的
sentimentality	[ˌsentɪmenˈtælti]	n.	多愁善感
strew	[struː]	v.	散播；撒满
lovesickness	[ˈlʌv ˌsɪknɪs]	n.	相思病
vanish	[ˈvænɪʃ]	v.	消失
ultima	[ˈʌltəmə]	adj.	最终的；最后的
Thule	[ˈθjuːliː]	n.	极北之地
engrave	[ɪnˈgreɪv]	v.	雕刻；铭记
complex	[ˈkɒmpleks]	adj.	复杂的；合成的
undertake	[ˌʌndəˈteɪk]	v.	承担，保证
accumulate	[əˈkjuːmjʊleɪt]	v.	累积；积聚
solitary	[ˈsɒlɪt(ə)ri]	adj.	孤独的；独居的
southmost	[ˈsaʊθˌməʊst]	adj.	最南的
indicate	[ˈɪndɪkeɪt]	v.	表明；指出
situate	[ˈsɪtʃʊeɪt]	v.	使位于；使处于
scatter	[ˈskætə]	v.	分散，散开
desolation	[ˌdesəˈleɪʃ(ə)n]	n.	荒芜；忧伤
jade	[dʒeɪd]	n.	翡翠

 Phrases and Expressions

- be famous for 因……而著名
- in the middle of 在……中间
- height above sea level 海拔高度
- as far as I know 据我所知；就我所知
- The Guest-Greeting Pine 迎客松
- The Guest's Companion Pine 陪客松
- The Seeing a-Friend-off Pine 送客松
- The Yearning-for-Guests Pine 望客松
- The Receptionist Pine 接引松
- The Sea-Surveying Pine 探海松
- consist of 由……构成
- different kinds of 各种各样
- set off 出发；引起
- enjoy themselves so much as to forget to go home 流连忘返
- due to 由于；归于

Appendix C 词汇表

- in fact 事实上，实际上
- come from 来自；出生于
- run out 耗尽；到期；伸向
- up to now 到目前为止
- faithful and unyielding 坚贞不屈
- head on 迎面地

Unit 5

 New Words

ancient	[ˈeɪnʃ(ə)nt]	adj. 古代的；古老的
admire	[ədˈmaɪə]	v. 钦佩；赞美；钦佩；称赞
persistence	[pəˈsɪst(ə)ns]	n. 持续
perseverance	[pɜːsɪˈvɪər(ə)ns]	n. 坚持不懈
pagoda	[pəˈɡəʊdə]	n. （东方寺院的）宝塔
strike	[straɪk]	v. 打，打击；敲，敲击
glory	[ˈɡlɔːri]	n. 光荣，荣誉；赞颂
prosperity	[prɒˈsperɪti]	n. 繁荣，成功
abound	[əˈbaʊnd]	v. 充满；富于
yield	[jiːld]	v. 生；产；结
excavate	[ˈekskəveɪt]	v. 挖掘；开凿
array	[əˈreɪ]	n. 数组，阵列；排列，列阵
vanguard	[ˈvænɡɑːd]	n. 先锋盾；前锋
chariot	[ˈtʃærɪət]	n. 二轮战车
armor	[ˈɑːmə]	n. [军] 装甲；盔甲 v. 为……装甲
gallop	[ˈɡæləp]	v. 飞驰，急速进行
distance	[ˈdɪst(ə)ns]	n. 距离
mansion	[ˈmænʃ(ə)n]	n. 大厦
pyramidal	[pɪˈræmɪd(ə)l]	adj. 锥体的；金字塔形的
granite	[ˈɡrænɪt]	n. 花岗岩
dock	[dɒk]	n. 码头；船坞
liberation	[lɪbəˈreɪʃ(ə)n]	n. 释放，解放
backward	[ˈbækwəd]	adj. 向后 adv. 向后地；相反地
ammunition	[æmjʊˈnɪʃ(ə)n]	n. 弹药；军火
boast	[bəʊst]	v. 以有……而自豪
catchword	[ˈkætʃwɜːd]	n. 标语，口号；流行语；口头禅
relevance	[ˈreləvəns]	n. 关联

281

brand	[brænd]	n.	商标，牌子；烙印
combination	[ˌkɒmbɪˈneɪʃ(ə)n]	n.	结合；组合；联合
patriotic	[ˌpeɪtrɪˈɒtɪk]	adj.	爱国的
recreation	[ˌrekrɪˈeɪʃ(ə)n]	n.	娱乐；消遣；休养
revolutionary	[ˌrevəˈluːʃ(ə)n(ə)ri]	n. 革命者 adj. 革命的	
designate	[ˈdezɪɡneɪt]	v.	指定；指派；把……定名为
promoter	[prəˈməʊtə]	n.	促进者；发起人
mountainous	[ˈmaʊntɪnəs]	adj.	多山的；巨大的
remote	[rɪˈməʊt]	n. 远程 adj. 遥远的；偏僻的	
sensible	[ˈsensɪb(ə)l]	adj.	明智的；合理的
sacrifice	[ˈsækrɪfaɪs]	n. 牺牲 v. 牺牲	
fleeting	[ˈfliːtɪŋ]	adj.	飞逝的；转瞬间的
sustainable	[səˈsteɪnəb(ə)l]	adj.	可以忍受的；可持续的
scattered	[ˈskætəd]	adj.	分散的；散乱的
potential	[pəˈtenʃl]	adj. 潜在的；可能的 n. 潜能；可能性	
squarely	[ˈskweəli]	adv.	直角地；诚实地；正好
drawback	[ˈdrɔːbæk]	n.	缺点，不利条件
devise	[dɪˈvaɪz]	n. 遗赠 vt. 设计；想出；遗赠给	
thrive	[θraɪv]	v.	繁荣，兴旺；茁壮成长
accordance	[əˈkɔːd(ə)ns]	n.	一致；和谐
milestone	[ˈmaɪlstəʊn]	n.	里程碑，划时代的事件
exclusively	[ɪkˈskluːsɪvli]	adv.	唯一地；专有地；排外地
abundant	[əˈbʌnd(ə)nt]	adj.	丰富的；充裕的；盛产
venue	[ˈvenjuː]	n.	发生地点；集合地点
testament	[ˈtestəm(ə)nt]	n.	确实的证明
enthusiastically	[ɪnˌθjuːzɪˈæstɪkəli]	adv.	热心地；满腔热情地
landmark	[ˈlæn(d)mɑːk]	n.	地标；里程碑；纪念碑
define	[dɪˈfaɪn]	v.	定义；使明确；规定
progressive	[prəˈɡresɪv]	n.	改革论者；进步分子
ecosystem	[ˈiːkəʊsɪstəm]	n.	生态系统
precipitous	[prɪˈsɪpɪtəs]	adj.	险峻的
dense	[dens]	adj.	稠密的；浓厚的；愚钝的
rugged	[ˈrʌɡɪd]	adj.	崎岖的

Appendix C 词汇表

suffering	[ˈsʌf(ə)rɪŋ]	n. 受难；苦楚 adj. 受苦的
scarce	[skeəs]	adj. 缺乏的，不足的
capitalism	[ˈkæpɪt(ə)lɪz(ə)m]	n. 资本主义
starvation	[staːˈveɪʃn]	n. 饿死；挨饿；绝食
Communism	[ˈkɒmjʊnɪz(ə)m]	n. 共产主义
annihilation	[ənaɪɪˈleɪʃ(ə)n]	n. 灭绝；消灭
painstaking	[ˈpeɪnzteɪkɪŋ]	n. 辛苦；勤勉 adj. 艰苦的；勤勉的
struggle	[ˈstrʌg(ə)l]	n. 努力，奋斗；竞争 v. 奋斗，努力；挣扎
backbone	[ˈbækbəʊn]	n. 支柱；骨干
expand	[ɪkˈspænd；ek-]	v. 扩张；发展
trek	[trek]	n. & v. 艰苦跋涉
augment	[ɔːgˈment]	n. 增加；增大 v. 增加；增大
blockade	[blɒˈkeɪd]	n. 阻塞 v. 封锁
summon	[ˈsʌmən]	v. 召唤；召集；鼓起
contemporary	[kənˈtemp(ə)r(ər)i]	adj. 当代的
terrain	[təˈreɪn]	n. 地形，地势；领域
acumen	[ˈækjʊmən；əˈkjuːmen]	n. 聪明，敏锐
plateau	[ˈplætəʊ]	n. 高原

 Phrases and Expressions

- on top of 在……之上
- figure out 解决；算出；想出；理解；断定
- the Xi'an City Wall 西安城墙
- the Dayan Pagoda 大雁塔
- Monk Xuan Zang 玄奘法师
- the Bell Tower 钟楼
- the Drum Tower 鼓楼
- Terracotta Warriors 陕西秦始皇陵兵马俑
- dagger-axe 戈
- the Warring States Period 战国
- the Huangpu River 黄浦江
- the Bund 上海外滩
- the Waibaidu Bridge 外白渡桥
- the Peace Hotel 和平饭店
- tell the time 报时
- speak of 证明；为……提供证据
- the ships at anchor 停着的船
- the Opium War 鸦片战争
- died as martyrs 壮烈牺牲
- a beacon tower 灯塔
- red scenic spots 红色旅游景点
- the Communist Party of China 中国共产党
- Gutian Meeting 古田会议
- the National Tourism Administration 国家旅游局
- soldier on 坚持着干；迎着困难干
- carry out 执行，实行；贯彻

283

- A Single Spark Can Start a Prairie Fire 星星之火，可以燎原
- set forth 陈述，提出；出发；宣布
- rely on 依靠，依赖
- the Long March 长征

Unit 6

New Words

menu	[ˈmenjuː]	n. 菜单
prefer	[prɪˈfɜː]	v. 更喜欢
appetizing	[ˈæpɪtaɪzɪŋ]	adj. 开胃的；促进食欲的
pancake	[ˈpænkeɪk]	n. 薄烤饼；粉饼
scallion	[ˈskæliən]	n. 青葱
incredible	[ɪnˈkredɪb(ə)l]	adj. 难以置信的，惊人的
handiwork	[ˈhændiwɜːk]	n. 手工艺
monster	[ˈmɒnstə]	n. 怪物
ugly	[ˈʌgli]	adj. 丑陋的
crab	[kræb]	n. 螃蟹；蟹肉
Soochow	[ˈsuːˈtʃaʊ]	n. 苏州
soya	[ˈsɔɪə]	n. 大豆
vinegar	[ˈvɪnɪgə]	n. 醋
plain	[pleɪn]	adj. 平的；简单的
delicious	[dɪˈlɪʃəs]	adj. 美味的；可口的
moderate	[ˈmɒd(ə)rət]	adj. 温和的；适度的
territory	[ˈterɪt(ə)ri]	n. 领土，领域；范围
fantastic	[fænˈtæstɪk]	adj. 极好的，极出色的
mouthwatering	[ˈmaʊθˌwɔːtərɪŋ]	adj. 令人垂涎的；美味的
greasy	[ˈgriːsi; -zi]	adj. 油腻的；含脂肪多的
aroma	[əˈrəʊmə]	n. 芳香
crispness	[ˈkrɪspnɪs]	n. 易碎；清新；酥脆
tenderness	[ˈtendənəs]	n. 软；柔和；敏感
pungent	[ˈpʌn(d)ʒ(ə)nt]	adj. 辛辣的
peninsula	[pɪˈnɪnsjʊlə]	n. 半岛
prolific	[prəˈlɪfɪk]	adj. 多产的
chili	[ˈtʃɪli]	n. 红辣椒，辣椒
pepper	[ˈpepə]	n. 胡椒

Appendix C 词汇表

prickly ash		n. 花椒
accompany	[əˈkʌmpəni]	v. 陪伴，伴随
ginger	[ˈdʒɪndʒə]	n. 姜
ferment	[fəˈment]	v. 使发酵；发酵
ingredient	[ɪnˈɡriːdɪənt]	n. 原料
pickle	[ˈpɪk(ə)l]	v. 泡；腌制
braise	[breɪz]	v. 炖；蒸
distinctively	[dɪsˈtɪŋktɪvli]	adv. 特殊地；区别地
originate	[əˈrɪdʒɪneɪt; ɒ-]	v. 发源；发生
adventurous	[ədˈventʃ(ə)rəs]	adj. 爱冒险的；危险的
palate	[ˈpælət]	n. 味觉；上颚
saute	[ˈsəʊteɪ]	v. 炒；嫩煎
stew	[stjuː]	v. 炖，炖汤；焖
artistic	[ɑːˈtɪstɪk]	adj. 艺术的；有美感的
meticulous	[məˈtɪkjələs]	adj. 一丝不苟的
mellow	[ˈmeləʊ]	adj. 圆润的，柔和的 v. 使成熟；使柔和
fragrance	[ˈfreɪɡr(ə)ns]	n. 香味，芬芳
nettlesome	[ˈnetlsəm]	adj. 恼人的
pre-paid	[prɪˈpeɪd]	adj. 提前支付的
pre-assigned	[prɪˈəsaɪnd]	adj. 预定的
preselected	[prɪˈsɪlektɪd]	adj. 预选好了的
surcharge	[ˈsɜːtʃɑːdʒ]	n. 附加费
buffet	[ˈbʊfeɪ; ˈbʌfeɪ]	n. 自助餐
atmosphere	[ˈætməsfɪə]	n. 气氛
authenticity	[ɔːθenˈtɪsɪti]	n. （风味）地道
fare	[feə]	n. 伙食，车费 v. 过日子
patronize	[ˈpætrənaɪz]	v. 光顾
premises	[ˈpremɪsɪz]	n. 餐馆，房屋
etiquette	[ˈetɪket; etɪˈket]	n. 礼节
protocol	[ˈprəʊtəkɒl]	n. 礼仪
elaborate	[ɪˈlæb(ə)rət]	adj. 精心准备的
usher	[ˈʌʃə]	n. & v. 引座
anteroom	[ˈæntɪruːm]	n. 前屋
nibble	[ˈnɪb(ə)l]	v. 吃，啃
setting	[ˈsetɪŋ]	n. 布置，环境

285

liquor	[ˈlɪkə]	n. 白酒
prescribed	[prɪˈskraɪbd]	adj. 预定了的
mushroom	[ˈmʌʃruːm; -rʊm]	n. 蘑菇 v. 雨后春笋般的出现
snack	[snæk]	n. 小吃

Phrases and Expressions

- be famous for 因……而著名
- Tasting is believing 百闻不如一尝
- a variety of 种种；各种各样的
- be divided into 被分成
- consist of 由……组成
- Confucius 孔子
- Mencius 孟子
- dietary requirements 进食要求
- in advance 预先地
- foot the bill 付账
- light conversation 轻松交谈
- a head table 主桌
- the seat of honor 主座
- seating plan 座次安排
- palate-stimulating sequence 开胃程序
- cold appetizers 开胃凉菜
- main courses 主菜
- catering services 餐饮服务

• • • • • Unit 7 • • • • •

New Words

receptionist	[rɪˈsepʃ(ə)nɪst]	n. 接待员
reservation	[rezəˈveɪʃ(ə)n]	n. 预约，预订；保留
suite	[swiːt]	n. 套房
requirement	[rɪˈkwaɪəm(ə)nt]	n. 要求；必需品
elevator	[ˈelɪveɪtə]	n. 电梯；升降机
available	[əˈveɪləb(ə)l]	adj. 可获得的；有空的
view	[vjuː]	n. 风景；视野；意见
noise	[nɒɪz]	n. 噪声；杂音
pool	[puːl]	n. 水塘；泳塘
hall	[hɔːl]	n. 前厅；大厅
procedure	[prəˈsiːdʒə]	n. 程序，手续；步骤
luggage	[ˈlʌɡɪdʒ]	n. 行李；皮箱
bellman	[ˈbelmən]	n. 行李员
immediately	[ɪˈmiːdɪətli]	adv. 立刻；马上
suitcase	[ˈsuːtkeɪs]	n. 手提箱；衣箱
valuable	[ˈvæljʊb(ə)l]	adj. 有价值的；贵重的

Appendix C 词汇表

breakable	[ˈbreɪkəb(ə)l]	adj. 易碎的
mega	[ˈmeɡə]	adj. 许多；宏大的
classify	[ˈklæsɪfaɪ]	v. 分类
location	[lə(ʊ)ˈkeɪʃ(ə)n]	n. 位置；地点
commercial	[kəˈmɜːʃ(ə)l]	adj. 商业的；营利的
accommodation	[əkɒməˈdeɪʃ(ə)n]	n. 膳宿；住处
resort	[rɪˈzɔːt]	n. 度假胜地
recreational	[rekrɪˈeɪʃənl]	adj. 娱乐的；消遣的
vacation	[vəˈkeɪʃn; veɪ-]	n. 假期
combine	[kəmˈbaɪn]	v. 联合；结合
luxury	[ˈlʌkʃ(ə)ri]	n. 奢侈，奢华；奢侈品
coziness	[ˈkəʊzɪnɪs]	n. 安逸，舒适；畅快
ideal	[aɪˈdɪəl; aɪˈdiːəl]	adj. 理想的；完美的
casino	[kəˈsiːnəʊ]	n. 俱乐部，赌场
gamble	[ˈɡæmb(ə)l]	n. 赌博，冒险，打赌
historic	[hɪˈstɒrɪk]	adj. 历史性的；有历史意义的
create	[kriːˈeɪt]	v. 创造；造成
essential	[ɪˈsenʃ(ə)l]	adj. 基本的；必要的
presentation	[prez(ə)nˈteɪʃ(ə)n]	n. 展示；陈述
curb	[kɜːb]	n. 抑制；控制
indispensable	[ɪndɪˈspensəb(ə)l]	n. 不可缺少的物或人
workout	[ˈwɜːkaʊt]	n. 锻炼；练习
facility	[fəˈsɪləti]	n. 设施；设备
snug	[snʌɡ]	adj. 紧身的
shuttle	[ˈʃʌt(ə)l]	n. 穿梭班机、公共汽车等
concierge	[ˈkɒnsɪeəʒ]	n. 门房；看门人
cab	[kæb]	n. 出租汽车
schlep	[ʃlep]	v. 拖曳；缓慢费力地行进
affordable	[əˈfɔːdəbəl]	adj. 负担得起的
range	[reɪn(d)ʒ]	n. 范围；幅度
undergo	[ʌndəˈɡəʊ]	v. 经历；忍受
gentrification	[dʒentrɪfɪˈkeɪʃən]	n. 中产阶级化
mosque	[mɒsk]	n. 清真寺
logistical	[ləˈdʒɪstɪkl]	adj. 物流的；物流业的
comprehensive	[kɒmprɪˈhensɪv]	adj. 综合的；广泛的

287

slum	[slʌm]	n. 贫民；贫民区
spot	[spɒt]	n. 地点 v. 认出
jostle	[ˈdʒɒs(ə)l]	v. 竞争，争夺；推挤
entertainment	[entəˈteɪnm(ə)nt]	n. 娱乐；款待
casino	[kəˈsiːnəʊ]	n. 俱乐部，赌场；娱乐场
thermostat	[ˈθɜːməstæt]	n. 恒温控制器；温度调节装置
collaborate	[kəˈlæbəreɪt]	v. 合作；勾结
ecosystem	[ˈiːkəʊsɪstəm]	n. 生态系统
leverage	[ˈlevərɪdʒ]	v. 利用；举债经营

 Phrases and Expressions

- Hilton Hotel 希尔顿大酒店
- single room 单人房，单人间
- twin room 双人房
- double room 双人房
- check in 报到；登记
- away from 远离；离开
- check out 结账；离开
- Bell Captain 礼宾；待者领班
- shoulder bag 手提包
- claim tay 行李标签
- in the broad sense 广义上（而言）
- range from... to... 范围从……到……
- focus on 集中于
- engage in 从事于（参加）
- tide over 克服；度过困难时期
- small bite 食品；小零食
- be placed 位于
- a dash of 少许；一点儿
- takes over 接管；接收
- get a bird's eye-view of 鸟瞰
- partner up with 和……进行合作

Unit 8

 New Words

airline	[ˈeəlaɪn]	n. 航空公司；航线
alternative	[ɔːlˈtɜːnətɪv; ɒl-]	n. 二中择一；选择
coach	[kəʊtʃ]	v. 旅客车厢；经济舱
fare	[feə]	n. 票价；费用
cancellation	[kænsəˈleɪʃ(ə)n]	n. 取消；删除
selection	[sɪˈlekʃ(ə)n]	n. 选择；挑选
vehicle	[ˈviːɪkl]	n. 车辆；交通工具
stereo	[ˈsterɪəʊ]	n. 立体声
Porsche	[ˈpɒrʃ]	n. 保时捷（德国名车品牌）

afford	[əˈfɔːd]	v．提供；买得起
insurance	[ɪnˈʃʊər(ə)ns]	n．保险
label	[ˈleɪb(ə)l]	n．标签；商标
anthropologist	[ˌænθrəˈpɒlədʒɪst]	n．人类学家
palaeolithic	[ˌpeɪliəˈlɪθɪk]	adj．旧石器时代的
neolithic	[ˌniːəˈlɪθɪk]	adj．新石器时代的
escalator	[ˈeskəleɪtə]	n．自动扶梯；电动扶梯
dweller	[ˈdwelə]	n．居民，居住者
extraordinary	[ɪkˈstrɔːd(ə)n(ə)ri]	adj．非凡的；特别的
mar	[mɑː]	v．损伤；糟蹋
deprive	[dɪˈpraɪv]	v．使丧失，剥夺
blur	[blɜː]	v．使……模糊不清
constantly	[ˈkɒnst(ə)ntli]	adv．不断地；时常地
smear	[smɪə]	v．弄脏；涂上
obsess	[əbˈses]	v．使……着迷；使……困扰
El Dorado	[ˌeldəˈrɑːdəʊ]	n．埃尔多拉多
Kabul	[ˈkɑːbəl; kəˈbuːl]	n．喀布尔（阿富汗的首都）
Irkutsk	[ɪəˈkuːtsk]	n．伊尔库茨克（苏联东西伯利亚城市）
urge	[ˈɜːdʒ]	v．催促；驱策
deserve	[dɪˈzɜːv]	v．应受，应得
remote	[rɪˈməʊt]	adj．遥远的；偏僻的
evocative	[ɪˈvɒkətɪv]	adj．唤起的；召唤的
suspend	[səˈspend]	v．使……延缓，推迟
weariness	[ˈwɪərɪnɪs]	n．疲劳；厌倦
sound	[saʊnd]	adj．酣（睡）的；健康的
complicate	[ˈkɒmplɪkeɪt]	v．使复杂化
strategy	[ˈstrætɪdʒi]	n．战略，策略
hassle	[ˈhæs(ə)l]	n．困难；麻烦
cherish	[ˈtʃerɪʃ]	v．珍爱
keepsake	[ˈkiːpseɪk]	n．纪念品
perk	[pɜːk]	n．小费；额外收入
elite	[eɪˈliːt]	n．精英；精华
tier	[tɪə]	n．层；等级
occasional	[əˈkeɪʒ(ə)n(ə)l]	adj．偶然的
entry-level	[ˈentrɪˌlevəl]	adj．入门的；初级的

priority	[praɪˈɒrɪti]	n. 优先；优先权
customize	[ˈkʌstəmaɪz]	v. 定做
liability	[laɪəˈbɪlɪti]	n. 倾向；可能性
reimbursement	[riːɪmˈbɜːsmənt]	n. 偿还；赔偿
toiletry	[ˈtɔɪlɪtri]	n. 化妆品；化妆用具
aggressive	[əˈgresɪv]	adj. 侵略性的；有进取心的
emergency	[ɪˈmɜːdʒ(ə)nsi]	n. 紧急情况；突发事件
siren	[ˈsaɪərən]	n. 警笛
blare	[bleə]	v. 发嘟嘟声；发出响而刺耳的声音

Phrases and Expressions

- make a reservation 预订；预约
- book up 订完；订光
- direct flight 直达班机
- first class 头等舱
- rental agency 租赁公司
- have in mind 考虑；想到
- air conditioning 空调
- back lot 露天区域；外景地
- rental agency 租赁公司
- get nothing for it 什么也得不到的
- get good gas mileage 低油耗；省油
- flat rate 统一费用
- cable railway 缆索铁路
- ski-lift 滑雪索道
- a bird's eye view of 鸟瞰

- even less 更不用说
- in particular 尤其，特别
- obsessed with 非常喜欢
- be bound to 必然；一定要
- hand down 把……传下去
- pat-down 搜身
- pull out 抽出；取出
- set off 出发；动身
- zip through 快速通过
- walk off with 偷走；顺手拿走
- Elite Treatment 贵宾待遇
- overhead bin 舱顶行李箱
- TSA（Transportation Security Administration）美国运输安全管理局

Unit 9

New Words

approximately	[əˈprɒksɪmətli]	adv. 大约，近似地；近于
coast	[kəʊst]	v. 滑行；沿岸航行；沿……岸航行 n. 海岸；滑坡
derive	[dɪˈraɪv]	v. 源于；得自；起源
rubber	[ˈrʌbə]	n. 橡胶；橡皮；合成橡胶；按摩师

Appendix C 词汇表

canyon	['kænjən]	n. 峡谷
tourist	['tʊərɪst]	n. 旅行者，观光客
hiking	['haɪkɪŋ]	n. 徒步旅行
sustainability	[sə'steɪnəbɪləti]	n. 持续性
ethics	['eθɪks]	n. 伦理观；道德标准
implementation	[ˌɪmplɪmen'teɪʃ(ə)n]	n. 实现；履行
millennium	[mɪ'lenɪrm]	n. 千年期；一千年
instrument	['ɪnstrʊm(ə)nt]	n. 仪器；乐器
foster	['fɒstə]	v. 培养；养育 adj. 收养的，养育的
affiliate	[ə'fɪlɪeɪt]	n. 联号；隶属的机构 v. 使附属；使紧密联系；加入；发生联系
religion	[rɪ'lɪdʒ(ə)n]	n. 宗教；宗教信仰
extract	['ekstrækt]	v. 提取；摘录 n. 汁；摘录
ratification	[ˌrætəfə'keɪʃən]	n. 批准；认可
debate	[dɪ'beɪt]	v. 辩论，争论 n. 辩论；辩论会
executive	[ɪg'zekjʊtɪv]	adj. 行政的；执行的 n. 总经理；执行者
programme	['prəʊgræm]	n. 计划；节目；程序 v. 规划编程；制作节目
voyage	['vɒɪdʒ]	n. 航行；旅行记 v. 航海；飞过；渡过
steamship	['stiːmʃɪp]	n. 轮船；汽船
pilgrim	['pɪlgrɪm]	n. 朝圣者；漫游者；（美）最初的移民 v. 去朝圣；漫游
innocent	['ɪnəs(ə)nt]	adj. 无辜的；无知的 n. 天真的人；笨蛋
echo	['ekəʊ]	v. 反射；重复；随声附和；发出回声 n. 回音；效仿
miracle	['mɪrək(ə)l]	n. 奇迹，奇迹般的人或物
gadgetry	['gædʒɪtri]	n. 小配件；小玩意

 Phrases and Expressions

- be situated off the west coast of 位于离……西海岸不远的
- derive... from 使……来源于……
- trading routes 贸易路线
- look forward to 盼望
- go down into 进入
- do a lot of hiking 徒步旅行
- sign up for 登记
- be responsible for 为……负责
- be committed to do sth. 致力于做某事
- contribute to 有助于，对……有贡献
- stem back to 起源于；上溯到
- be composed of 由……组成

- at the dawn of 在……的黎明
- leisure curiosity 休闲性好奇
- hark back to 回到
- an echo of the past 对过去的回应
- the sweep of technological change 科技变革的影响
- renewed values 重新审视的价值观

Unit 10

 New Words

community	[kəˈmjuːnɪti]	n. 社区；[生态] 群落；共同体；团体
flea	[fliː]	n. 跳蚤；低廉的旅馆
stuff	[stʌf]	n. 东西；材料；填充物 v. 塞满；让吃饱；吃得过多
utensil	[juːˈtens(ə)l]	n. 用具，器皿
haggle	[ˈhæg(ə)l]	n. 讨价还价；争论 v. 乱劈；乱砍；争论
thrift	[θrɪft]	n. 节俭；节约；[植] 海石竹
neighborhood	[ˈneɪbə,hʊd]	n. 附近；街坊；接近
jogger	[ˈdʒɒgə]	n. 慢跑者
barbershop	[ˈbɑːbəʃɒp]	n. 理发店 adj. 有男声合唱之和声的
gossip	[ˈgɒsɪp]	n. 传闻；随笔；爱说长道短的人 v. 闲聊；传播流言蜚语
paradise	[ˈpærədaɪs]	n. 天堂
accessory	[əkˈses(ə)ri]	n. 配件；附件 adj. 副的；同谋的；附属的
advantage	[ədˈvɑːntɪdʒ]	n. 优势；利益 v. 有利于；使处于优势；获利
fabulous	[ˈfæbjʊləs]	adj. 难以置信的；极好的
evolve	[ɪˈvɒlv]	vi. 进展；进化；逐步形成
souvenir	[ˌsuːvəˈnɪə]	n. 纪念品；礼物 v. 把……留作纪念
dynasty	[ˈdɪnəsti]	n. 王朝，朝代
indispensable	[ˌɪndɪˈspensəb(ə)l]	adj. 不可缺少的；责无旁贷的 n. 不可缺少之物或人
refund	[rɪˈfʌnd]	v. 退还；偿还 n. 退款
reputation	[ˌrepjʊˈteɪʃ(ə)n]	n. 名声；声望
elegance	[ˈelɪg(ə)ns]	n. 典雅；高雅

merchandise	[ˈmɜːtʃ(ə)ndaɪs; -z]	n. 商品；货物 v. 买卖；推销；经商
bustling	[ˈbʌslɪŋ]	adj. 熙熙攘攘的；忙乱的
plaza	[ˈplɑːzə]	n. 广场；购物中心
whet	[wet]	v. 刺激；促进 n. 开胃物；刺激物
appetite	[ˈæpɪtaɪt]	n. 食欲；嗜好
vogue	[vəʊg]	n. 时尚，流行 adj. 时髦的，流行的
fabric	[ˈfæbrɪk]	n. 织物；布；构造
undergo	[ˌʌndəˈgəʊ]	v. 经受；忍受
outlets	[ˈaʊtˌlet]	n. 出路；销售点
anchovy	[ˈæntʃəvɪ; ænˈtʃəʊvɪ]	n. 凤尾鱼；鳀鱼
embroidery	[ɪmˈbrɔɪd(ə)rɪ; em-]	n. 刺绣；刺绣品；粉饰
tapestry	[ˈtæpɪstrɪ]	n. 织锦；挂毯；绣帷；用挂毯装饰
sculpture	[ˈskʌlptʃə]	n. & v. 雕塑；雕刻；刻蚀

 Phrases and Expressions

- get involved in 卷入的；参与的；与……有密切关联的；
- be familiar with 熟悉；熟知
- get rid of 扔掉；丢弃
- used to do sth. 过去常常/过去曾做某事
- be into sth. 对某事很感兴趣；极喜欢某事
- in the middle of 中部；中央
- hang out 闲逛，逗留
- close off 隔绝；封锁
- each other 彼此；互相
- be interested in 感兴趣的；关心的

- be famous for 因为……而出名
- wander around 闲逛
- be filled with 充满……
- feel like doing sth. 想做（喜欢）做某事
- flea market 跳蚤市场，专门卖旧货的市场
- be divided into 把……分成
- at present 当时，目前
- in abundance 大量的，丰富充足的
- on the grand scale 大规模
- as well as 也

Appendix D
世界著名景观中英文对照

 1. 中国 China

颐和园	the Summer Palace
故宫博物院	the Palace Museum
香山公园	Xiangshan Park
天安门广场	Tian'anmen Square
人民英雄纪念碑	Monument of the People's Heroes
北海	Beihai Park
雍和宫	Yonghe Lamasery
长城	the Great Wall
八达岭长城	Great Wall at Badaling or Badaling Great Wall
居庸关	Juyongguan Pass or Juyonguan Great Wall
慕田峪长城	Great Wall at Mutianyu
天安门广场	Tian'anmen Square
人民大会堂	the Great Hall of the People
人民英雄纪念碑	Monument to the People's Heroes
琉璃厂	Glass Street
昆明湖	Kunming Lake
北海公园	Beihai Park
白马寺	White Horse Temple
天坛	Temple of Heaven
紫禁城	the Forbidden City
避暑山庄	the Imperial Mountain Summer Resort
毛主席纪念堂	Chairman Mao Zedong Memorial Hall
革命历史博物馆	the Museum of Revolutionary History
紫金山天文台	Purple and Gold Hills Observatory
周口店北京猿人遗址	Zhoukoudian: Home of the Peking Man
黄果树瀑布	Huangguoshu Falls

Appendix D 世界著名景观中英文对照

西山晴雪	the Sunny Western Hills after Snow
龙门石窟	Longmen Stone Cave
苏州园林	Suzhou Gardens
庐山	Lushan Mountain
天池	Heaven Pool
蓬莱水城	Penglai Water City
大雁塔	Big Wild Goose Pagoda
华山	Huashan Mountain
峨眉山	Emei Mountain
石林	Stone Forest
白云山	White Cloud Mountain
布达拉宫	Potala Palace
大运河	The Grand Canal
滇池	Dianchi Lake
杜甫草堂	Du Fu Cottage
都江堰	Dujiang Dam
鼓浪屿	Gulangyu Islet
观音阁	Goddess of Mercy Pavilion
甘露寺	Sweet Dew Temple
黄花岗七十二烈士墓	Mausoleum of the 72 Martyrs
华清池	Huaqing Hot Spring
昭君墓	Zhaojun's Tomb
越秀公园	Yuexiu Park
岳阳楼	Yueyang Tower
南湖公园	South Lake Park
中山公园	Zhongshan Park
武侯祠	Temple of Marquis
漓江	Lijiang River
寒山寺	Hanshan Temple
静心斋	Heart-East Study
黄鹤楼	Yellow Crane Tower
黄山	Mount Huangshan
天下第一关	the First Pass under Heaven
桂林山水	Guilin Scenery with Hills and Waters
秦始皇兵马俑博物馆	Qinshihuang's Mausoleum and Terra-cotta Army

2. 国外 Overseas

日本富士山	Fujiyama, Japan
印度泰姬陵	Taj Mahal, India
柬埔寨吴哥窟	Angkor Wat, Cambodia
印度尼西亚巴厘岛	Bali, Indonesia
印度尼西亚波罗浮屠	Borobudur, Indonesia
新加坡圣淘沙	Sentosa, Singapore
泰国芭提雅海滩	Pattaya Beach, Thailand
伊拉克巴比伦遗迹	Babylon, Iraq
土耳其圣索非亚教堂	Mosque of St., Sophia in Istanbul (Constantinople), Turkey
埃及苏伊士运河	Suez Canal, Egypt
埃及阿斯旺大坝	Aswan High Dam, Egypt
肯尼亚内罗毕国家公园	Nairobi National Park, Kenya
南非好望角	Cape of Good Hope, South Africa
撒哈拉大沙漠	Sahara Desert
埃及金字塔	Pyramids, Egypt
埃及尼罗河	The Nile, Egypt
大堡礁	Great Barrier Reef
澳大利亚悉尼歌剧院	Sydney Opera House, Australia
艾尔斯巨石	Ayers Rock
库克山	Mount Cook
复活节岛	Easter Island
法国巴黎圣母院	Notre-Dame de Paris, France
法国埃菲尔铁塔	Effiel Tower, France
法国凯旋门	Arch of Triumph, France
法国爱丽舍宫	Elysee Palace, France
法国卢浮宫	Louvre, France
德国科隆大教堂	Kolner Dom, Koln, Germany
意大利比萨斜塔	Leaning Tower of Pisa, Italy
意大利古罗马圆形剧场	Colosseum in Rome, Italy
意大利威尼斯	Venice, Italy
希腊帕台农神庙	Parthenon Temple, Greece

Appendix D 世界著名景观中英文对照

俄罗斯莫斯科红场	Red Square in Moscow, Russia
英国伦敦大笨钟	Big Ben in London, England
英国白金汉宫	Buckingham Palace, England
英国海德公园	Hyde Park, England
英国伦敦塔桥	London Tower Bridge, England
英国威斯敏斯特大教堂	Westminster Abbey, England
摩洛哥蒙特卡洛	Monte Carlo, Monaco
美国尼亚加拉大瀑布	Niagara Falls, New York State, USA
美国夏威夷火奴鲁鲁	Honolulu, Hawaii, USA
巴拿马大运河	Panama Canal
美国黄石国家公园	Yellowstone National Park, USA
美国纽约自由女神像	Statue of Liberty, New York City, USA
美国纽约时代广场	Times Square, New York City, USA
美国华盛顿白宫	The White House, Washington D.C., USA
美国纽约中央公园	Central Park, New York City, USA
美国亚利桑那州大峡谷	Grand Canyon, Arizona, USA
美国加利福尼亚好莱坞	Hollywood, California, USA
美国内华达拉斯维加斯	Las Vegas, Nevada, USA
美国佛罗里达迈阿密	Miami, Florida, USA
纽约大都会艺术博物馆	Metropolitan Museum of Art, New York City, USA
墨西哥阿卡普尔科	Acapulco, Mexico
墨西哥库斯科	Cuzco, Mexico

Appendix E
中国菜名中英文对照

 1. 头盘，凉菜类 Appetizers and Salads

拌豆腐丝	Shredded Tofu with Sauce
白切鸡	Boiled Chicken with Sauce
拌双耳	Tossed Black and White Fungus
冰镇芥兰	Chinese Broccoli with Wasabi
朝鲜辣白菜	Korean Cabbage in Chili Sauce
川北凉粉	Clear Noodles in Chili Sauce
刺身凉瓜	Bitter Melon with Wasabi
夫妻肺片	Pork Lungs in Chili Sauce
干拌牛舌	Ox Tongue in Chili Sauce
姜汁皮蛋	Preserved Eggs in Ginger Sauce
酱香猪蹄	Pig Feet Seasoned with Soy Sauce
酱肘花	Sliced Pork in Soy Sauce
老北京豆酱	Traditional Beijing Bean Paste
老醋泡花生	Peanuts Pickled in Aged Vinegar
凉拌金针菇	Golden Mushrooms and Mixed Vegetables
凉拌西芹云耳	Celery with White Fungus
卤水大肠	Marinated Pork Intestines
卤水豆腐	Marinated Tofu
卤水拼盘	Marinated Meat Combination
麻辣肚丝	Shredded Pig Tripe in Chili Sauce
美味牛筋	Beef Tendon
蜜汁叉烧	Honey-Stewed BBQ Pork
皮蛋豆腐	Tofu with Preserved Eggs
乳猪拼盘	Roast Suckling Pig
五香牛肉	Spicy Roast Beef
香葱酥鱼	Crispy Crucian Carp in Scallion Oil

298

Appendix E 中国菜名中英文对照

琥珀核桃	Honeyed Walnuts
杭州凤鹅	Pickled Goose, Hangzhou Style
八宝菠菜	Spinach with Eight Delicacies
家常皮冻	Pork Skin Aspic
大拉皮	Tossed Mung Clear Noodles in Sauce
糖蒜	Sweet Garlic

 ## 2. 肉类 Meat

白菜豆腐焖酥肉	Braised Pork Cubes with Tofu and Chinese Cabbage
鲍鱼红烧肉	Braised Pork with Abalone
川味小炒	Shredded Pork with Vegetables, Sichuan Style
地瓜烧肉	Stewed Diced Pork and Sweet Potatoes
东坡方肉	Braised Dongpo Pork
冬菜扣肉	Braised Pork with Preserved Vegetables
方竹笋炖肉	Braised Pork with Bamboo Shoots
干煸小猪腰	Fried Pig Kidney with Onion
干豆角回锅肉	Sautéed Spicy Pork with Dried Beans
咕噜肉	Gulaorou (Sweet and Sour Pork with Fat)
红烧狮子头	Stewed Pork Ball in Brown Sauce
脆皮乳猪	Crispy BBQ Suckling Pig
回锅肉片	Sautéed Sliced Pork with Pepper and Chili
木耳肉片	Sautéed Sliced Pork with Black Fungus
酱烧排骨	Braised Spare Ribs in Brown Sauce
酱猪手	Braised Pig Feet in Brown Sauce
椒盐肉排	Spare Ribs with Spicy Salt
京酱肉丝	Sautéed Shredded Pork in Sweet Bean Sauce
蜜汁烧小肉排	Stewed Spare Ribs in Honey Sauce
木须肉	Sautéed Sliced Pork, Eggs and Black Fungus
南瓜香芋蒸排骨	Steamed Spare Ribs with Pumpkin and Taro
砂锅海带炖排骨	Stewed Spare Ribs with Kelp en Casserole
砂锅排骨土豆	Stewed Spare Ribs with Potatoes en Casserole
鱼香肉丝	Yu-Shiang Shredded Pork (Sautéed with Spicy Garlic Sauce)
糖醋里脊	Fried Sweet and Sour Tenderloin (Lean Meat)
水晶肘	Stewed Pork Hock

299

九转大肠	Braised Intestines in Brown Sauce
四喜丸子	Four-Joy Meatballs
软炸里脊	Soft-Fried Pork Filet
东坡肘子	Braised Dongpo Pork Hock with Brown Sauce
川式红烧肉	Braised Pork，Sichuan Style
蚂蚁上树	Sautéed Vermicelli with Spicy Minced
猪肉炖粉条	Braised Pork with Vermicelli
XO酱炒牛柳条	Sautéed Beef Filet in XO Sauce
爆炒牛肋骨	Sautéed Beef Ribs
葱爆肥牛	Sautéed Beef with Scallion
番茄炖牛腩	Braised Beef Brisket with Tomato
干煸牛肉丝	Sautéed Shredded Beef in Chili Sauce
胡萝卜炖牛肉	Braised Beef with Carrots
土豆炒牛柳条	Sautéed Beef Filet with Potatoes
红烧牛蹄筋	Braised Beef Tendon in Brown Sauce
葱爆羊肉	Sautéed Lamb Slices with Scallion
大蒜羊仔片	Sautéed Lamb Filet with Garlic
红焖羊排	Braised Lamb Chops with Carrots
葱煸羊腩	Sautéed Diced Lamb with Scallion
烤羊里脊	Roast Lamb Tenderloin
烤羊腿	Roast Lamb Leg
涮羊肉	Mongolian Hot Pot
红烧羊肉	Braised Lamb in Brown Sauce
烤全羊	Roast Whole Lamb
孜然羊肉	Fried Lamb with Cumin
羊蝎子	Lamb Spine Hot Pot

3. 家禽类 Poultry

扒鸡腿	Grilled Chicken Legs
脆皮鸡	Crispy Chicken
干锅鸡	Griddle Cooked Chicken with Pepper
干锅鸡胗	Griddle Cooked Chicken Gizzard
宫保鸡丁	Kung Pao Chicken
四川辣子鸡	Sauteed Diced Chicken with Chili and Pepper，Sichuan Style

Appendix E 中国菜名中英文对照

酥炸鸡胸	Deep-Fried Crispy Chicken Breast
干烧鸡	Dry-Braised Chicken in Chili Sauce
柠檬鸡	Sauteed Chicken with Lemon
三杯鸡	Stewed Chicken with Three Cups Sauce
糖醋鸡块	Braised Chicken in Sweet and Sour Sauce
四川樟茶鸭	Smoked Duck, Sichuan Style
香熏鸭腰	Fragrant Smoked Duck Kernel
芥末鸭掌	Duck Feet with Mustard
北京烤鸭	Beijing Roast Duck
火燎鸭心	Sauteed Duck Hearts
酱爆鸭片	Sauteed Sliced Duck in Soy Sauce
脆皮乳鸽	Crispy Pigeon
咸鸭蛋	Salted Duck Egg
卤蛋	Marinated Egg
煮鸡蛋	Boiled Egg
糟蛋	Egg Preserved in Rice Wine
荷包蛋	Poached Egg
韭菜炒鸡蛋	Scrambled Egg with Leek
葱花炒鸡蛋	Scrambled Egg with Scallion
蛤蜊蒸蛋	Steamed Egg with Clams

 4. Seafood 海鲜类

红烧鲍翅燕	Braised Abalone, Shark's Fin and Bird's Nest
红烧鲍鱼	Braised Abalone
鲍汁牛肝菌	Braised Boletus in Abalone Sauce
白玉蒸扇贝	Steamed Scallops with Tofu
宫保鲜带子	Kung Pao Scallops
扇贝（蒜茸蒸，XO 炒，豉汁蒸）	Scallop in Shell (Steamed with Garlic/Sautéed with XO Sauce /Steamed with Black Bean Sauce)
干煎带鱼	Deep-Fried Ribbonfish
多宝鱼（清蒸，豉汁蒸 过桥）	Turbot (Steamed/Steamed with Black Bean Sauce/ Boiled)
芝麻炸多春鱼	Deep-Fried Shisamo with Sesame
松鼠桂鱼	Sweet and Sour Mandarin Fish
豆腐烧鱼	Fried Fish with Tofu

葱烧海参	Braised Sea Cucumber with Scallion
豉油王蒸鲈鱼	Steamed Perch in Black Bean Sauce
葱姜肉蟹	Sauteed Crab with Ginger and Scallion
红烧甲鱼	Braised Turtle in Brown Sauce
香辣蟹	Sauteed Crab in Hot Spicy Sauce
香油蟮糊	Braised Shredded Eel with Sesame Oil
澳洲龙虾（刺身，上汤焗，椒盐）	Australian Lobster (Sashimi/ in Chicken Consomm / Fried with Spicy Salt)
干烧大虾	Dry-Braised Prawn with Ham and Asparagus
宫保虾仁	Kung Pao Shrimps
油焖大虾	Braised Prawns
煎银鳕鱼	Pan-Fried Codfish Filet
香烧鱿鱼	Braised Squid
酸菜鱼	Boiled Fish with Pickled Cabbage and Chili
西湖醋鱼	West Lake Fish in Vinegar Gravy
咖喱虾	Curry Shrimps
什烩干贝	Sautéed Scallops with Mixed Vegetable
清蒸石斑鱼	Steamed Sea Bass
清蒸龙利	Steamed Flounder

5. Vegetables 蔬菜类

豪油冬菇	Oyster Sauce Mushroom
红烧豆腐	Fried Tofu
炒素丁	Vegetable Roll
罗汉腐皮卷	Vegetable Egg Roll
素咕噜肉	Vegetarian Sweet and Sour
蒸山水豆腐	Steam Tofu
鲜菇扒菜胆	Mushroom Tender Green
炒杂菜	Mixed Green Tender
清炒芥兰	Chinese Green Tender
盐水菜心	Salt Green Tender
干扁四季豆	String Bean Western Style
上汤芥菜胆	Mustard Green Tender
砂锅三菌	Braised Assorted Mushrooms en Casserole

Appendix E 中国菜名中英文对照

烧汁烩南野山菌	Braised Mushrooms in BBQ Sauce
剁椒土豆丝	Sautéed Shredded Potato with Chopped Chili Pepper
干煸扁豆	Dry-Fried French Beans
清炒丝瓜	Sautéed Sponge Gourd
醋熘豆芽	Fried Bean Sprouts with Vinegar Sauce
地三鲜	Sautéed Potato, Green Pepper and Eggplant
酱烧茄子	Braised Eggplant with Soy Bean Paste
红烧日本豆腐	Braised Japanese Tofu with Vegetables
家常豆腐	Fried Tofu, Home Style

6. Pasta and Rice 主食类

稀饭	Rice Porridge	白饭	Plain White Rice
八宝饭	Eight Delicacies Rice	油饭	Glutinous Oil Rice
糯米饭	Glutinous Rice	卤肉饭	Braised Pork Rice
蛋炒饭	Fried Rice with Egg	地瓜粥	Congee with Sweet Potato Congee
小米金瓜粥	Millet Congee with Pumpkin	绿豆粥	Congee with Mung Bean Congee
腊八粥	Porridge with Nuts and Dried Fruits	地瓜粥	Sweet Potato Congee
馄饨面	Wonton & Noodles	刀削面	Sliced Noodles
麻辣面	Spicy Hot Noodles	麻酱面	Sesame paste Noodles
鸭肉面	Duck with Noodles	鳝鱼面	Eel Noodles
乌龙面	Seafood Noodles	牡蛎细面	Oyster Thin Noodles
板条	Flat Noodles	米粉	Rice Noodles
炒米粉	Fried Rice Noodles	冬粉	Green Bean Noodle
烧饼	Clay Oven Rolls	油条	Fried Bread Stick
韭菜盒	Fried Leek Dumplings	水饺	Boiled Dumplings
蒸饺	Steamed Dumplings	馒头	Steamed Buns
饭团	Rice and Vegetable Roll	春卷	Spring Rolls
蛋卷	Chicken Rolls	碗糕	Salty Rice Pudding
筒仔米糕	Rice Tube Pudding	红豆糕	Red Bean Cake
绿豆糕	Bean Paste Cake	糯米糕	Glutinous Rice Cakes
萝卜糕	Fried White Radish Patty	芋头糕	Taro Cake
肉圆	Taiwanese Meatballs	水晶饺	Pyramid Dumplings

7. Soups 汤羹类

鱼丸汤	Fish Ball Soup	贡丸汤	Meat Ball Doup
蛋花汤	Egg & Vegetable Soup	蛤蜊汤	Clams Soup
牡蛎汤	Oyster Soup	紫菜汤	Seaweed Soup
酸辣汤	Sweet & Sour Soup	馄饨汤	Wonton Soup
猪肠汤	Pork Intestine Soup	肉羹汤	Pork Thick Soup
鱿鱼汤	Squid Soup	花枝羹	Squid Thick Soup

 ### 8. Desserts 甜品类

布丁	Pudding	爱玉	Vegetarian Gelatin
糖葫芦	Tomatoes on Sticks	长寿桃	Longevity Peaches
芝麻球	Glutinous Rice Sesame Balls	麻花	Hemp Flowers
绵绵冰	Mein Mein Ice	麦角冰	Oatmeal Ice
地瓜冰	Sweet Potato Ice	红豆牛奶冰	Red Bean with Milk Ice
八宝冰	Eight Treasures Ice	豆花	Tofu Pudding
蜜糖龟苓膏	Guiling Jelly (Chinese Herbal Jelly) Served with Honey		

 ### 9. Alcohol and Drinks 酒水类

甘蔗汁	Sugar Cane Juice	酸梅汁	Plum Juice
杨桃汁	Star Fruit Juice	青草茶	Herb Juice
果醋	Apple Cider Vinegar	露露	Lulu Almond Juice
山楂醋	Hawthorn Vinegar	矿泉水	Spring Water
中国酒	Chinese Alcoholic Drinks		

Appendix F
常用公共标识语中英文对照

 1. 公共场所标志

中文	英文	中文	英文
营业时间	Business Hours	办公时间	Office Hours
入口	Entrance	出口	Exit
推	Push	拉	Pull
此路不通	Shut	开	On
关	Off	营业	Open
暂停	Pause	关闭	Stop
下班	Closed	失物招领处	Lost and Found
油漆未干	Wet Paint	危险	Danger
安全第一	Safety First	加油站	Gas Station
禁止吸烟	No Smoking	请勿拍照	No Photographing
游人止步	No Visitors	禁止入内	No Entry
闲人免进	No Admittance	禁止通行	No Passing
不准垂钓	No Angling	禁止打猎	Shooting Prohibited
招聘	Hands Wanted	职工专用	Staff Only
勿乱扔杂物	No Litter	不准张贴	No Bills
请勿用手触摸	Hands Off	保持安静	Keep Silence
降价出售	On Sale	恕不出售	Not for Sale
对号入座	Seat by Number	谨防扒手	Beware of Pickpocket
爱护公共财物	Protect Public Property	售票处	Ticket Office
行李存放处	Luggage Depository	来宾登记	Visitors Please Register
免费入场	Admission Free	自行车存车处	Bike Park（ing）
妇女、儿童优先	Children and Women First	禁止携犬入内	Dogs Not Allowed
男厕所	Men's/Gentlemen Room	女厕所	Women's/ Ladies Room
（厕所）有人	Occupied	（厕所）无人	Vacant

2. 行车标志

停车处	Parking Lot	免费通行	Toll Free
单行道	One-Way Street	靠右/左	Keep Right/Left
快车先行	Give Way	只准公共汽车通过	Buses Only
禁止超车	Do Not Pass	禁止鸣喇叭	No Honking
禁止掉头	No U Turn	校内禁止骑车	No Cycling in the School
减速行驶	Reduced Speed Now	马路施工，请绕行	Road Up. Detour

3. 产品说明标志

易碎	Fragile	置于阴凉处	In Shade
此面朝上	This Side Up	小心轻放	Handle with Care
避光保存	Keep in Dark Place	有毒/毒品	Poison
防潮	Guard against Damp	保持干燥	Keep Dry
切勿近火	Keep Away From Fire	灭火专用	For Use Only in Case of Fire
此处插入	Insert Here	此处开启	Open Here
此处撕开	Split Here		

Appendix G
酒店词汇

 1. 酒店部门

前厅部	Front Office	礼宾部	Concierge
客房部	Housekeeping	餐饮部	Food and Beverage
市场营销部	Marketing Department	公关部	Public Relations Department
人力资源部	Human Resources Department	培训部	Training Department
财务部	Financial Department	成本部	Cost-Control Department
审计部	Auditor Department	采购部	Purchasing Department
医务室	Clinic	行政办公室	Executive Office
工程部	Engineering Department	安保部	Security
信息中心	IT Office		

 2. 酒店职位

总经理	General Manager	大堂经理	Lounge Manager
部门经理	Department Manager	主管	Supervisor
领班	Captain	女礼宾员	Door Girl
礼宾司	Door Man	服务员	Attendant
行李员	Bellman	接单员	Order Taker
收银员	Cashier	行政总厨	Executive Chef
厨师	Chef	西饼主管	Chief Baker
酒水部经理	Beverage Manager	调酒师	Bartender
酒吧服务员	Barman	服务员	Waiter & Waitress
传菜员	Pantry Man	实习生	Trainee

 3. 酒店区域

问询处	Information Desk	接待室	Reception Office
售报处	News Stand	邮局服务处	Postal Service
小卖部	Shop	酒吧间	Bar

洗衣房	Laundry	休息厅	Lounge
屋顶花园	Roof Garden	桌球房	Billiard-Room
健身中心	Health Club	餐厅	Dining-Room, Dining Hall
行李房/存衣处	Cloak-Room	地下室	Basement
精品商场	Boutique	大堂吧	Lobby Lounge
行政酒廊	Executive Lounge	地窖	Cellar
杂物室	Broom Closet	（英）底层，一楼	Ground Floor
（英）二楼，（美）一楼	First Floor	（英）三楼，（美）二楼	Second Floor

4. 酒店常用物品

卫生纸	Toilet Tissue	毛巾	Towel
面巾	Face Towel	浴巾	Bath Towel
浴袍	Bathrobe	睡袍	Evening Gown
淋浴帽	Shower Cap	指甲挫	Nail File
剃须刀	Razor	梳子	Comb
沐浴露	Bath Foam	化妆品	Cosmetics
香皂	Soap	牙膏	Tooth Paste
牙刷	Tooth Brush	浴盆	Bath Tub
窗帘	Curtain	垃圾桶	Rubbish Bin
废纸篓	Waste-Paper Basket	蚊香	Mosquito Incense
电热水壶	Electric Kettle	圆珠笔	Ball Pen
电视遥控器	TV Remove Control	电熨斗	Electric Iron
针线包	Sewing Kit	电吹风	Hair Dryer
鞋篓	Shoe Basket	剪刀	Scissors
中央空调系统	Central Air-Conditioning System	应急电筒	Flashlight
单人床	Single Bed	双人床	Double Bed
成对床	Twin Beds	被子	Quilt
毯子	Blanket	床单	Sheet
床罩	Bedspread	毛巾被	Cotton Terry Blanket
枕头	Pillow		

5. 酒店业务常用词汇

租金	Rent	账单	Bill
市价	Market Price	支票	Check，Cheque
价目表	Price List	硬币	Coin
纸币	Note	收费	Charge
换钱	Change Money	房价	Room Rate
预付	Prepaid	兑换处	Cashier's desk
兑换率	Rate of Exchange	身份证	Identification Card
退房时间	Check-Out Time	签字	Sign
表格	Form	预订	Reservation
押金	Advance Deposit	订房	Booking
小费	Tip	政府税	Government Tax
延期	Postpone	取消	Cancel
更改	Amendment	国籍	Nationality
永久地址	Permanent Address	信用卡	Credit Card
有效的	Valid		

Reference

［1］赛静，张亲青，徐艳．实用旅游英语［M］．合肥：合肥工业大学出版社，2005．
［2］孙一文，于春雨．旅游英语［M］．北京：北京理工大学出版社，2011．
［3］李洪涛．旅游英语．快易通［M］．北京：北京邮电大学出版社，2005．
［4］高文知．酒店情景英语［M］．北京：北京大学出版社，2013．
［5］朱华．导游英语［M］．北京：高等教育出版社，2013．
［6］LiveABC．美语会话全集——观光旅游［M］．北京：科学出版社，2010．
［7］钱玲，李启金．旅游情境英语［M］．北京：旅游教育出版社，2011．
［8］杨红．实用旅游英语［M］．北京：知识产权出版社，2010．
［9］教育部教材编写组．旅游英语［M］．北京：高等教育出版社，2002．
［10］陈昕．旅游英语［M］．北京：人民邮电出版社，2011．
［11］崔进，刘云，魏昆．新编旅游英语［M］．武汉：武汉大学出版社，2003．
［12］刘会，张海让．导游英语［M］．天津：天津科技翻译出版公司，2006．
［13］李德荣，俞理明．导游英语［M］．上海：上海交通大学出版社，2003．